MARK ANDREW SMITH
PAUL MAYBURY

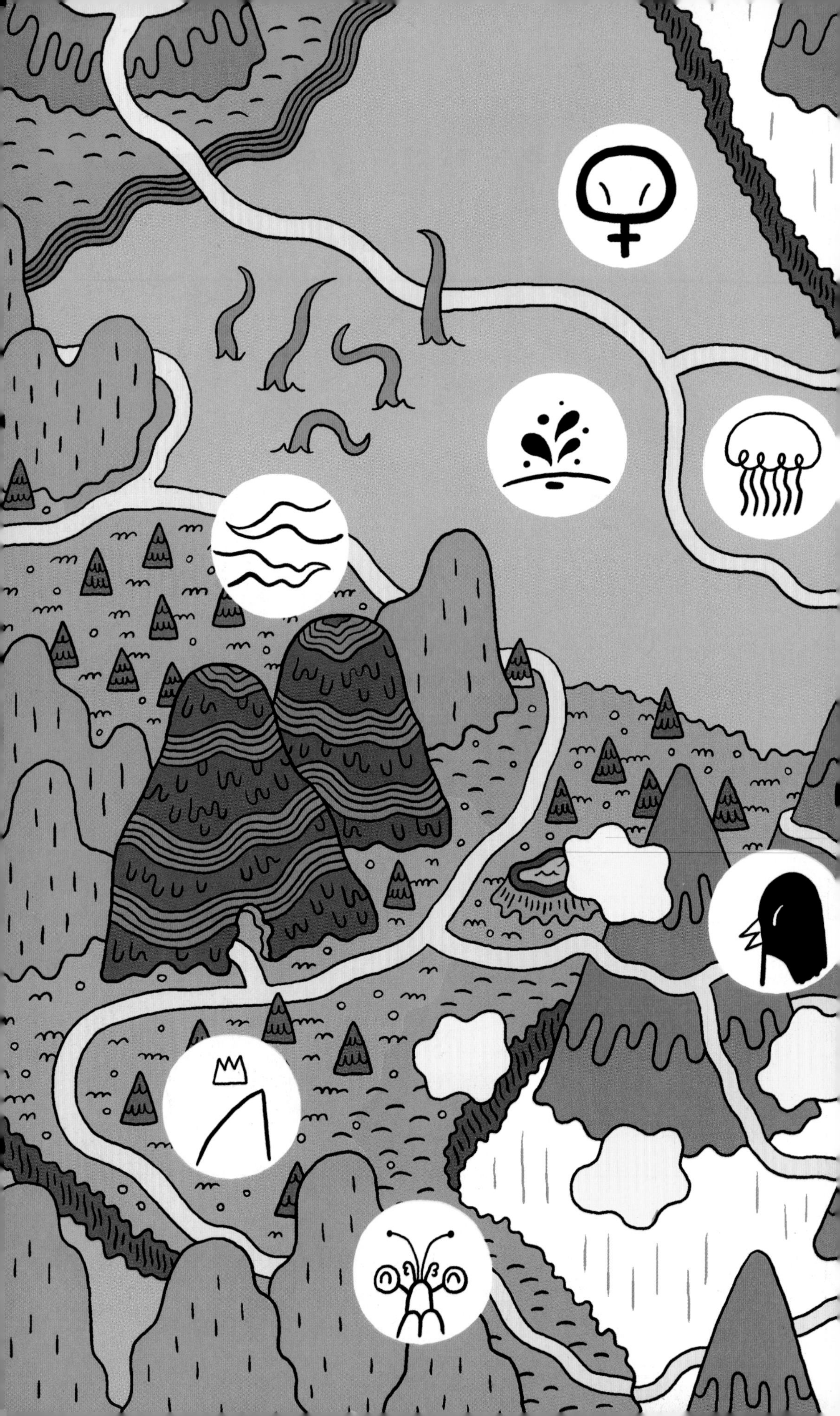

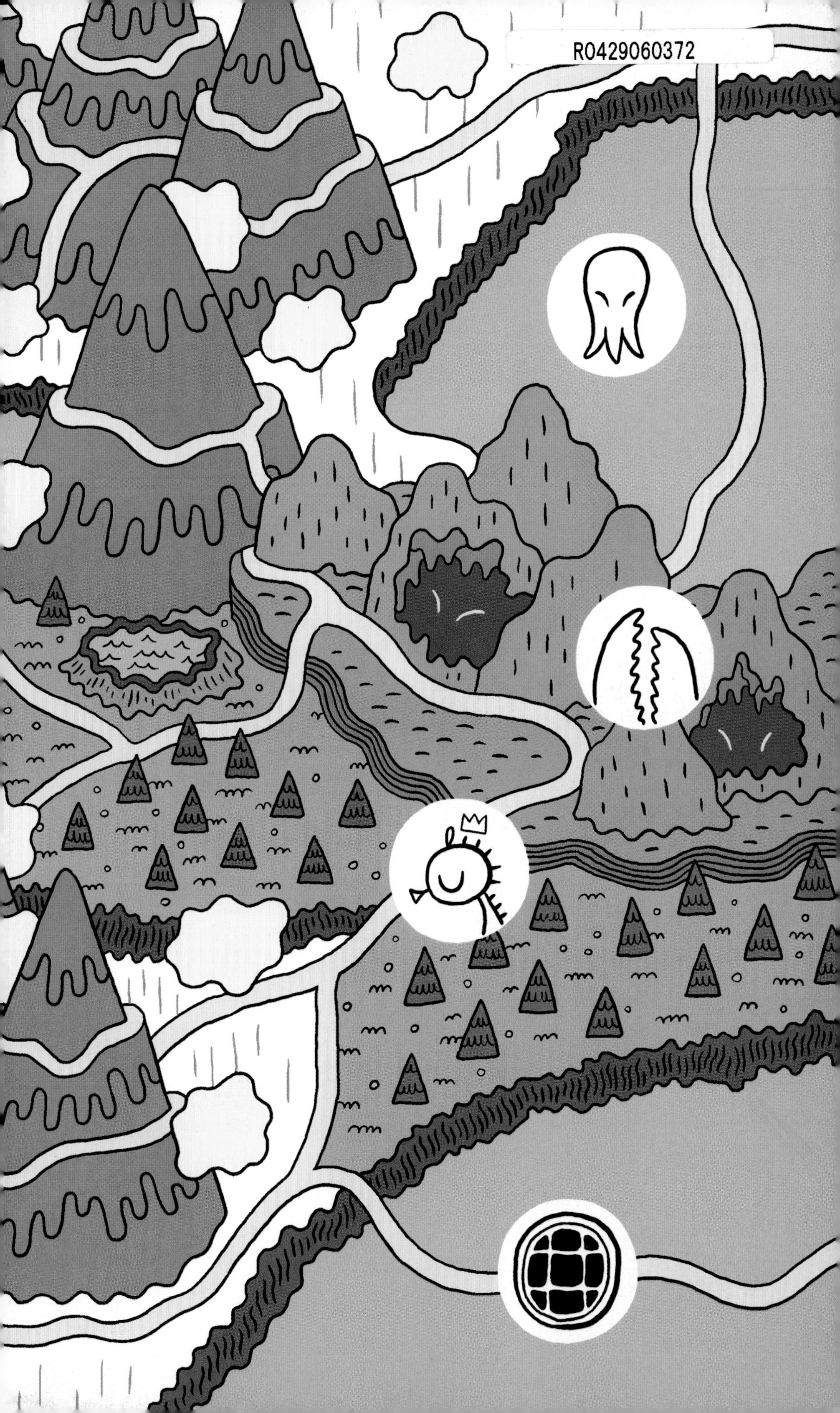

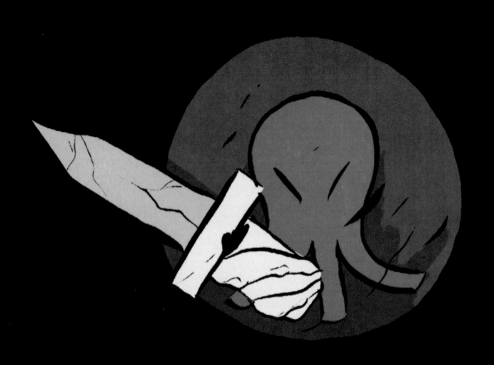

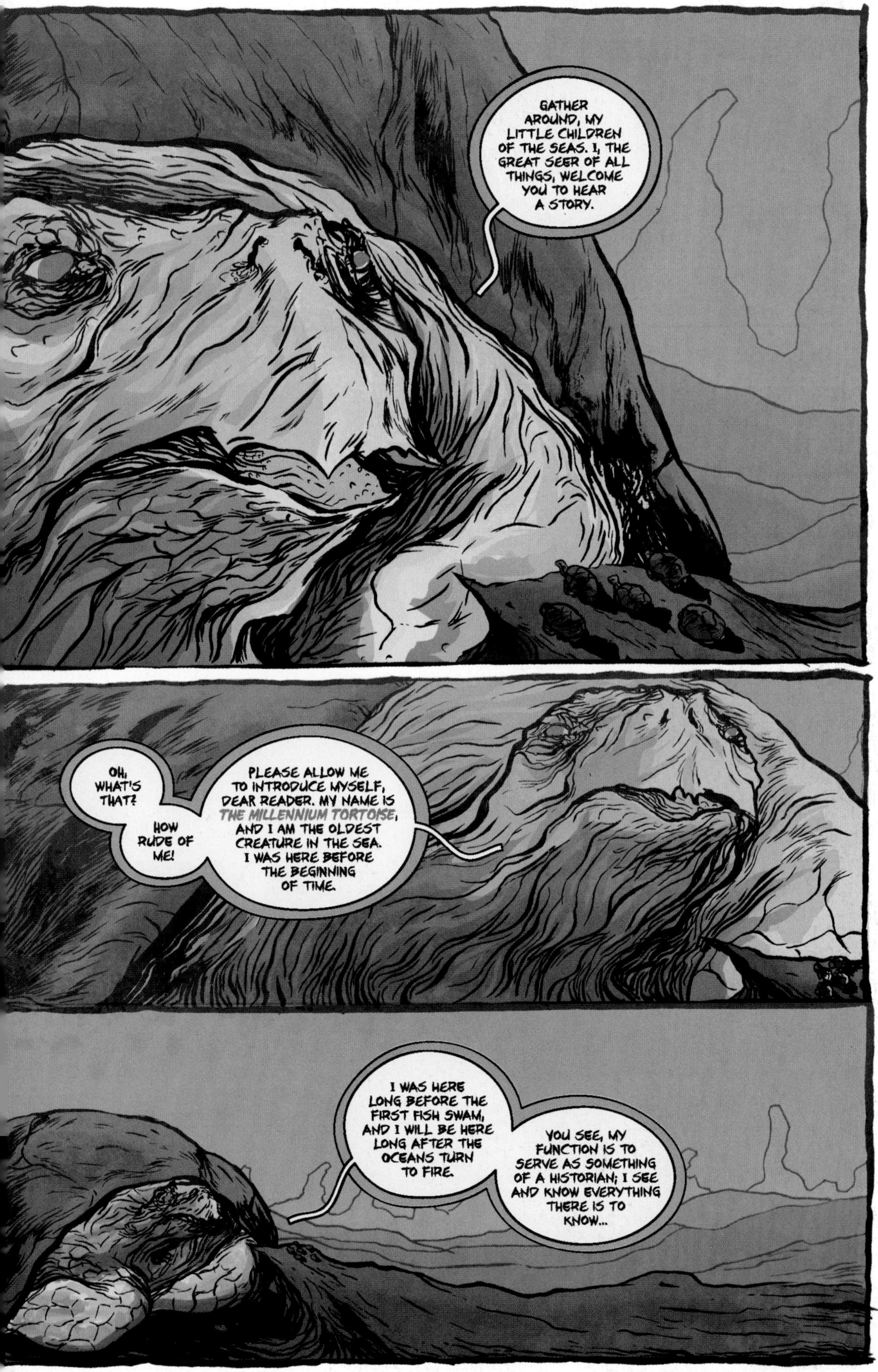
GATHER AROUND, MY LITTLE CHILDREN OF THE SEAS. I, THE GREAT SEER OF ALL THINGS, WELCOME YOU TO HEAR A STORY.
OH, WHAT'S THAT?
HOW RUDE OF ME!
PLEASE ALLOW ME TO INTRODUCE MYSELF, DEAR READER. MY NAME IS THE MILLENNIUM TORTOISE, AND I AM THE OLDEST CREATURE IN THE SEA. I WAS HERE BEFORE THE BEGINNING OF TIME.
I WAS HERE LONG BEFORE THE FIRST FISH SWAM, AND I WILL BE HERE LONG AFTER THE OCEANS TURN TO FIRE.
YOU SEE, MY FUNCTION IS TO SERVE AS SOMETHING OF A HISTORIAN; I SEE AND KNOW EVERYTHING THERE IS TO KNOW...

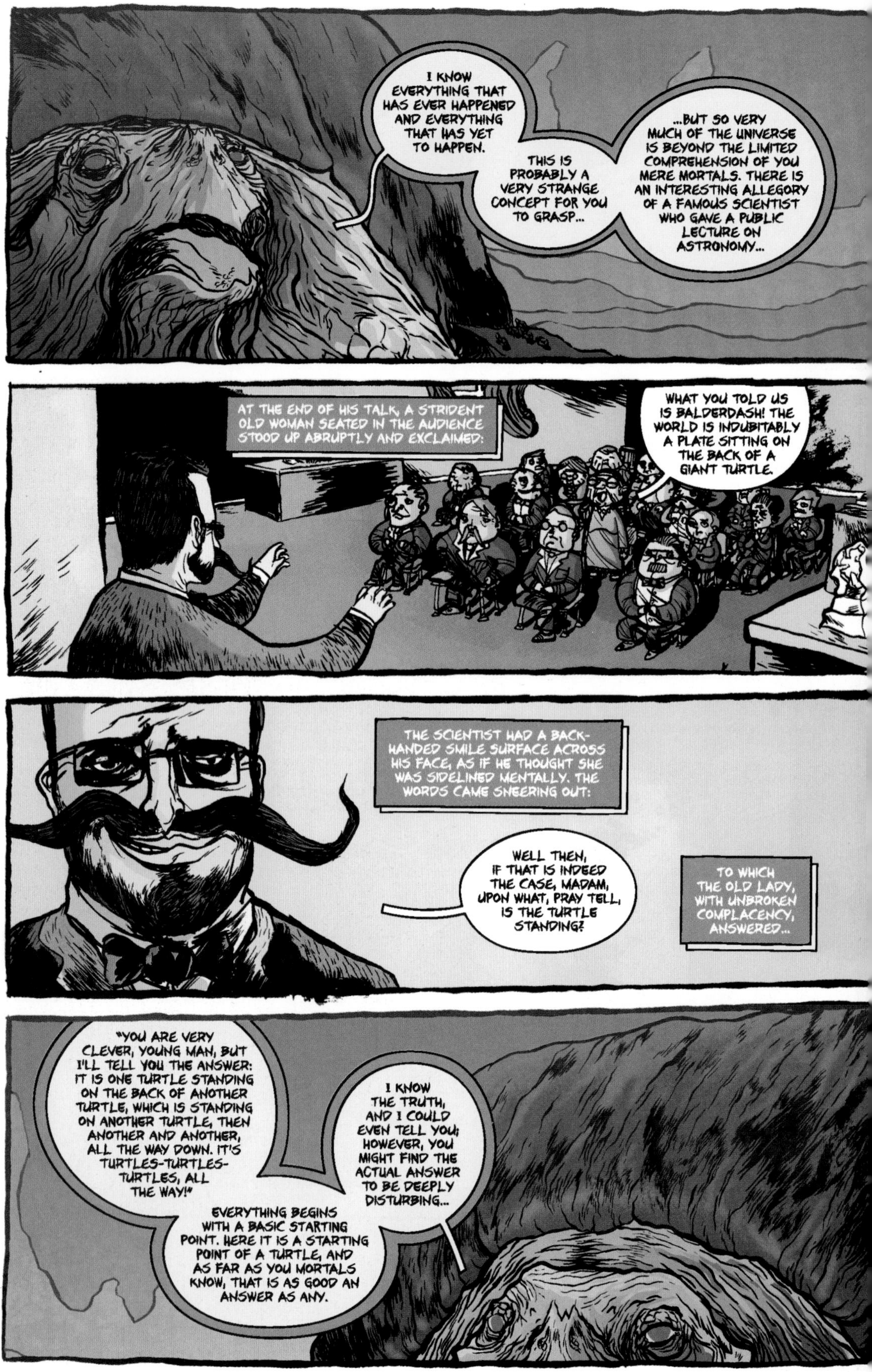
I KNOW EVERYTHING THAT HAS EVER HAPPENED AND EVERYTHING THAT HAS YET TO HAPPEN.
THIS IS PROBABLY A VERY STRANGE CONCEPT FOR YOU TO GRASP...
...BUT SO VERY MUCH OF THE UNIVERSE IS BEYOND THE LIMITED COMPREHENSION OF YOU MERE MORTALS. THERE IS AN INTERESTING ALLEGORY OF A FAMOUS SCIENTIST WHO GAVE A PUBLIC LECTURE ON ASTRONOMY...
AT THE END OF HIS TALK, A STRIDENT OLD WOMAN SEATED IN THE AUDIENCE STOOD UP ABRUPTLY AND EXCLAIMED:
WHAT YOU TOLD US IS BALDERDASH! THE WORLD IS INDUBITABLY A PLATE SITTING ON THE BACK OF A GIANT TURTLE.
THE SCIENTIST HAD A BACK-HANDED SMILE SURFACE ACROSS HIS FACE, AS IF HE THOUGHT SHE WAS SIDELINED MENTALLY. THE WORDS CAME SNEERING OUT:
WELL THEN, IF THAT IS INDEED THE CASE, MADAM, UPON WHAT, PRAY TELL, IS THE TURTLE STANDING?
TO WHICH THE OLD LADY, WITH UNBROKEN COMPLACENCY, ANSWERED...
"YOU ARE VERY CLEVER, YOUNG MAN, BUT I'LL TELL YOU THE ANSWER: IT IS ONE TURTLE STANDING ON THE BACK OF ANOTHER TURTLE, WHICH IS STANDING ON ANOTHER TURTLE, THEN ANOTHER AND ANOTHER, ALL THE WAY DOWN. IT'S TURTLES-TURTLES-TURTLES, ALL THE WAY!"
EVERYTHING BEGINS WITH A BASIC STARTING POINT. HERE IT IS A STARTING POINT OF A TURTLE, AND AS FAR AS YOU MORTALS KNOW, THAT IS AS GOOD AN ANSWER AS ANY.
I KNOW THE TRUTH, AND I COULD EVEN TELL YOU; HOWEVER, YOU MIGHT FIND THE ACTUAL ANSWER TO BE DEEPLY DISTURBING...

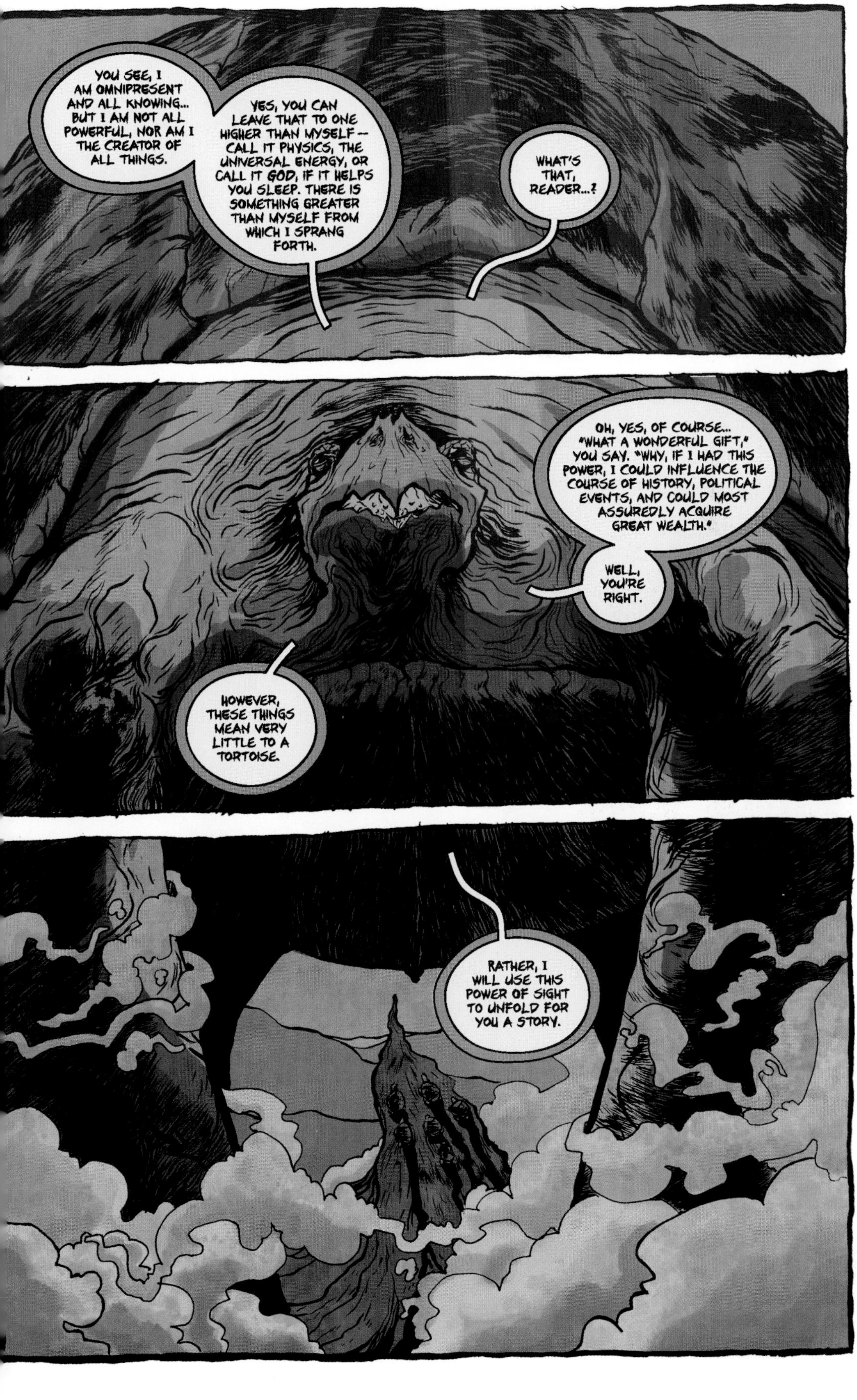
YOU SEE, I AM OMNIPRESENT AND ALL KNOWING... BUT I AM NOT ALL POWERFUL, NOR AM I THE CREATOR OF ALL THINGS.
YES, YOU CAN LEAVE THAT TO ONE HIGHER THAN MYSELF -- CALL IT PHYSICS, THE UNIVERSAL ENERGY, OR CALL IT GOD, IF IT HELPS YOU SLEEP. THERE IS SOMETHING GREATER THAN MYSELF FROM WHICH I SPRANG FORTH.
WHAT'S THAT, READER...?
OH, YES, OF COURSE... "WHAT A WONDERFUL GIFT," YOU SAY. "WHY, IF I HAD THIS POWER, I COULD INFLUENCE THE COURSE OF HISTORY, POLITICAL EVENTS, AND COULD MOST ASSUREDLY ACQUIRE GREAT WEALTH."
WELL, YOU'RE RIGHT.
HOWEVER, THESE THINGS MEAN VERY LITTLE TO A TORTOISE.
RATHER, I WILL USE THIS POWER OF SIGHT TO UNFOLD FOR YOU A STORY.

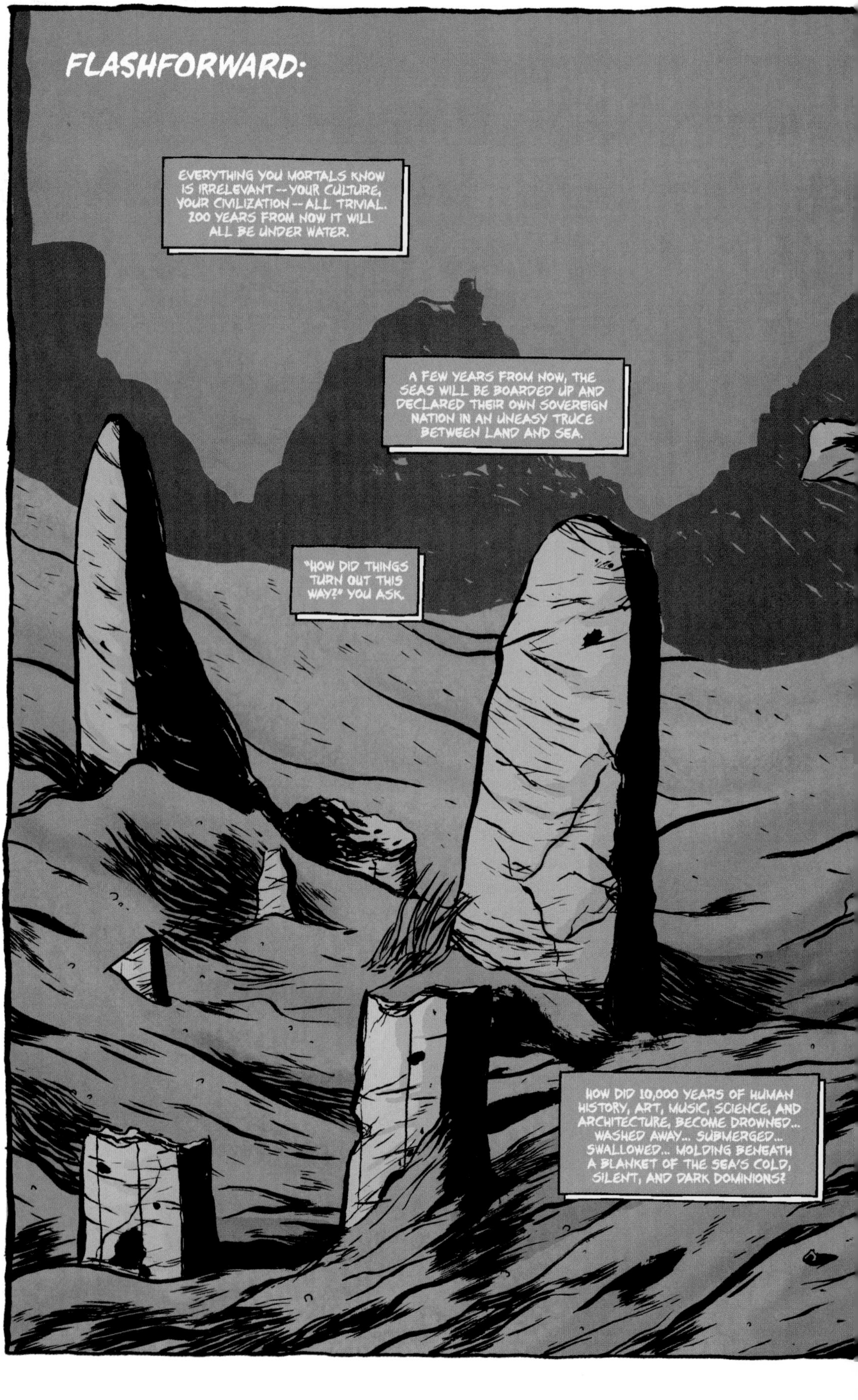
FLASHFORWARD:
EVERYTHING YOU MORTALS KNOW IS IRRELEVANT -- YOUR CULTURE, YOUR CIVILIZATION -- ALL TRIVIAL. 200 YEARS FROM NOW IT WILL ALL BE UNDER WATER.
A FEW YEARS FROM NOW, THE SEAS WILL BE BOARDED UP AND DECLARED THEIR OWN SOVEREIGN NATION IN AN UNEASY TRUCE BETWEEN LAND AND SEA.
"HOW DID THINGS TURN OUT THIS WAY?" YOU ASK.
HOW DID 10,000 YEARS OF HUMAN HISTORY, ART, MUSIC, SCIENCE, AND ARCHITECTURE, BECOME DROWNED... WASHED AWAY... SUBMERGED... SWALLOWED... MOLDING BENEATH A BLANKET OF THE SEA'S COLD, SILENT, AND DARK DOMINIONS?

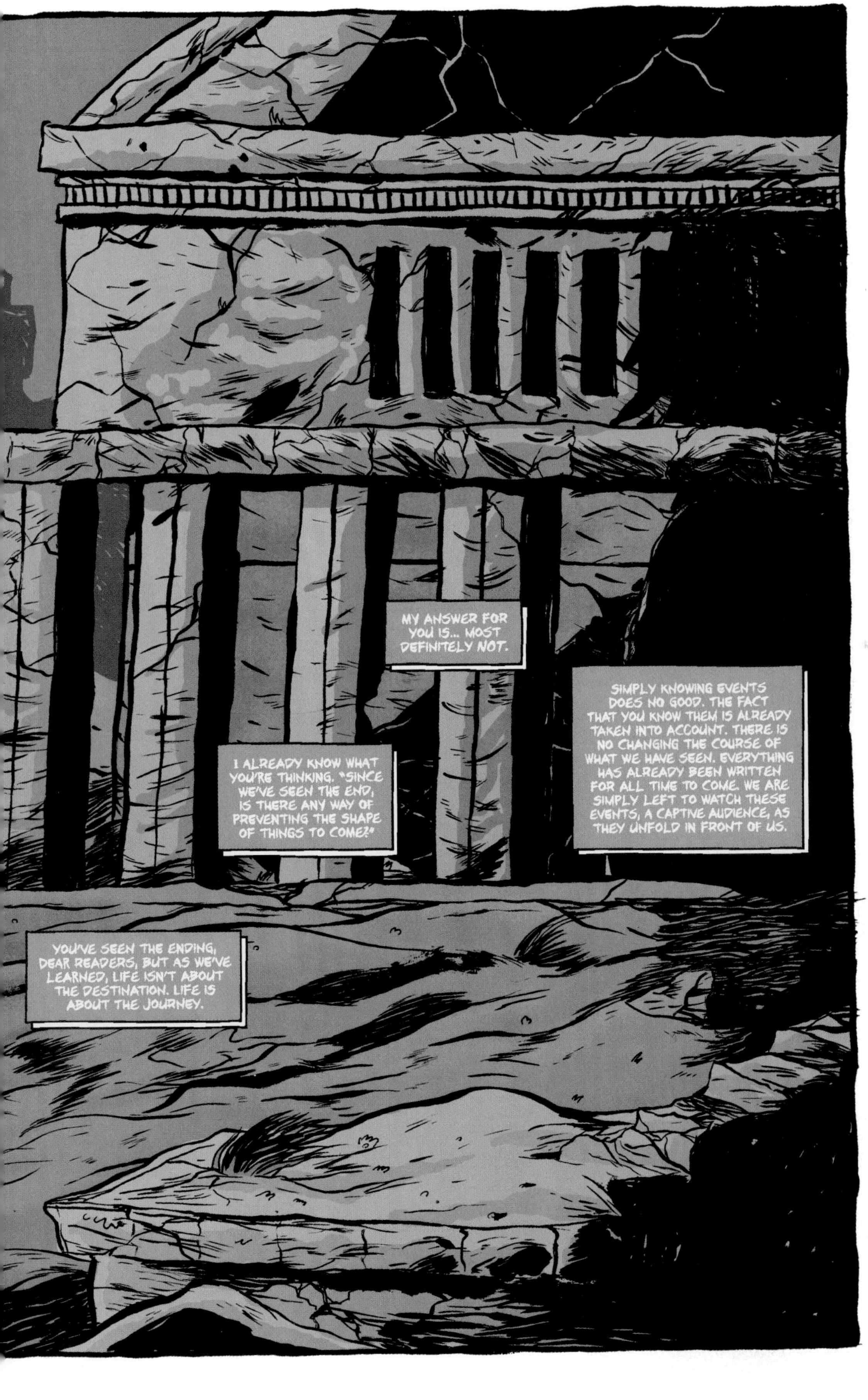
MY ANSWER FOR YOU IS... MOST DEFINITELY NOT.
I ALREADY KNOW WHAT YOU'RE THINKING. "SINCE WE'VE SEEN THE END, IS THERE ANY WAY OF PREVENTING THE SHAPE OF THINGS TO COME?"
SIMPLY KNOWING EVENTS DOES NO GOOD. THE FACT THAT YOU KNOW THEM IS ALREADY TAKEN INTO ACCOUNT. THERE IS NO CHANGING THE COURSE OF WHAT WE HAVE SEEN. EVERYTHING HAS ALREADY BEEN WRITTEN FOR ALL TIME TO COME. WE ARE SIMPLY LEFT TO WATCH THESE EVENTS, A CAPTIVE AUDIENCE, AS THEY UNFOLD IN FRONT OF US.
YOU'VE SEEN THE ENDING, DEAR READERS, BUT AS WE'VE LEARNED, LIFE ISN'T ABOUT THE DESTINATION. LIFE IS ABOUT THE JOURNEY.

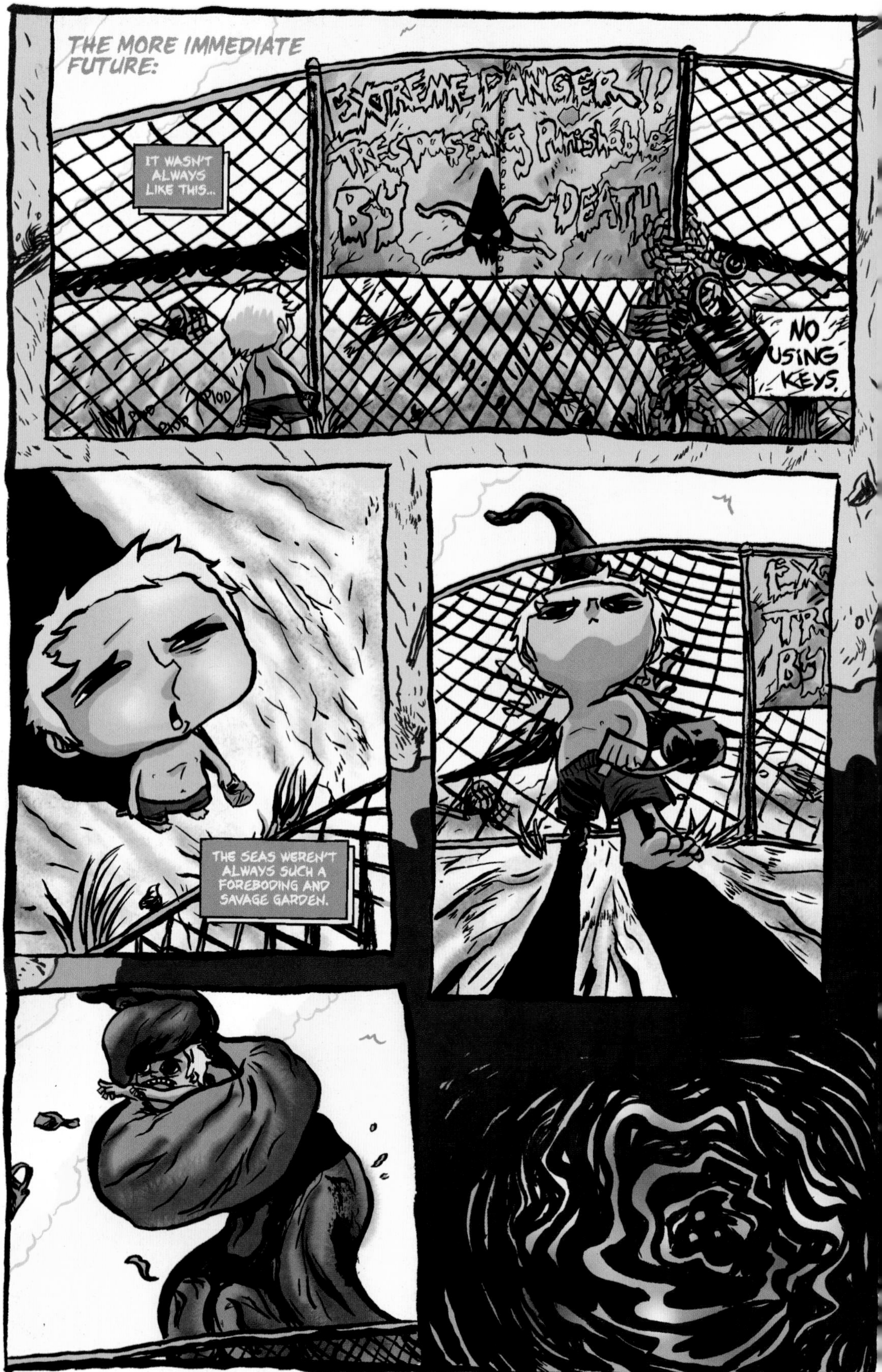
THE MORE IMMEDIATE FUTURE:
EXTREME DANGER!!
Trespassing Punishable
BY DEATH
IT WASN'T ALWAYS LIKE THIS...
NO USING KEYS
PLOD
PLOD
PLOD
THE SEAS WEREN'T ALWAYS SUCH A FOREBODING AND SAVAGE GARDEN.

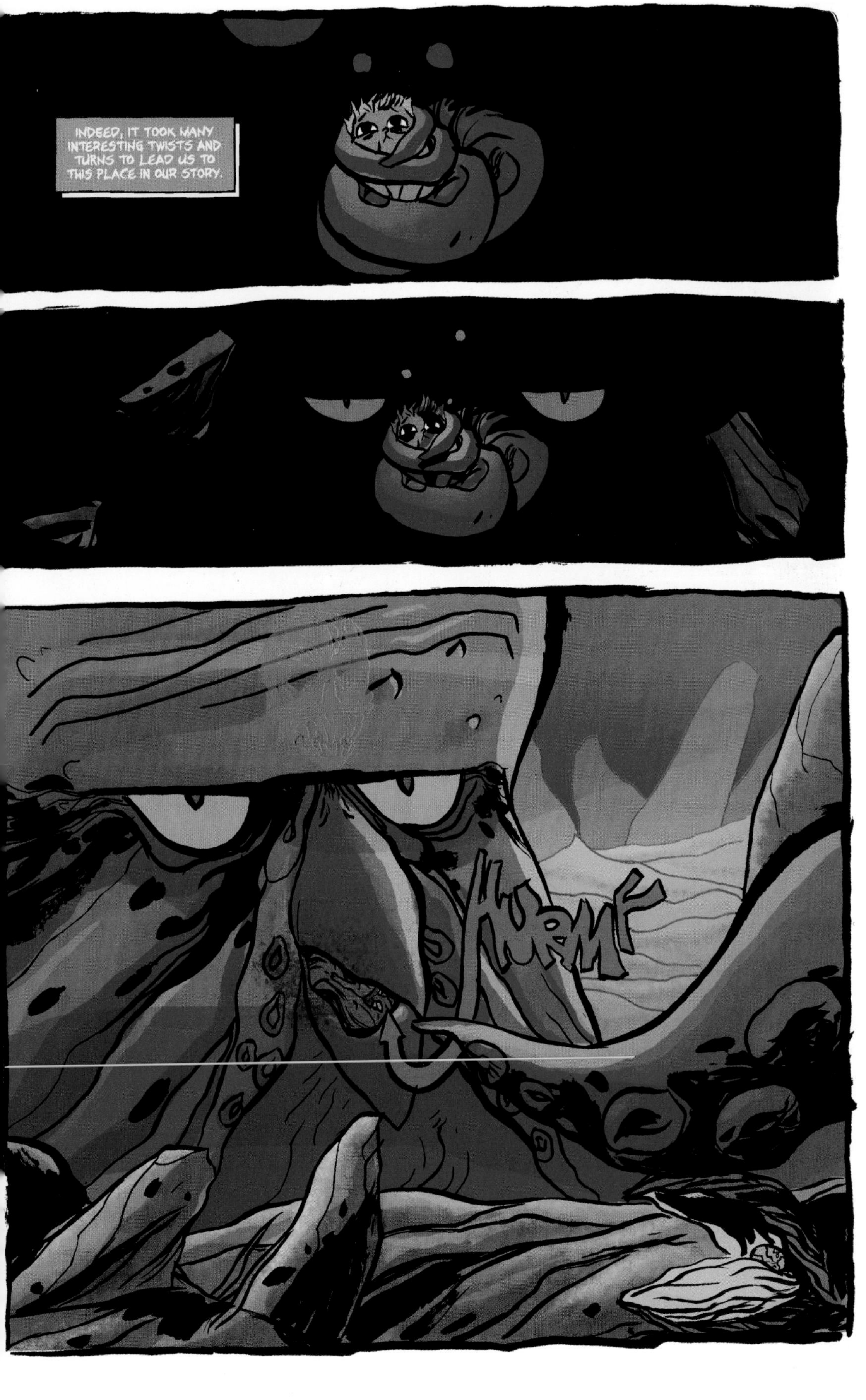
INDEED, IT TOOK MANY INTERESTING TWISTS AND TURNS TO LEAD US TO THIS PLACE IN OUR STORY.
HURMF

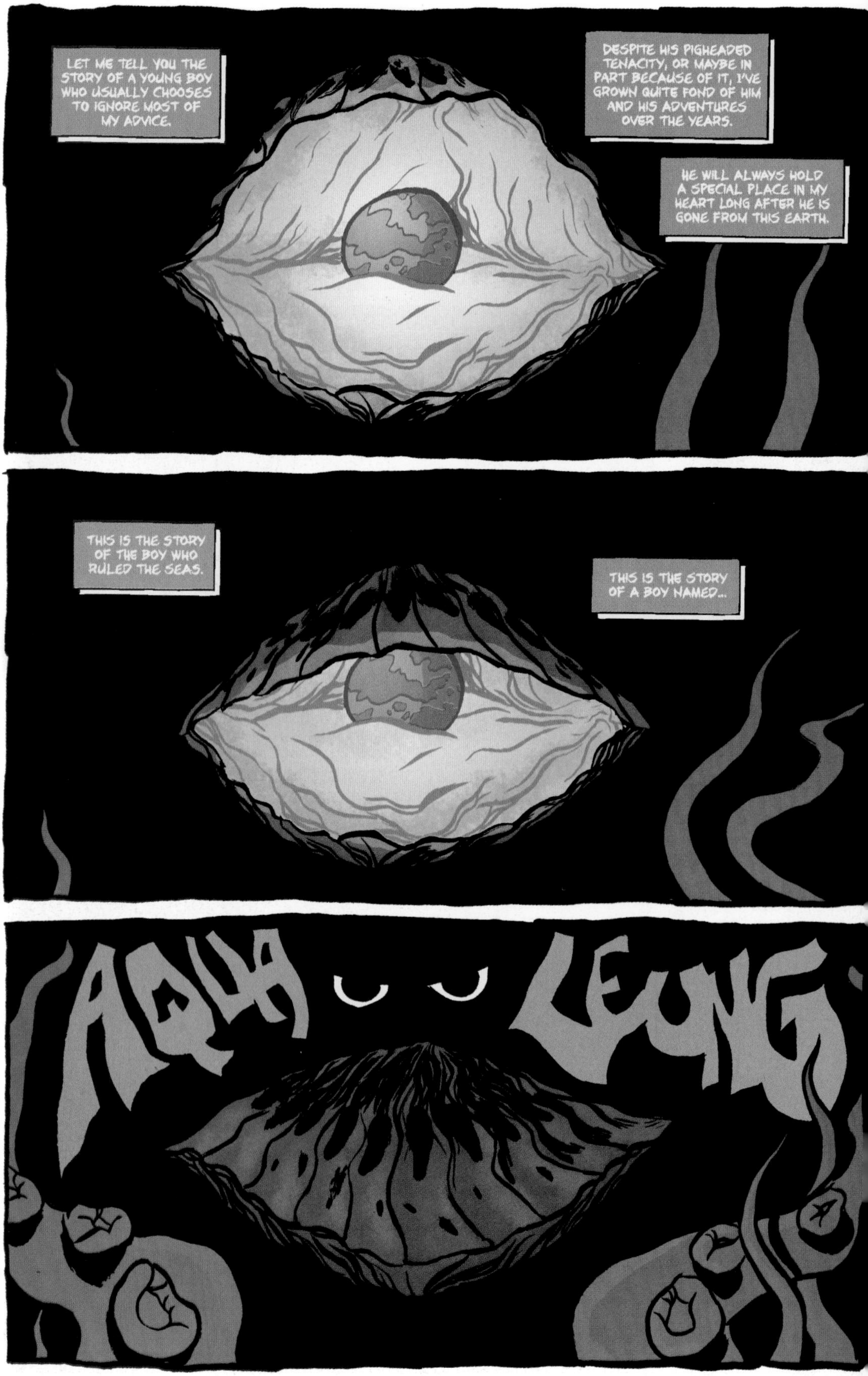
LET ME TELL YOU THE STORY OF A YOUNG BOY WHO USUALLY CHOOSES TO IGNORE MOST OF MY ADVICE.
DESPITE HIS PIGHEADED TENACITY, OR MAYBE IN PART BECAUSE OF IT, I'VE GROWN QUITE FOND OF HIM AND HIS ADVENTURES OVER THE YEARS.
HE WILL ALWAYS HOLD A SPECIAL PLACE IN MY HEART LONG AFTER HE IS GONE FROM THIS EARTH.
THIS IS THE STORY OF THE BOY WHO RULED THE SEAS.
THIS IS THE STORY OF A BOY NAMED...
AQUA LEUNG

CREATED + PRODUCED BY
MARK ANDREW SMITH & PAUL MAYBURY
COLORS BY RUSS LOWERY
LETTERS + LOGO BY FONOGRAFIKS
EDITED BY DJ KIRKBRIDE & CASSANDRA PASLEY
BOOK DESIGN BY THOMAS MAUER

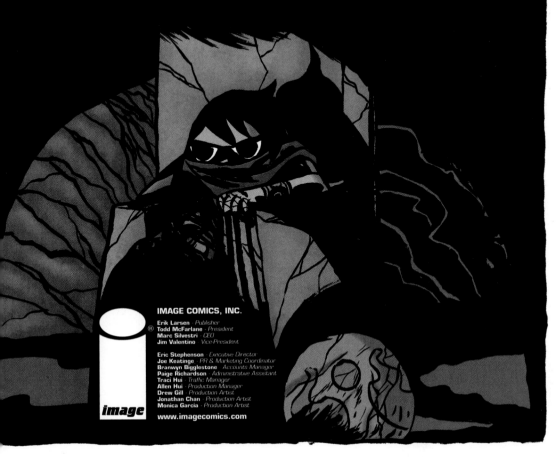

IMAGE COMICS, INC.

Erik Larsen - *Publisher*
Todd McFarlane - *President*
Marc Silvestri - *CEO*
Jim Valentino - *Vice-President*

Eric Stephenson - *Executive Director*
Joe Keatinge - *PR & Marketing Coordinator*
Branwyn Bigglestone - *Accounts Manager*
Paige Richardson - *Administrative Assistant*
Traci Hui - *Traffic Manager*
Allen Hui - *Production Manager*
Drew Gill - *Production Artist*
Jonathan Chan - *Production Artist*
Monica Garcia - *Production Artist*

www.imagecomics.com

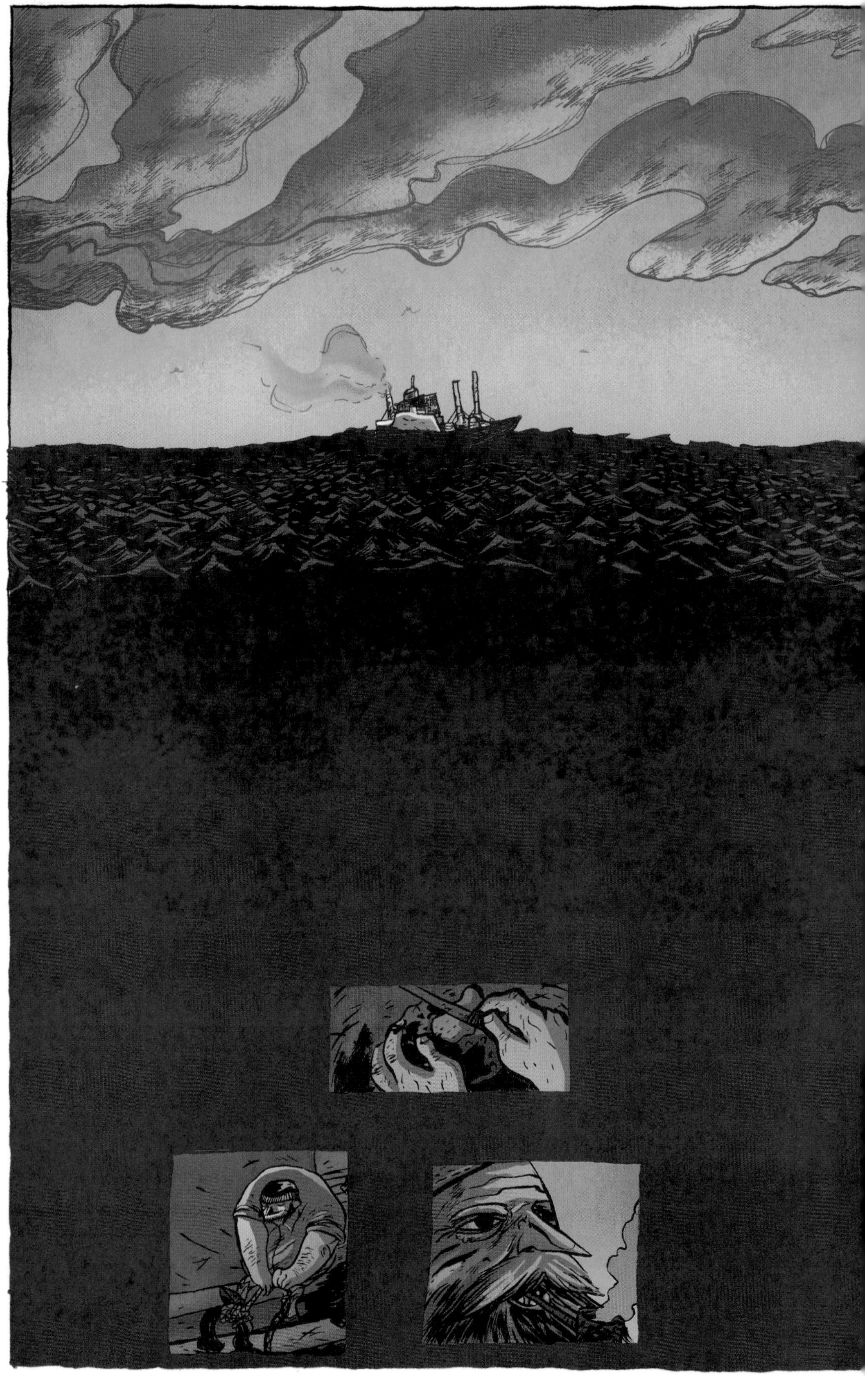

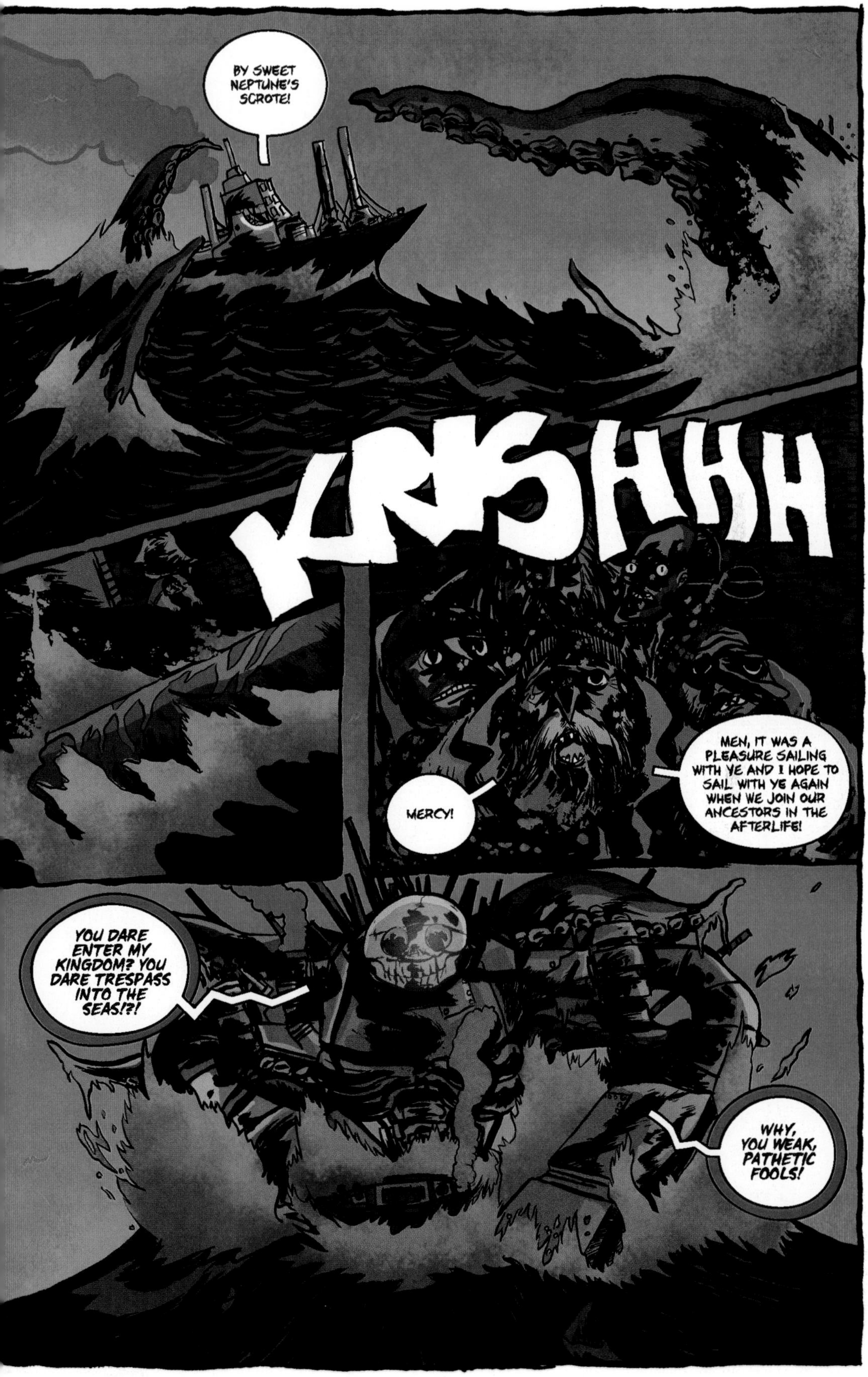
BY SWEET NEPTUNE'S SCROTE!
KRSHHH
MERCY!
MEN, IT WAS A PLEASURE SAILING WITH YE AND I HOPE TO SAIL WITH YE AGAIN WHEN WE JOIN OUR ANCESTORS IN THE AFTERLIFE!
YOU DARE ENTER MY KINGDOM? YOU DARE TRESPASS INTO THE SEAS!?!
WHY, YOU WEAK, PATHETIC FOOLS!

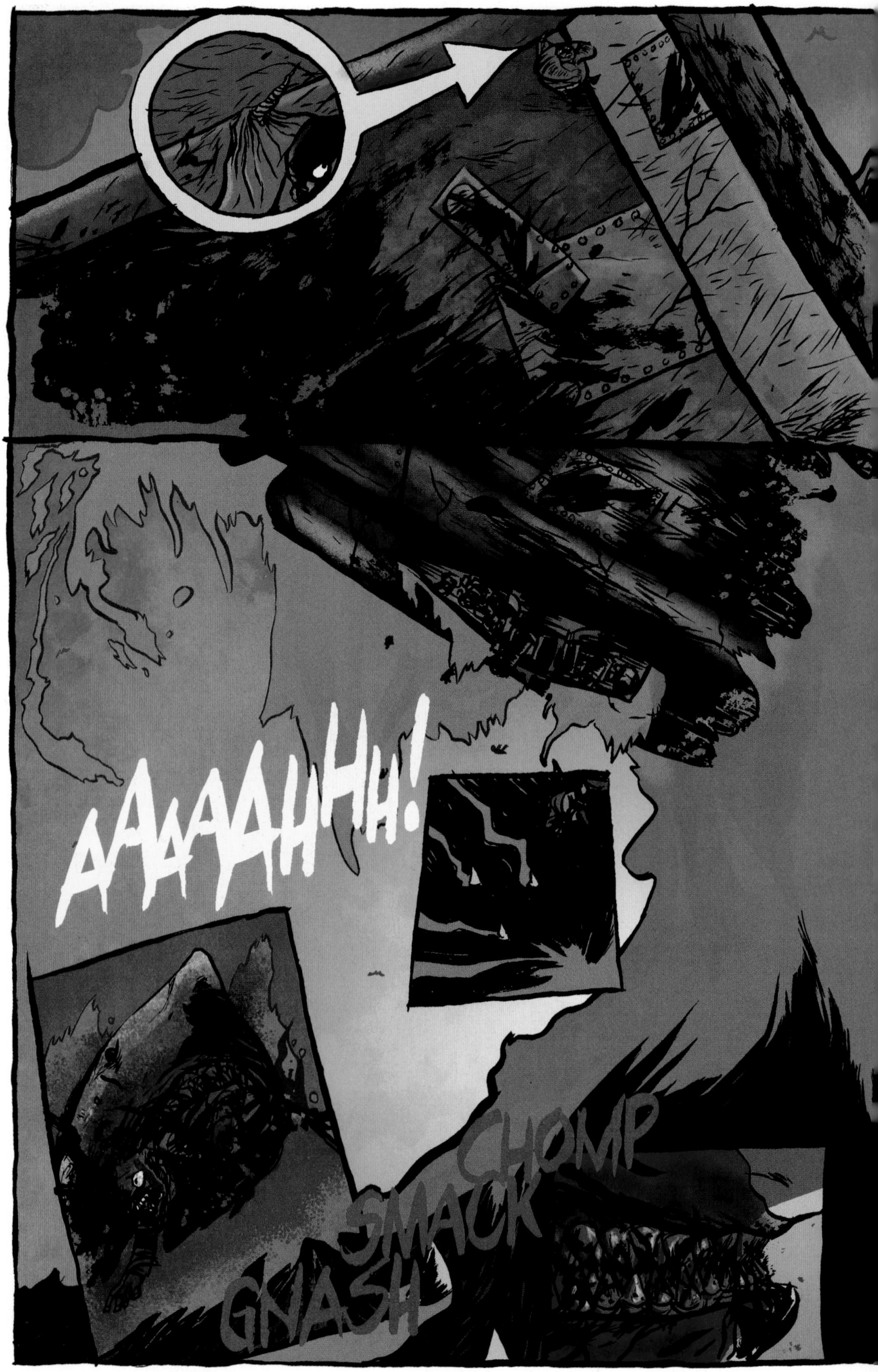

AAAAAHHH!
CHOMP
SMACK
GNASH

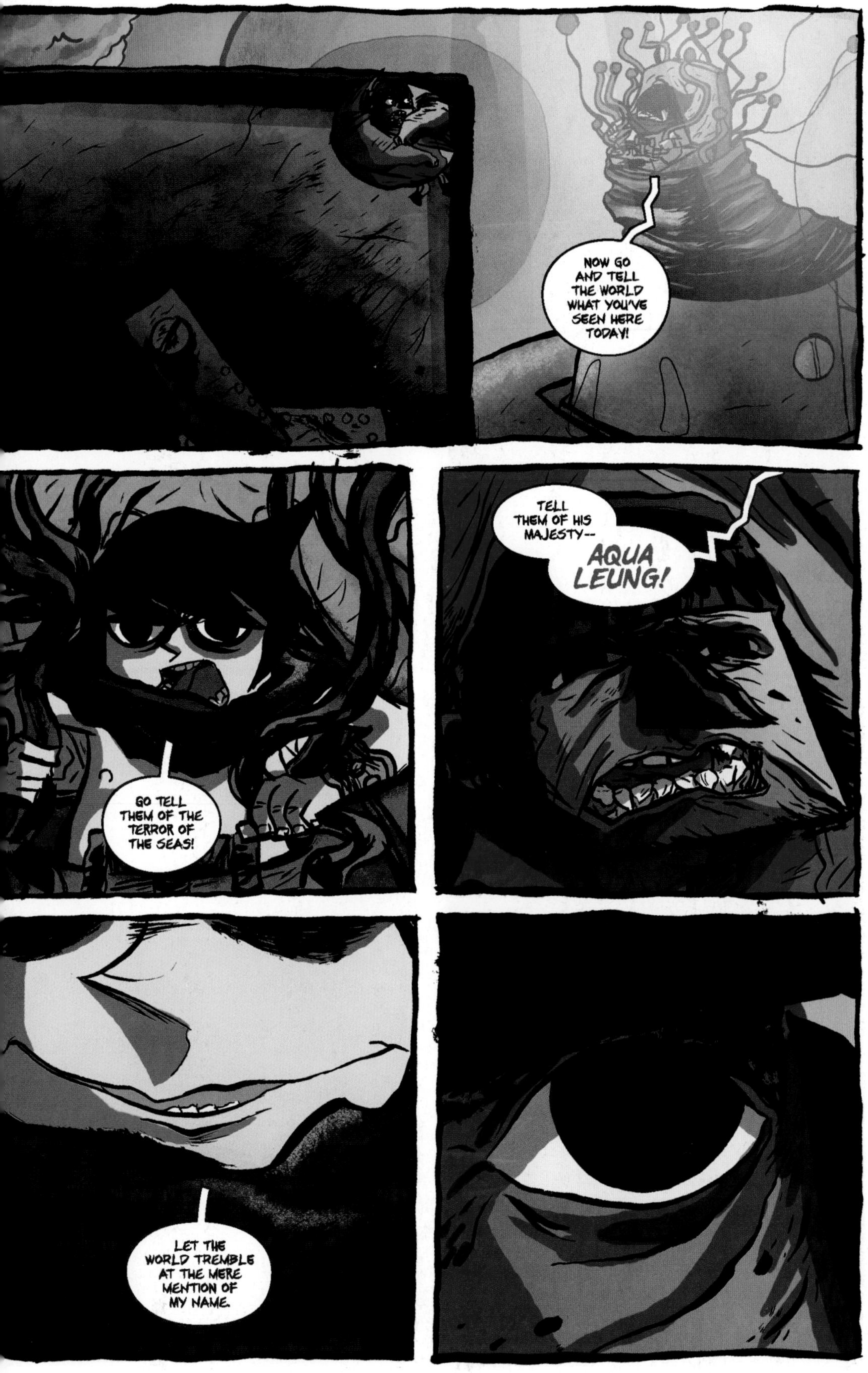
NOW GO AND TELL THE WORLD WHAT YOU'VE SEEN HERE TODAY!
GO TELL THEM OF THE TERROR OF THE SEAS!
TELL THEM OF HIS MAJESTY--
AQUA LEUNG!
LET THE WORLD TREMBLE AT THE MERE MENTION OF MY NAME.

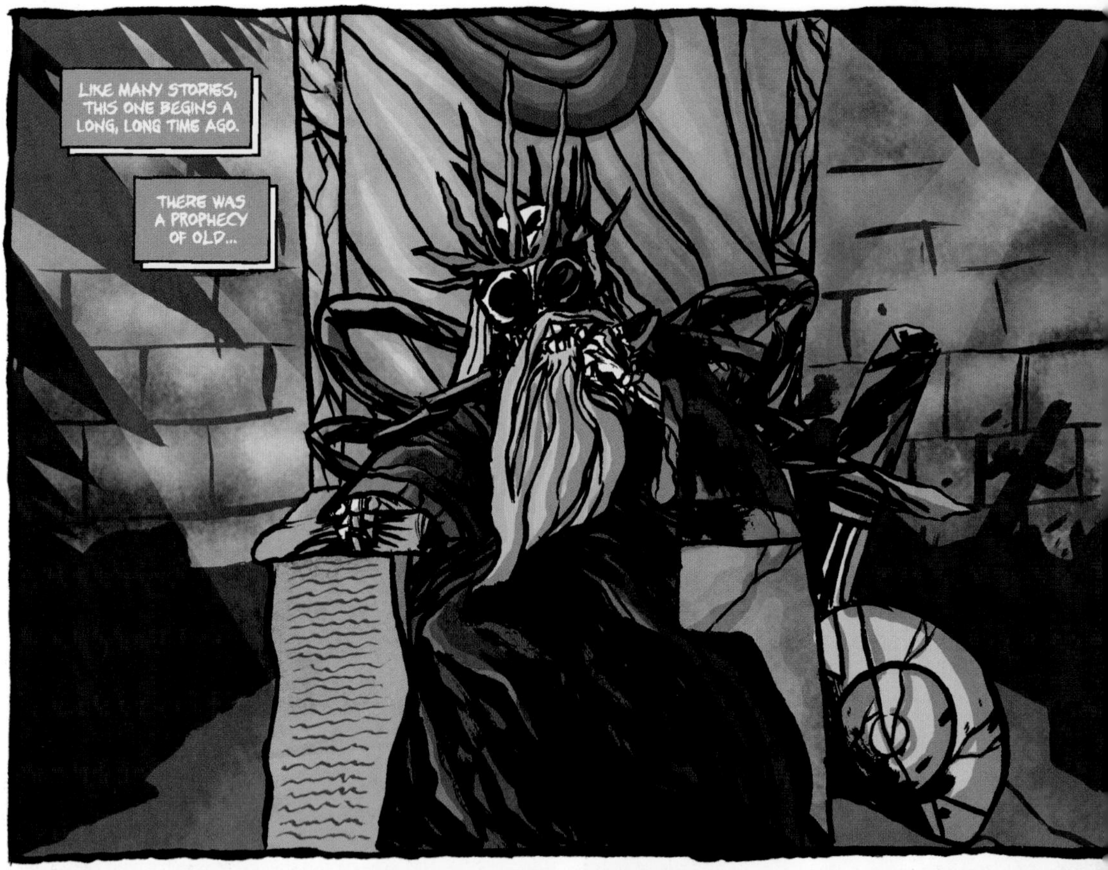
LIKE MANY STORIES, THIS ONE BEGINS A LONG, LONG TIME AGO.
THERE WAS A PROPHECY OF OLD...

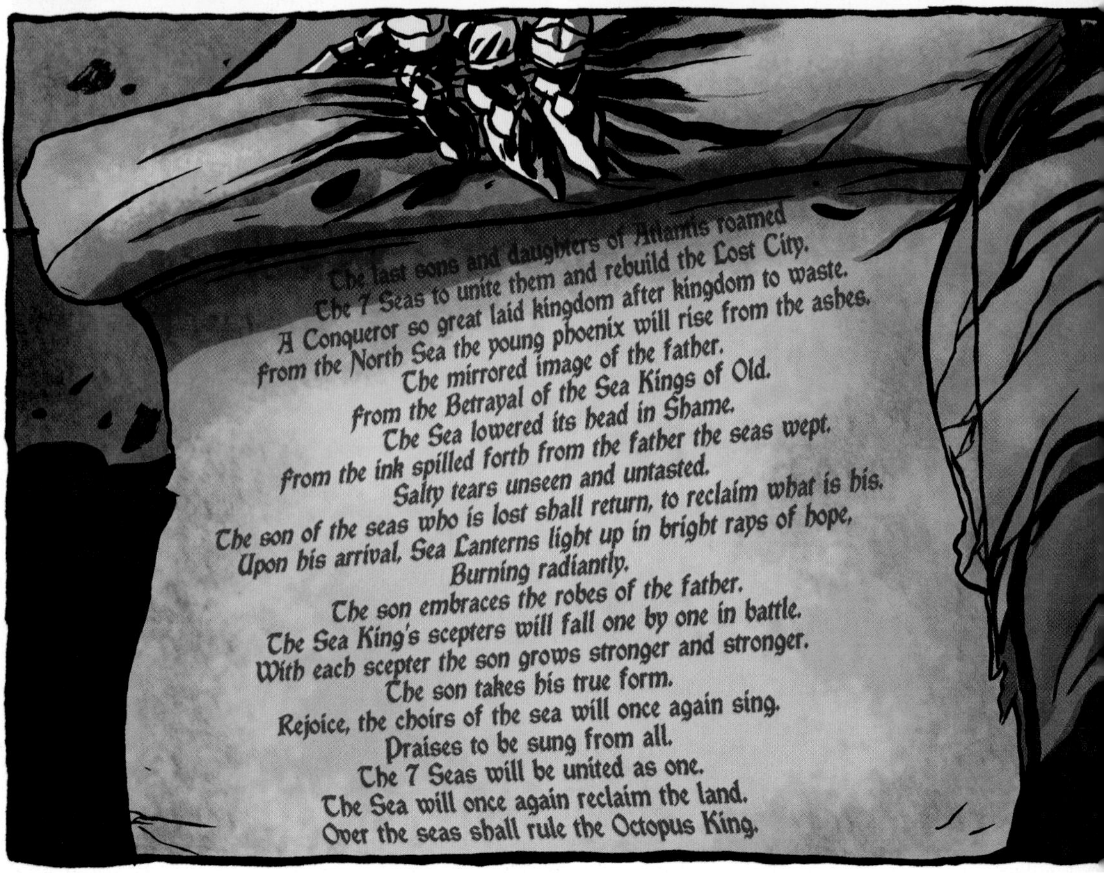
The last sons and daughters of Atlantis roamed
The 7 Seas to unite them and rebuild the Lost City.
A Conqueror so great laid kingdom after kingdom to waste.
From the North Sea the young phoenix will rise from the ashes.
The mirrored image of the father.
From the Betrayal of the Sea Kings of Old.
The Sea lowered its head in Shame.
From the ink spilled forth from the father the seas wept.
Salty tears unseen and untasted.
The son of the seas who is lost shall return, to reclaim what is his.
Upon his arrival, Sea Lanterns light up in bright rays of hope,
Burning radiantly.
The son embraces the robes of the father.
The Sea King's scepters will fall one by one in battle.
With each scepter the son grows stronger and stronger.
The son takes his true form.
Rejoice, the choirs of the sea will once again sing.
Praises to be sung from all.
The 7 Seas will be united as one.
The Sea will once again reclaim the land.
Over the seas shall rule the Octopus King.

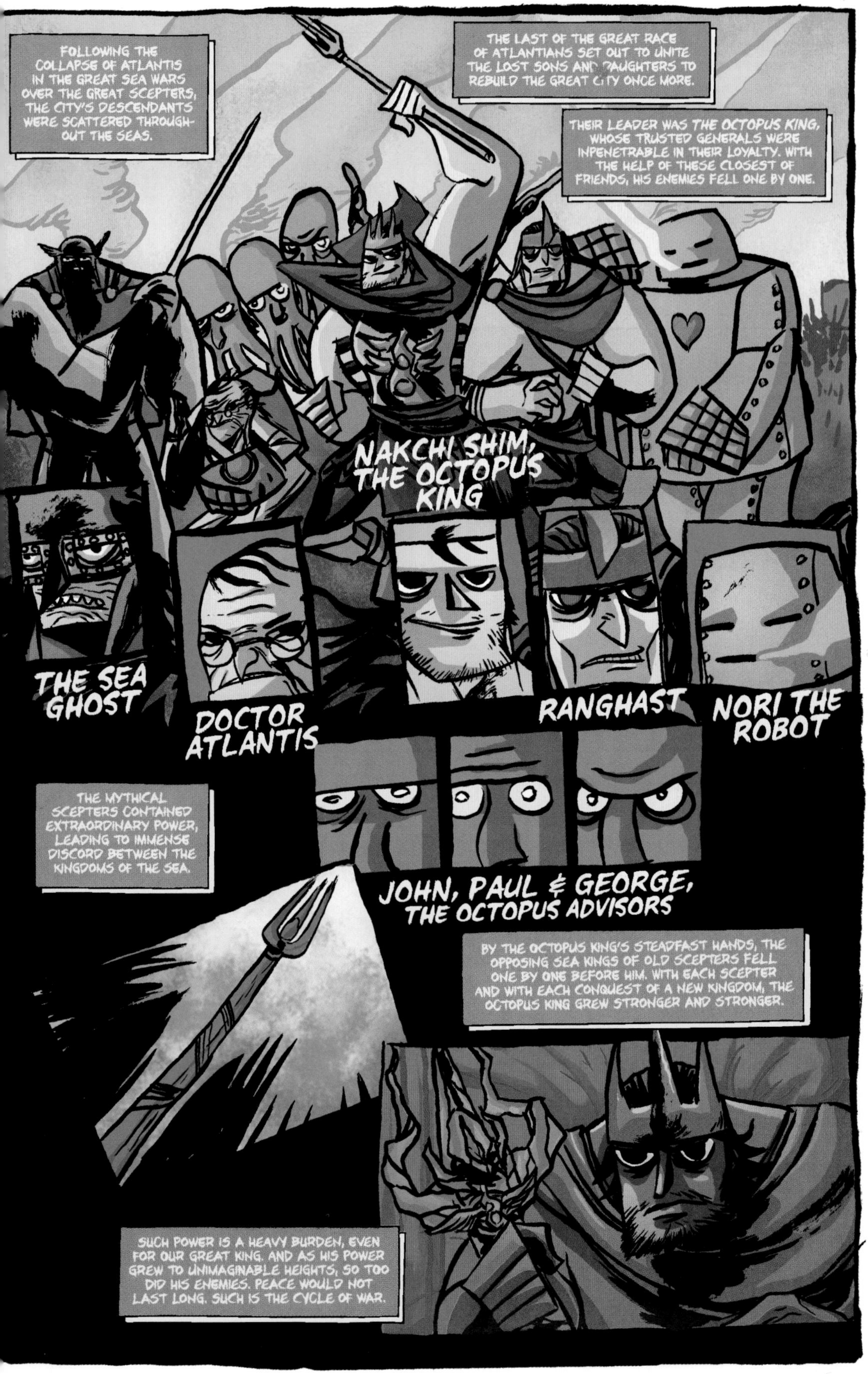
FOLLOWING THE COLLAPSE OF ATLANTIS IN THE GREAT SEA WARS OVER THE GREAT SCEPTERS, THE CITY'S DESCENDANTS WERE SCATTERED THROUGH-OUT THE SEAS.
THE LAST OF THE GREAT RACE OF ATLANTIANS SET OUT TO UNITE THE LOST SONS AND DAUGHTERS TO REBUILD THE GREAT CITY ONCE MORE.
THEIR LEADER WAS THE OCTOPUS KING, WHOSE TRUSTED GENERALS WERE INPENETRABLE IN THEIR LOYALTY. WITH THE HELP OF THESE CLOSEST OF FRIENDS, HIS ENEMIES FELL ONE BY ONE.
NAKCHI SHIM, THE OCTOPUS KING
THE SEA GHOST
DOCTOR ATLANTIS
RANGHAST
NORI THE ROBOT
THE MYTHICAL SCEPTERS CONTAINED EXTRAORDINARY POWER, LEADING TO IMMENSE DISCORD BETWEEN THE KINGDOMS OF THE SEA.
JOHN, PAUL & GEORGE, THE OCTOPUS ADVISORS
BY THE OCTOPUS KING'S STEADFAST HANDS, THE OPPOSING SEA KINGS OF OLD SCEPTERS FELL ONE BY ONE BEFORE HIM. WITH EACH SCEPTER AND WITH EACH CONQUEST OF A NEW KINGDOM, THE OCTOPUS KING GREW STRONGER AND STRONGER.
SUCH POWER IS A HEAVY BURDEN, EVEN FOR OUR GREAT KING. AND AS HIS POWER GREW TO UNIMAGINABLE HEIGHTS, SO TOO DID HIS ENEMIES. PEACE WOULD NOT LAST LONG. SUCH IS THE CYCLE OF WAR.

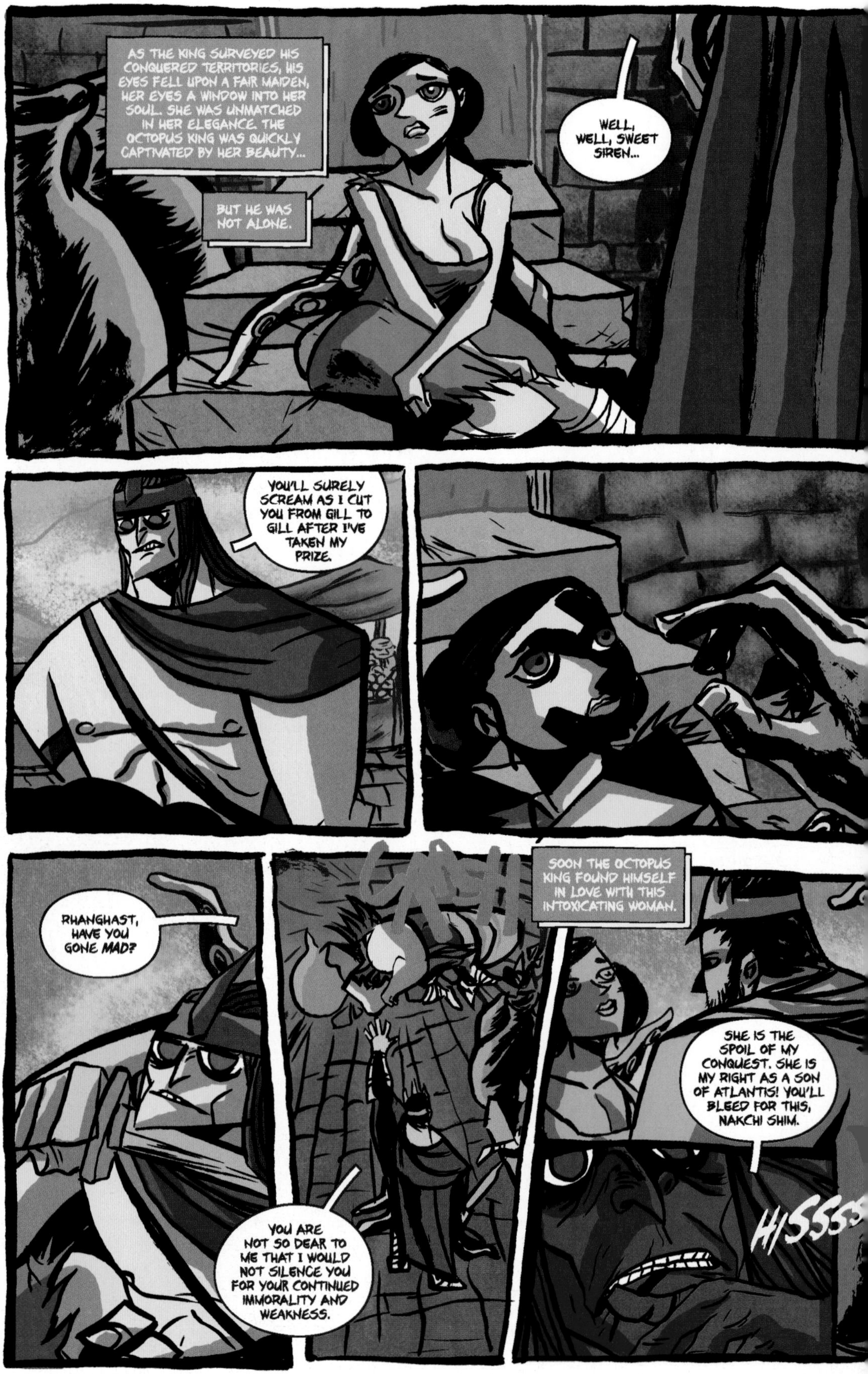
AS THE KING SURVEYED HIS CONQUERED TERRITORIES, HIS EYES FELL UPON A FAIR MAIDEN, HER EYES A WINDOW INTO HER SOUL. SHE WAS UNMATCHED IN HER ELEGANCE. THE OCTOPUS KING WAS QUICKLY CAPTIVATED BY HER BEAUTY...
BUT HE WAS NOT ALONE.
WELL, WELL, SWEET SIREN...
YOU'LL SURELY SCREAM AS I CUT YOU FROM GILL TO GILL AFTER I'VE TAKEN MY PRIZE.
RHANGHAST, HAVE YOU GONE MAD?
YOU ARE NOT SO DEAR TO ME THAT I WOULD NOT SILENCE YOU FOR YOUR CONTINUED IMMORALITY AND WEAKNESS.
SOON THE OCTOPUS KING FOUND HIMSELF IN LOVE WITH THIS INTOXICATING WOMAN.
SHE IS THE SPOIL OF MY CONQUEST. SHE IS MY RIGHT AS A SON OF ATLANTIS! YOU'LL BLEED FOR THIS, NAKCHI SHIM.
HISSSS

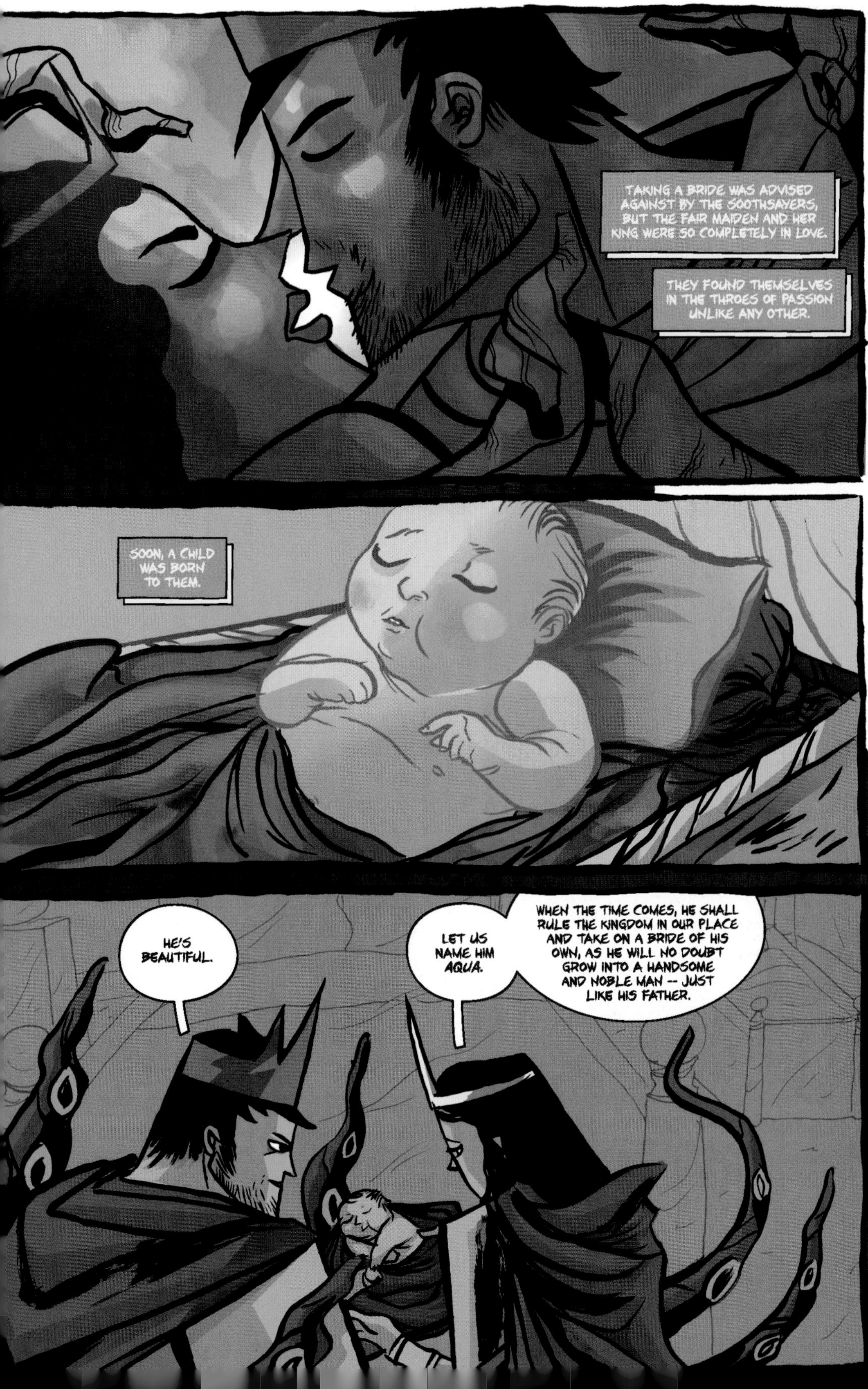
TAKING A BRIDE WAS ADVISED AGAINST BY THE SOOTHSAYERS, BUT THE FAIR MAIDEN AND HER KING WERE SO COMPLETELY IN LOVE.
THEY FOUND THEMSELVES IN THE THROES OF PASSION UNLIKE ANY OTHER.
SOON, A CHILD WAS BORN TO THEM.
HE'S BEAUTIFUL.
LET US NAME HIM AQUA.
WHEN THE TIME COMES, HE SHALL RULE THE KINGDOM IN OUR PLACE AND TAKE ON A BRIDE OF HIS OWN, AS HE WILL NO DOUBT GROW INTO A HANDSOME AND NOBLE MAN -- JUST LIKE HIS FATHER.

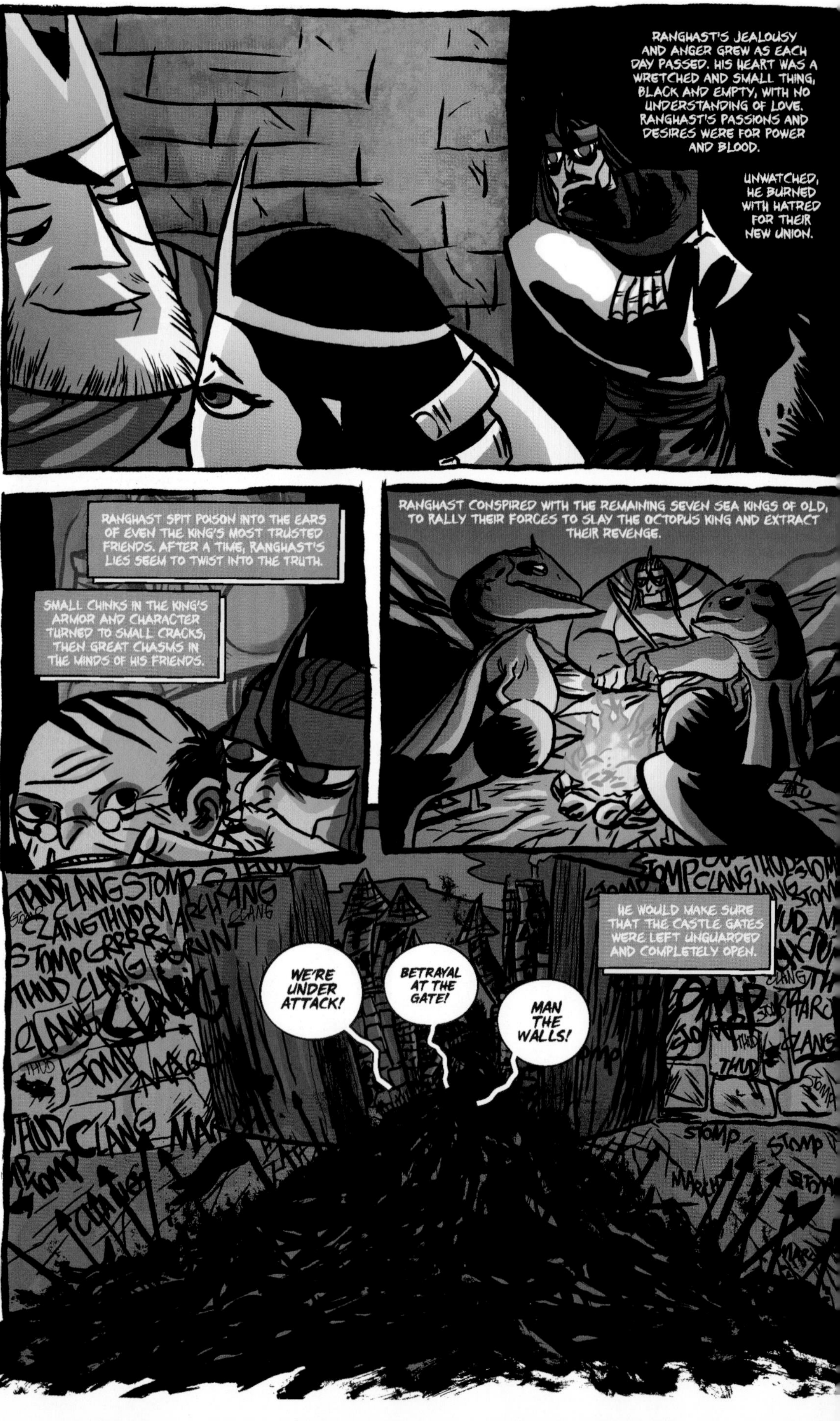
RANGHAST'S JEALOUSY AND ANGER GREW AS EACH DAY PASSED. HIS HEART WAS A WRETCHED AND SMALL THING, BLACK AND EMPTY, WITH NO UNDERSTANDING OF LOVE. RANGHAST'S PASSIONS AND DESIRES WERE FOR POWER AND BLOOD.
UNWATCHED, HE BURNED WITH HATRED FOR THEIR NEW UNION.
RANGHAST SPIT POISON INTO THE EARS OF EVEN THE KING'S MOST TRUSTED FRIENDS. AFTER A TIME, RANGHAST'S LIES SEEM TO TWIST INTO THE TRUTH.
SMALL CHINKS IN THE KING'S ARMOR AND CHARACTER TURNED TO SMALL CRACKS, THEN GREAT CHASMS IN THE MINDS OF HIS FRIENDS.
RANGHAST CONSPIRED WITH THE REMAINING SEVEN SEA KINGS OF OLD, TO RALLY THEIR FORCES TO SLAY THE OCTOPUS KING AND EXTRACT THEIR REVENGE.
THUD CLANG STOMP CLANG
STOMP CLANG THUD
HE WOULD MAKE SURE THAT THE CASTLE GATES WERE LEFT UNGUARDED AND COMPLETELY OPEN.
WE'RE UNDER ATTACK!
BETRAYAL AT THE GATE!
MAN THE WALLS!
THUD CLANG
STOMP STOMP

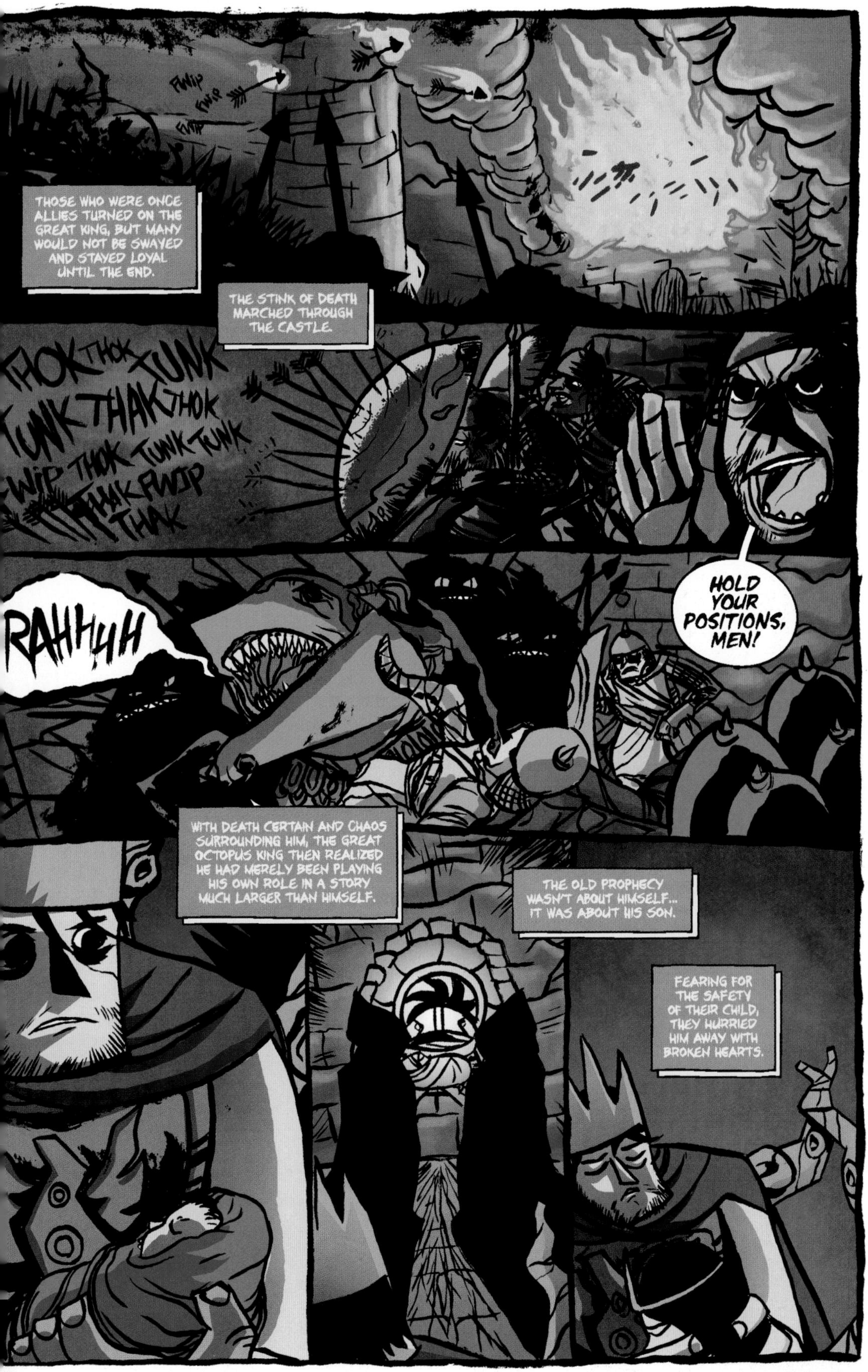
FWIP
FWIP
FWIP
THOSE WHO WERE ONCE ALLIES TURNED ON THE GREAT KING, BUT MANY WOULD NOT BE SWAYED AND STAYED LOYAL UNTIL THE END.
THE STINK OF DEATH MARCHED THROUGH THE CASTLE.
THOK THOK TUNK TUNK THAK THOK FWIP THOK TUNK TUNK THAK FWIP THAK
HOLD YOUR POSITIONS, MEN!
RAHHHH
WITH DEATH CERTAIN AND CHAOS SURROUNDING HIM, THE GREAT OCTOPUS KING THEN REALIZED HE HAD MERELY BEEN PLAYING HIS OWN ROLE IN A STORY MUCH LARGER THAN HIMSELF.
THE OLD PROPHECY WASN'T ABOUT HIMSELF... IT WAS ABOUT HIS SON.
FEARING FOR THE SAFETY OF THEIR CHILD, THEY HURRIED HIM AWAY WITH BROKEN HEARTS.

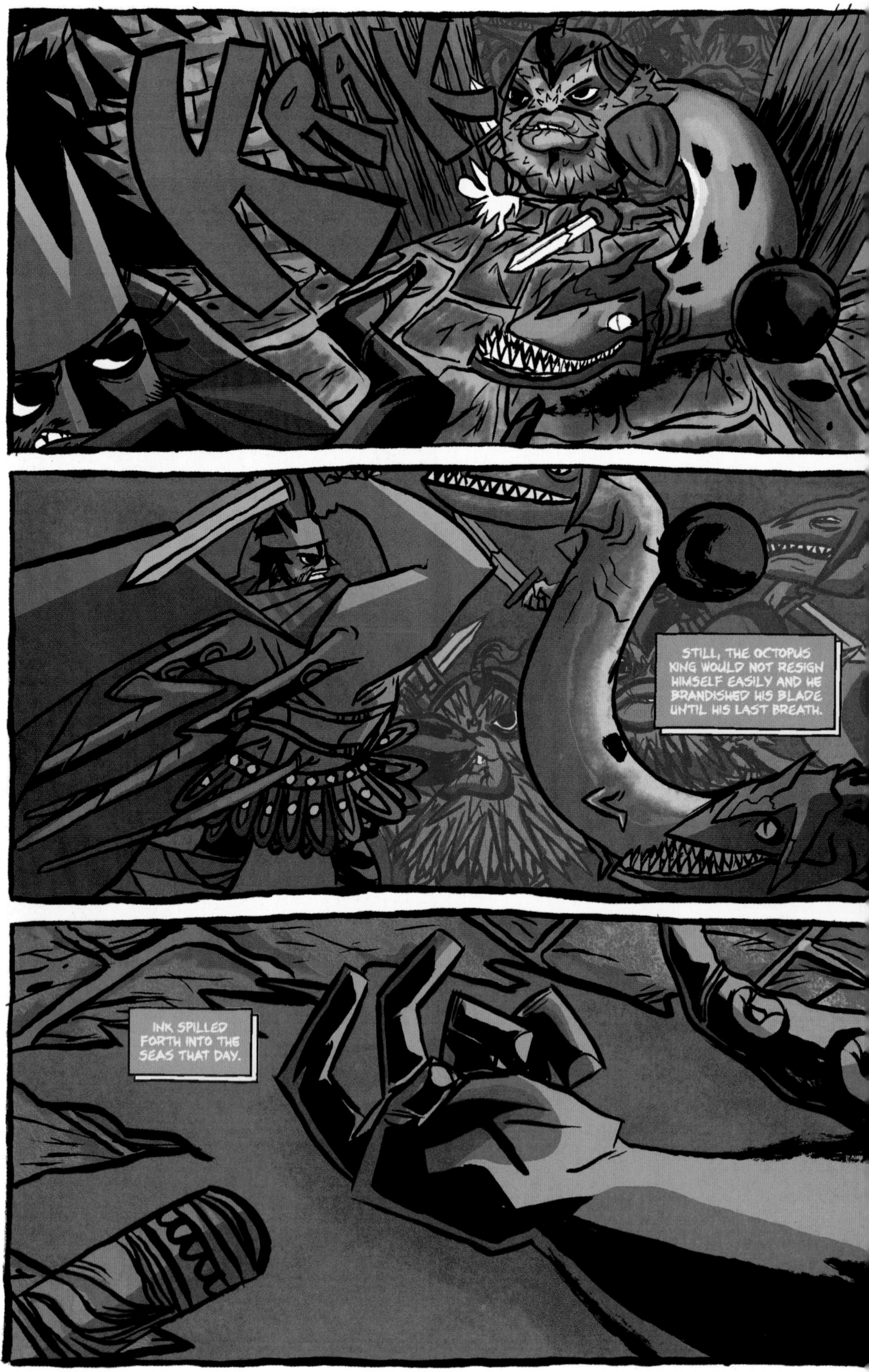

KRAK
STILL, THE OCTOPUS KING WOULD NOT RESIGN HIMSELF EASILY AND HE BRANDISHED HIS BLADE UNTIL HIS LAST BREATH.
INK SPILLED FORTH INTO THE SEAS THAT DAY.

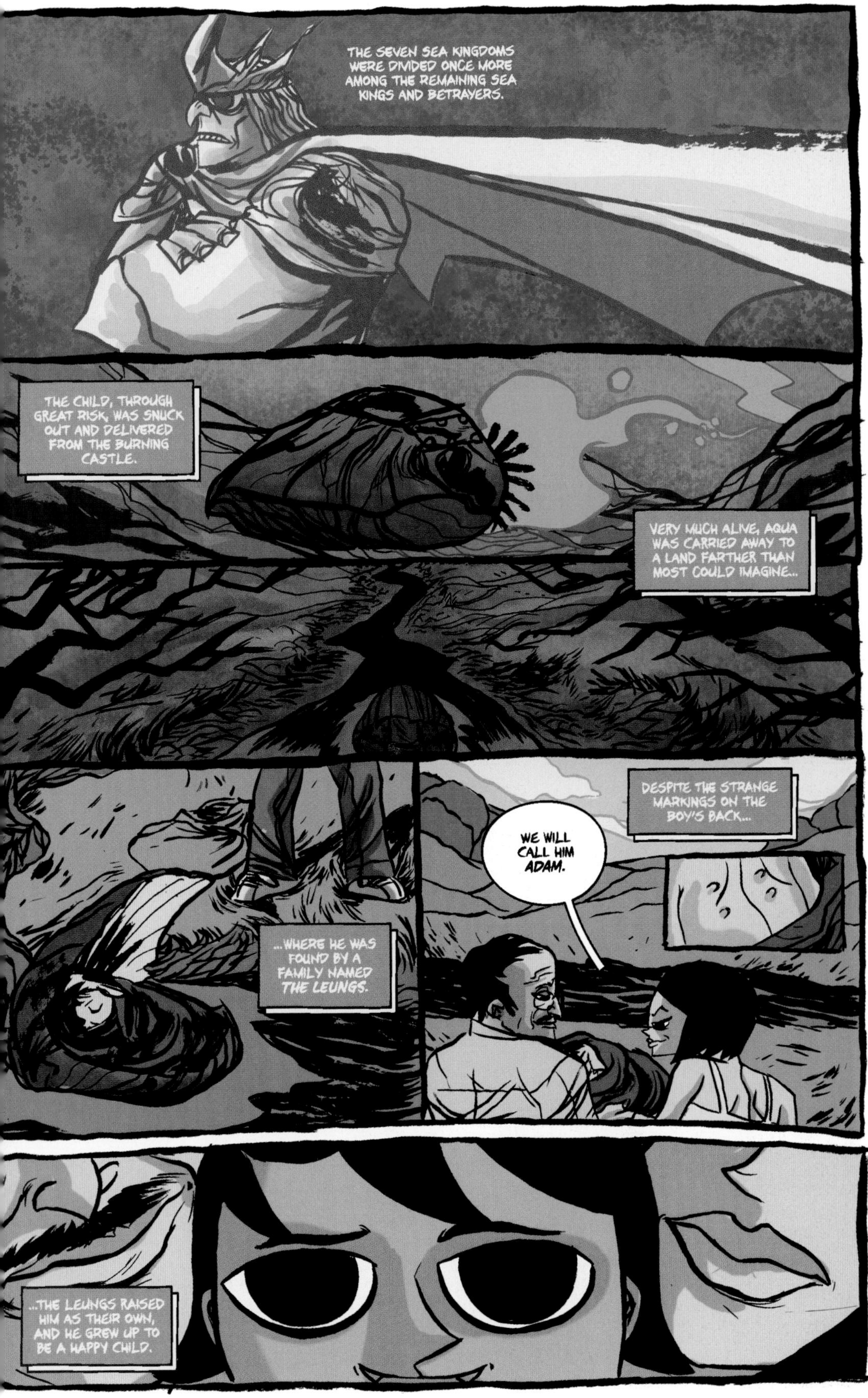

THE SEVEN SEA KINGDOMS WERE DIVIDED ONCE MORE AMONG THE REMAINING SEA KINGS AND BETRAYERS.
THE CHILD, THROUGH GREAT RISK, WAS SNUCK OUT AND DELIVERED FROM THE BURNING CASTLE.
VERY MUCH ALIVE, AQUA WAS CARRIED AWAY TO A LAND FARTHER THAN MOST COULD IMAGINE...
...WHERE HE WAS FOUND BY A FAMILY NAMED THE LEUNGS.
DESPITE THE STRANGE MARKINGS ON THE BOY'S BACK...
WE WILL CALL HIM ADAM.
...THE LEUNGS RAISED HIM AS THEIR OWN, AND HE GREW UP TO BE A HAPPY CHILD.

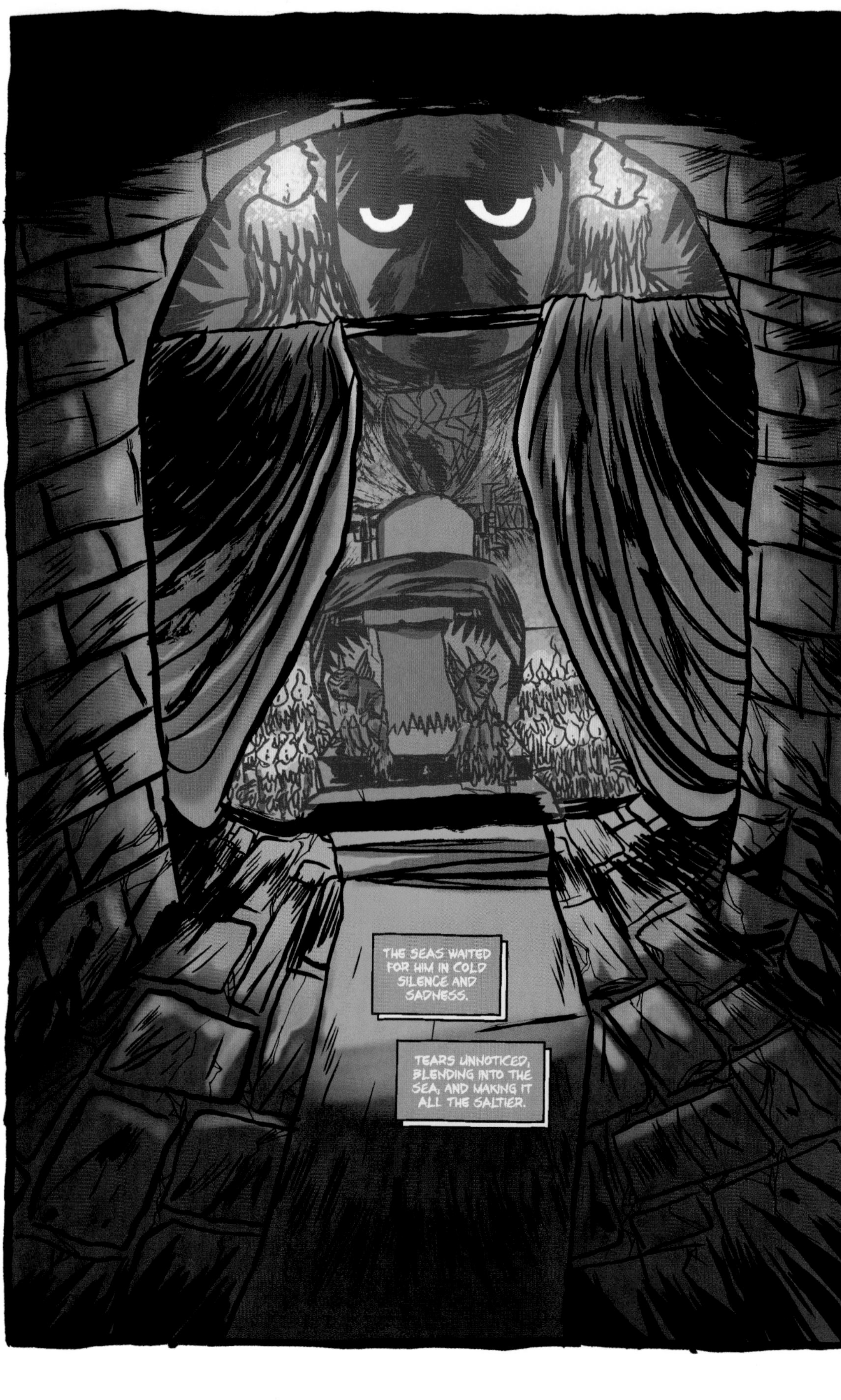
THE SEAS WAITED FOR HIM IN COLD SILENCE AND SADNESS.
TEARS UNNOTICED, BLENDING INTO THE SEA, AND MAKING IT ALL THE SALTIER.

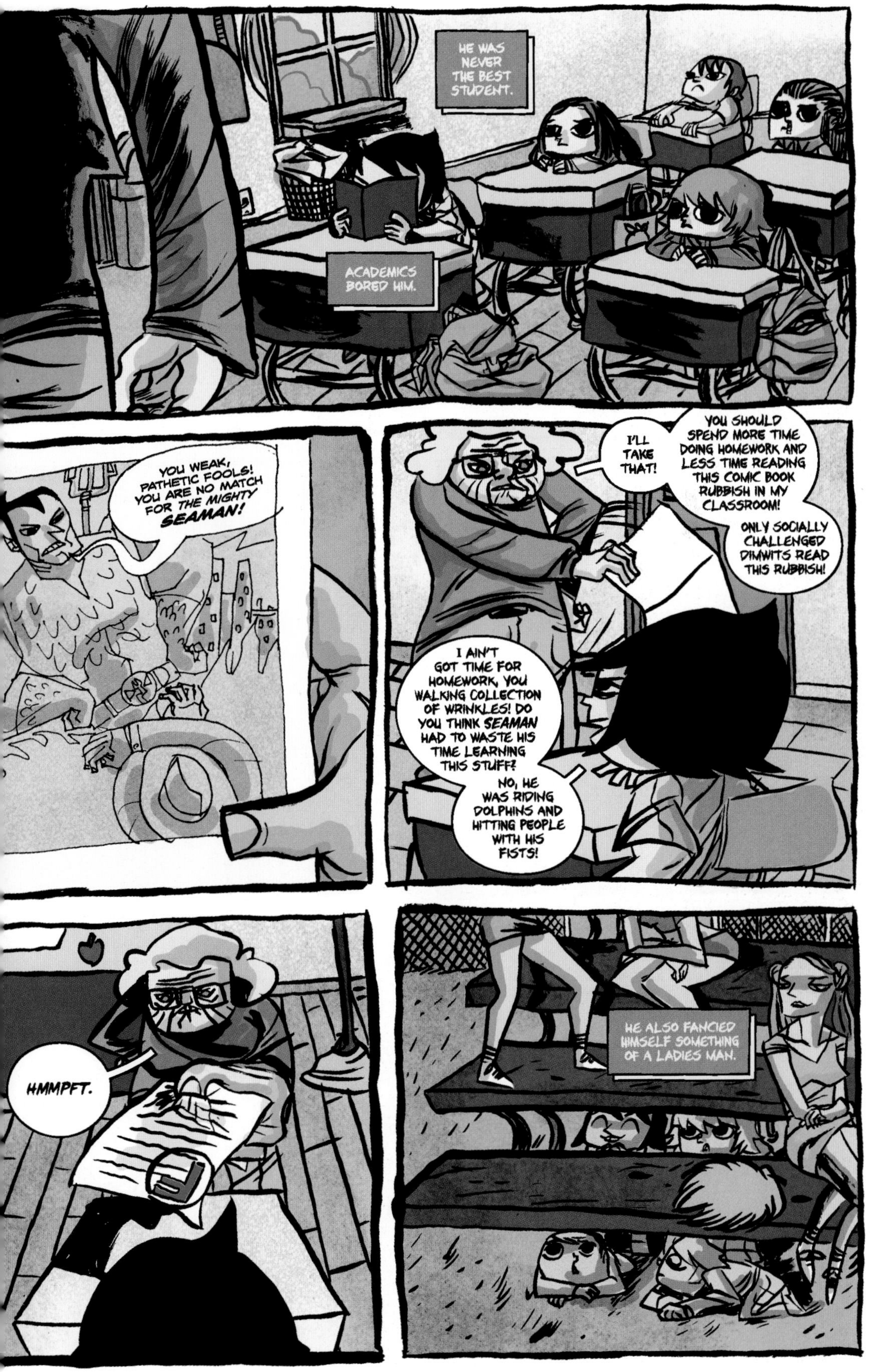
HE WAS NEVER THE BEST STUDENT.
ACADEMICS BORED HIM.
YOU WEAK, PATHETIC FOOLS! YOU ARE NO MATCH FOR THE MIGHTY SEAMAN!
I'LL TAKE THAT!
YOU SHOULD SPEND MORE TIME DOING HOMEWORK AND LESS TIME READING THIS COMIC BOOK RUBBISH IN MY CLASSROOM!
ONLY SOCIALLY CHALLENGED DIMWITS READ THIS RUBBISH!
I AIN'T GOT TIME FOR HOMEWORK, YOU WALKING COLLECTION OF WRINKLES! DO YOU THINK SEAMAN HAD TO WASTE HIS TIME LEARNING THIS STUFF?
NO, HE WAS RIDING DOLPHINS AND HITTING PEOPLE WITH HIS FISTS!
HMMPFT.
HE ALSO FANCIED HIMSELF SOMETHING OF A LADIES MAN.

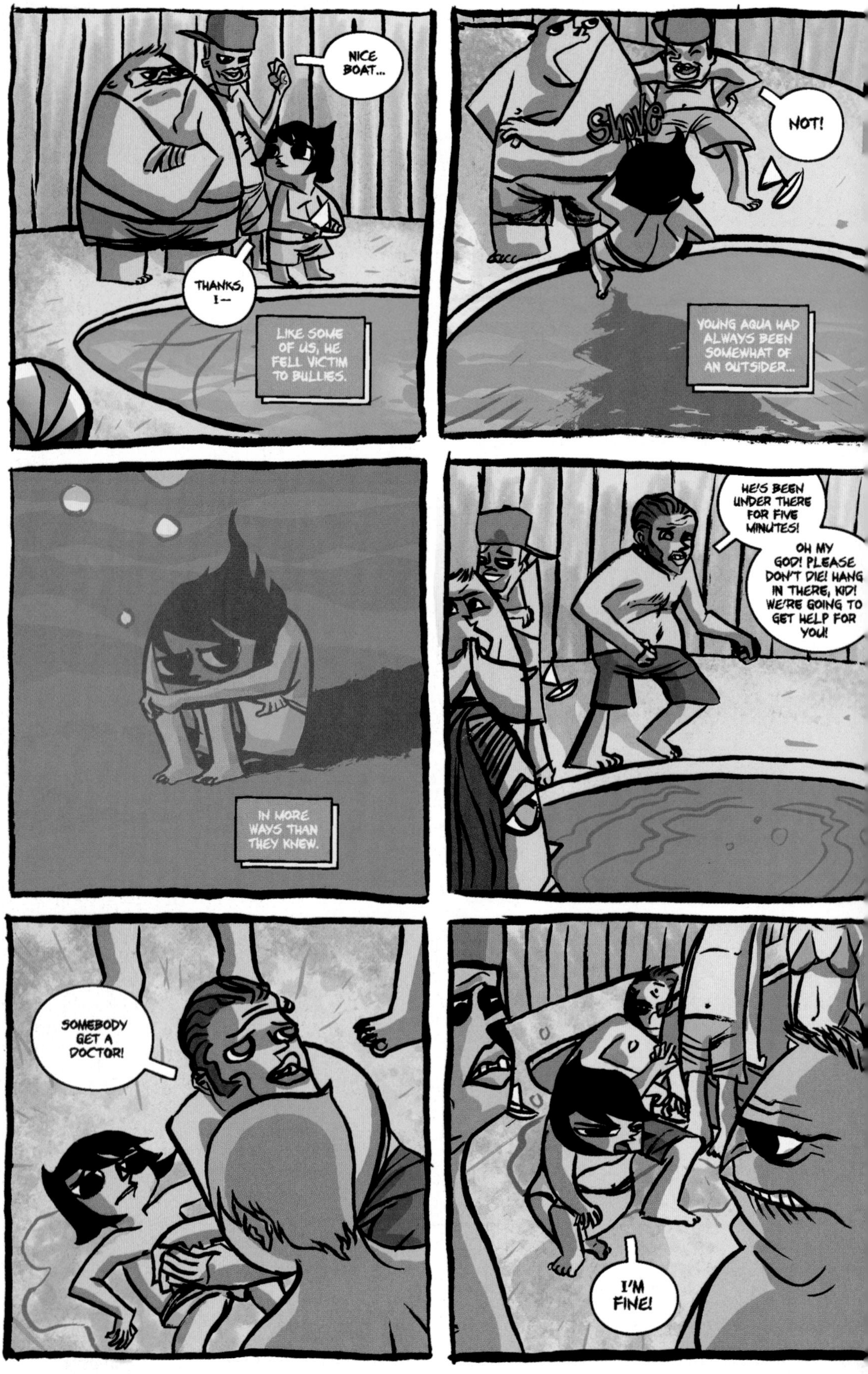

NICE BOAT...
THANKS, I--
LIKE SOME OF US, HE FELL VICTIM TO BULLIES.
NOT!
Shove
YOUNG AQUA HAD ALWAYS BEEN SOMEWHAT OF AN OUTSIDER...
IN MORE WAYS THAN THEY KNEW.
HE'S BEEN UNDER THERE FOR FIVE MINUTES!
OH MY GOD! PLEASE DON'T DIE! HANG IN THERE, KID! WE'RE GOING TO GET HELP FOR YOU!
SOMEBODY GET A DOCTOR!
I'M FINE!

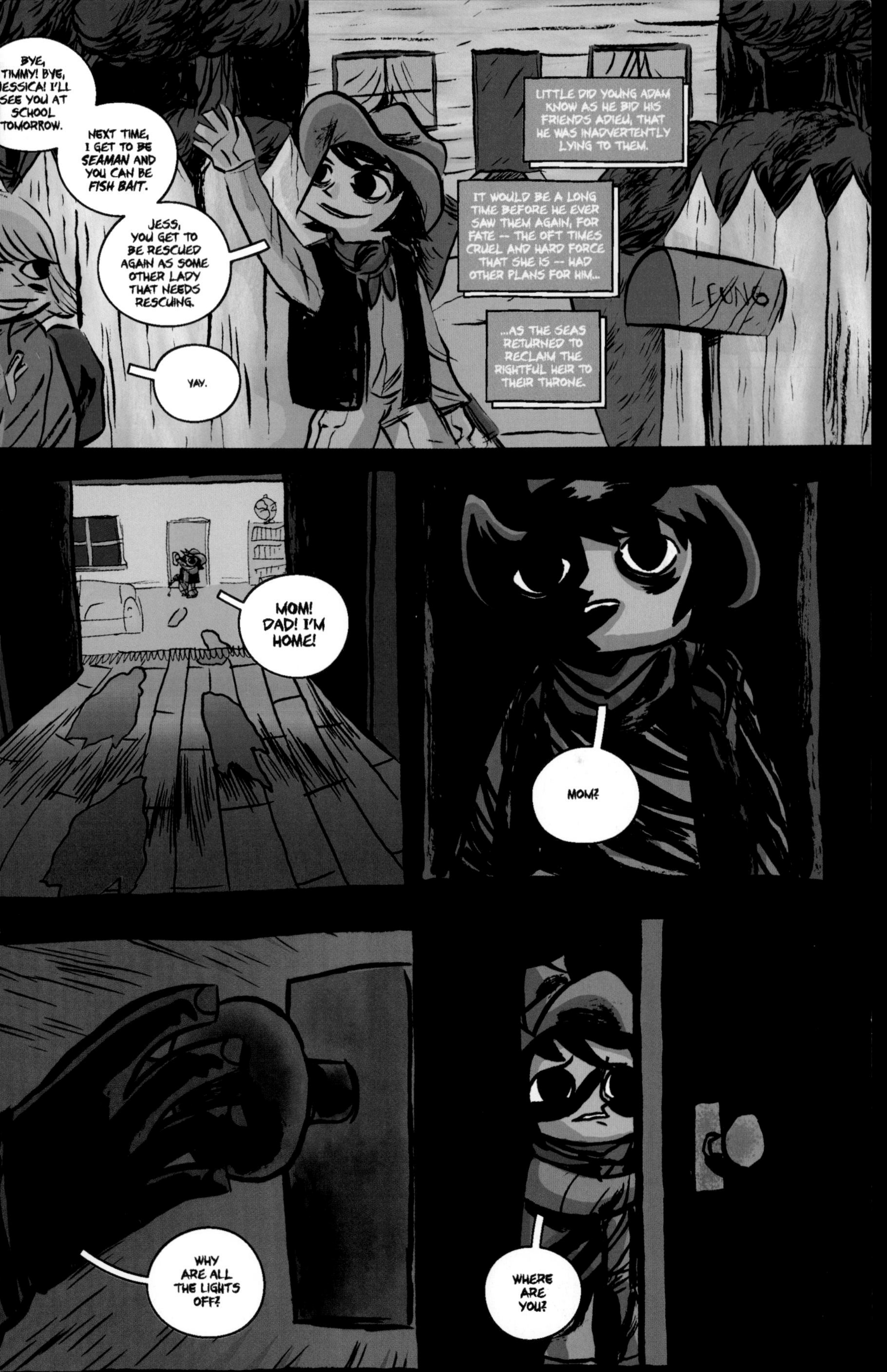
BYE, TIMMY! BYE, JESSICA! I'LL SEE YOU AT SCHOOL TOMORROW.
NEXT TIME, I GET TO BE SEAMAN AND YOU CAN BE FISH BAIT.
JESS, YOU GET TO BE RESCUED AGAIN AS SOME OTHER LADY THAT NEEDS RESCUING.
YAY.
LITTLE DID YOUNG ADAM KNOW AS HE BID HIS FRIENDS ADIEU, THAT HE WAS INADVERTENTLY LYING TO THEM.
IT WOULD BE A LONG TIME BEFORE HE EVER SAW THEM AGAIN, FOR FATE -- THE OFT TIMES CRUEL AND HARD FORCE THAT SHE IS -- HAD OTHER PLANS FOR HIM...
...AS THE SEAS RETURNED TO RECLAIM THE RIGHTFUL HEIR TO THEIR THRONE.
LEUNG
MOM! DAD! I'M HOME!
MOM?
WHY ARE ALL THE LIGHTS OFF?
WHERE ARE YOU?

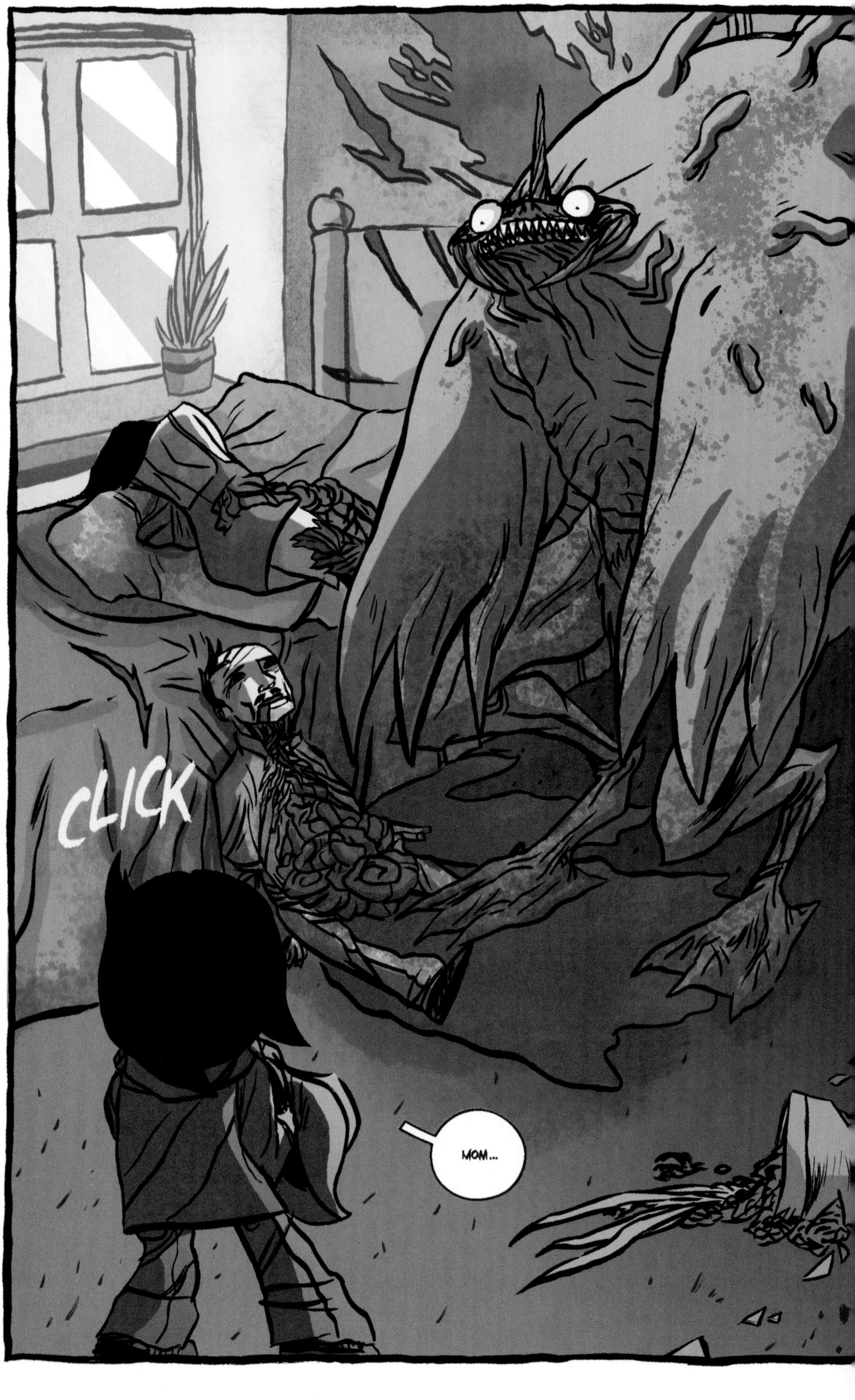
CLICK
MOM...

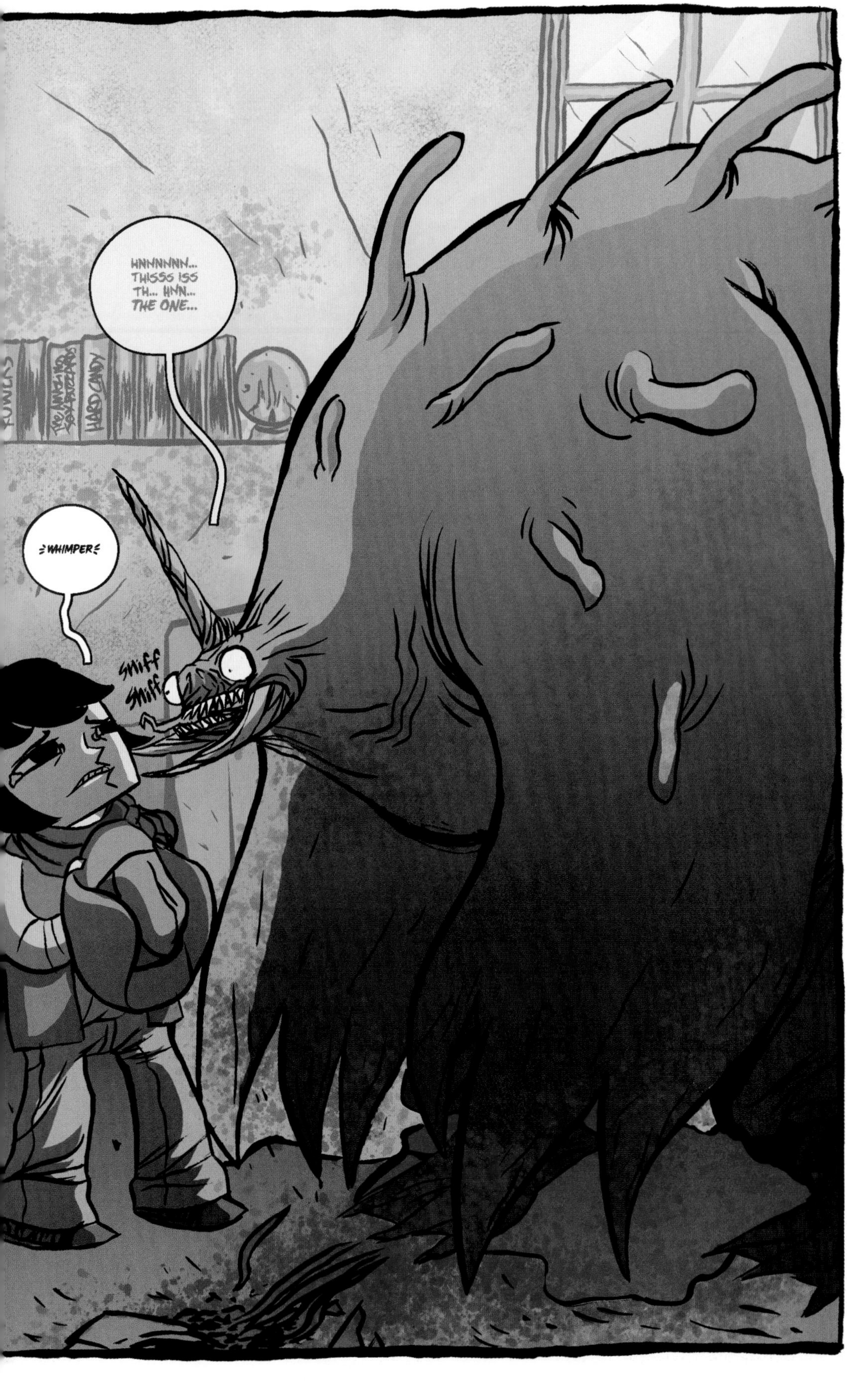
HNNNNNN... THISSS ISS TH... HNN... THE ONE...
HARD CANDY
WHIMPER
SNIFF SNIFF

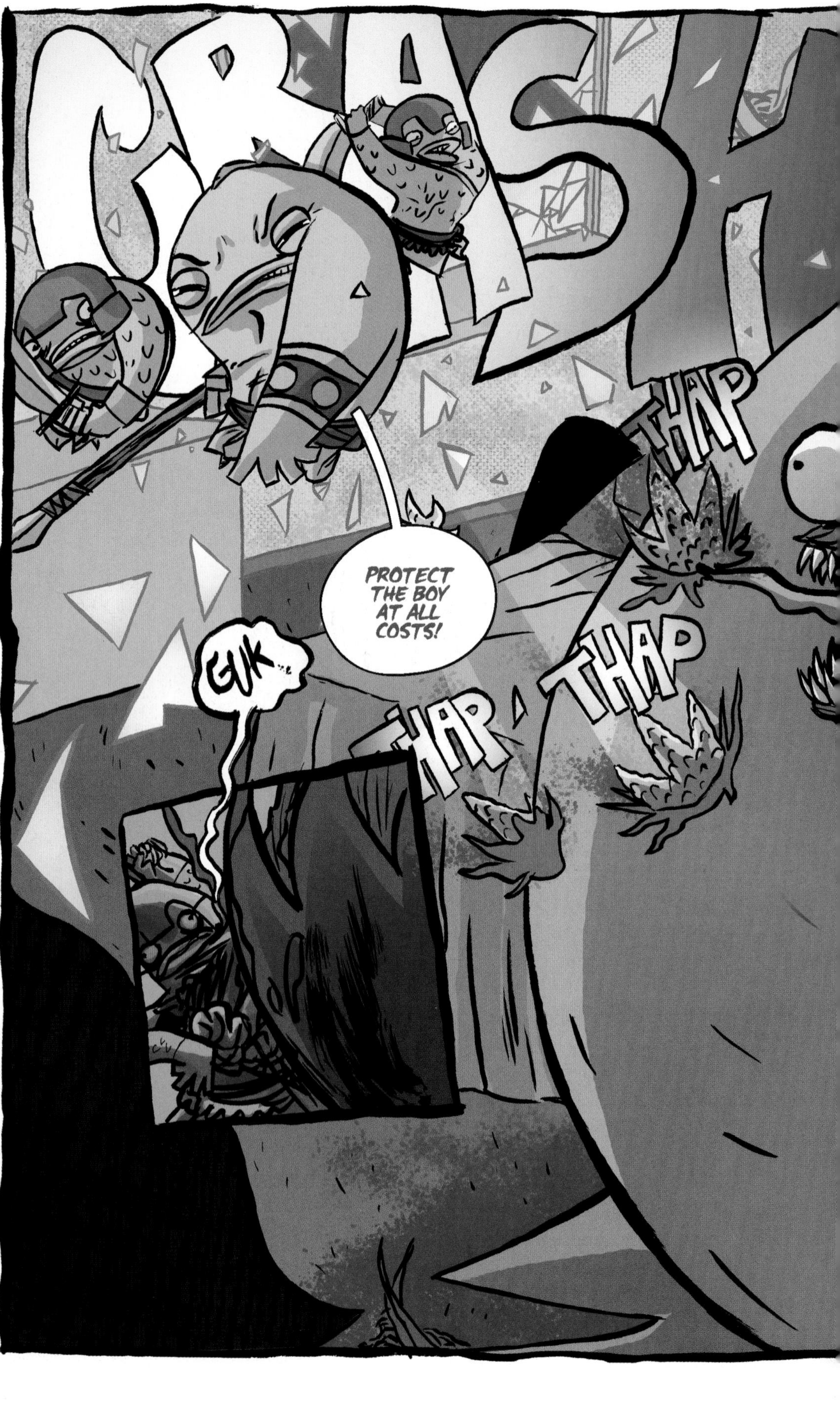
CRASH
PROTECT THE BOY AT ALL COSTS!
THAP
GUK
THAP
THAP

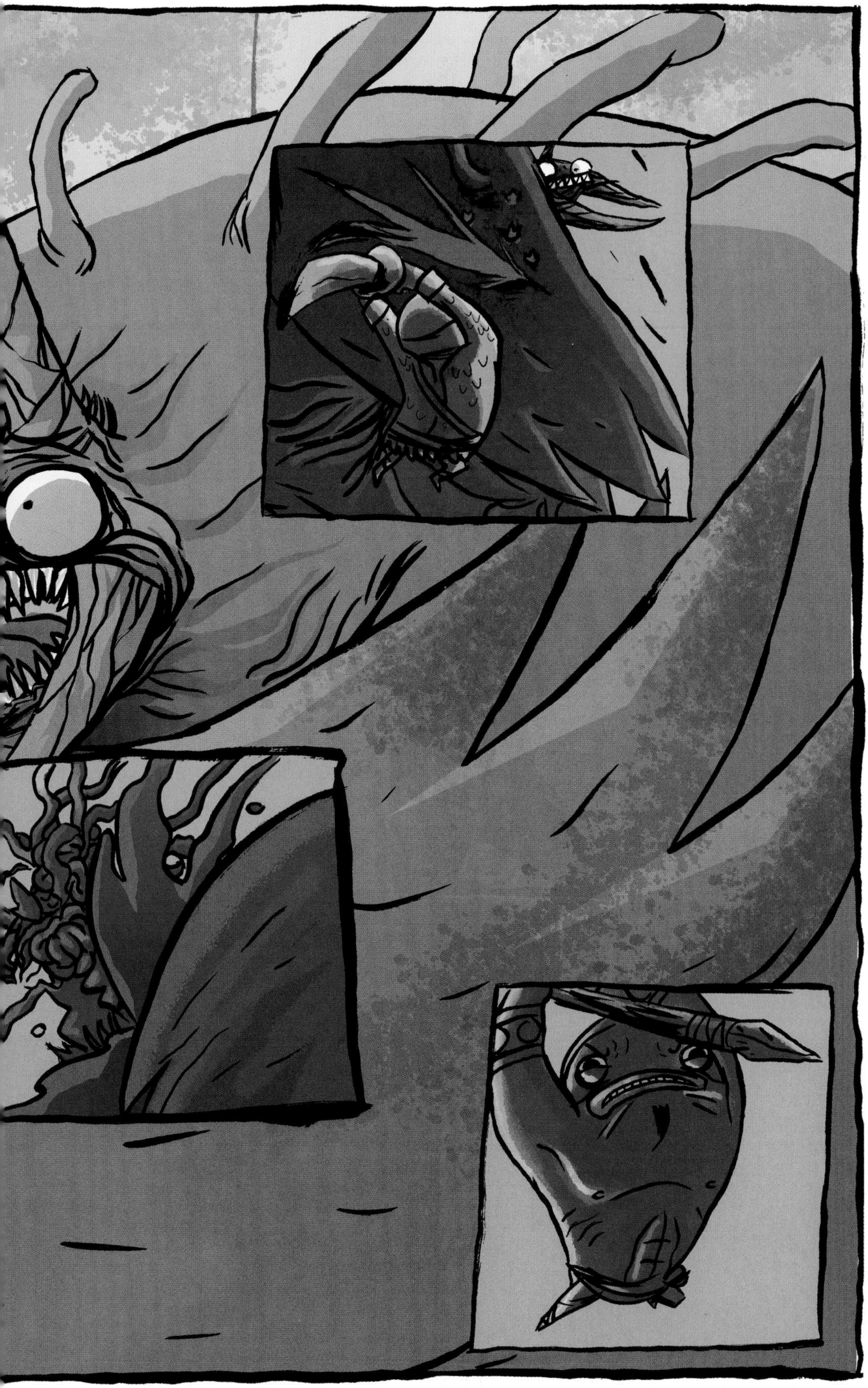

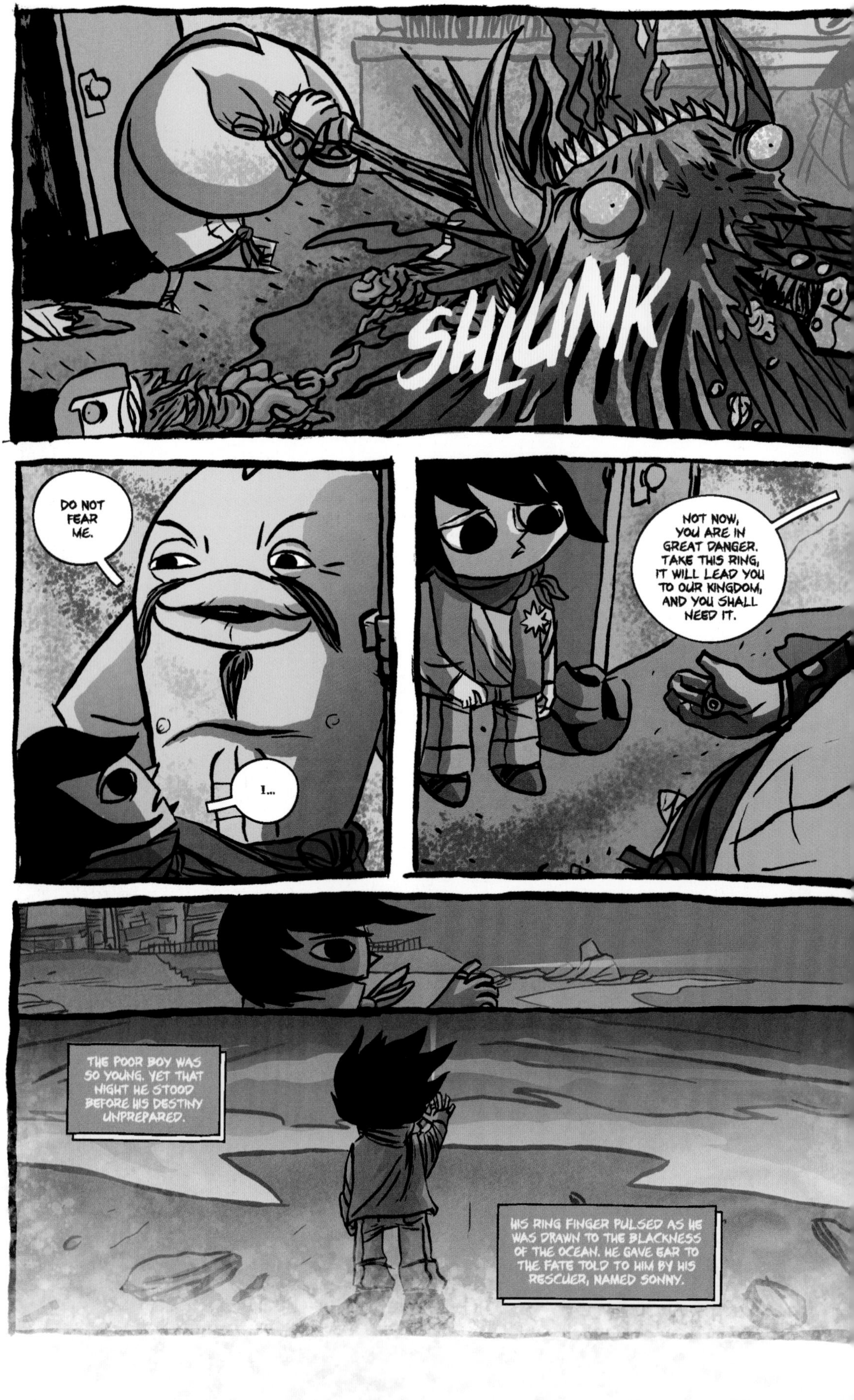
SHLUNK
DO NOT FEAR ME.
I...
NOT NOW, YOU ARE IN GREAT DANGER. TAKE THIS RING, IT WILL LEAD YOU TO OUR KINGDOM, AND YOU SHALL NEED IT.
THE POOR BOY WAS SO YOUNG, YET THAT NIGHT HE STOOD BEFORE HIS DESTINY UNPREPARED.
HIS RING FINGER PULSED AS HE WAS DRAWN TO THE BLACKNESS OF THE OCEAN. HE GAVE EAR TO THE FATE TOLD TO HIM BY HIS RESCUER, NAMED SONNY.

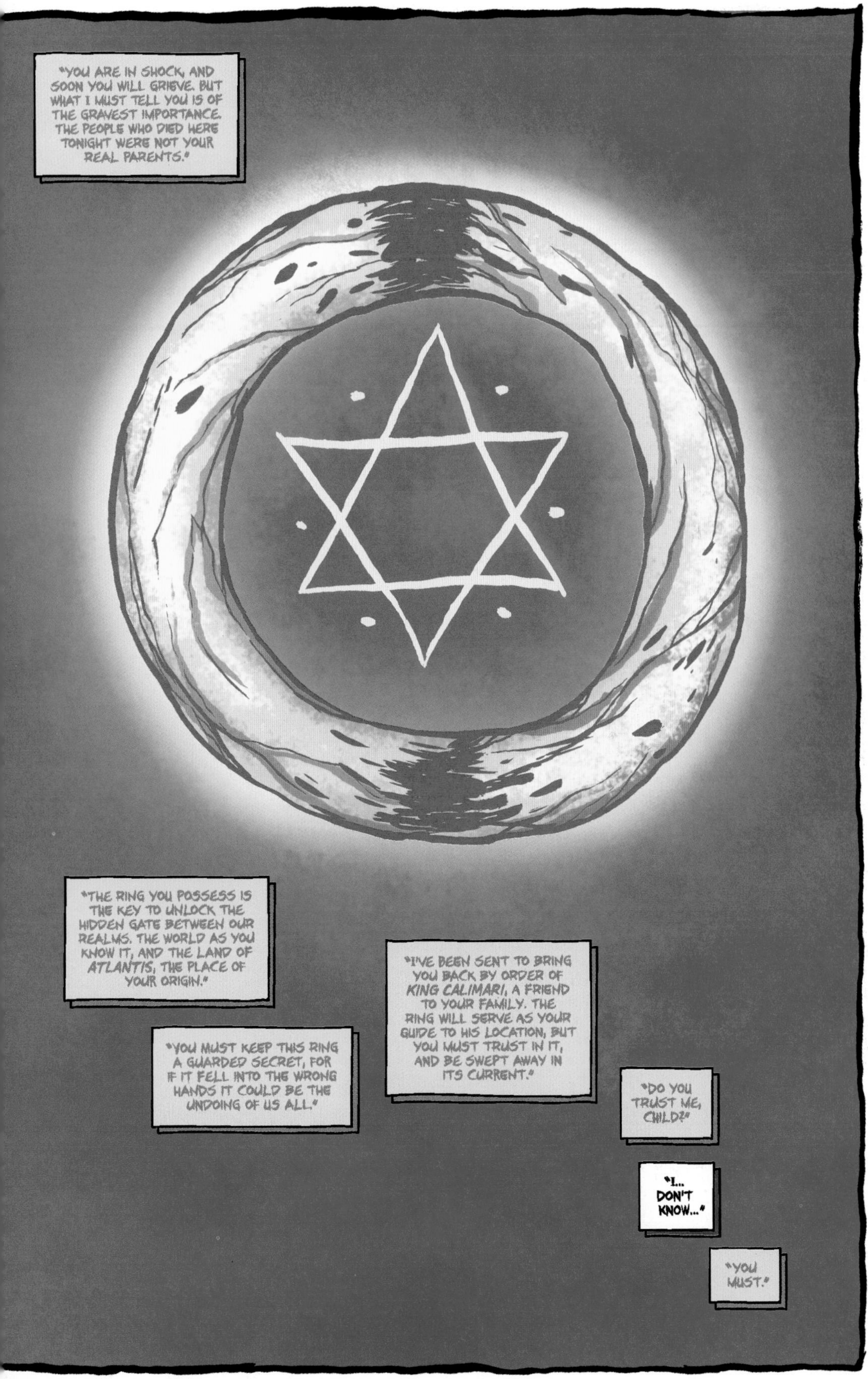
"YOU ARE IN SHOCK, AND SOON YOU WILL GRIEVE. BUT WHAT I MUST TELL YOU IS OF THE GRAVEST IMPORTANCE. THE PEOPLE WHO DIED HERE TONIGHT WERE NOT YOUR REAL PARENTS."
"THE RING YOU POSSESS IS THE KEY TO UNLOCK THE HIDDEN GATE BETWEEN OUR REALMS. THE WORLD AS YOU KNOW IT, AND THE LAND OF *ATLANTIS*, THE PLACE OF YOUR ORIGIN."
"YOU MUST KEEP THIS RING A GUARDED SECRET, FOR IF IT FELL INTO THE WRONG HANDS IT COULD BE THE UNDOING OF US ALL."
"I'VE BEEN SENT TO BRING YOU BACK BY ORDER OF *KING CALIMARI*, A FRIEND TO YOUR FAMILY. THE RING WILL SERVE AS YOUR GUIDE TO HIS LOCATION, BUT YOU MUST TRUST IN IT, AND BE SWEPT AWAY IN ITS CURRENT."
"DO YOU TRUST ME, CHILD?"
"I... DON'T KNOW..."
"YOU MUST."

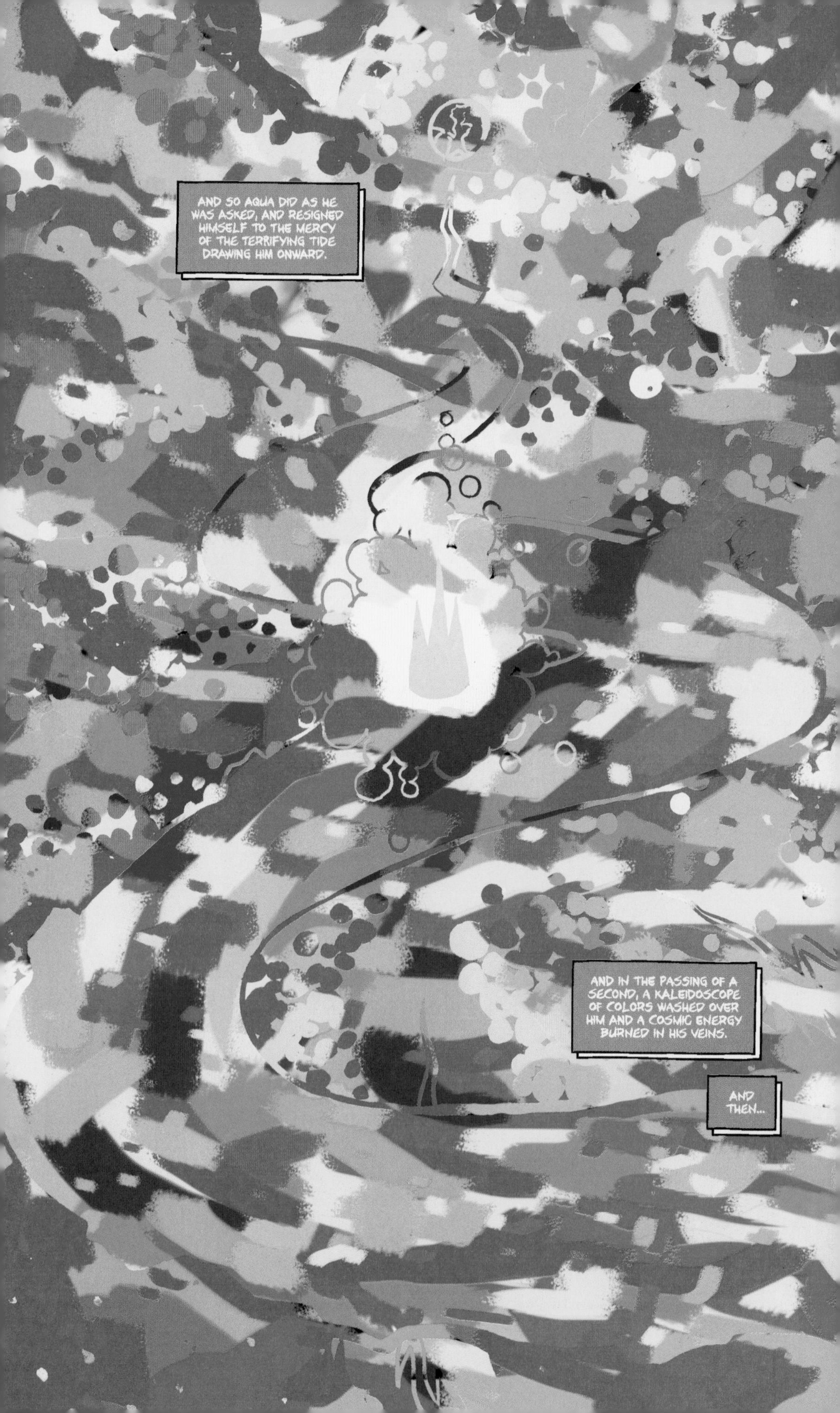
AND SO AQUA DID AS HE WAS ASKED, AND RESIGNED HIMSELF TO THE MERCY OF THE TERRIFYING TIDE DRAWING HIM ONWARD.
AND IN THE PASSING OF A SECOND, A KALEIDOSCOPE OF COLORS WASHED OVER HIM AND A COSMIC ENERGY BURNED IN HIS VEINS.
AND THEN...

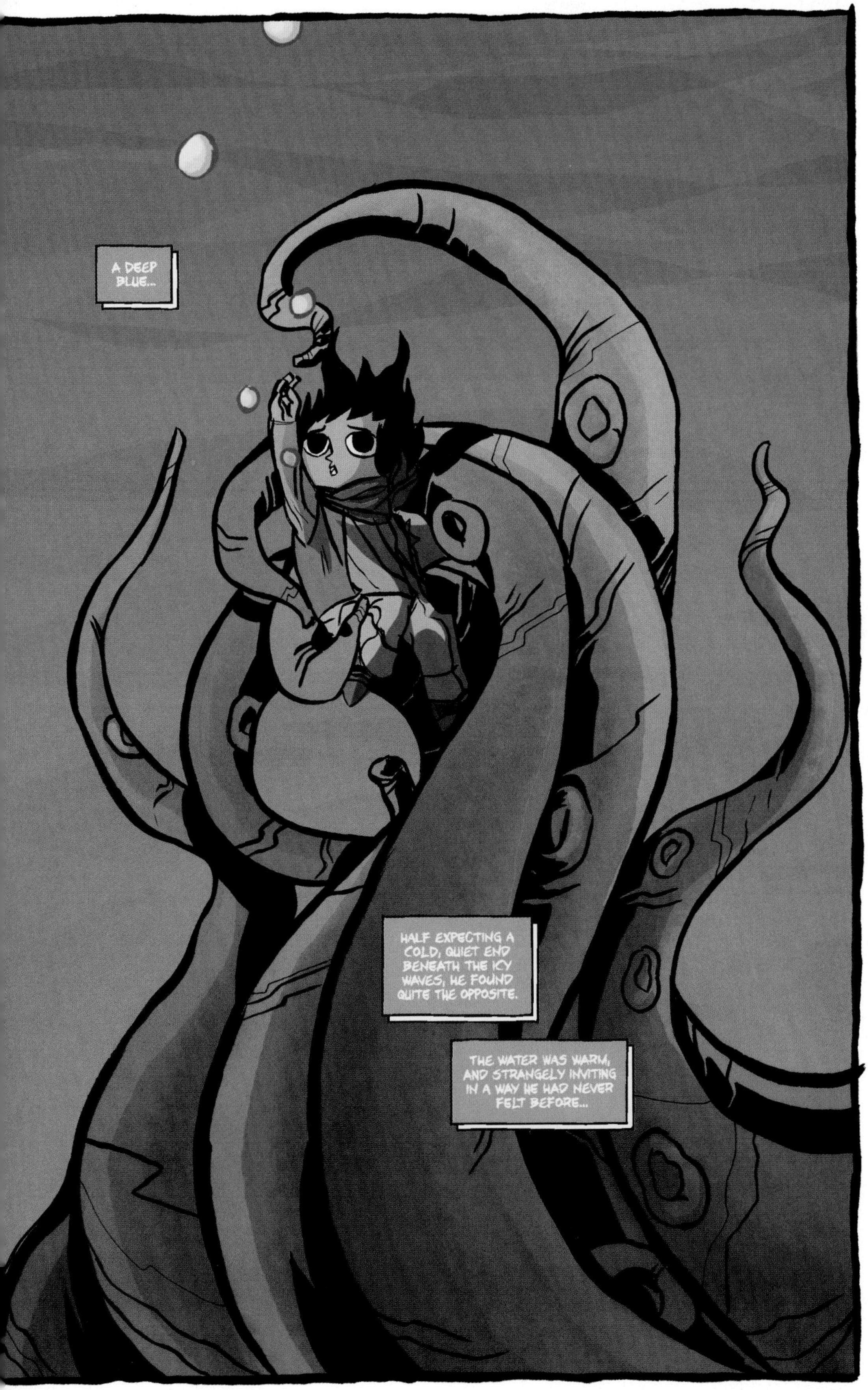
A DEEP BLUE...
HALF EXPECTING A COLD, QUIET END BENEATH THE ICY WAVES, HE FOUND QUITE THE OPPOSITE.
THE WATER WAS WARM, AND STRANGELY INVITING IN A WAY HE HAD NEVER FELT BEFORE...

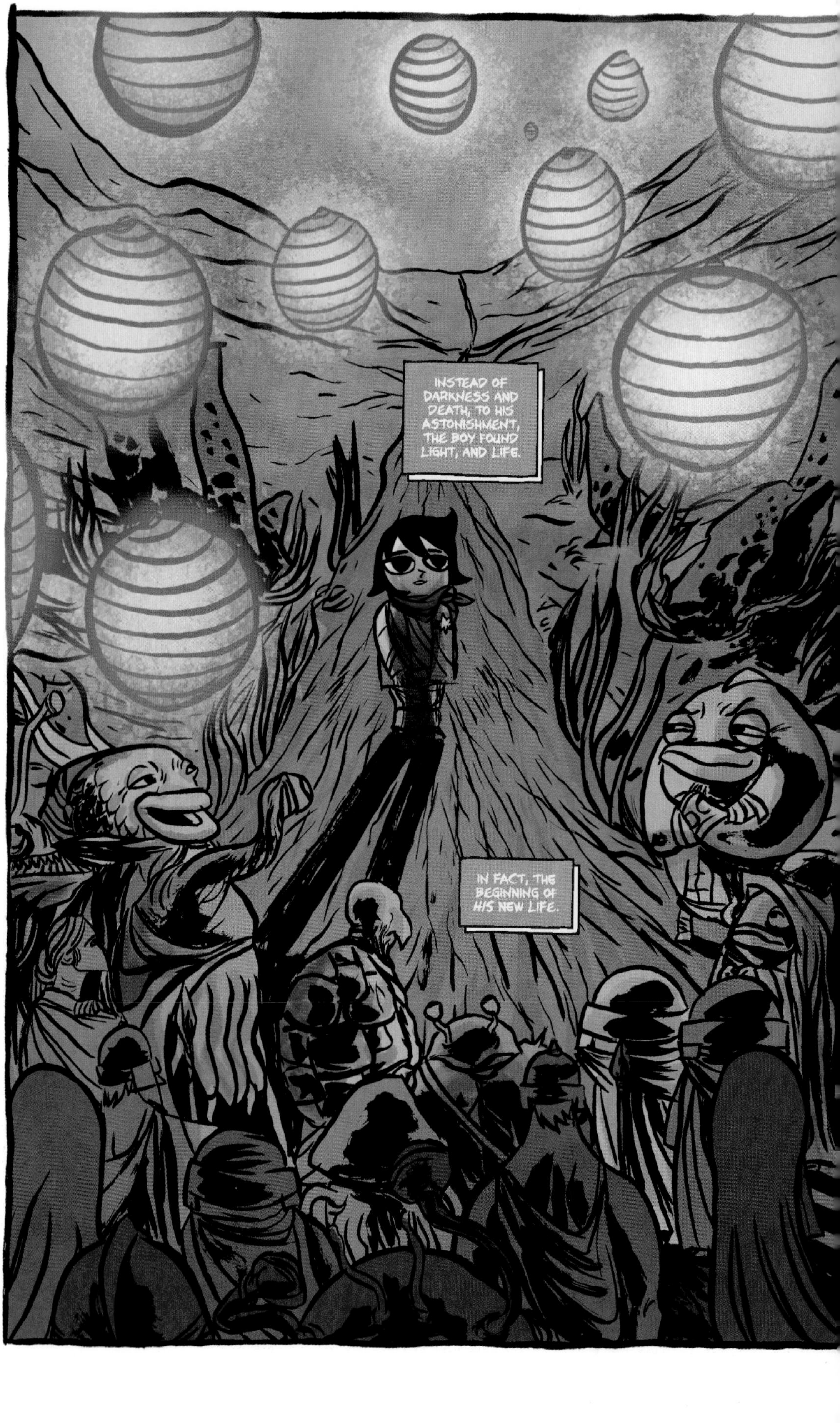
INSTEAD OF DARKNESS AND DEATH, TO HIS ASTONISHMENT, THE BOY FOUND LIGHT, AND LIFE.
IN FACT, THE BEGINNING OF HIS NEW LIFE.

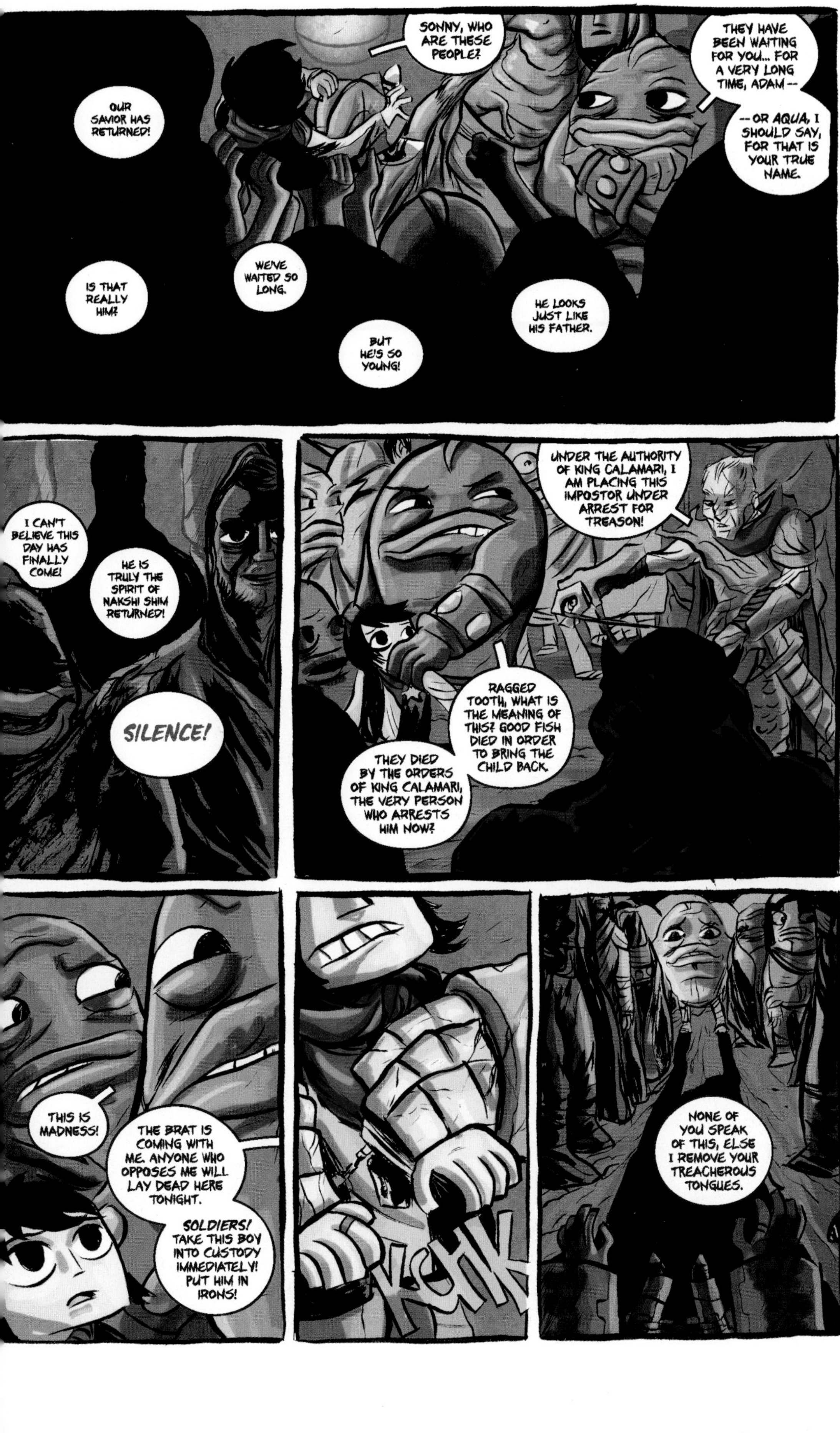

SONNY, WHO ARE THESE PEOPLE?
THEY HAVE BEEN WAITING FOR YOU... FOR A VERY LONG TIME, ADAM --
-- OR AQUA, I SHOULD SAY, FOR THAT IS YOUR TRUE NAME.
OUR SAVIOR HAS RETURNED!
IS THAT REALLY HIM?
WE'VE WAITED SO LONG.
BUT HE'S SO YOUNG!
HE LOOKS JUST LIKE HIS FATHER.
I CAN'T BELIEVE THIS DAY HAS FINALLY COME!
HE IS TRULY THE SPIRIT OF NAKSHI SHIM RETURNED!
SILENCE!
UNDER THE AUTHORITY OF KING CALAMARI, I AM PLACING THIS IMPOSTOR UNDER ARREST FOR TREASON!
RAGGED TOOTH, WHAT IS THE MEANING OF THIS? GOOD FISH DIED IN ORDER TO BRING THE CHILD BACK.
THEY DIED BY THE ORDERS OF KING CALAMARI, THE VERY PERSON WHO ARRESTS HIM NOW?
THIS IS MADNESS!
THE BRAT IS COMING WITH ME. ANYONE WHO OPPOSES ME WILL LAY DEAD HERE TONIGHT.
SOLDIERS! TAKE THIS BOY INTO CUSTODY IMMEDIATELY! PUT HIM IN IRONS!
KSHK
NONE OF YOU SPEAK OF THIS, ELSE I REMOVE YOUR TREACHEROUS TONGUES.

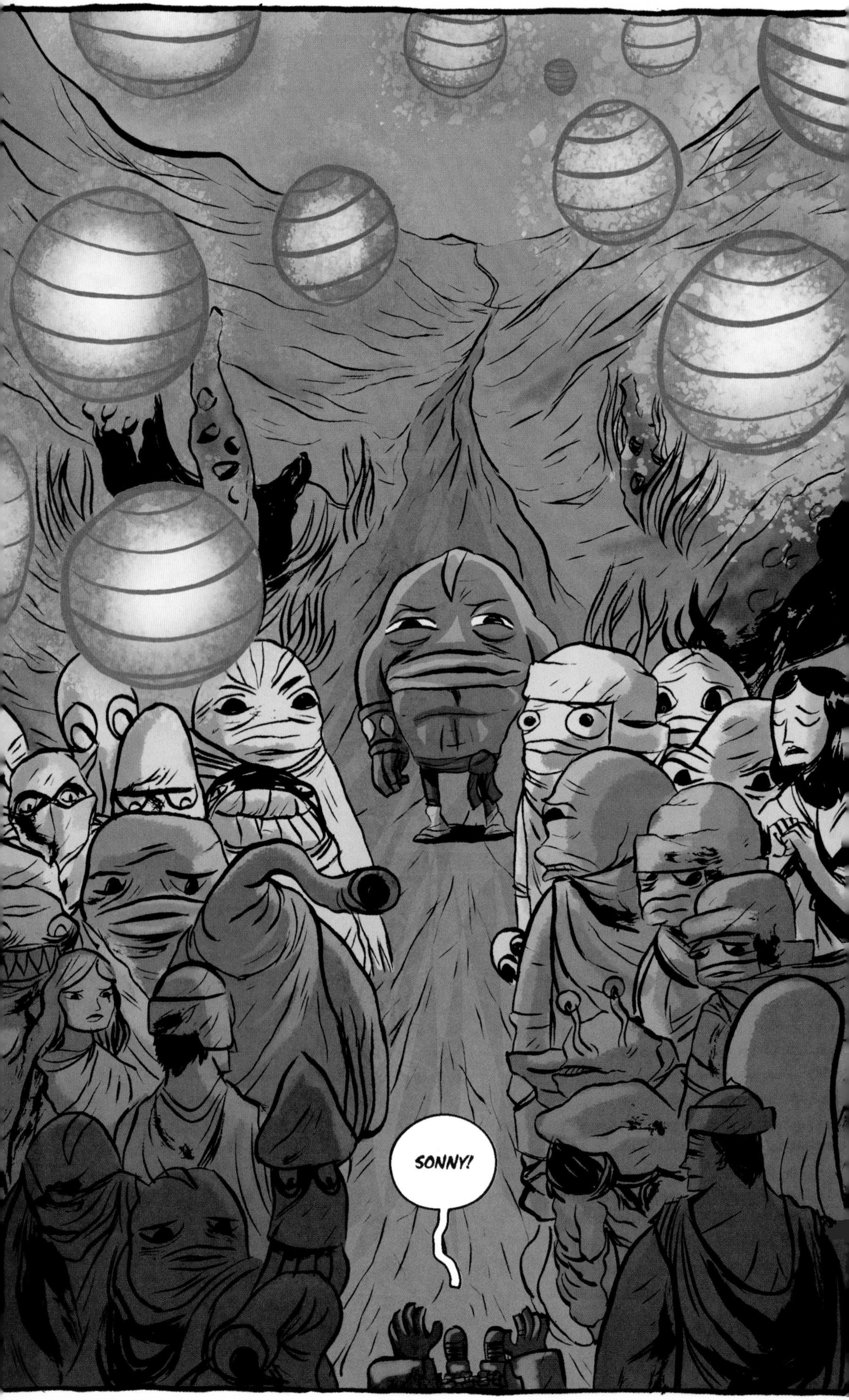
SONNY!

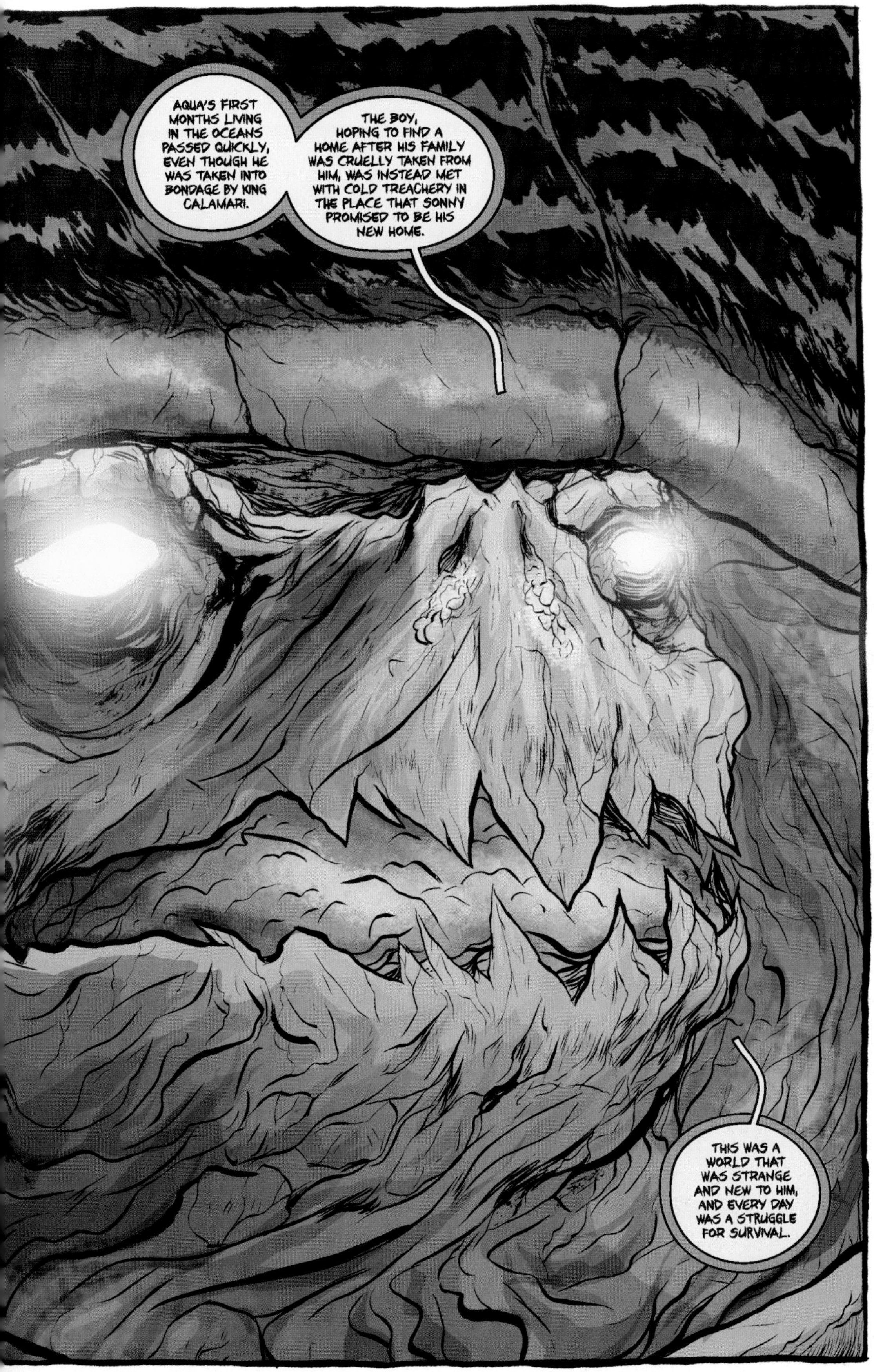
AQUA'S FIRST MONTHS LIVING IN THE OCEANS PASSED QUICKLY, EVEN THOUGH HE WAS TAKEN INTO BONDAGE BY KING CALAMARI.
THE BOY, HOPING TO FIND A HOME AFTER HIS FAMILY WAS CRUELLY TAKEN FROM HIM, WAS INSTEAD MET WITH COLD TREACHERY IN THE PLACE THAT SONNY PROMISED TO BE HIS NEW HOME.
THIS WAS A WORLD THAT WAS STRANGE AND NEW TO HIM, AND EVERY DAY WAS A STRUGGLE FOR SURVIVAL.

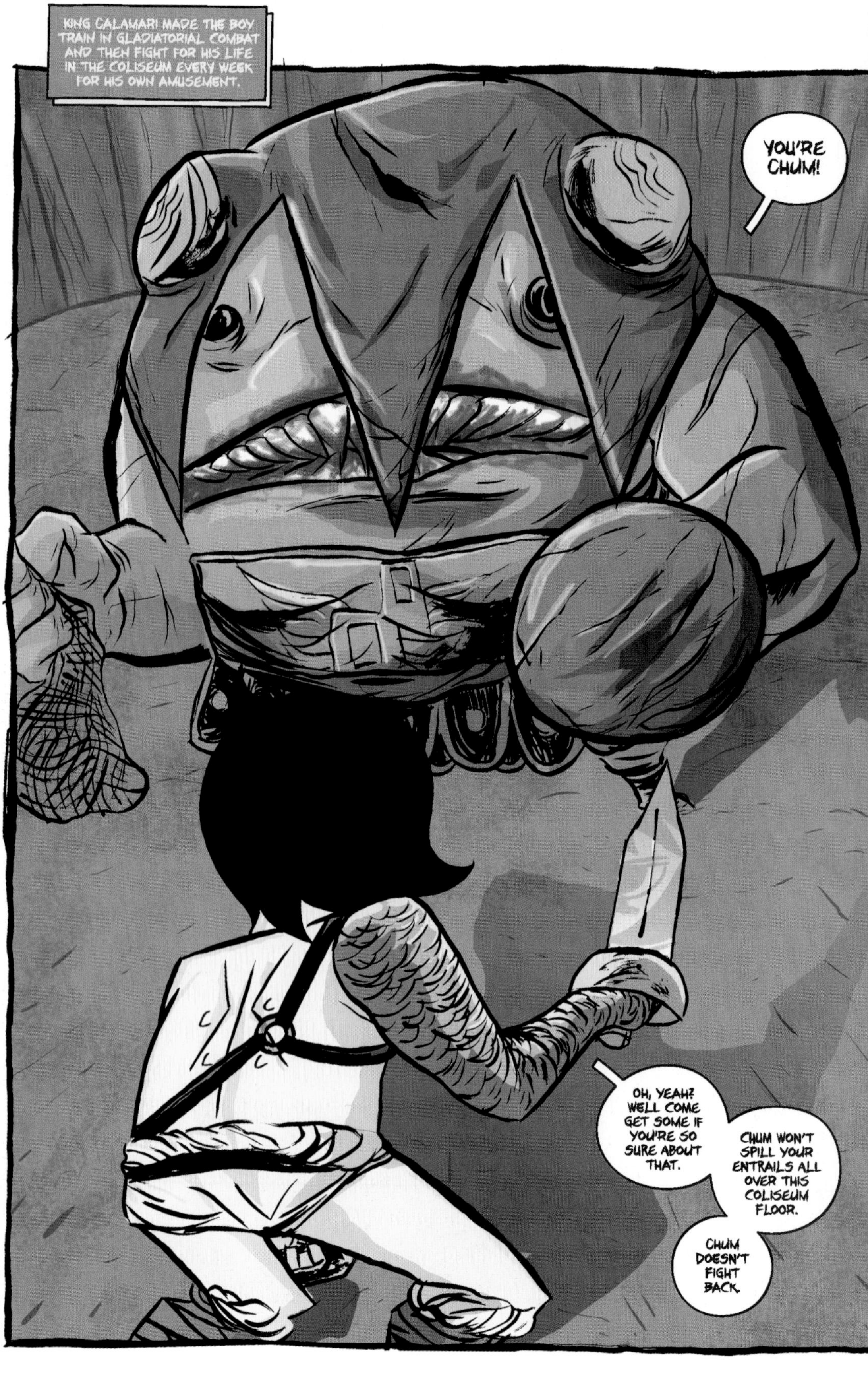
KING CALAMARI MADE THE BOY TRAIN IN GLADIATORIAL COMBAT AND THEN FIGHT FOR HIS LIFE IN THE COLISEUM EVERY WEEK FOR HIS OWN AMUSEMENT.
YOU'RE CHUM!
OH, YEAH? WELL COME GET SOME IF YOU'RE SO SURE ABOUT THAT.
CHUM WON'T SPILL YOUR ENTRAILS ALL OVER THIS COLISEUM FLOOR.
CHUM DOESN'T FIGHT BACK.

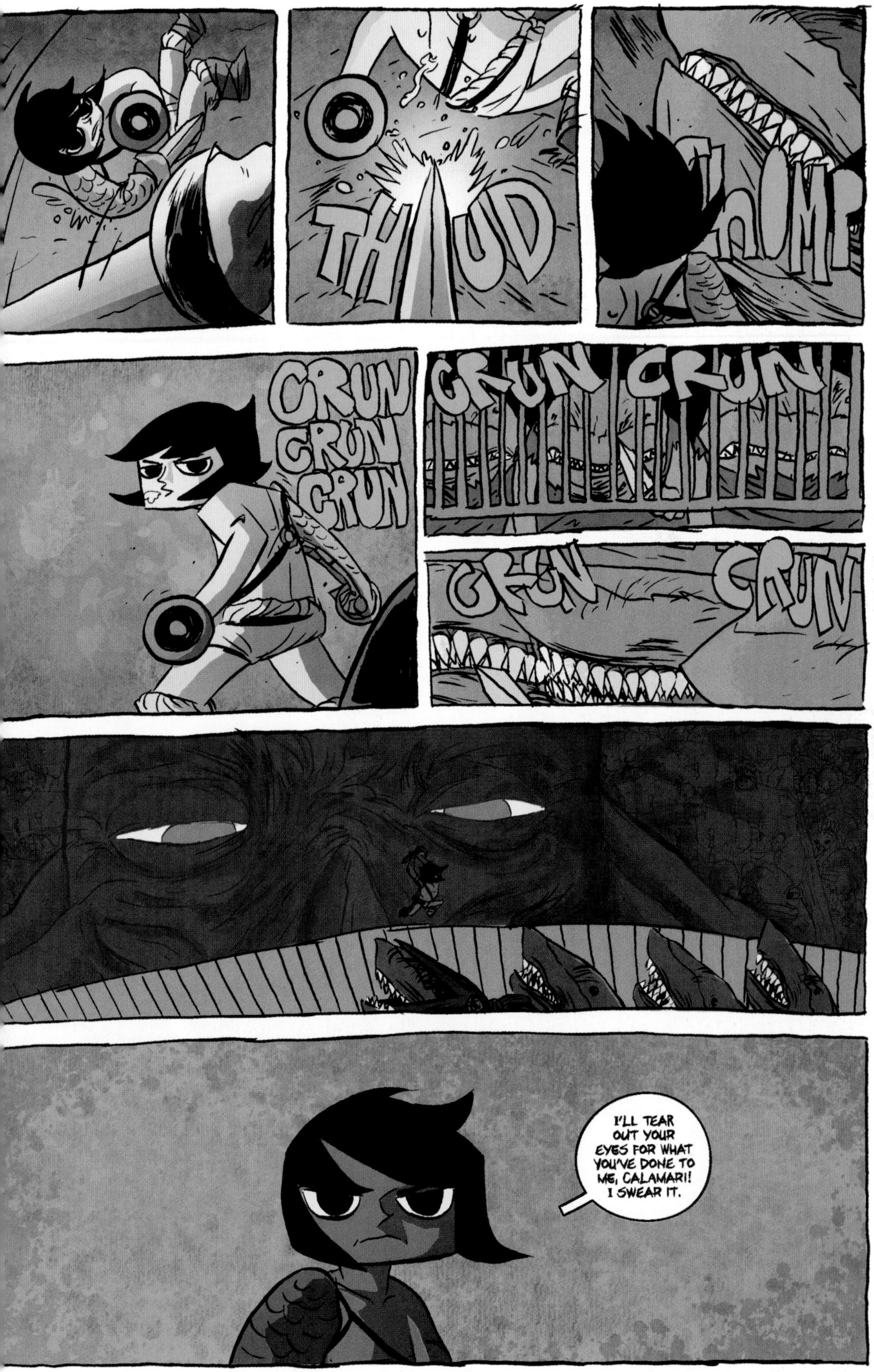
THUD
CRUN
CRUN
CRUN
CRUN
CRUN
CRUN
CRUN
CRUN
I'LL TEAR OUT YOUR EYES FOR WHAT YOU'VE DONE TO ME, CALAMARI! I SWEAR IT.

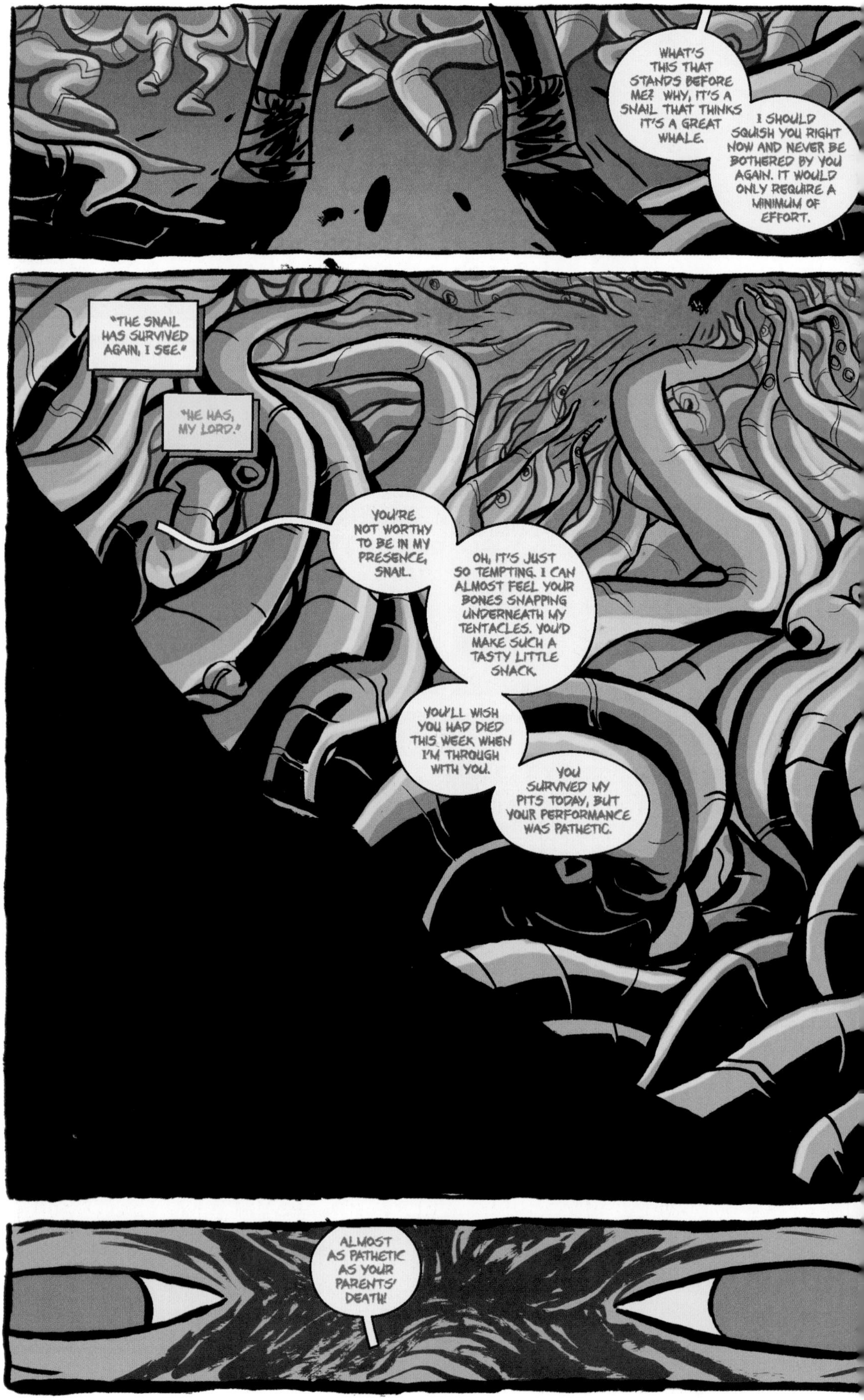
WHAT'S THIS THAT STANDS BEFORE ME? WHY, IT'S A SNAIL THAT THINKS IT'S A GREAT WHALE.
I SHOULD SQUISH YOU RIGHT NOW AND NEVER BE BOTHERED BY YOU AGAIN. IT WOULD ONLY REQUIRE A MINIMUM OF EFFORT.
"THE SNAIL HAS SURVIVED AGAIN, I SEE."
"HE HAS, MY LORD."
YOU'RE NOT WORTHY TO BE IN MY PRESENCE, SNAIL.
OH, IT'S JUST SO TEMPTING. I CAN ALMOST FEEL YOUR BONES SNAPPING UNDERNEATH MY TENTACLES. YOU'D MAKE SUCH A TASTY LITTLE SNACK.
YOU'LL WISH YOU HAD DIED THIS WEEK WHEN I'M THROUGH WITH YOU.
YOU SURVIVED MY PITS TODAY, BUT YOUR PERFORMANCE WAS PATHETIC.
ALMOST AS PATHETIC AS YOUR PARENTS' DEATH!

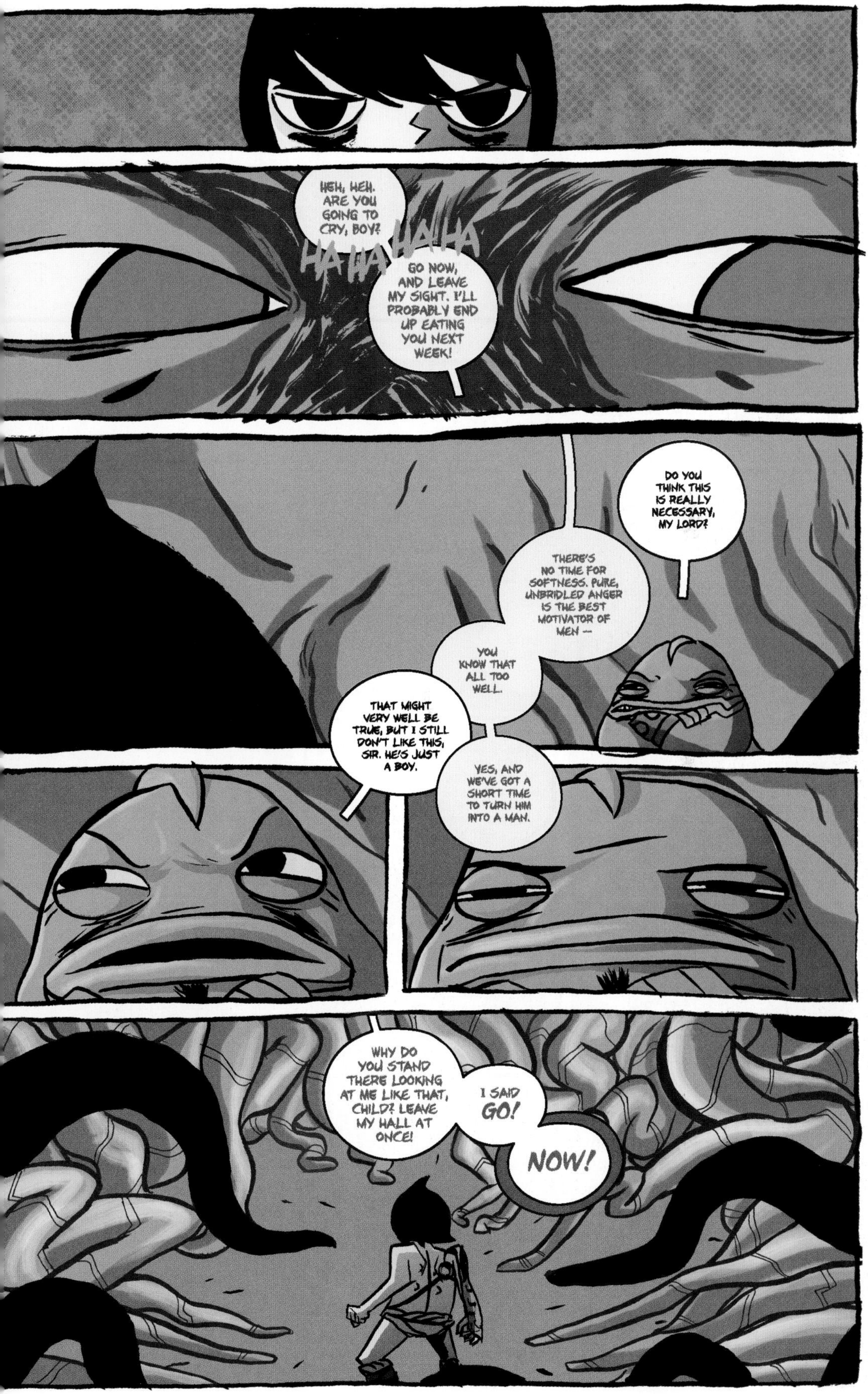
HEH, HEH. ARE YOU GOING TO CRY, BOY?
HA HA HA HA
GO NOW, AND LEAVE MY SIGHT. I'LL PROBABLY END UP EATING YOU NEXT WEEK!
DO YOU THINK THIS IS REALLY NECESSARY, MY LORD?
THERE'S NO TIME FOR SOFTNESS. PURE, UNBRIDLED ANGER IS THE BEST MOTIVATOR OF MEN --
YOU KNOW THAT ALL TOO WELL.
THAT MIGHT VERY WELL BE TRUE, BUT I STILL DON'T LIKE THIS, SIR. HE'S JUST A BOY.
YES, AND WE'VE GOT A SHORT TIME TO TURN HIM INTO A MAN.
WHY DO YOU STAND THERE LOOKING AT ME LIKE THAT, CHILD? LEAVE MY HALL AT ONCE!
I SAID GO!
NOW!

=SOB=

OH, IT'S YOU.

WHEN I WAS YOUNG, I TOO CAME TO KNOW DEATH.

IT IS THE TRADITION OF MY PEOPLE THAT ONLY THE STRONGEST OF OUR OFFSPRING SHALL LIVE.

IT IS THE TEST OF OUR YOUNG TO KILL THEIR SIBLINGS AND STAND ALONE, STRONG. I HAD TWO BROTHERS. I MURDERED THEM WITH MY OWN HANDS IN MY MOTHER'S BELLY... BEFORE I'D EVEN ENTERED THIS WORLD, MY HANDS WERE STAINED WITH BLOOD.

IT WAS EITHER THEM OR ME. THEIR DEATH WAS THE ONLY PATH TO MY SURVIVAL. BY KILLING THEM, I CHOSE LIFE.

THAT'S TERRIBLE!

IT IS THE WAY OF THINGS. I KNOW DEATH NOW, AND I DO NOT FEAR IT.

YOU WEEP FOR YOUR LOVED ONES AND FOR YOUR IMPRISONMENT. EVEN IF THE BARS ON YOUR WINDOWS CEASED TO EXIST, YOU WOULD NOT FIND FREEDOM OR SOLACE. YOU MUST ACCEPT WHAT HAS COME TO PASS AND WHAT HAS NOT BUT INEVITABLY WILL. THE LIFE YOU KNEW BEFORE IS GONE, AND YOU WILL NOT SURVIVE IF YOU DO NOT EMBRACE THE NEW ONE BEFORE YOU.

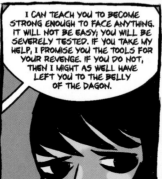

I CAN TEACH YOU TO BECOME STRONG ENOUGH TO FACE ANYTHING. IT WILL NOT BE EASY; YOU WILL BE SEVERELY TESTED. IF YOU TAKE MY HELP, I PROMISE YOU THE TOOLS FOR YOUR REVENGE. IF YOU DO NOT, THEN I MIGHT AS WELL HAVE LEFT YOU TO THE BELLY OF THE DAGON.

I WANT TO BE STRONG... LIKE YOU.

HA! EXCELLENT, YOUNG GUPPY! THERE IS HOPE FOR YOU YET. YOUR TRAINING BEGINS AT DAWN.

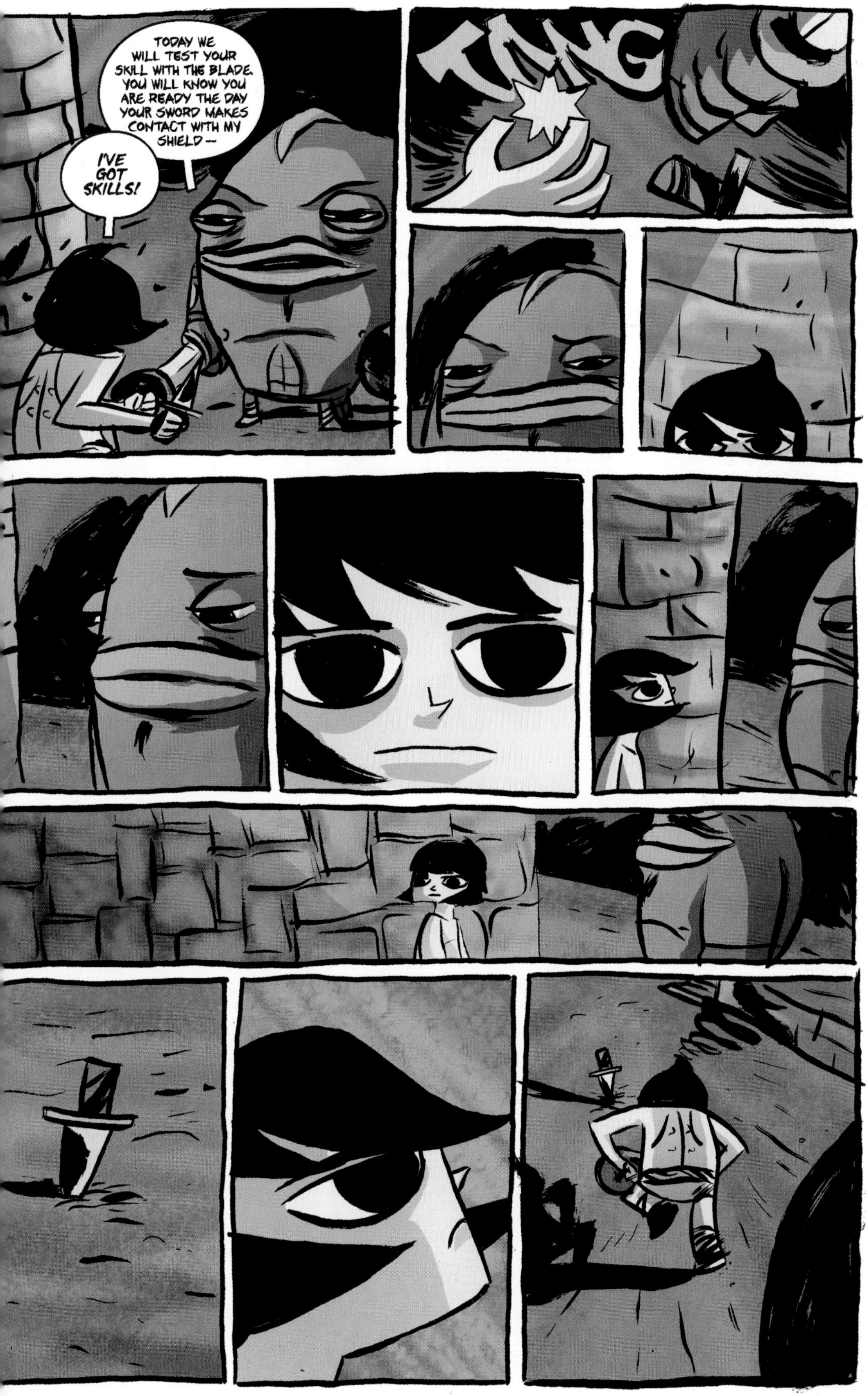
TODAY WE WILL TEST YOUR SKILL WITH THE BLADE. YOU WILL KNOW YOU ARE READY THE DAY YOUR SWORD MAKES CONTACT WITH MY SHIELD --
I'VE GOT SKILLS!

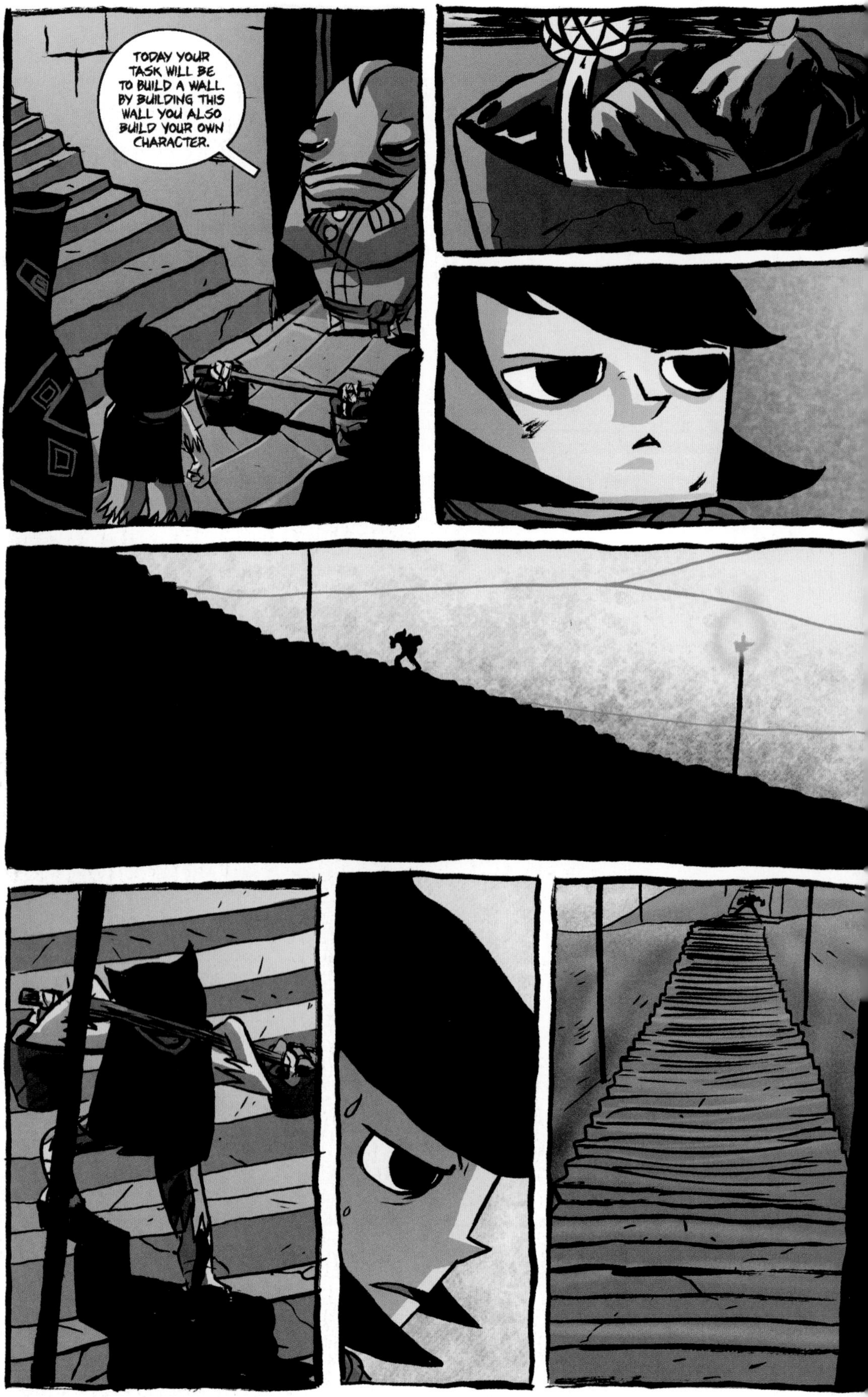
TODAY YOUR TASK WILL BE TO BUILD A WALL. BY BUILDING THIS WALL YOU ALSO BUILD YOUR OWN CHARACTER.

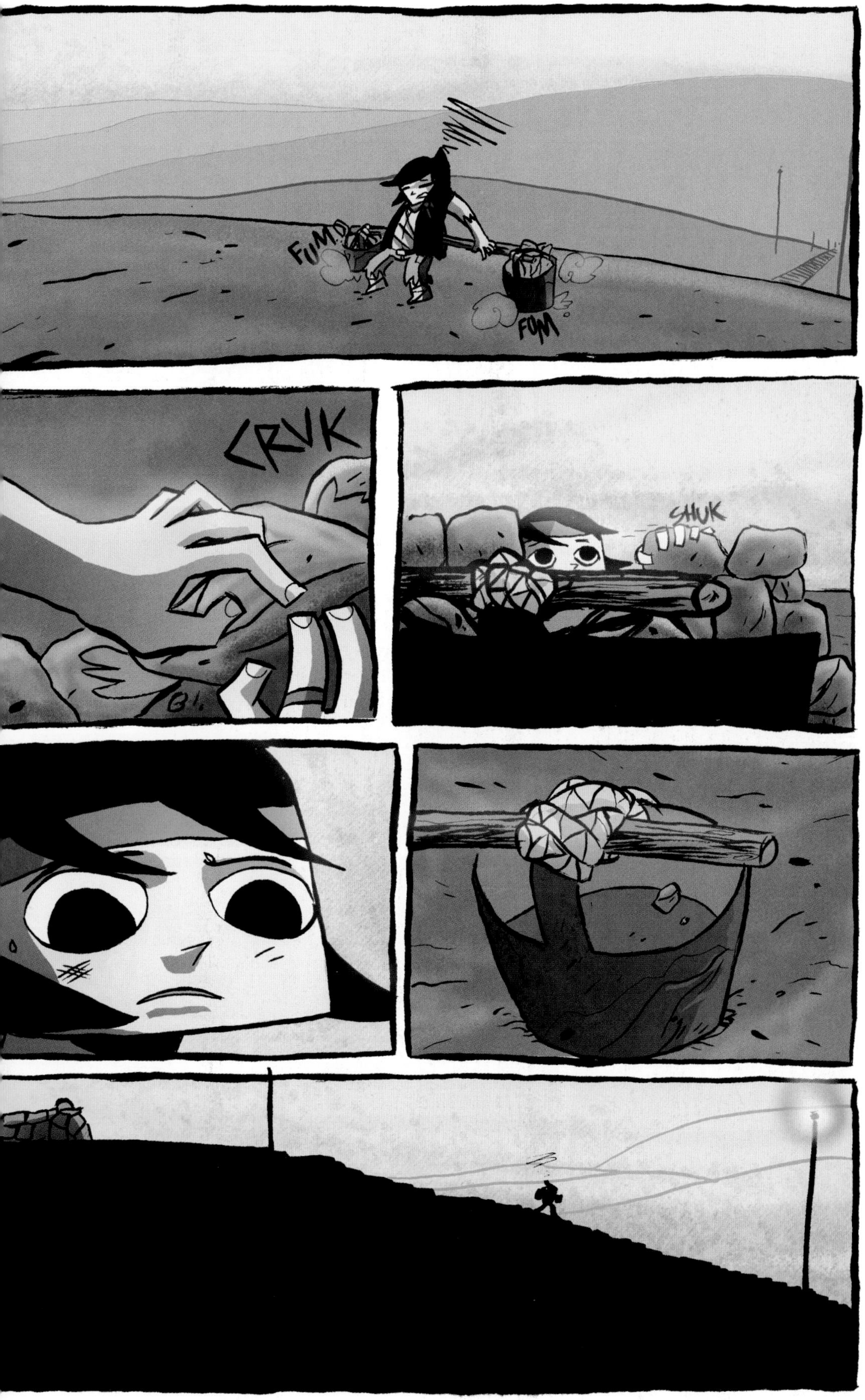

FUMP
FUM
CRUK
SHUK

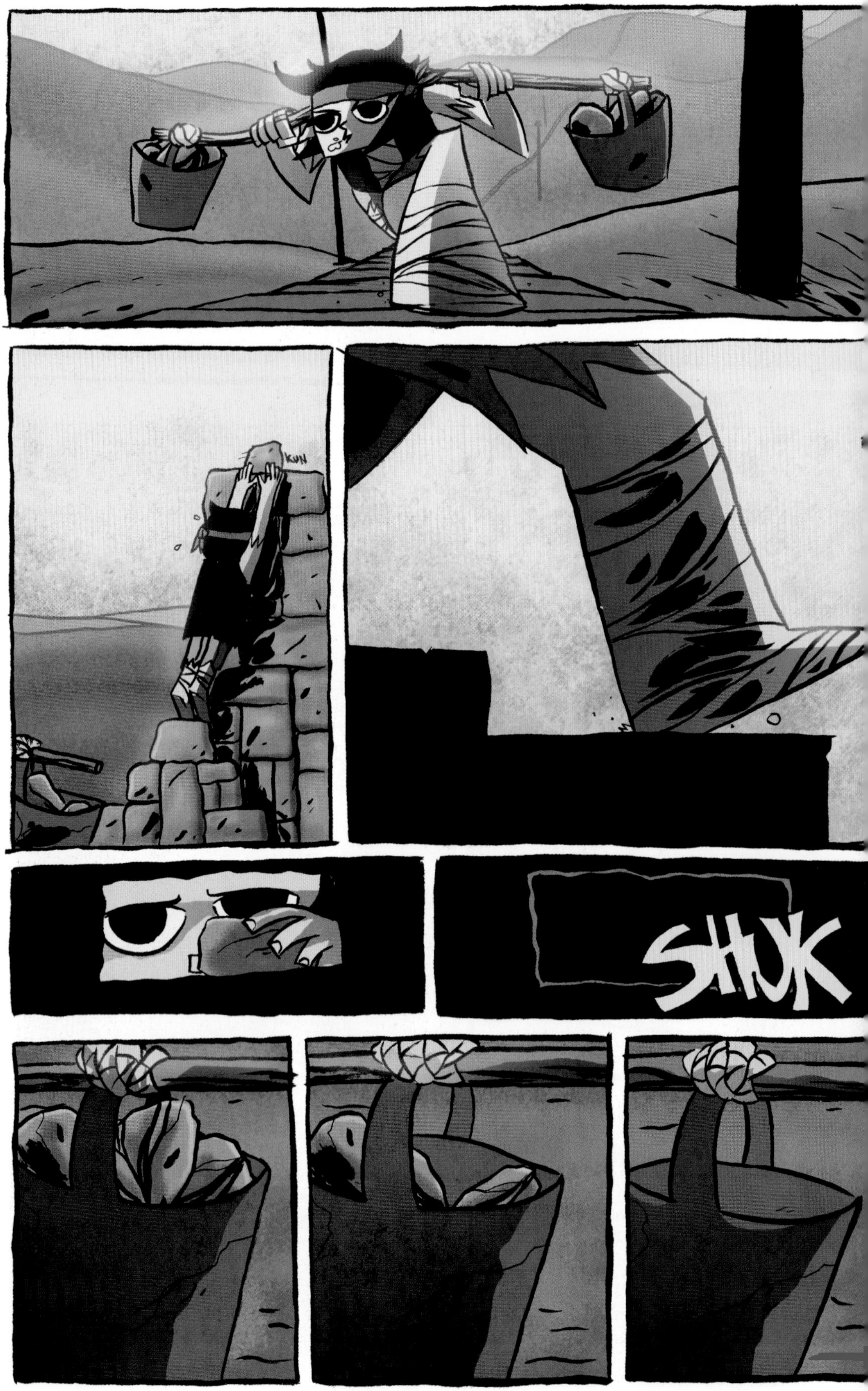
KUN
SHUK

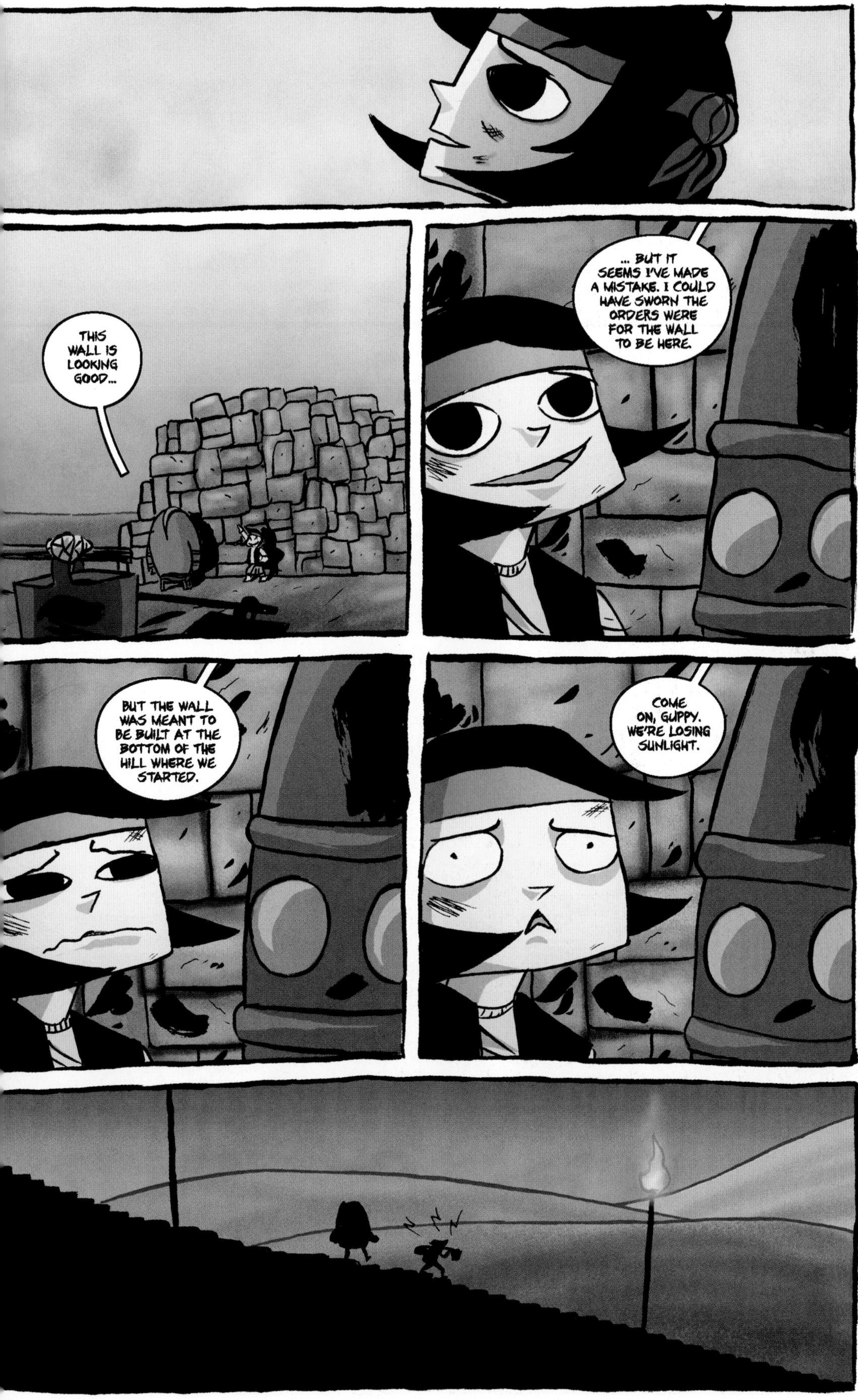
THIS WALL IS LOOKING GOOD...
... BUT IT SEEMS I'VE MADE A MISTAKE. I COULD HAVE SWORN THE ORDERS WERE FOR THE WALL TO BE HERE.
BUT THE WALL WAS MEANT TO BE BUILT AT THE BOTTOM OF THE HILL WHERE WE STARTED.
COME ON, GUPPY. WE'RE LOSING SUNLIGHT.

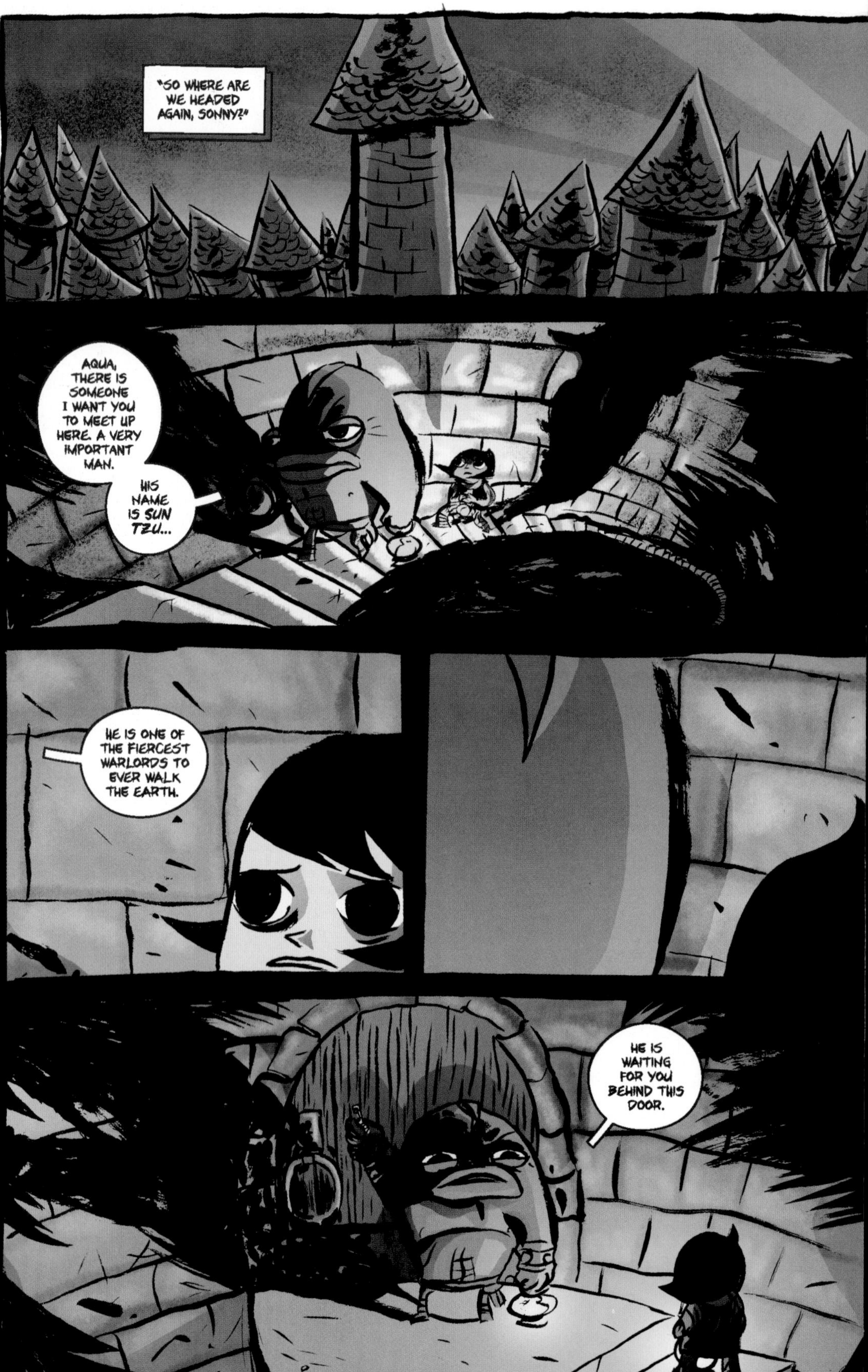
"SO WHERE ARE WE HEADED AGAIN, SONNY?"
AQUA, THERE IS SOMEONE I WANT YOU TO MEET UP HERE. A VERY IMPORTANT MAN.
HIS NAME IS SUN TZU...
HE IS ONE OF THE FIERCEST WARLORDS TO EVER WALK THE EARTH.
HE IS WAITING FOR YOU BEHIND THIS DOOR.

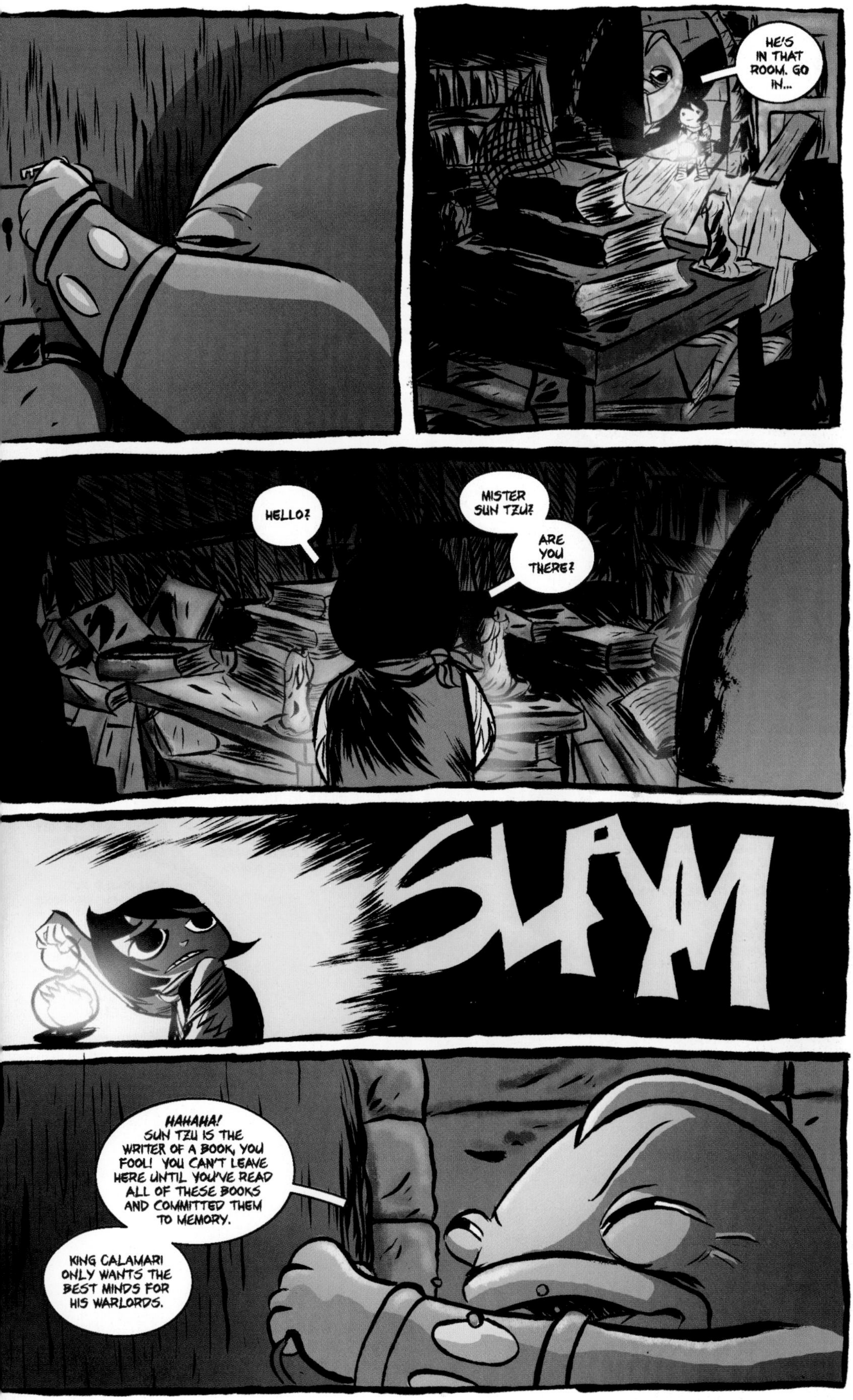
HE'S IN THAT ROOM. GO IN...
HELLO?
MISTER SUN TZU?
ARE YOU THERE?
SLAM
HAHAHA! SUN TZU IS THE WRITER OF A BOOK, YOU FOOL! YOU CAN'T LEAVE HERE UNTIL YOU'VE READ ALL OF THESE BOOKS AND COMMITTED THEM TO MEMORY.
KING CALAMARI ONLY WANTS THE BEST MINDS FOR HIS WARLORDS.

A MONTH LATER:

"OKAY, GUPPY. I WILL ASK YOU A SERIES OF QUESTIONS IN THE AREAS OF HISTORY, CLASSICS, AND WAR. ARE YOU READY FOR YOUR FIRST QUESTION?"

"I AM."

"WHO WAS THE FIRST FOUNDER OF THE EASTERN SEA COLONIES?"

BY EASTERN ACCOUNTS OR NORTHERN ACCOUNTS?

NORTHERN.

NUUIN THE FOURTH.

OKAY, GOOD.

NOW FOR YOUR SECOND QUESTION.

IN THE BOOK, *THE LONG JOURNEY OF ARNUS FAULSTON*, WHAT DOES PAPHOSGILL STEAL FROM THE KRAKEN'S GARDEN?

SHE STEALS THE KRAKEN'S EGGS.

YOU'RE RIGHT FOR A SECOND TIME.

YOU'RE INVADING AN ENEMY'S CASTLE. THE MAIN GATES ARE WIDE OPEN. DO YOU GO IN?

WHEN INVADING AN ENEMY'S CASTLE, YOU MUST ALWAYS BE WARY OF BEING CAUGHT IN A TRAP, SUCH AS A SALLY PORT. HERE YOUR ENEMIES CAN LURE YOU INSIDE THE CASTLE THROUGH A NARROW AREA AND THEN CLOSE THE DOORS BEHIND YOU. THESE AREAS CAN BE FILLED WITH MANY SURPRISES FOR THE ENEMY TO USE AS THEY ROUTE BEHIND YOU AND ATTACK.

I WOULD SEND AN EMISSARY, DISGUISED AS A GENERAL, INTO THE SALLY PORT TO TEST IT AND TO MAKE SURE THAT IT'S SAFE. THEN PROCEED.

VERY GOOD.

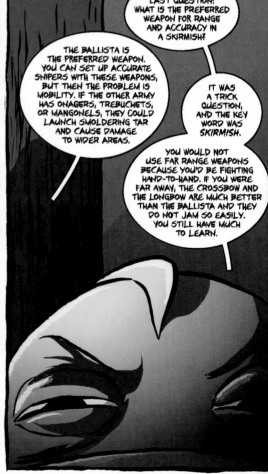

LAST QUESTION: WHAT IS THE PREFERRED WEAPON FOR RANGE AND ACCURACY IN A SKIRMISH?

THE BALLISTA IS THE PREFERRED WEAPON. YOU CAN SET UP ACCURATE SNIPERS WITH THESE WEAPONS, BUT THEN THE PROBLEM IS MOBILITY. IF THE OTHER ARMY HAS ONAGERS, TREBUCHETS, OR MANGONELS, THEY COULD LAUNCH SMOLDERING TAR AND CAUSE DAMAGE TO WIDER AREAS.

IT WAS A TRICK QUESTION, AND THE KEY WORD WAS SKIRMISH.

YOU WOULD NOT USE FAR RANGE WEAPONS BECAUSE YOU'D BE FIGHTING HAND-TO-HAND. IF YOU WERE FAR AWAY, THE CROSSBOW AND THE LONGBOW ARE MUCH BETTER THAN THE BALLISTA AND THEY DO NOT JAM SO EASILY. YOU STILL HAVE MUCH TO LEARN.

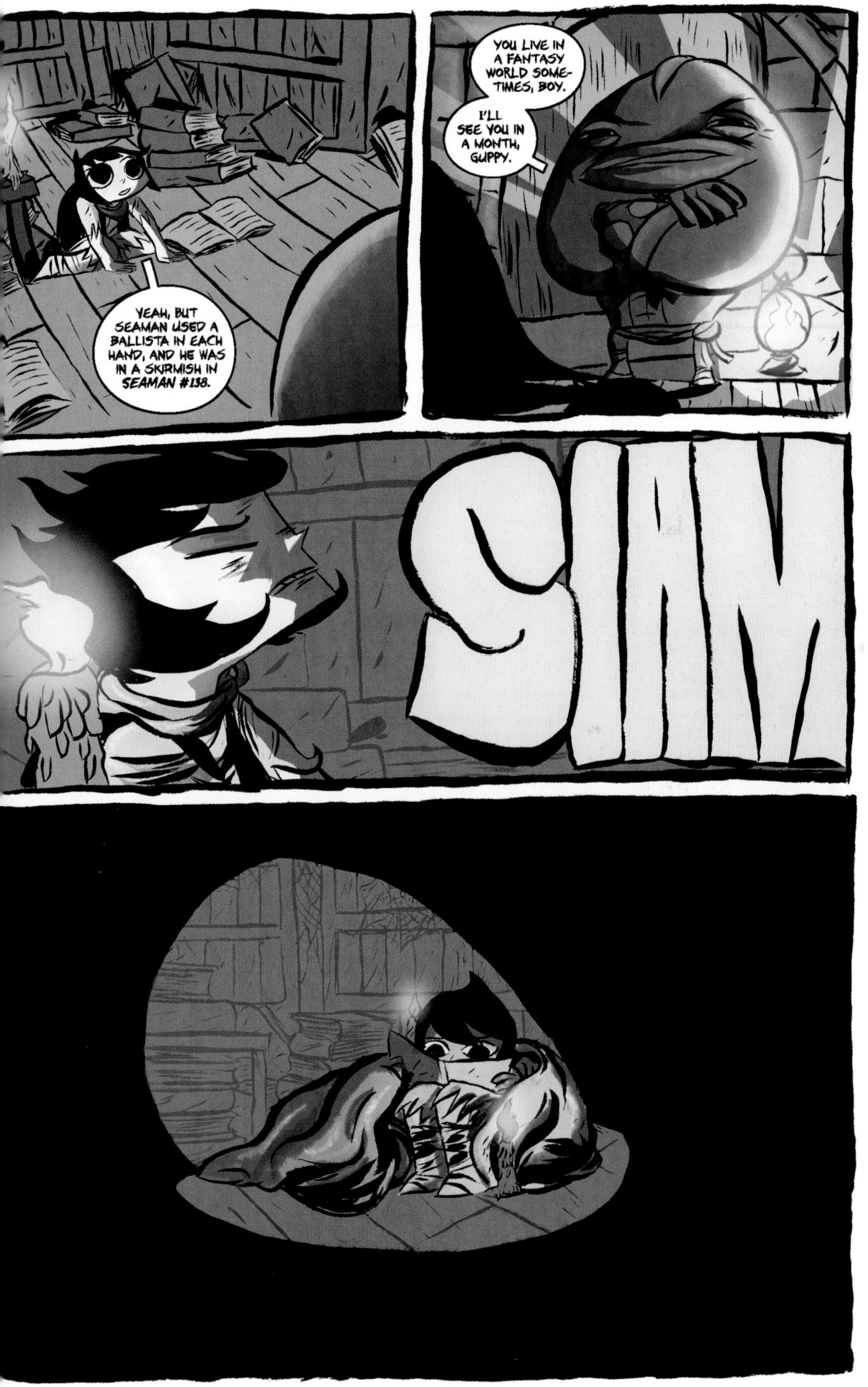
YEAH, BUT SEAMAN USED A BALLISTA IN EACH HAND, AND HE WAS IN A SKIRMISH IN SEAMAN #138.
YOU LIVE IN A FANTASY WORLD SOMETIMES, BOY.
I'LL SEE YOU IN A MONTH, GUPPY.
SLAM

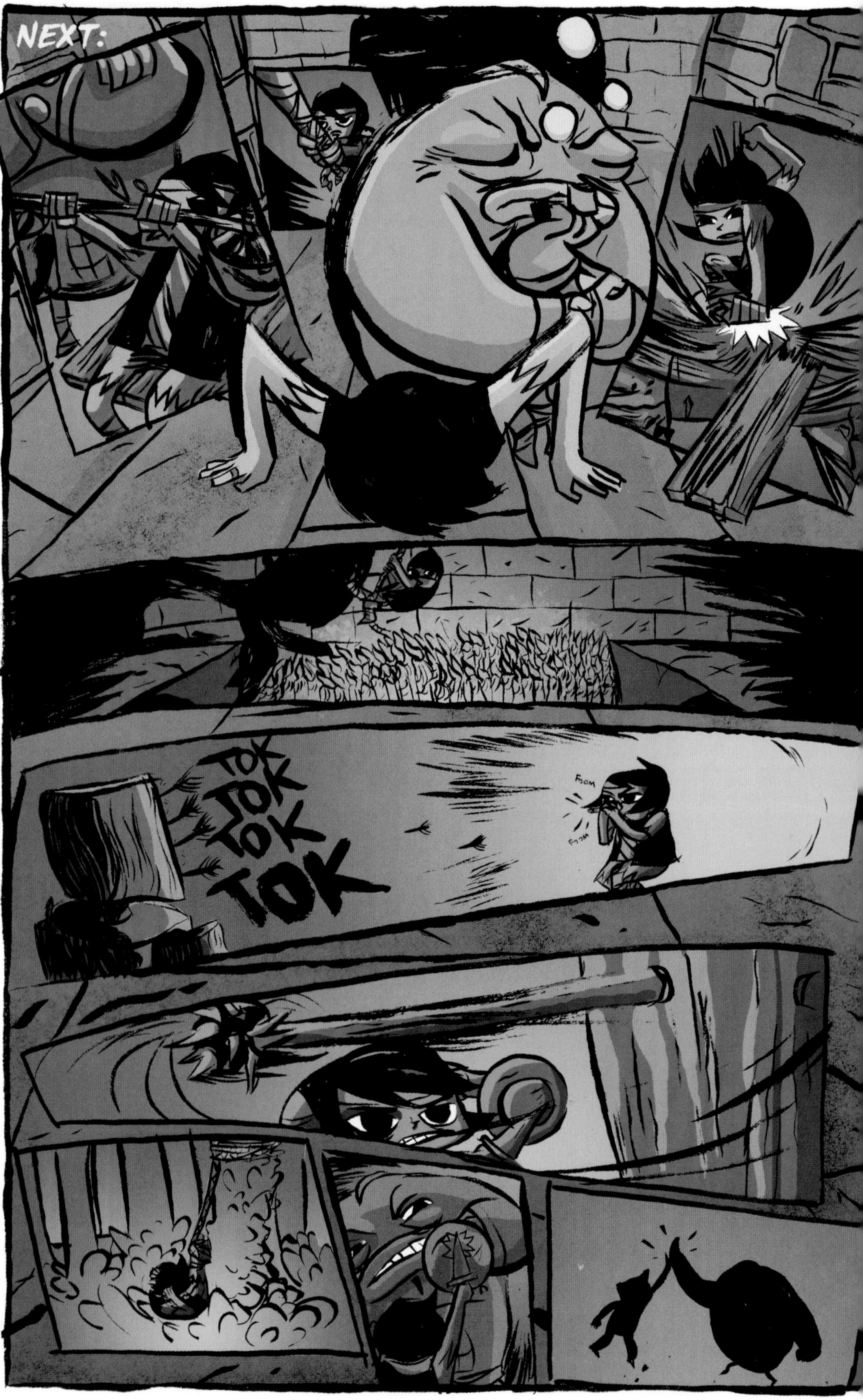
NEXT:
TOK
TOK
TOK
TOK

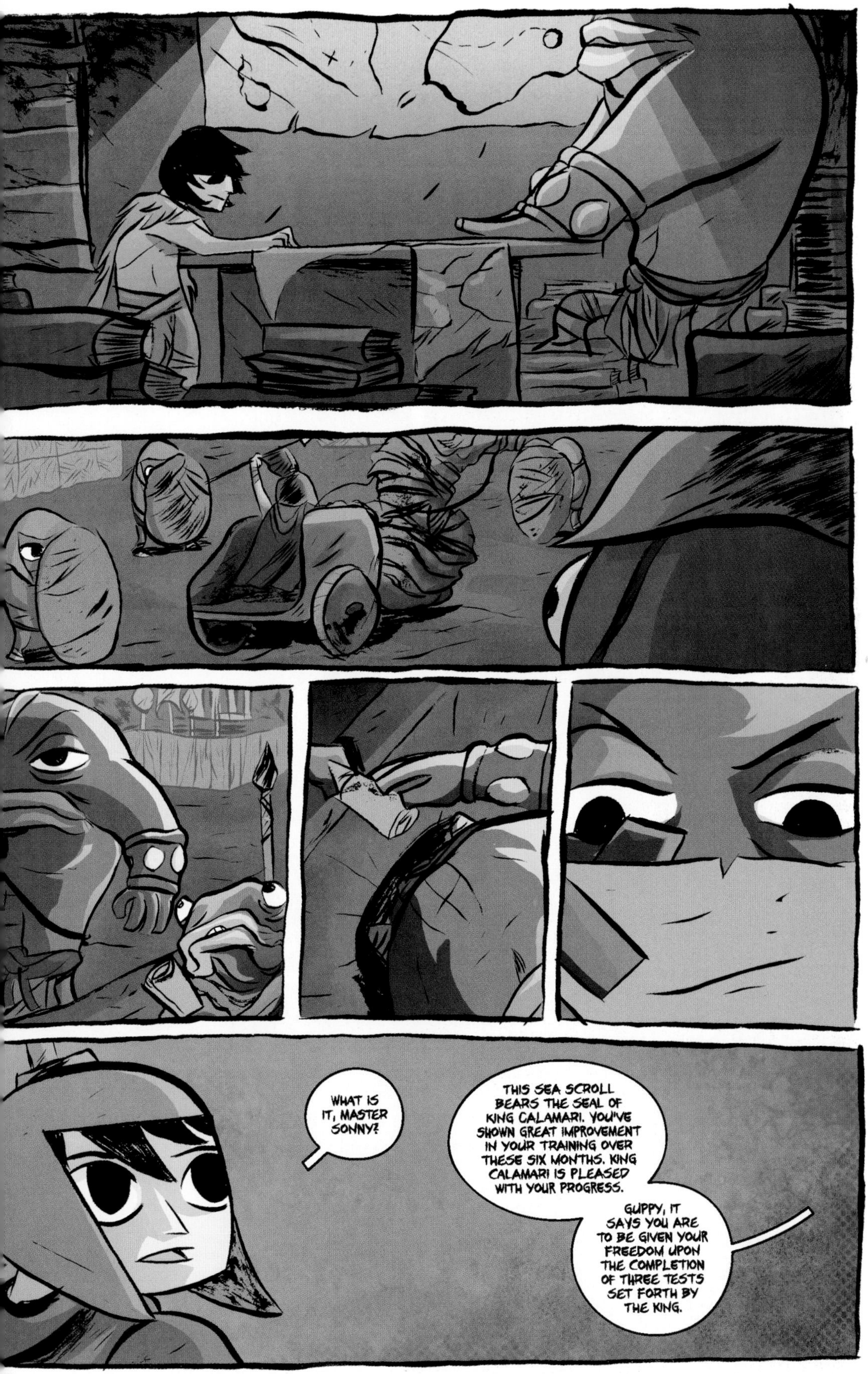
WHAT IS IT, MASTER SONNY?
THIS SEA SCROLL BEARS THE SEAL OF KING CALAMARI. YOU'VE SHOWN GREAT IMPROVEMENT IN YOUR TRAINING OVER THESE SIX MONTHS. KING CALAMARI IS PLEASED WITH YOUR PROGRESS.
GUPPY, IT SAYS YOU ARE TO BE GIVEN YOUR FREEDOM UPON THE COMPLETION OF THREE TESTS SET FORTH BY THE KING.

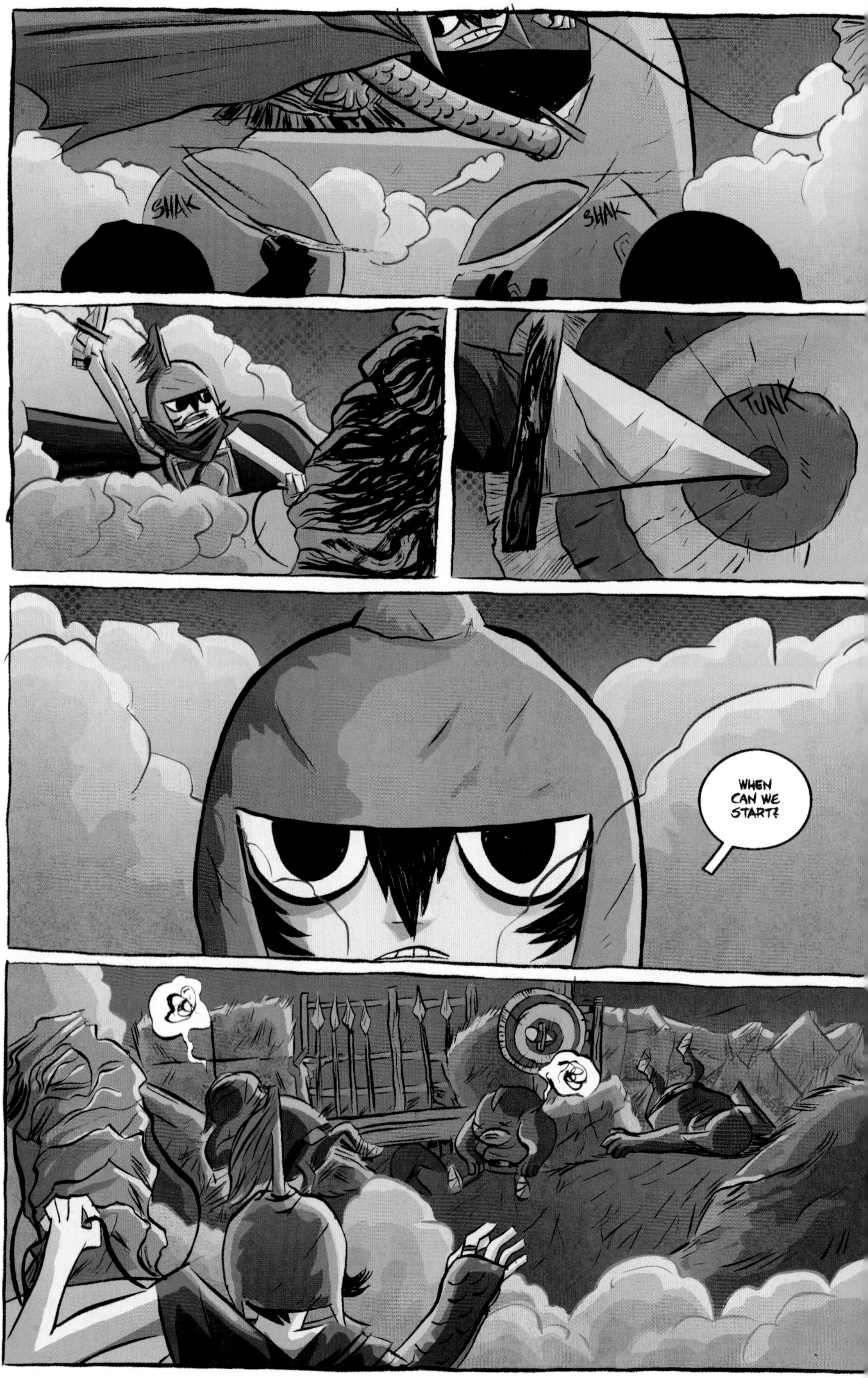
SHAK
SHAK
TUNK
WHEN CAN WE START?

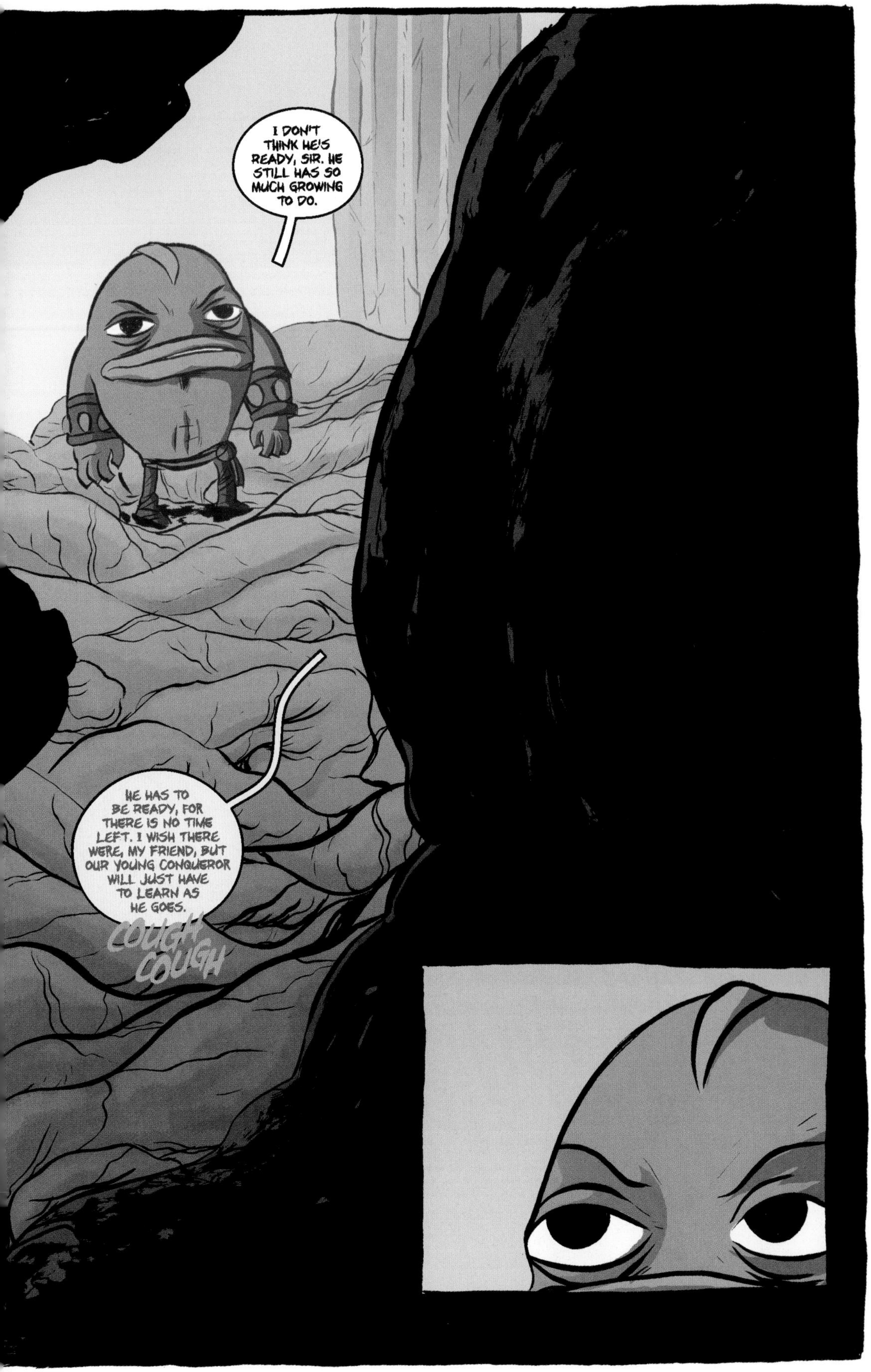
I DON'T THINK HE'S READY, SIR. HE STILL HAS SO MUCH GROWING TO DO.
HE HAS TO BE READY, FOR THERE IS NO TIME LEFT. I WISH THERE WERE, MY FRIEND, BUT OUR YOUNG CONQUEROR WILL JUST HAVE TO LEARN AS HE GOES.
COUGH COUGH

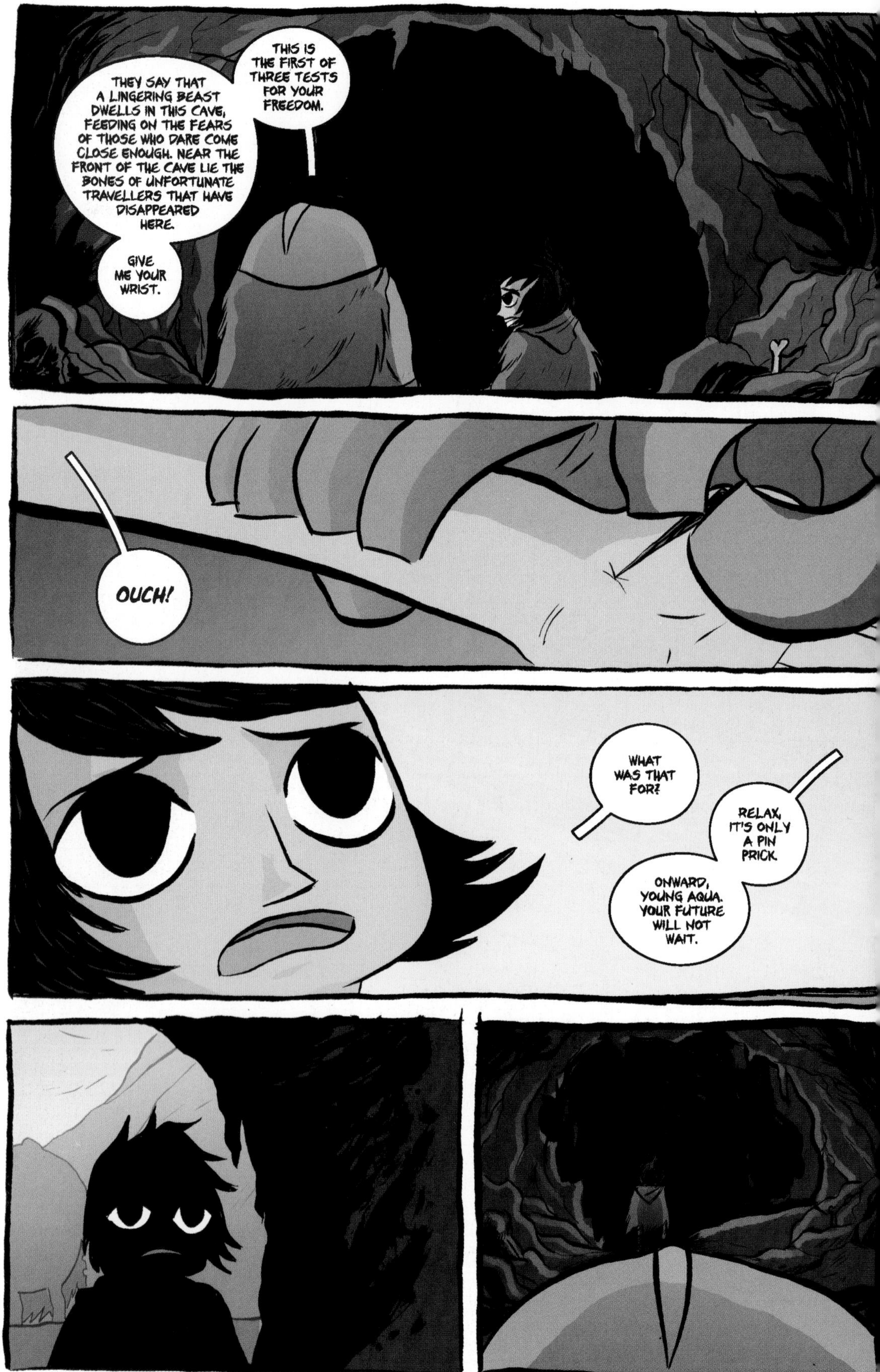
THEY SAY THAT A LINGERING BEAST DWELLS IN THIS CAVE, FEEDING ON THE FEARS OF THOSE WHO DARE COME CLOSE ENOUGH. NEAR THE FRONT OF THE CAVE LIE THE BONES OF UNFORTUNATE TRAVELLERS THAT HAVE DISAPPEARED HERE.
THIS IS THE FIRST OF THREE TESTS FOR YOUR FREEDOM.
GIVE ME YOUR WRIST.
OUCH!
WHAT WAS THAT FOR?
RELAX, IT'S ONLY A PIN PRICK.
ONWARD, YOUNG AQUA. YOUR FUTURE WILL NOT WAIT.

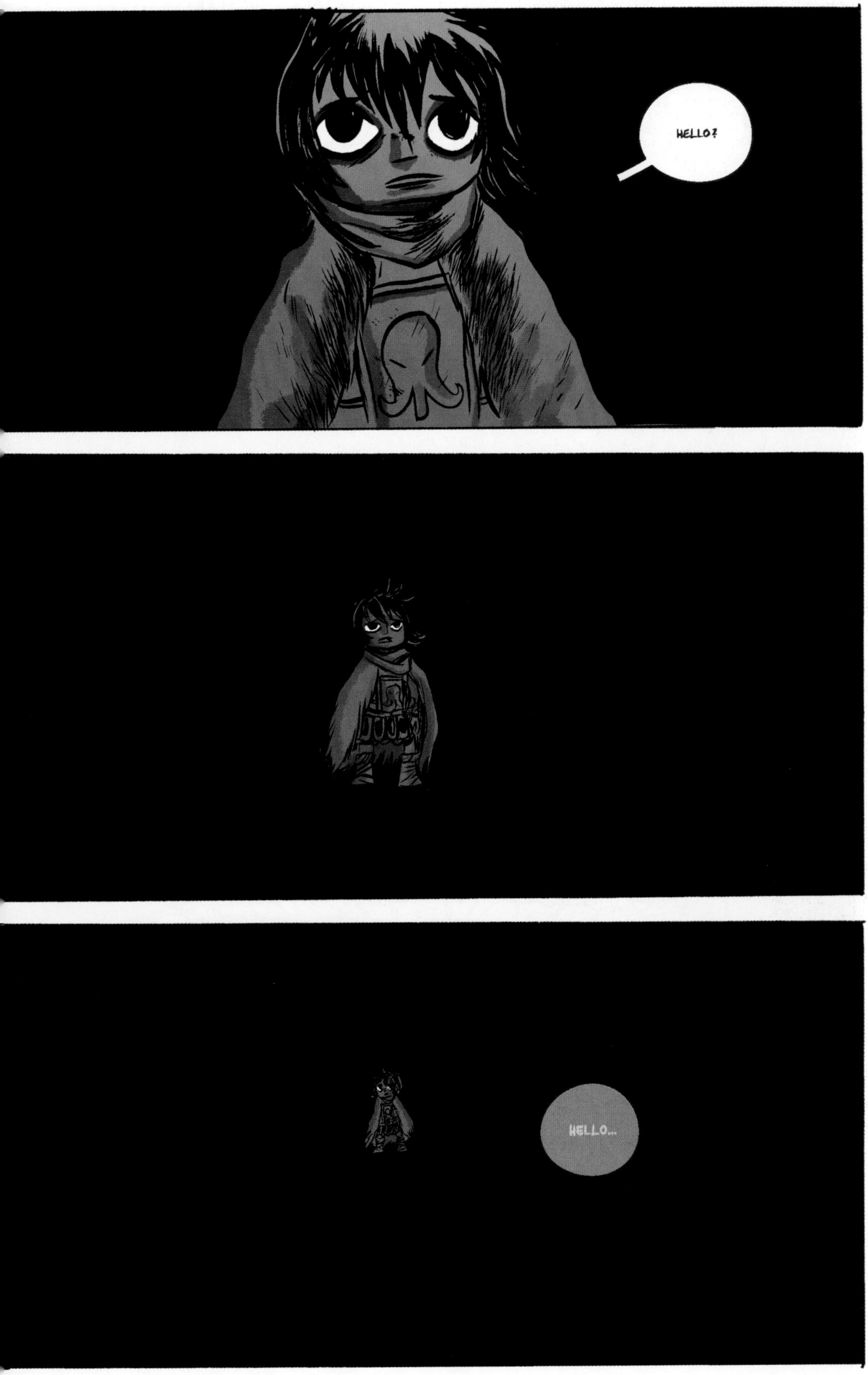
HELLO?
HELLO...

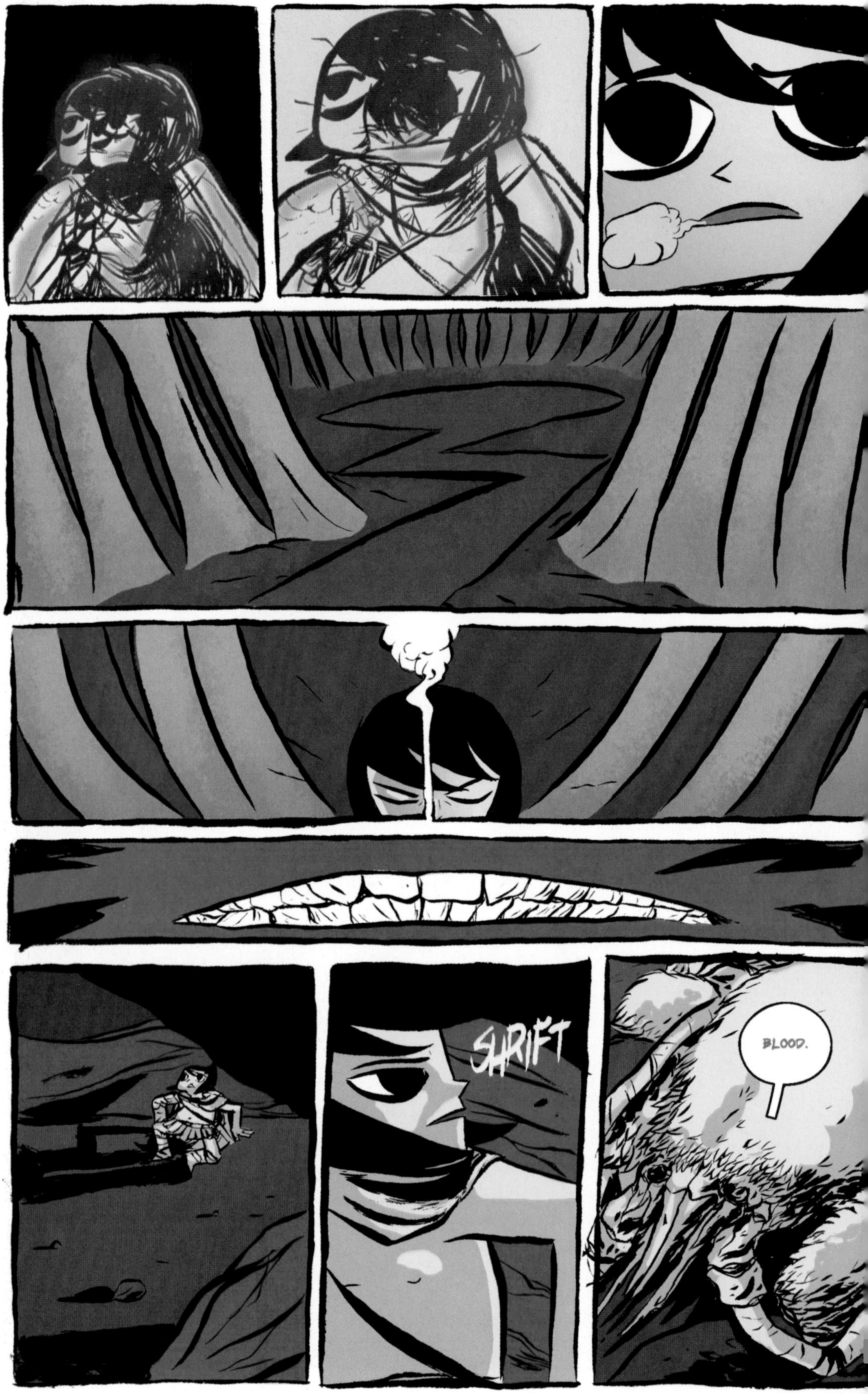
SHRIFT
BLOOD.

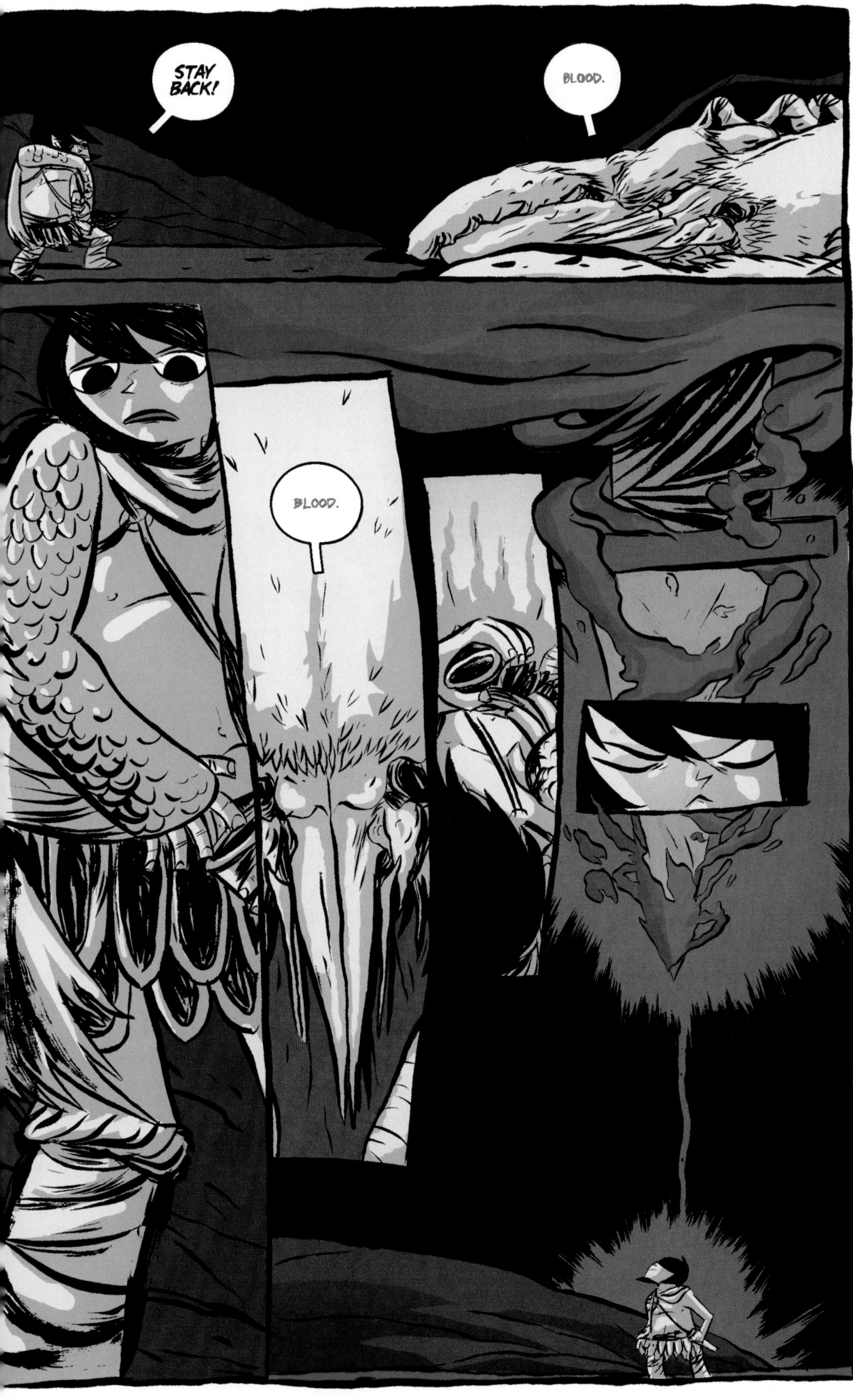
STAY BACK!
BLOOD.
BLOOD.

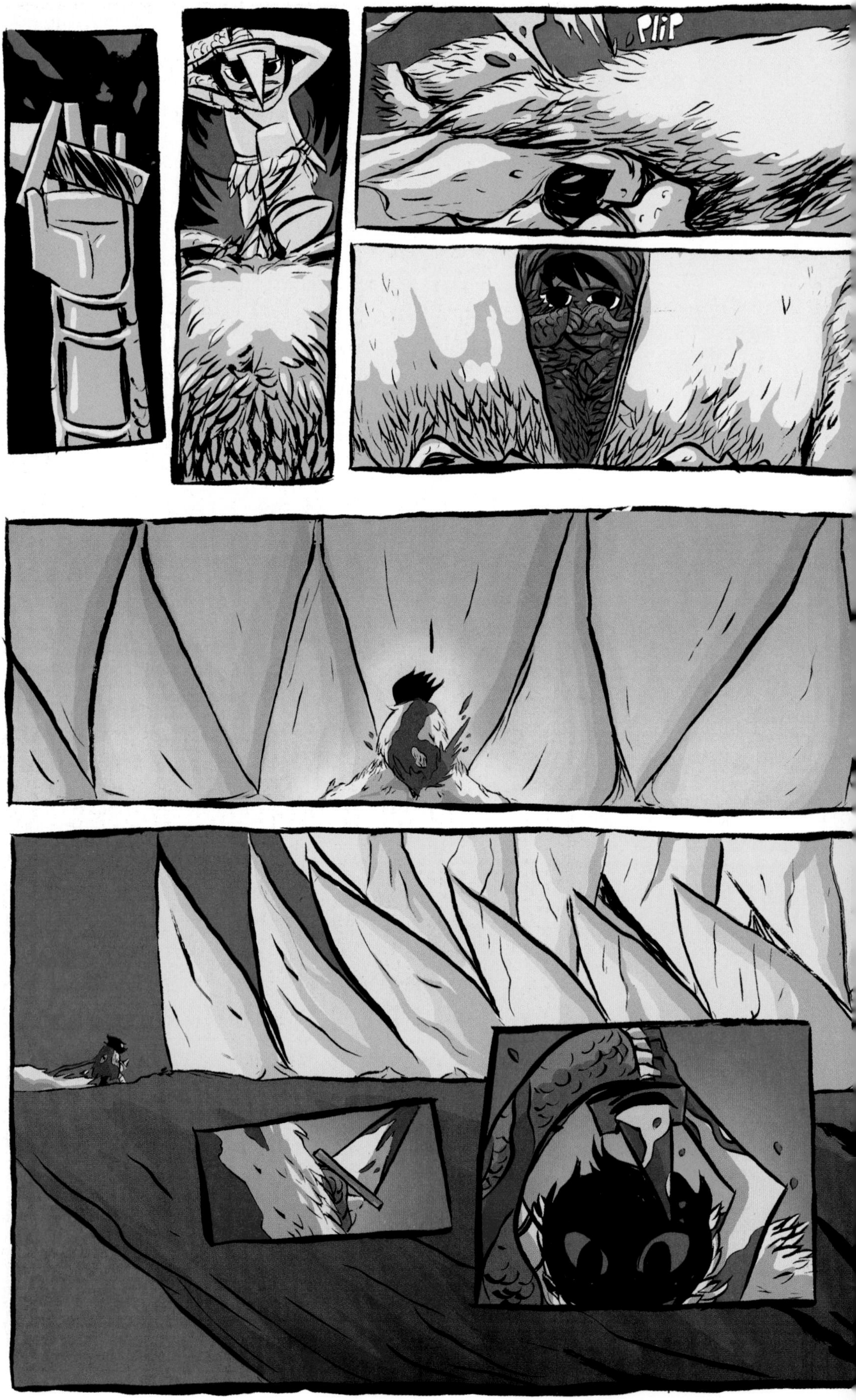
PLIP

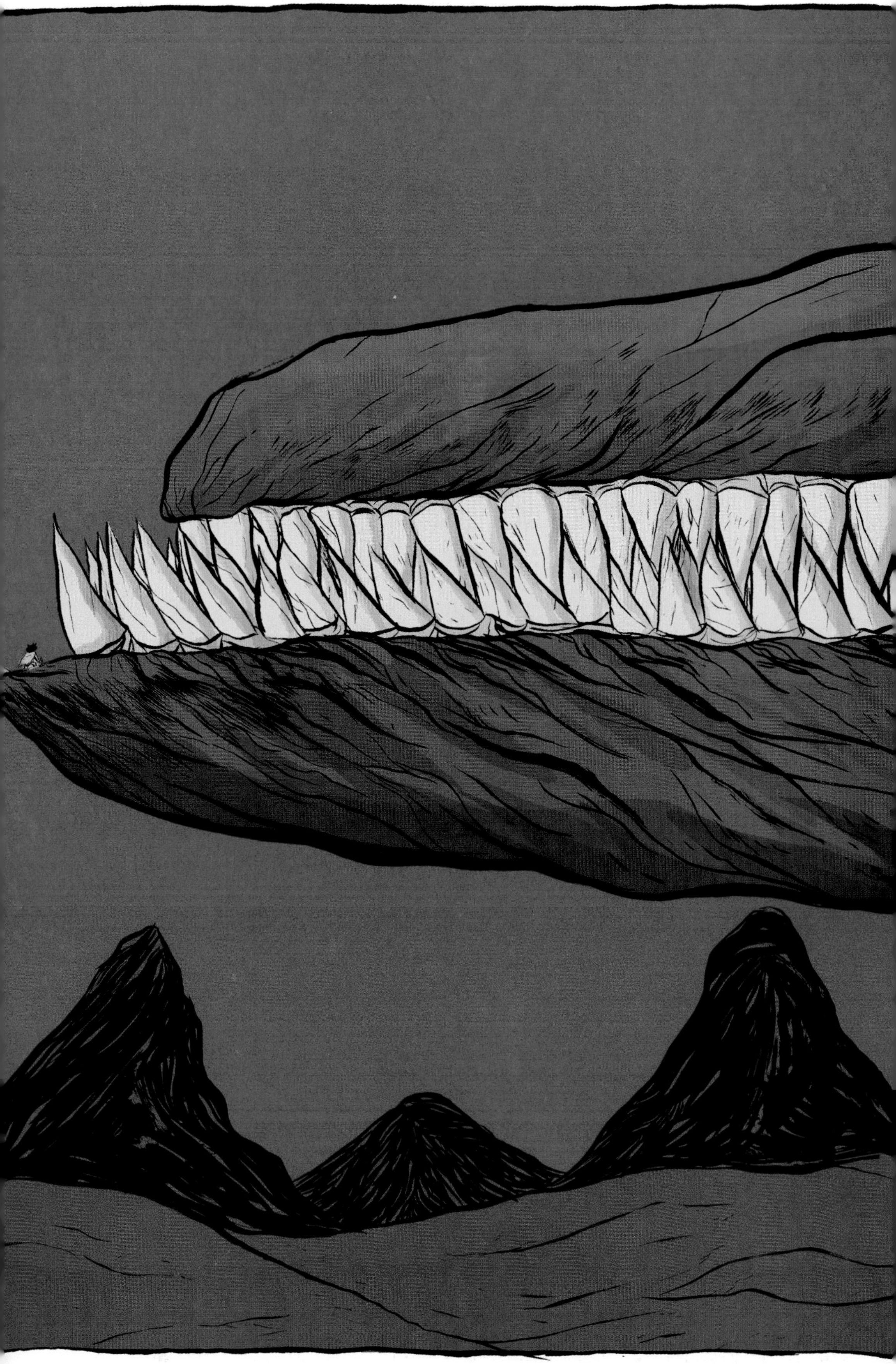

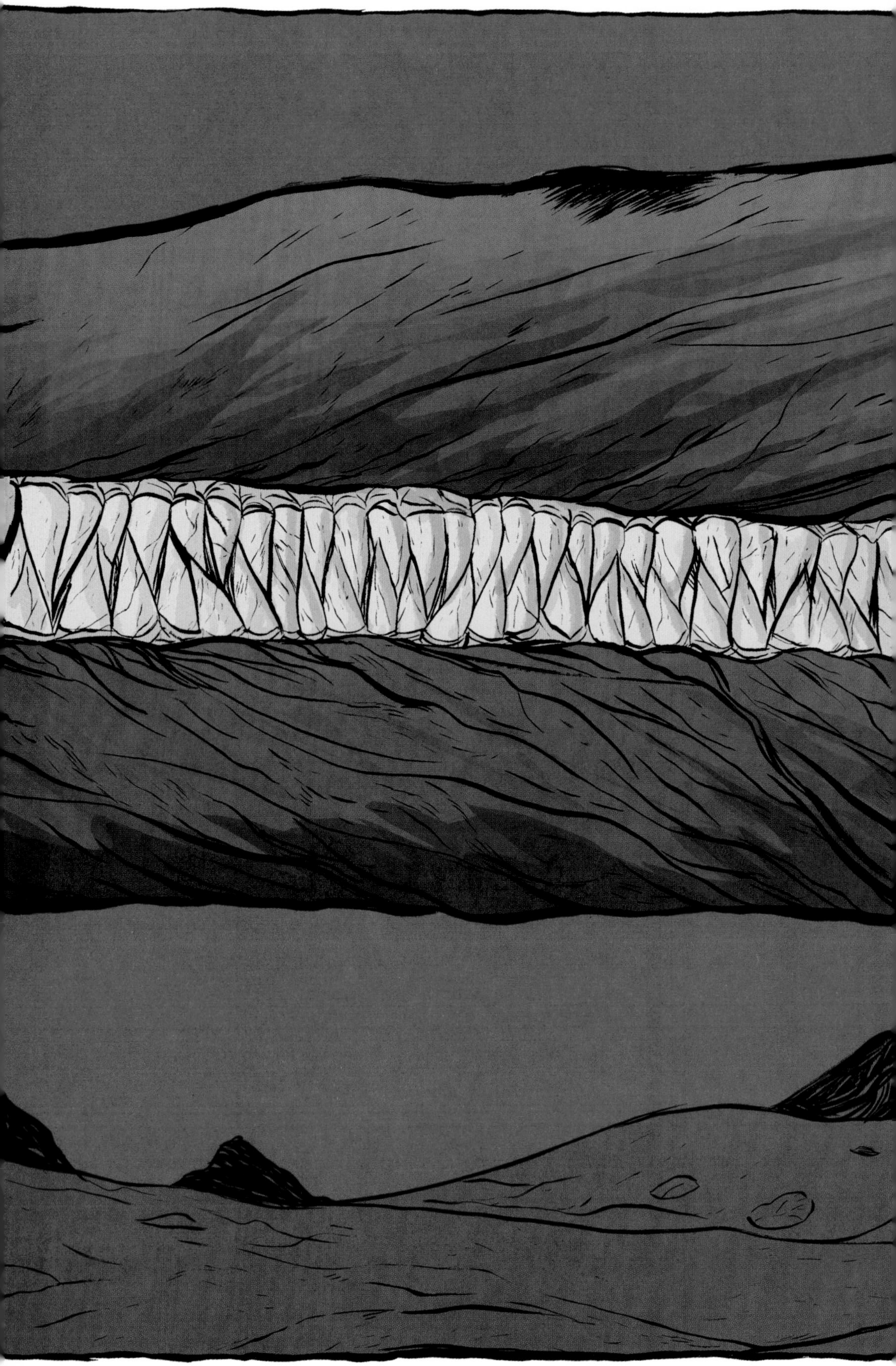

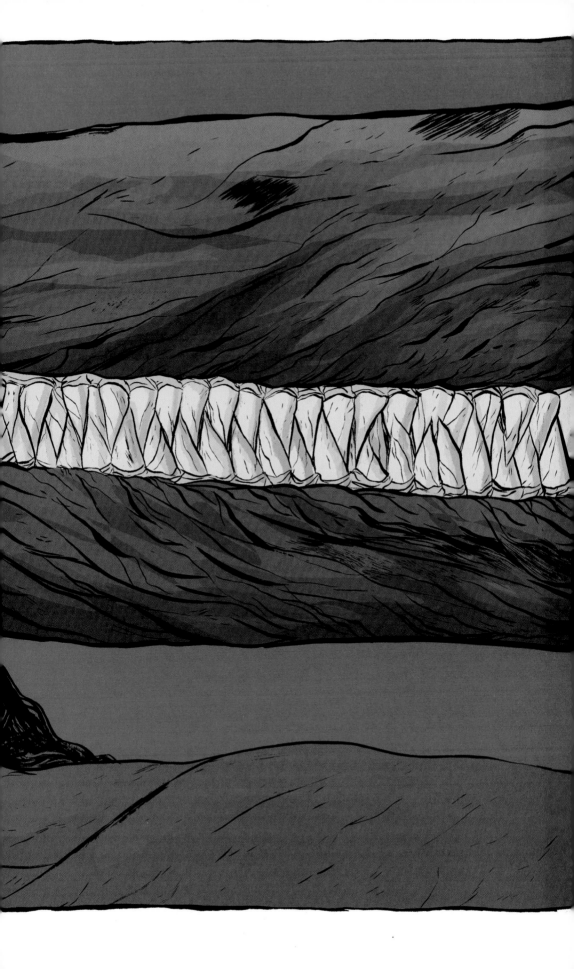

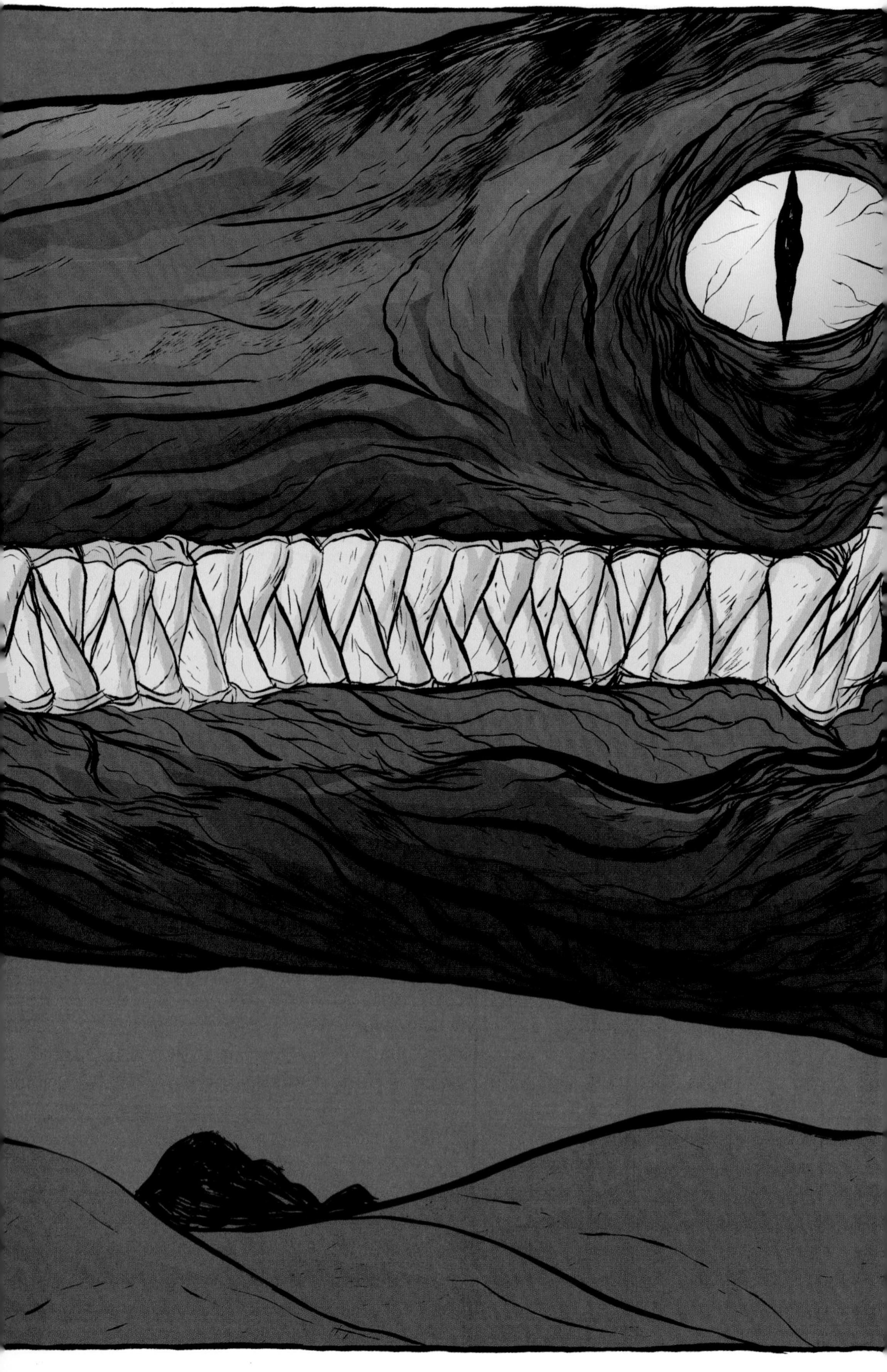

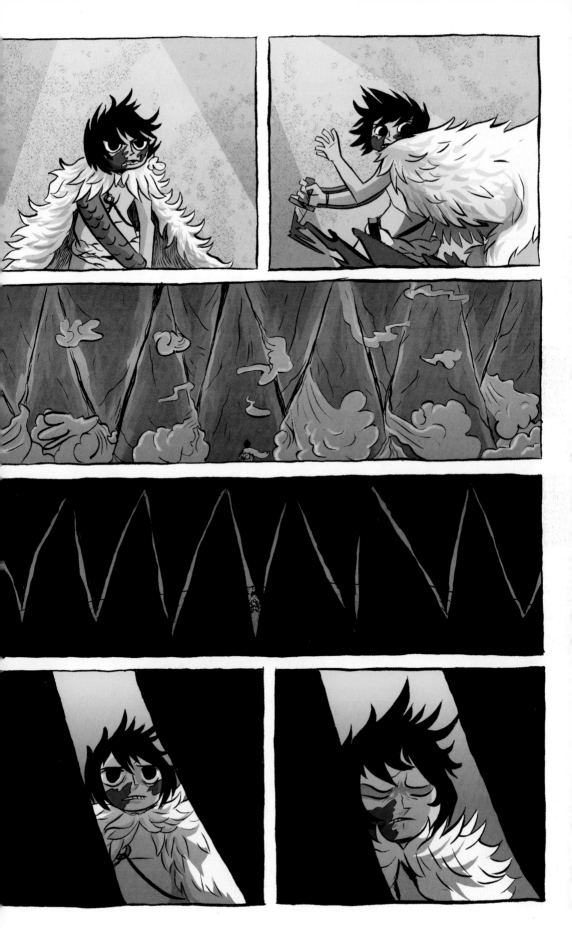

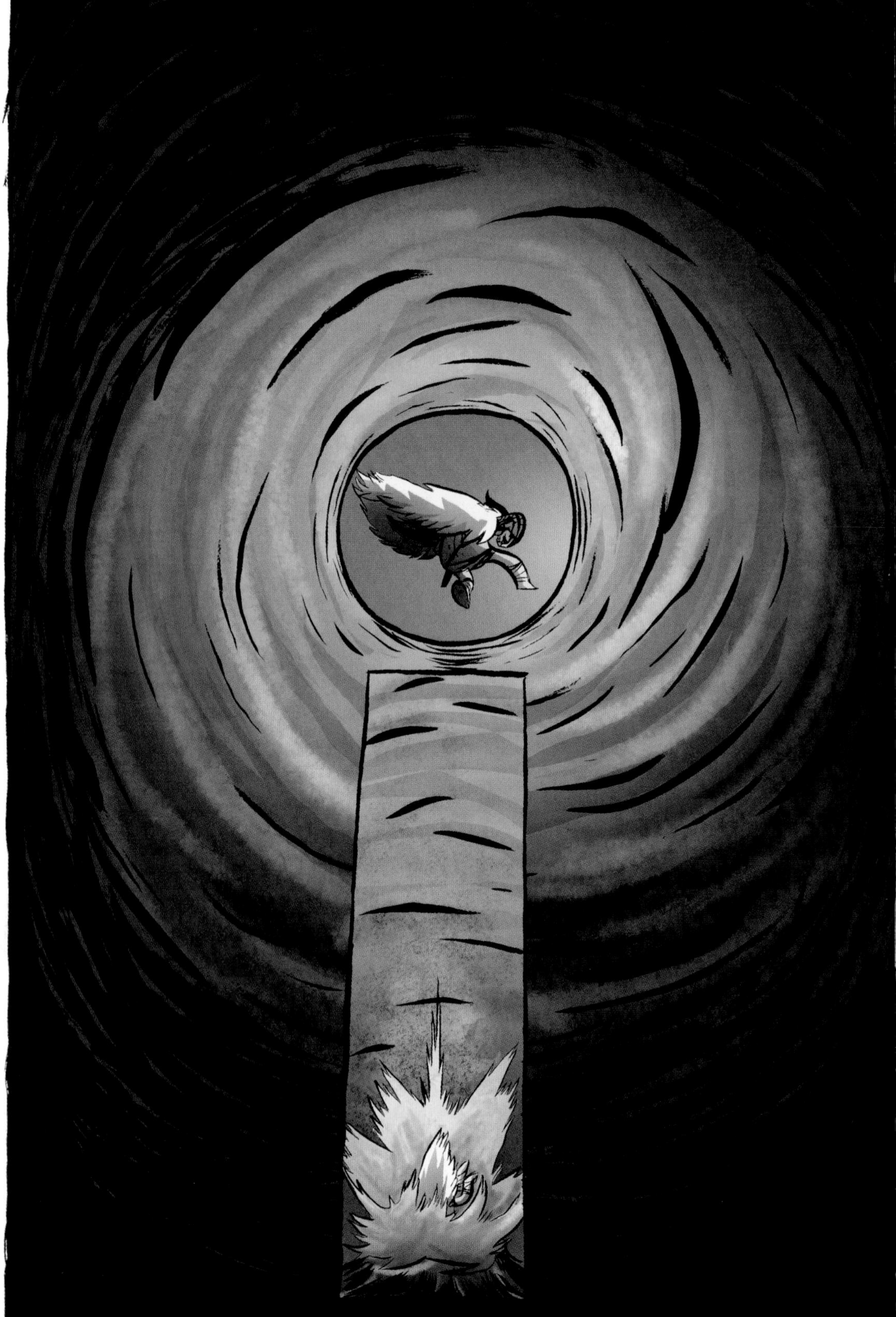

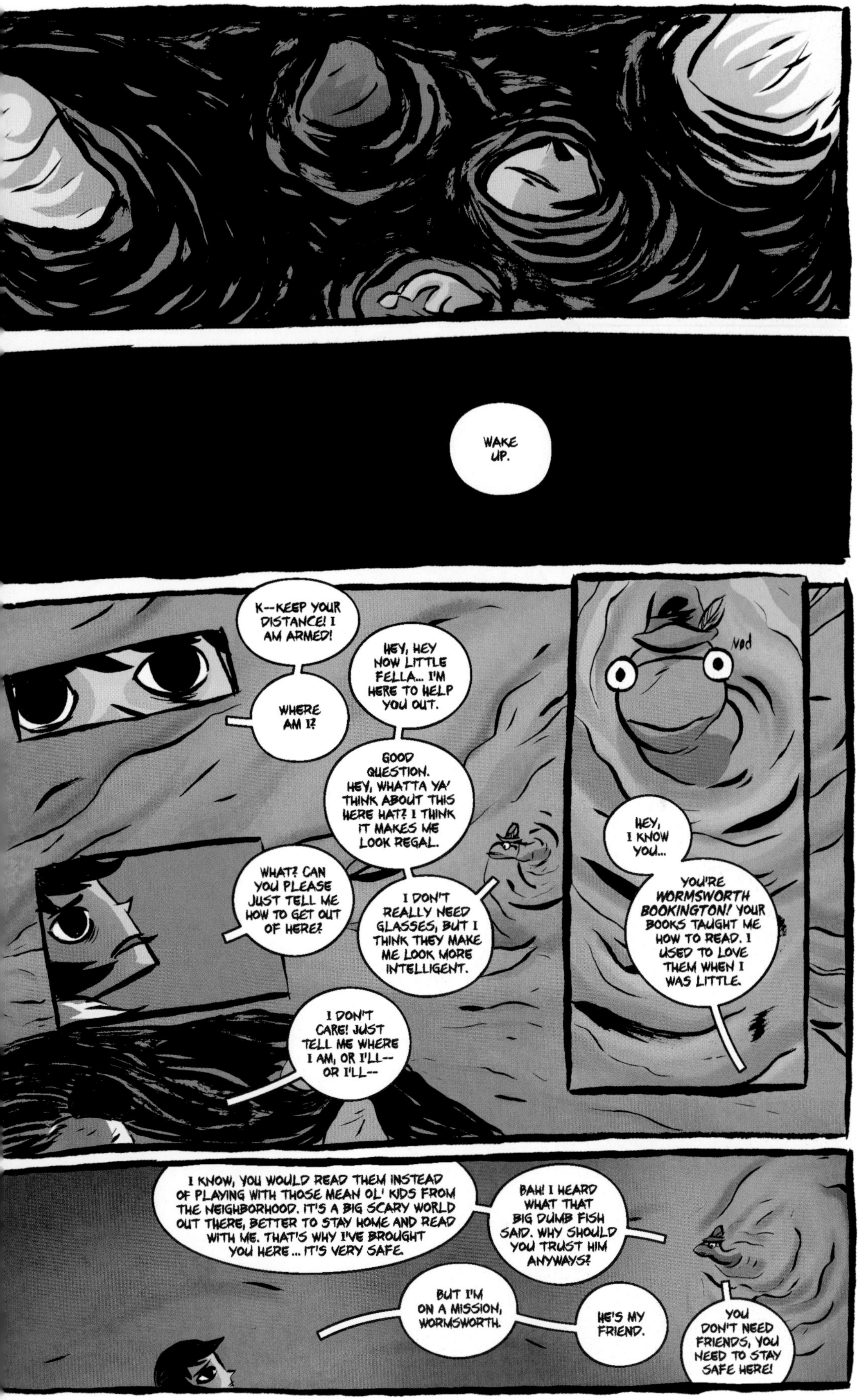
WAKE UP.
K--KEEP YOUR DISTANCE! I AM ARMED!
WHERE AM I?
HEY, HEY NOW LITTLE FELLA... I'M HERE TO HELP YOU OUT.
GOOD QUESTION. HEY, WHATTA YA' THINK ABOUT THIS HERE HAT? I THINK IT MAKES ME LOOK REGAL.
WHAT? CAN YOU PLEASE JUST TELL ME HOW TO GET OUT OF HERE?
I DON'T REALLY NEED GLASSES, BUT I THINK THEY MAKE ME LOOK MORE INTELLIGENT.
I DON'T CARE! JUST TELL ME WHERE I AM, OR I'LL-- OR I'LL--
nod
HEY, I KNOW YOU...
YOU'RE WORMSWORTH BOOKINGTON! YOUR BOOKS TAUGHT ME HOW TO READ. I USED TO LOVE THEM WHEN I WAS LITTLE.
I KNOW, YOU WOULD READ THEM INSTEAD OF PLAYING WITH THOSE MEAN OL' KIDS FROM THE NEIGHBORHOOD. IT'S A BIG SCARY WORLD OUT THERE, BETTER TO STAY HOME AND READ WITH ME. THAT'S WHY I'VE BROUGHT YOU HERE... IT'S VERY SAFE.
BAH! I HEARD WHAT THAT BIG DUMB FISH SAID. WHY SHOULD YOU TRUST HIM ANYWAYS?
BUT I'M ON A MISSION, WORMSWORTH.
HE'S MY FRIEND.
YOU DON'T NEED FRIENDS, YOU NEED TO STAY SAFE HERE!

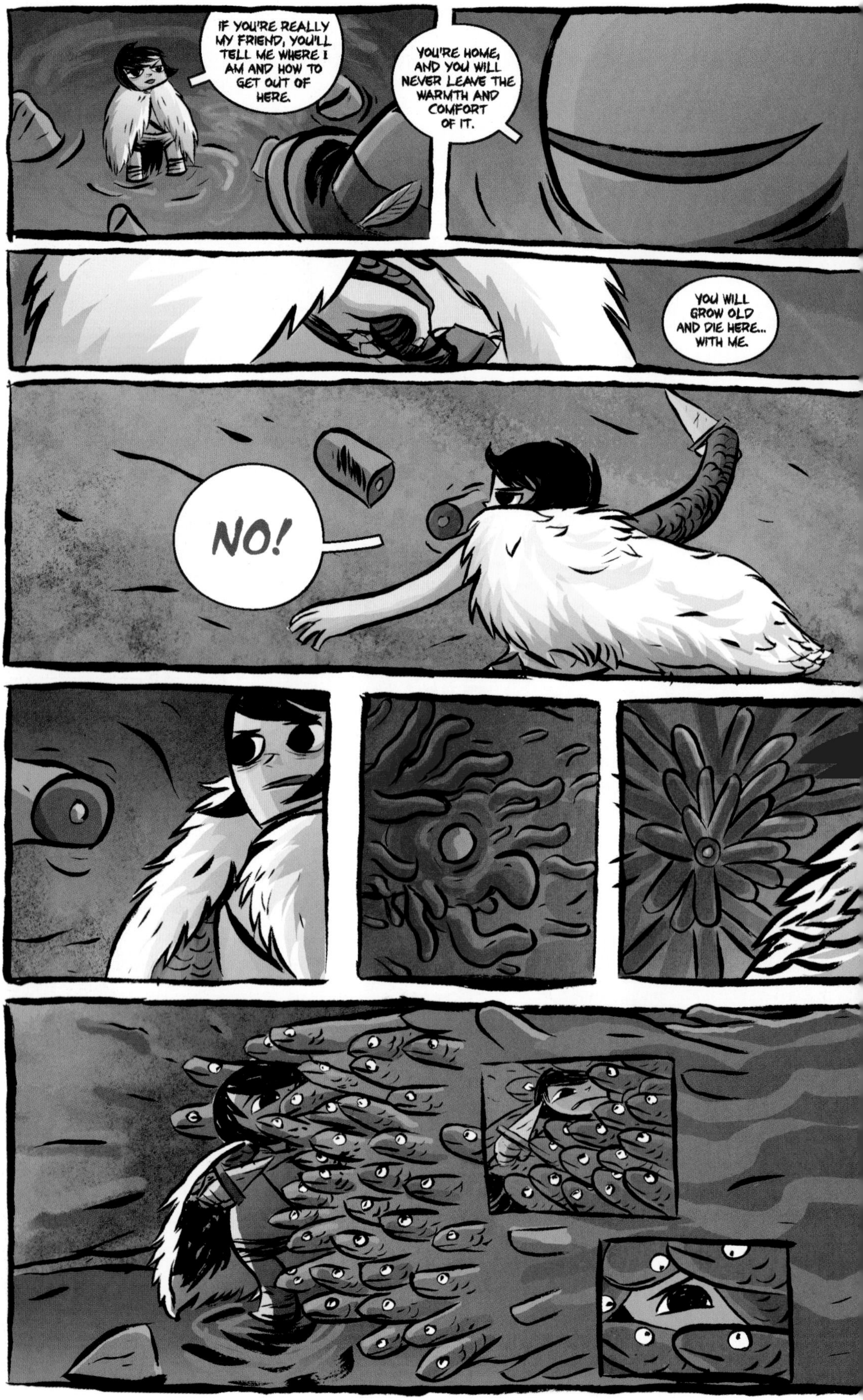
IF YOU'RE REALLY MY FRIEND, YOU'LL TELL ME WHERE I AM AND HOW TO GET OUT OF HERE.
YOU'RE HOME, AND YOU WILL NEVER LEAVE THE WARMTH AND COMFORT OF IT.
YOU WILL GROW OLD AND DIE HERE... WITH ME.
NO!

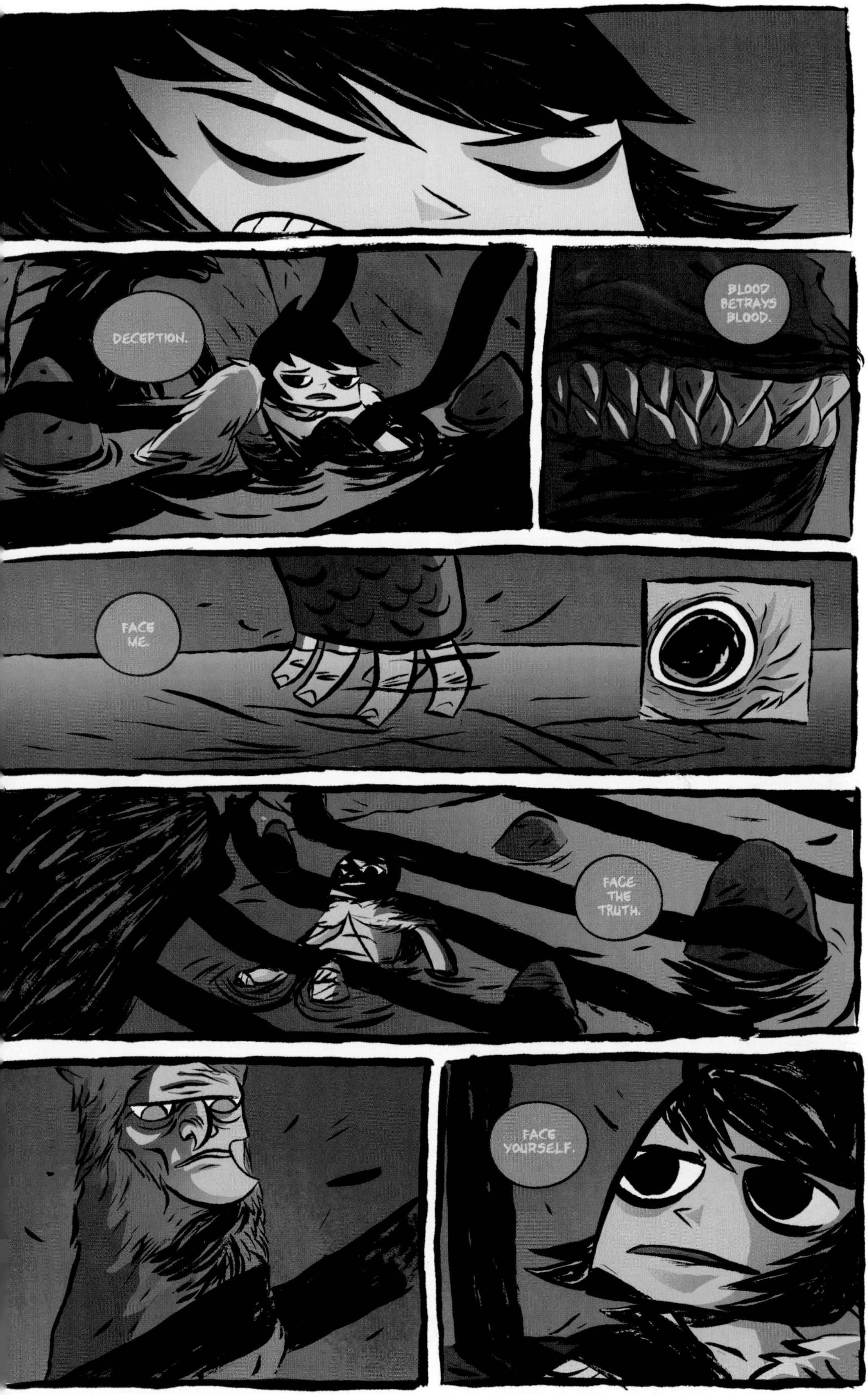
DECEPTION.
BLOOD BETRAYS BLOOD.
FACE ME.
FACE THE TRUTH.
FACE YOURSELF.

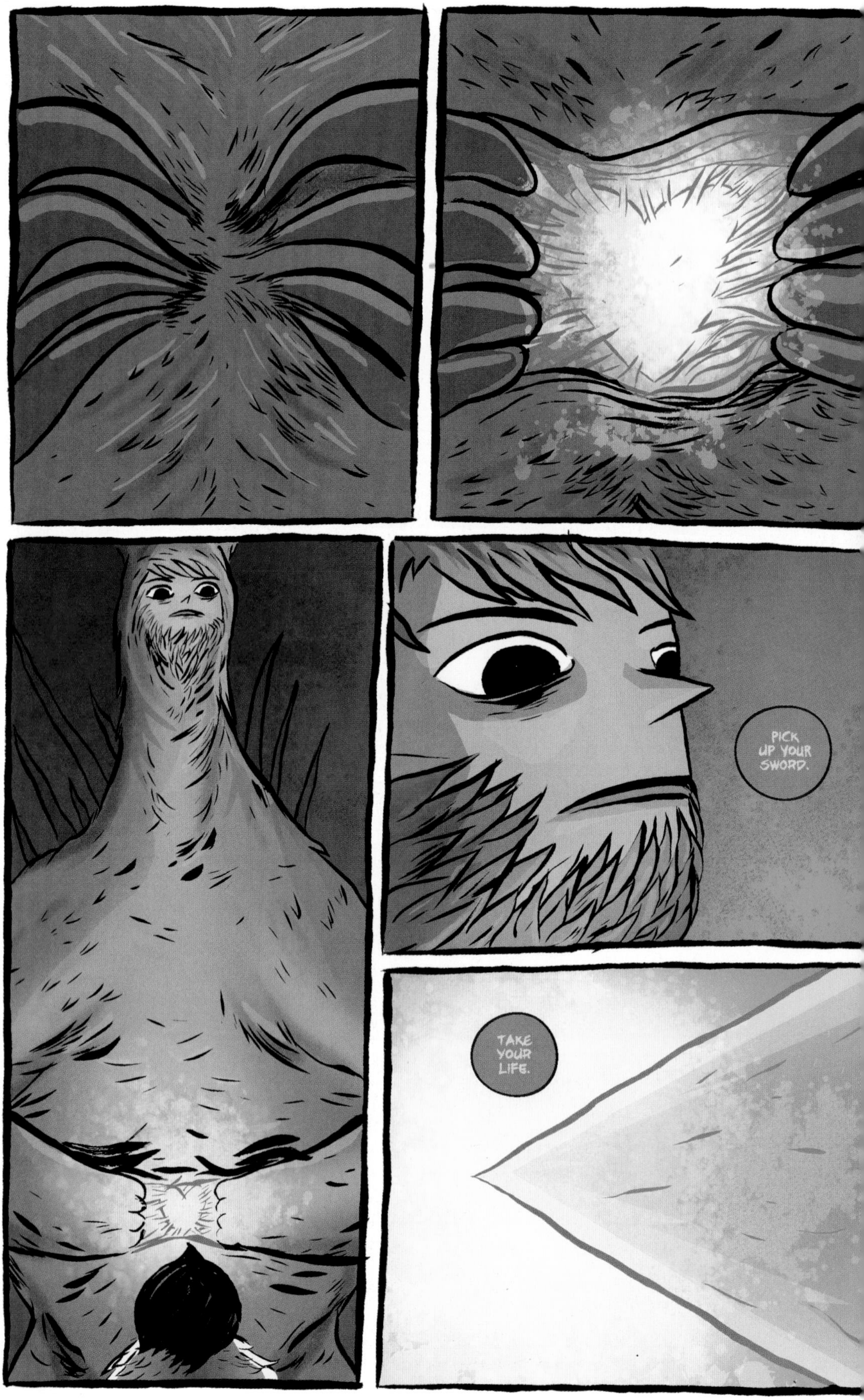
PICK UP YOUR SWORD.
TAKE YOUR LIFE.

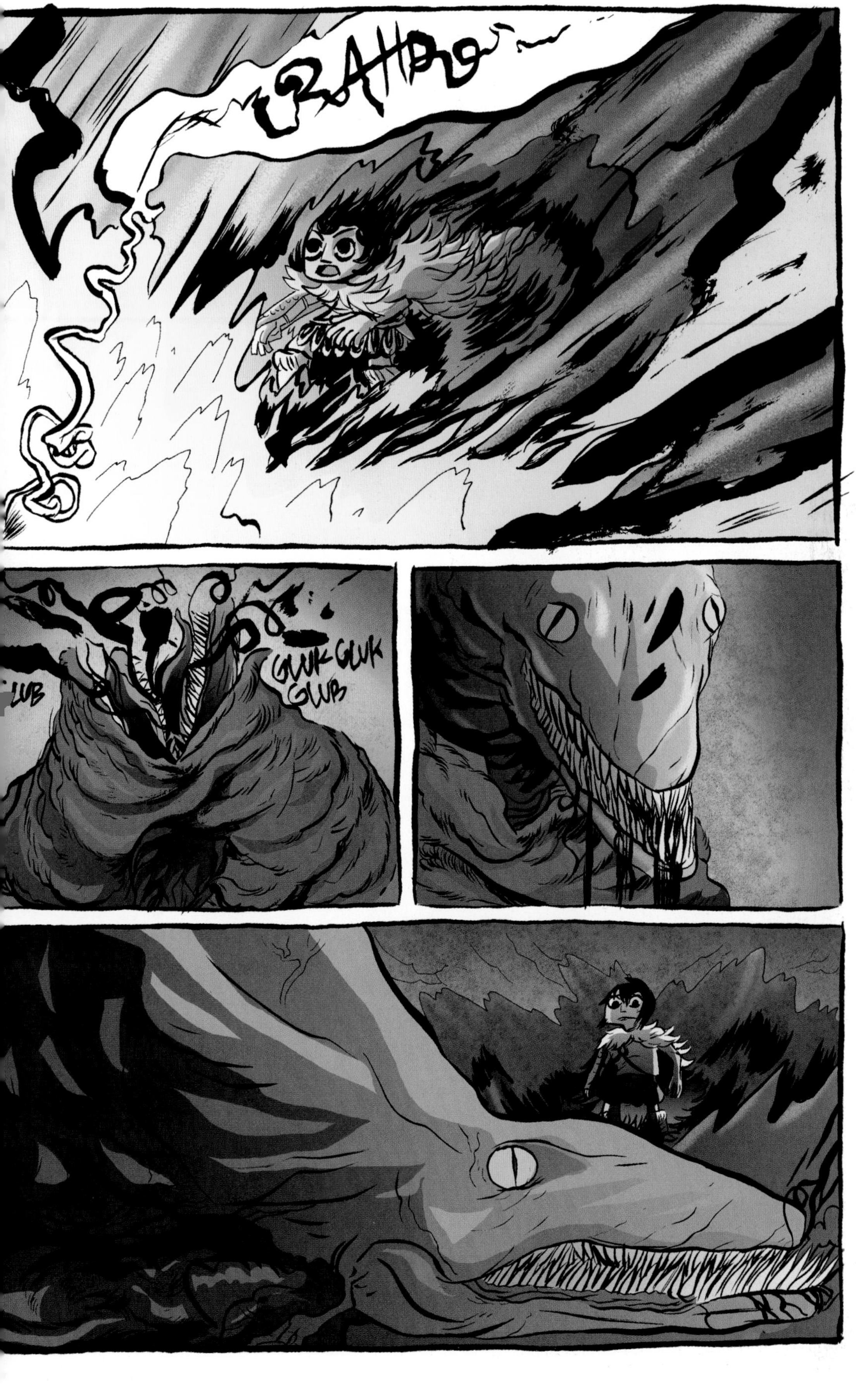
CRAHRO
GLUB
GLUK GLUK
GLUB

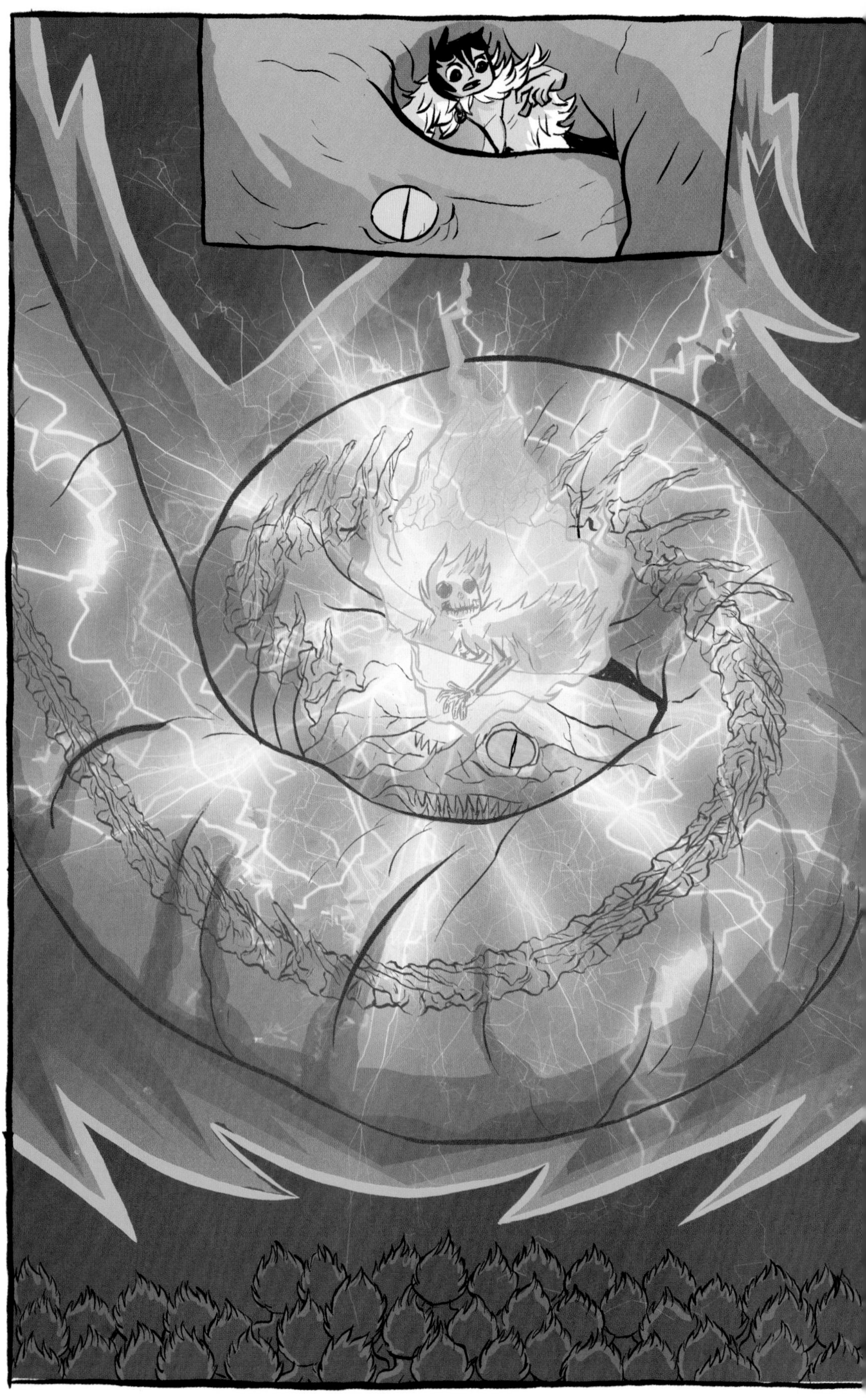

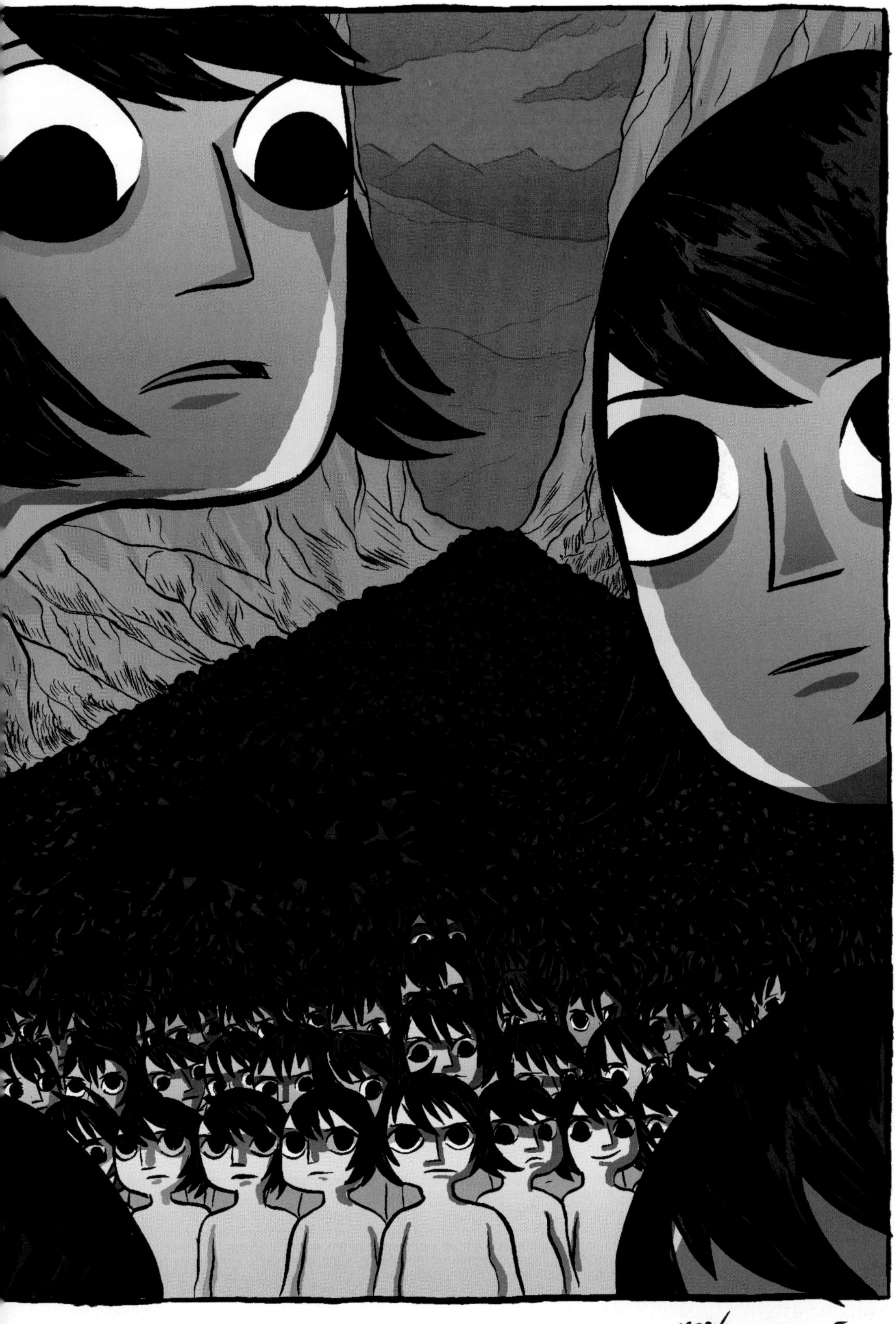

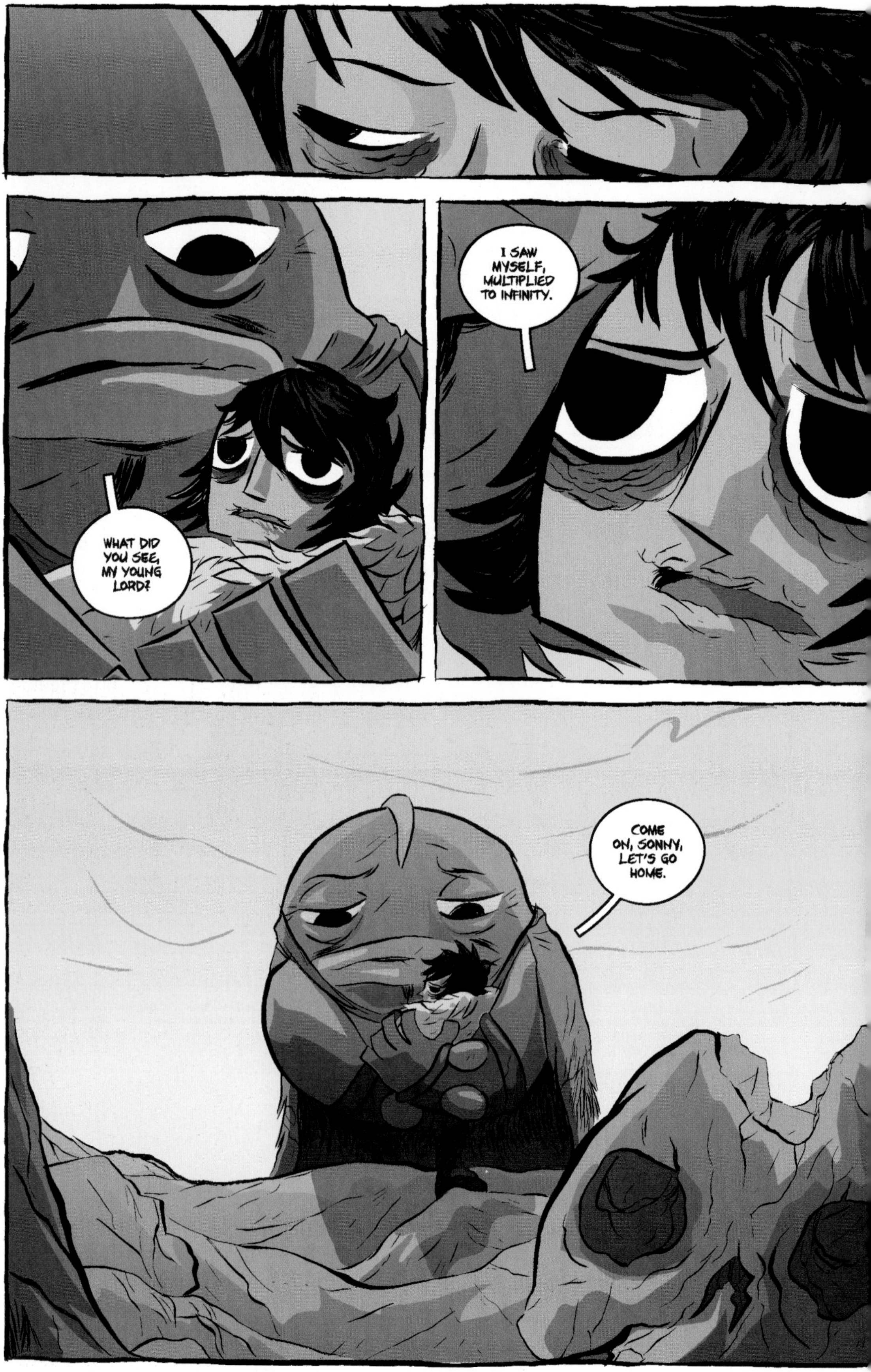
WHAT DID YOU SEE, MY YOUNG LORD?
I SAW MYSELF, MULTIPLIED TO INFINITY.
COME ON, SONNY, LET'S GO HOME.

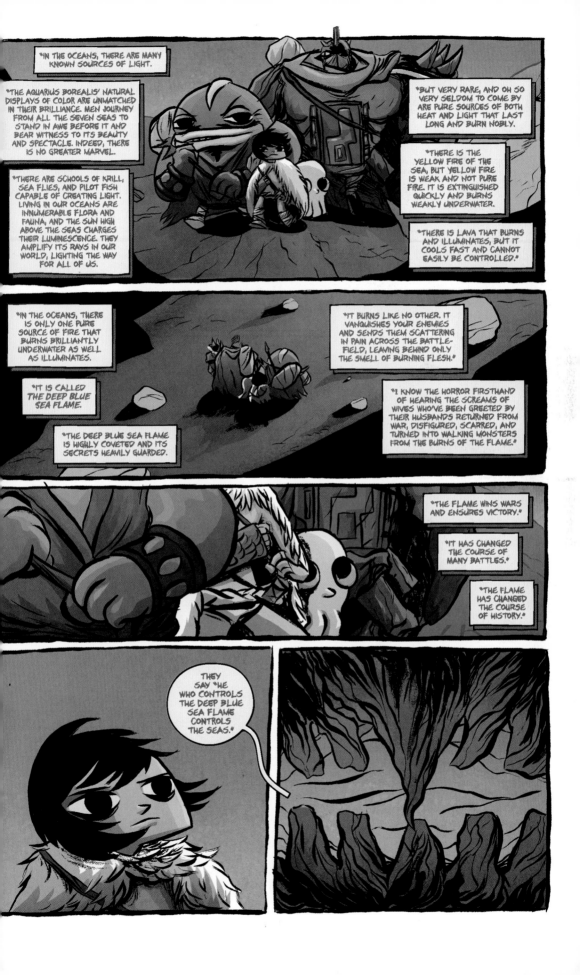

"IN THE OCEANS, THERE ARE MANY KNOWN SOURCES OF LIGHT.

"THE AQUARIUS BOREALIS' NATURAL DISPLAYS OF COLOR ARE UNMATCHED IN THEIR BRILLIANCE. MEN JOURNEY FROM ALL THE SEVEN SEAS TO STAND IN AWE BEFORE IT AND BEAR WITNESS TO ITS BEAUTY AND SPECTACLE. INDEED, THERE IS NO GREATER MARVEL.

"THERE ARE SCHOOLS OF KRILL, SEA FLIES, AND PILOT FISH CAPABLE OF CREATING LIGHT. LIVING IN OUR OCEANS ARE INNUMERABLE FLORA AND FAUNA, AND THE SUN HIGH ABOVE THE SEAS CHARGES THEIR LUMINESCENCE. THEY AMPLIFY ITS RAYS IN OUR WORLD, LIGHTING THE WAY FOR ALL OF US.

"BUT VERY RARE, AND OH SO VERY SELDOM TO COME BY ARE PURE SOURCES OF BOTH HEAT AND LIGHT THAT LAST LONG AND BURN NOBLY.

"THERE IS THE YELLOW FIRE OF THE SEA, BUT YELLOW FIRE IS WEAK AND NOT PURE AND IS EXTINGUISHED QUICKLY AND BURNS WEAKLY UNDERWATER.

"THERE IS LAVA THAT BURNS AND ILLUMINATES, BUT IT COOLS FAST AND CANNOT EASILY BE CONTROLLED."

"IN THE OCEANS, THERE IS ONLY ONE PURE SOURCE OF FIRE THAT BURNS BRILLIANTLY UNDERWATER AS WELL AS ILLUMINATES.

"IT IS CALLED THE DEEP BLUE SEA FLAME.

"THE DEEP BLUE SEA FLAME IS HIGHLY COVETED AND ITS SECRETS HEAVILY GUARDED.

"IT BURNS LIKE NO OTHER. IT VANQUISHES YOUR ENEMIES AND SENDS THEM SCATTERING IN PAIN ACROSS THE BATTLE-FIELD, LEAVING BEHIND ONLY THE SMELL OF BURNING FLESH."

"I KNOW THE HORROR FIRSTHAND OF HEARING THE SCREAMS OF WIVES WHO'VE BEEN GREETED BY THEIR HUSBANDS RETURNED FROM WAR, DISFIGURED, SCARRED, AND TURNED INTO WALKING MONSTERS FROM THE BURNS OF THE FLAME."

"THE FLAME WINS WARS AND ENSURES VICTORY."

"IT HAS CHANGED THE COURSE OF MANY BATTLES."

"THE FLAME HAS CHANGED THE COURSE OF HISTORY."

THEY SAY "HE WHO CONTROLS THE DEEP BLUE SEA FLAME CONTROLS THE SEAS."

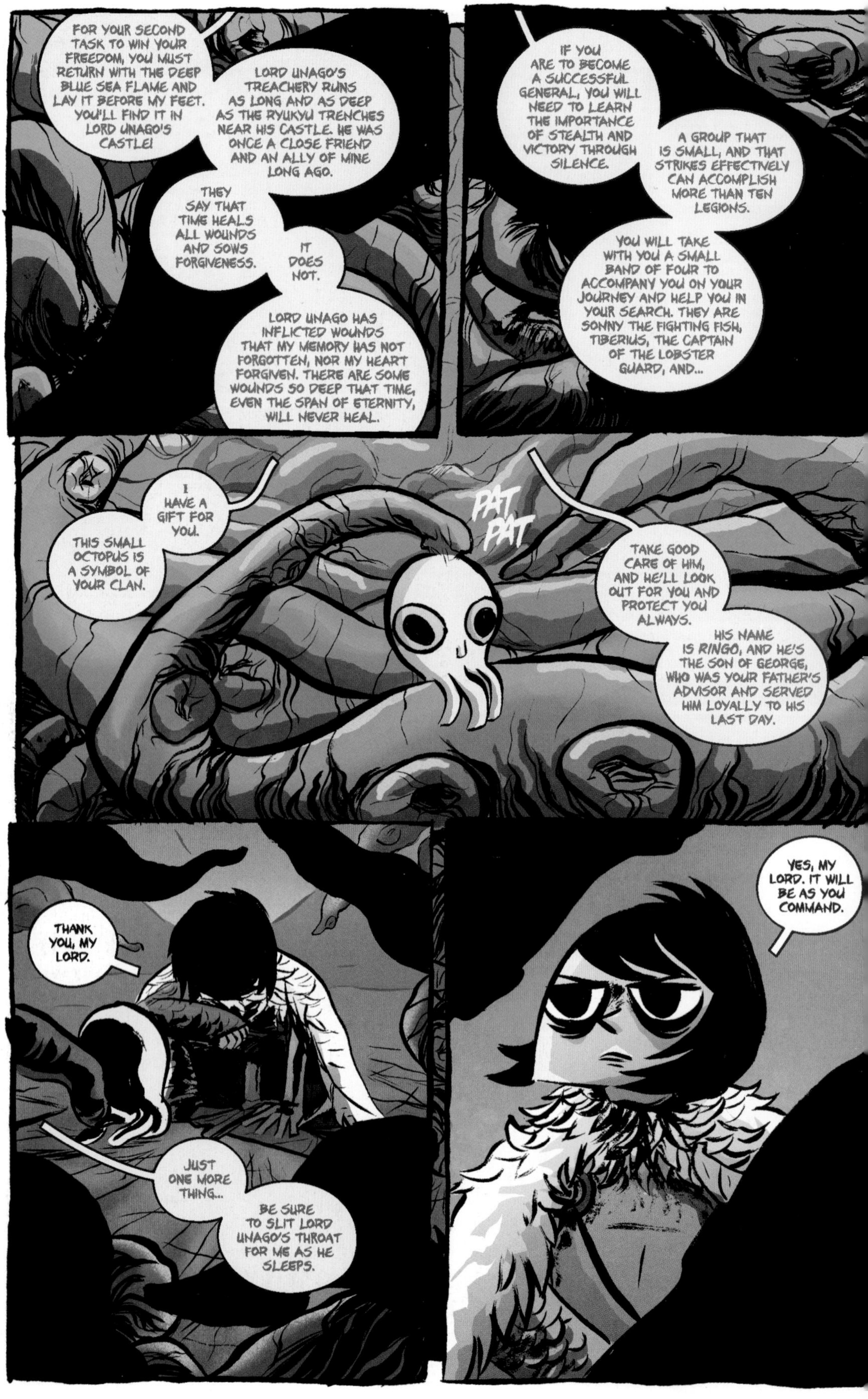
FOR YOUR SECOND TASK TO WIN YOUR FREEDOM, YOU MUST RETURN WITH THE DEEP BLUE SEA FLAME AND LAY IT BEFORE MY FEET. YOU'LL FIND IT IN LORD UNAGO'S CASTLE!
LORD UNAGO'S TREACHERY RUNS AS LONG AND AS DEEP AS THE RYUKYU TRENCHES NEAR HIS CASTLE. HE WAS ONCE A CLOSE FRIEND AND AN ALLY OF MINE LONG AGO.
THEY SAY THAT TIME HEALS ALL WOUNDS AND SOWS FORGIVENESS.
IT DOES NOT.
LORD UNAGO HAS INFLICTED WOUNDS THAT MY MEMORY HAS NOT FORGOTTEN, NOR MY HEART FORGIVEN. THERE ARE SOME WOUNDS SO DEEP THAT TIME, EVEN THE SPAN OF ETERNITY, WILL NEVER HEAL.
IF YOU ARE TO BECOME A SUCCESSFUL GENERAL, YOU WILL NEED TO LEARN THE IMPORTANCE OF STEALTH AND VICTORY THROUGH SILENCE.
A GROUP THAT IS SMALL, AND THAT STRIKES EFFECTIVELY CAN ACCOMPLISH MORE THAN TEN LEGIONS.
YOU WILL TAKE WITH YOU A SMALL BAND OF FOUR TO ACCOMPANY YOU ON YOUR JOURNEY AND HELP YOU IN YOUR SEARCH. THEY ARE SONNY THE FIGHTING FISH, TIBERIUS, THE CAPTAIN OF THE LOBSTER GUARD, AND...
I HAVE A GIFT FOR YOU.
THIS SMALL OCTOPUS IS A SYMBOL OF YOUR CLAN.
PAT PAT
TAKE GOOD CARE OF HIM, AND HE'LL LOOK OUT FOR YOU AND PROTECT YOU ALWAYS.
HIS NAME IS *RINGO*, AND HE'S THE SON OF GEORGE, WHO WAS YOUR FATHER'S ADVISOR AND SERVED HIM LOYALLY TO HIS LAST DAY.
THANK YOU, MY LORD.
JUST ONE MORE THING...
BE SURE TO SLIT LORD UNAGO'S THROAT FOR ME AS HE SLEEPS.
YES, MY LORD. IT WILL BE AS YOU COMMAND.

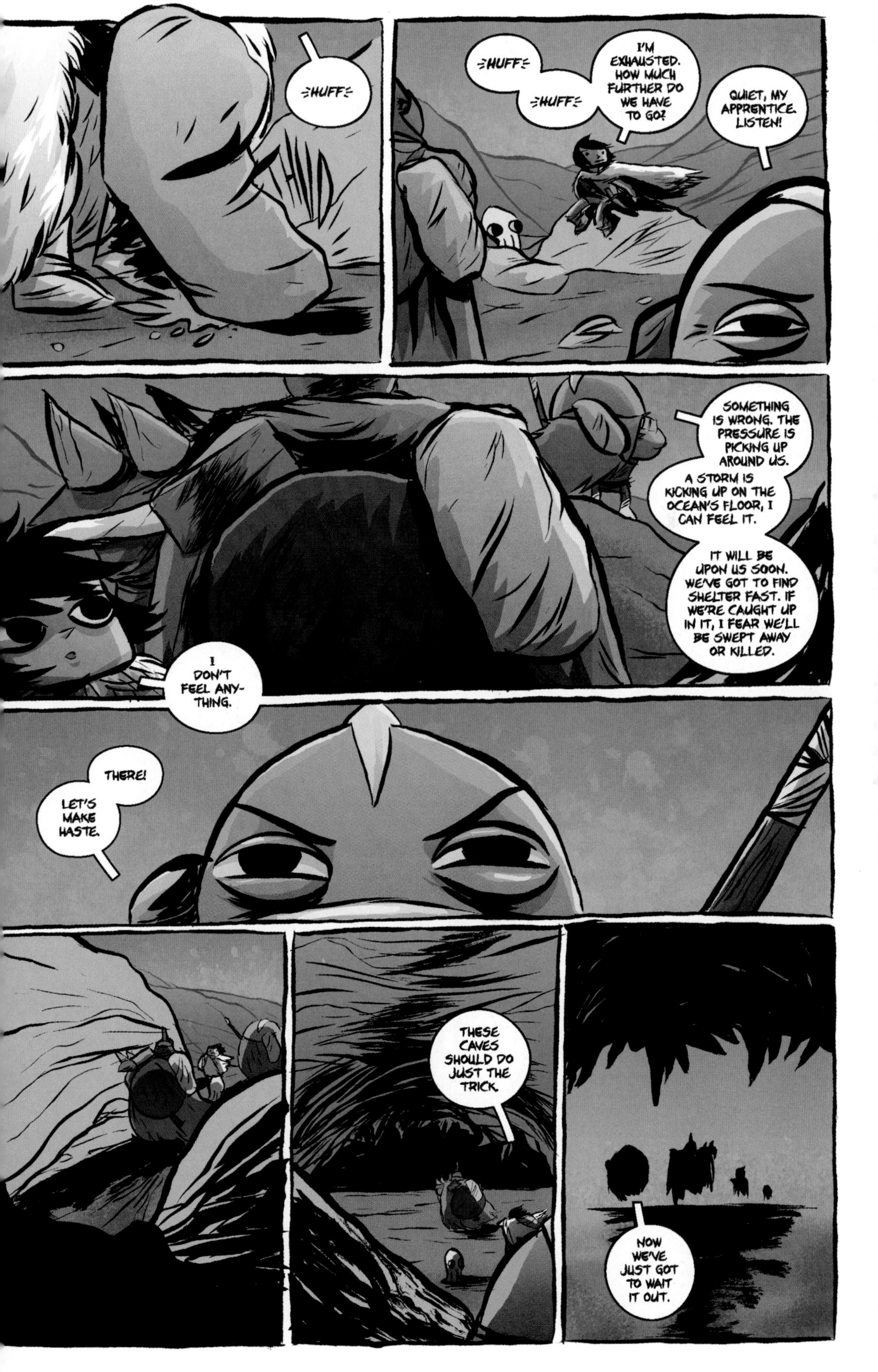

HUFF
HUFF
HUFF
I'M EXHAUSTED. HOW MUCH FURTHER DO WE HAVE TO GO?
QUIET, MY APPRENTICE. LISTEN!
SOMETHING IS WRONG. THE PRESSURE IS PICKING UP AROUND US.
A STORM IS KICKING UP ON THE OCEAN'S FLOOR, I CAN FEEL IT.
IT WILL BE UPON US SOON. WE'VE GOT TO FIND SHELTER FAST. IF WE'RE CAUGHT UP IN IT, I FEAR WE'LL BE SWEPT AWAY OR KILLED.
I DON'T FEEL ANY-THING.
THERE!
LET'S MAKE HASTE.
THESE CAVES SHOULD DO JUST THE TRICK.
NOW WE'VE JUST GOT TO WAIT IT OUT.

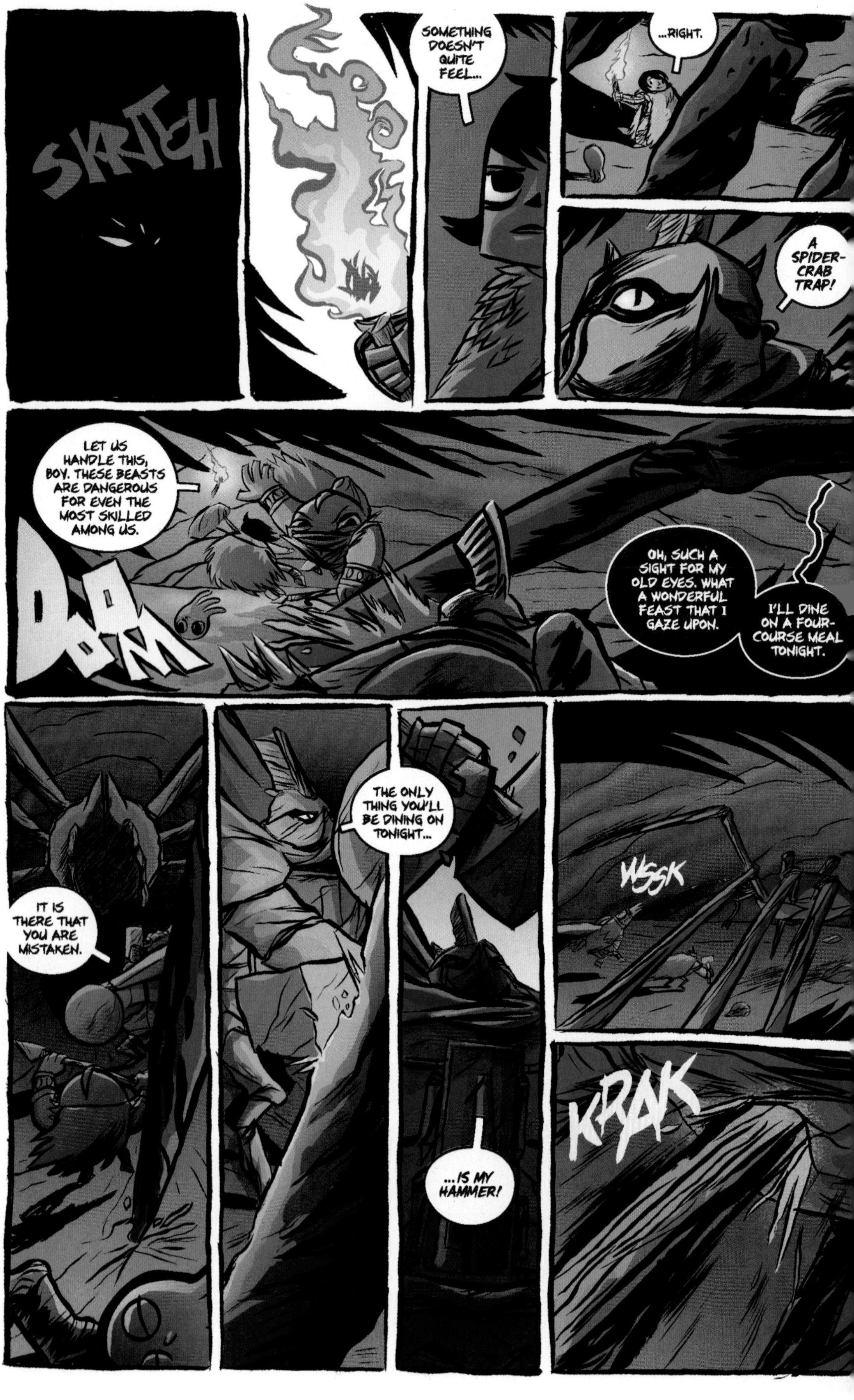
SKRITCH
SOMETHING DOESN'T QUITE FEEL...
...RIGHT.
A SPIDER-CRAB TRAP!
LET US HANDLE THIS, BOY. THESE BEASTS ARE DANGEROUS FOR EVEN THE MOST SKILLED AMONG US.
DOOM
OH, SUCH A SIGHT FOR MY OLD EYES. WHAT A WONDERFUL FEAST THAT I GAZE UPON.
I'LL DINE ON A FOUR-COURSE MEAL TONIGHT.
IT IS THERE THAT YOU ARE MISTAKEN.
THE ONLY THING YOU'LL BE DINING ON TONIGHT...
...IS MY HAMMER!
WSSK
KRAK

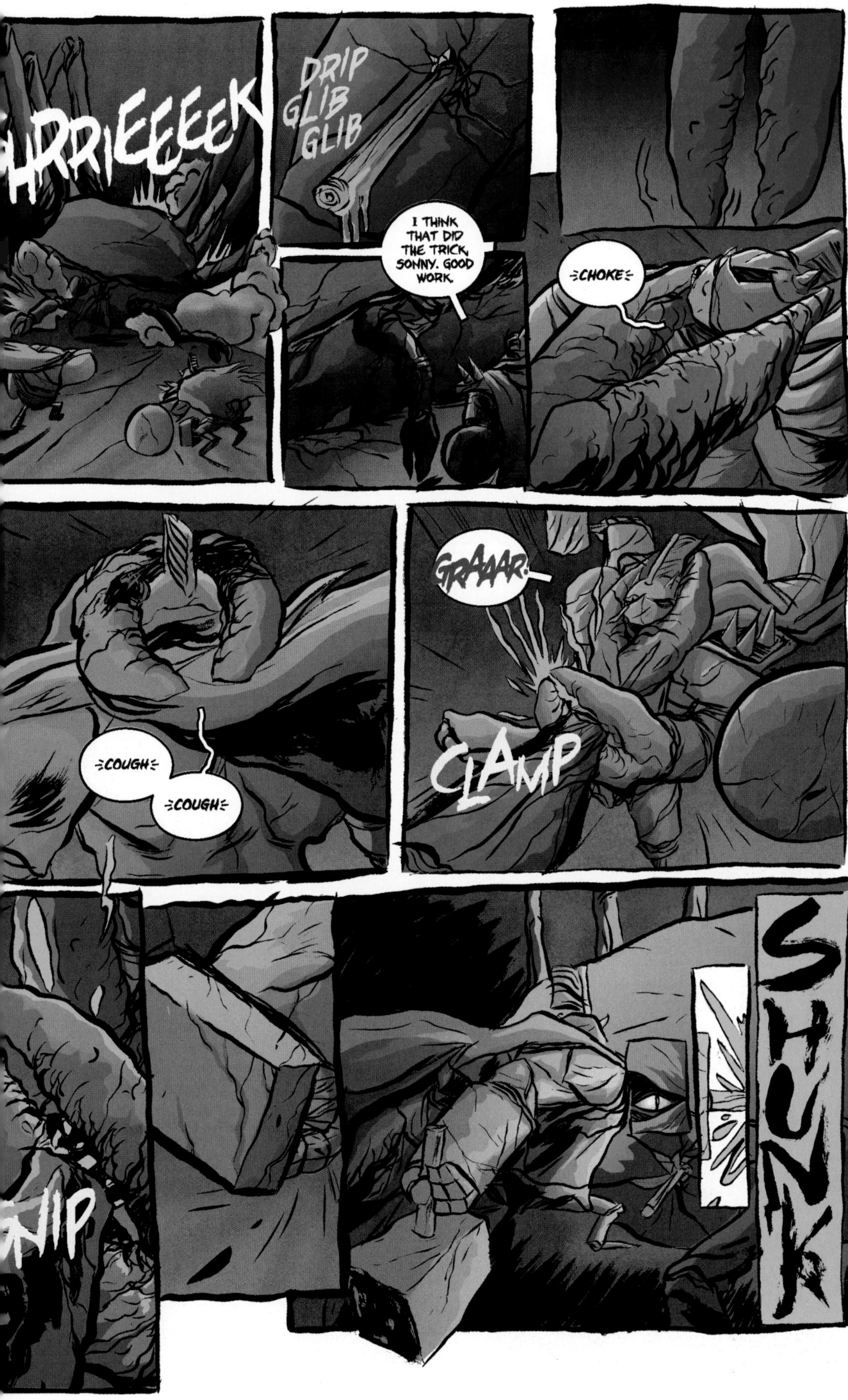
SHRIEEEEEK
DRIP
GLIB
GLIB
I THINK THAT DID THE TRICK, SONNY. GOOD WORK.
CHOKE
COUGH
COUGH
GRAAAR
CLAMP
SNIP
SHUNK

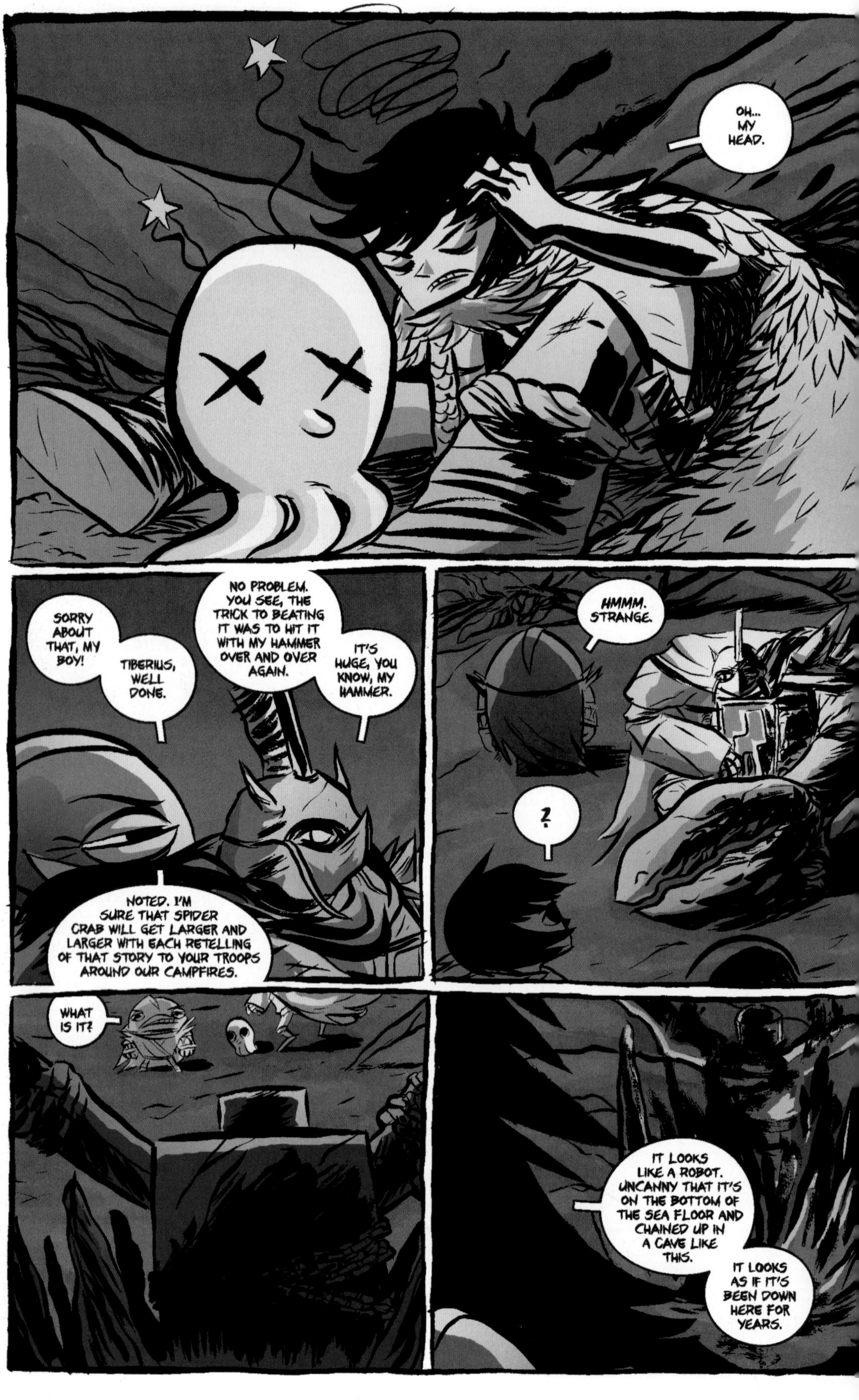
OH... MY HEAD.
SORRY ABOUT THAT, MY BOY!
TIBERIUS, WELL DONE.
NO PROBLEM. YOU SEE, THE TRICK TO BEATING IT WAS TO HIT IT WITH MY HAMMER OVER AND OVER AGAIN.
IT'S HUGE, YOU KNOW, MY HAMMER.
NOTED. I'M SURE THAT SPIDER CRAB WILL GET LARGER AND LARGER WITH EACH RETELLING OF THAT STORY TO YOUR TROOPS AROUND OUR CAMPFIRES.
HMMM. STRANGE.
?
WHAT IS IT?
IT LOOKS LIKE A ROBOT. UNCANNY THAT IT'S ON THE BOTTOM OF THE SEA FLOOR AND CHAINED UP IN A CAVE LIKE THIS.
IT LOOKS AS IF IT'S BEEN DOWN HERE FOR YEARS.

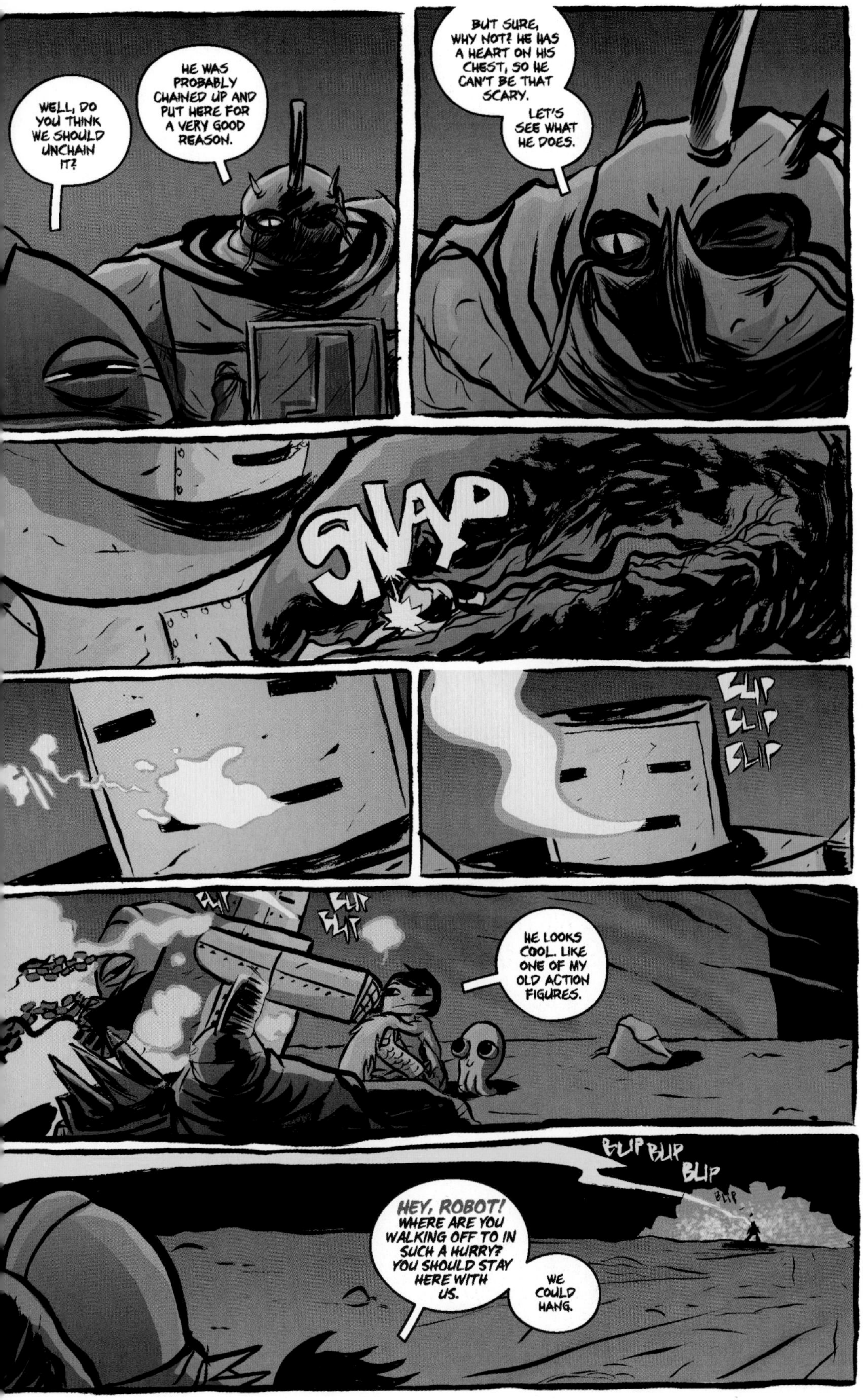
WELL, DO YOU THINK WE SHOULD UNCHAIN IT?
HE WAS PROBABLY CHAINED UP AND PUT HERE FOR A VERY GOOD REASON.
BUT SURE, WHY NOT? HE HAS A HEART ON HIS CHEST, SO HE CAN'T BE THAT SCARY.
LET'S SEE WHAT HE DOES.
SNAP
BLIP BLIP BLIP
BLIP BLIP
HE LOOKS COOL. LIKE ONE OF MY OLD ACTION FIGURES.
BLIP BLIP BLIP
BLIP
HEY, ROBOT! WHERE ARE YOU WALKING OFF TO IN SUCH A HURRY? YOU SHOULD STAY HERE WITH US.
WE COULD HANG.

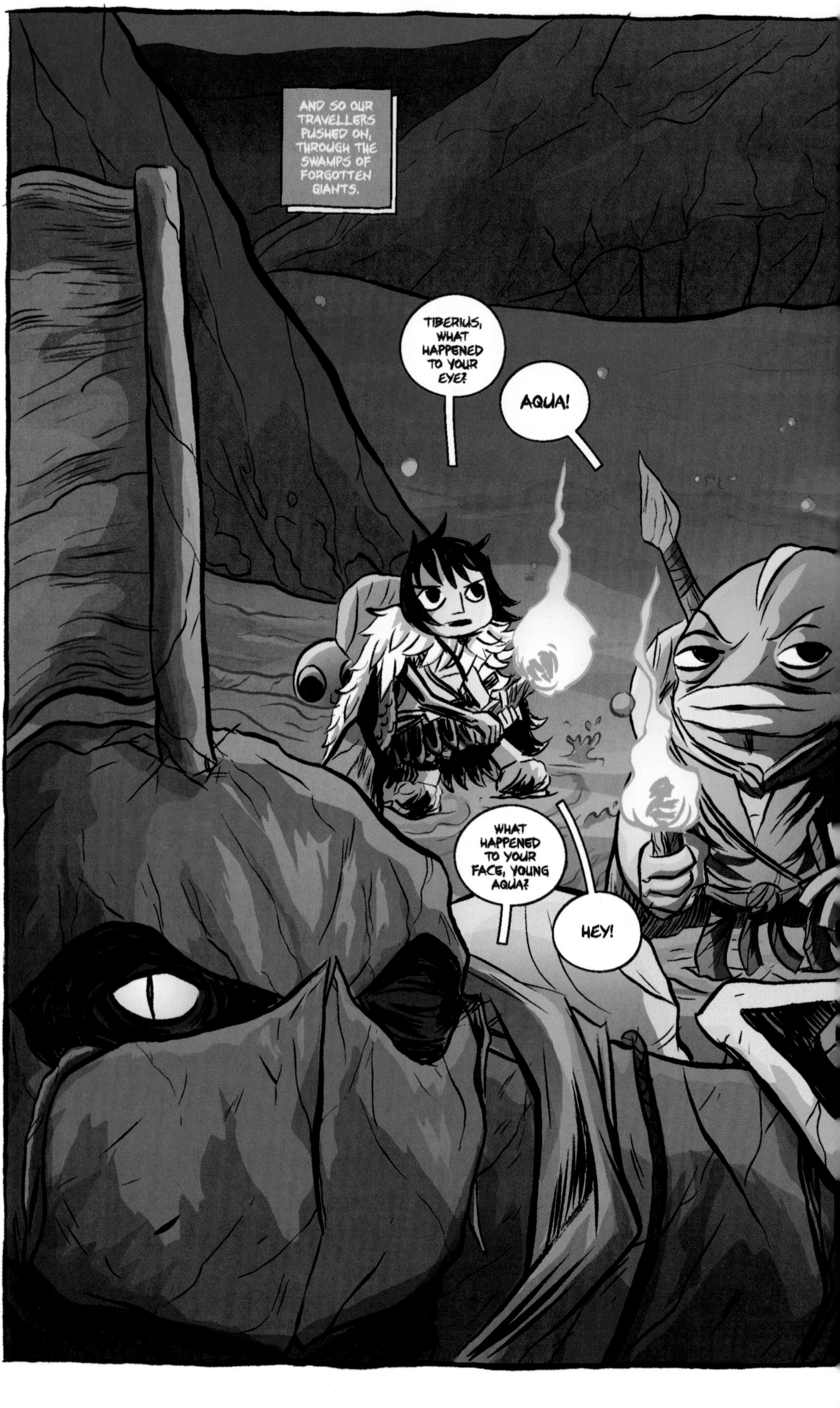
AND SO OUR TRAVELLERS PUSHED ON, THROUGH THE SWAMPS OF FORGOTTEN GIANTS.
TIBERIUS, WHAT HAPPENED TO YOUR EYE?
AQUA!
WHAT HAPPENED TO YOUR FACE, YOUNG AQUA?
HEY!

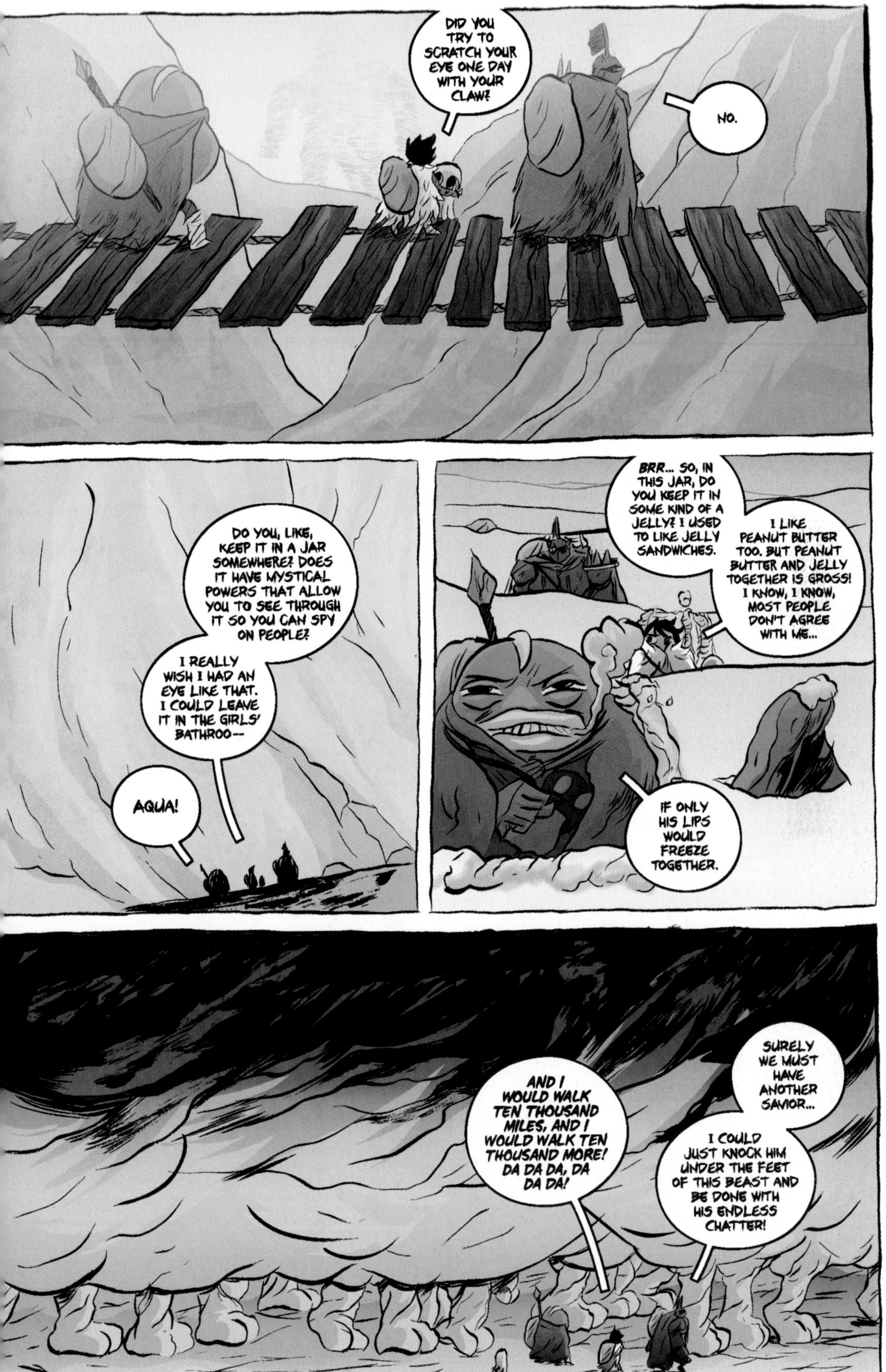
DID YOU TRY TO SCRATCH YOUR EYE ONE DAY WITH YOUR CLAW?
NO.
DO YOU, LIKE, KEEP IT IN A JAR SOMEWHERE? DOES IT HAVE MYSTICAL POWERS THAT ALLOW YOU TO SEE THROUGH IT SO YOU CAN SPY ON PEOPLE?
I REALLY WISH I HAD AN EYE LIKE THAT. I COULD LEAVE IT IN THE GIRLS' BATHROO--
AQUA!
BRR... SO, IN THIS JAR, DO YOU KEEP IT IN SOME KIND OF A JELLY? I USED TO LIKE JELLY SANDWICHES.
I LIKE PEANUT BUTTER TOO. BUT PEANUT BUTTER AND JELLY TOGETHER IS GROSS! I KNOW, I KNOW, MOST PEOPLE DON'T AGREE WITH ME...
IF ONLY HIS LIPS WOULD FREEZE TOGETHER.
AND I WOULD WALK TEN THOUSAND MILES, AND I WOULD WALK TEN THOUSAND MORE! DA DA DA, DA DA DA!
SURELY WE MUST HAVE ANOTHER SAVIOR...
I COULD JUST KNOCK HIM UNDER THE FEET OF THIS BEAST AND BE DONE WITH HIS ENDLESS CHATTER!

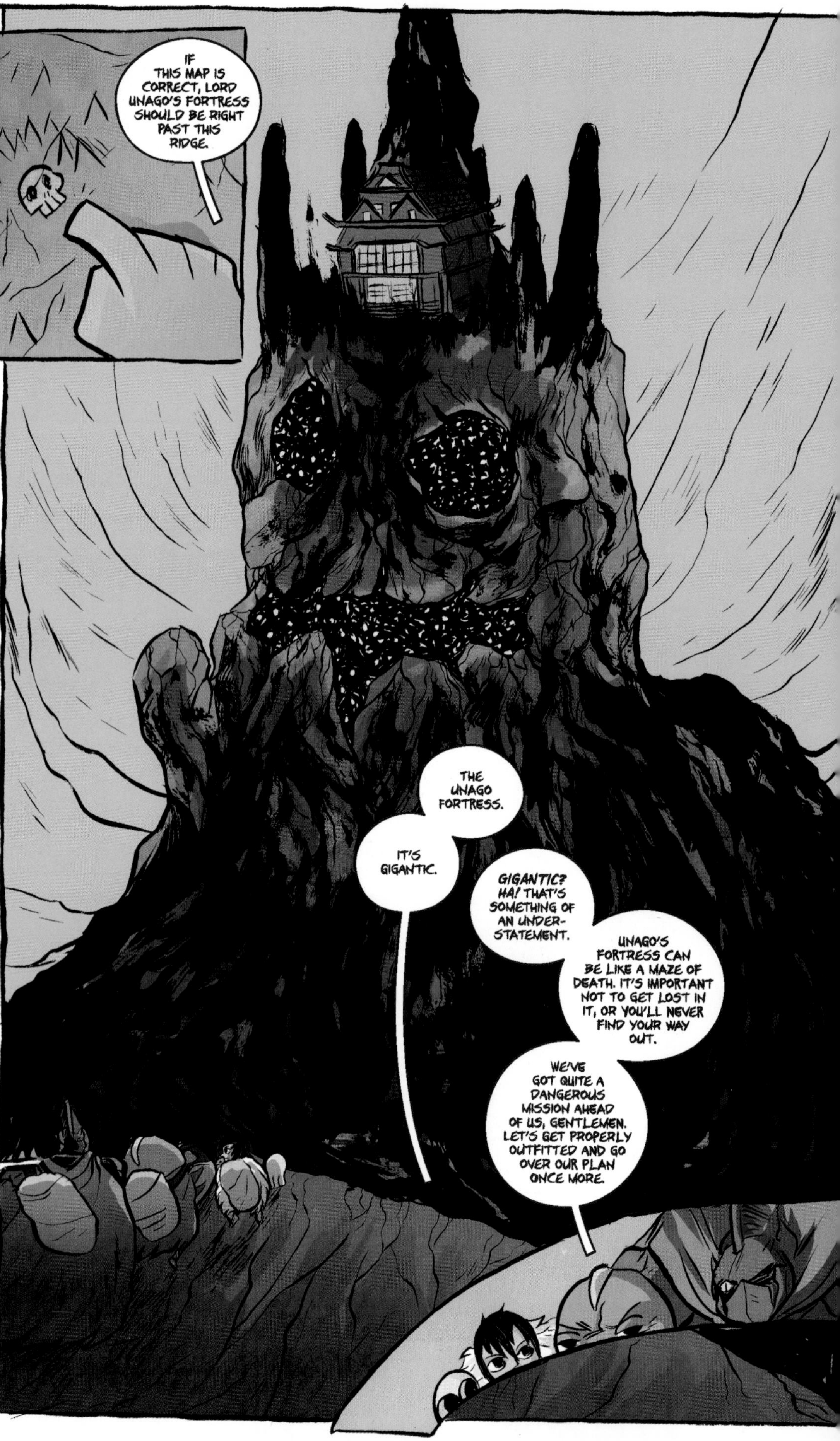
IF THIS MAP IS CORRECT, LORD UNAGO'S FORTRESS SHOULD BE RIGHT PAST THIS RIDGE.
THE UNAGO FORTRESS.
IT'S GIGANTIC.
GIGANTIC? HA! THAT'S SOMETHING OF AN UNDER-STATEMENT.
UNAGO'S FORTRESS CAN BE LIKE A MAZE OF DEATH. IT'S IMPORTANT NOT TO GET LOST IN IT, OR YOU'LL NEVER FIND YOUR WAY OUT.
WE'VE GOT QUITE A DANGEROUS MISSION AHEAD OF US, GENTLEMEN. LET'S GET PROPERLY OUTFITTED AND GO OVER OUR PLAN ONCE MORE.

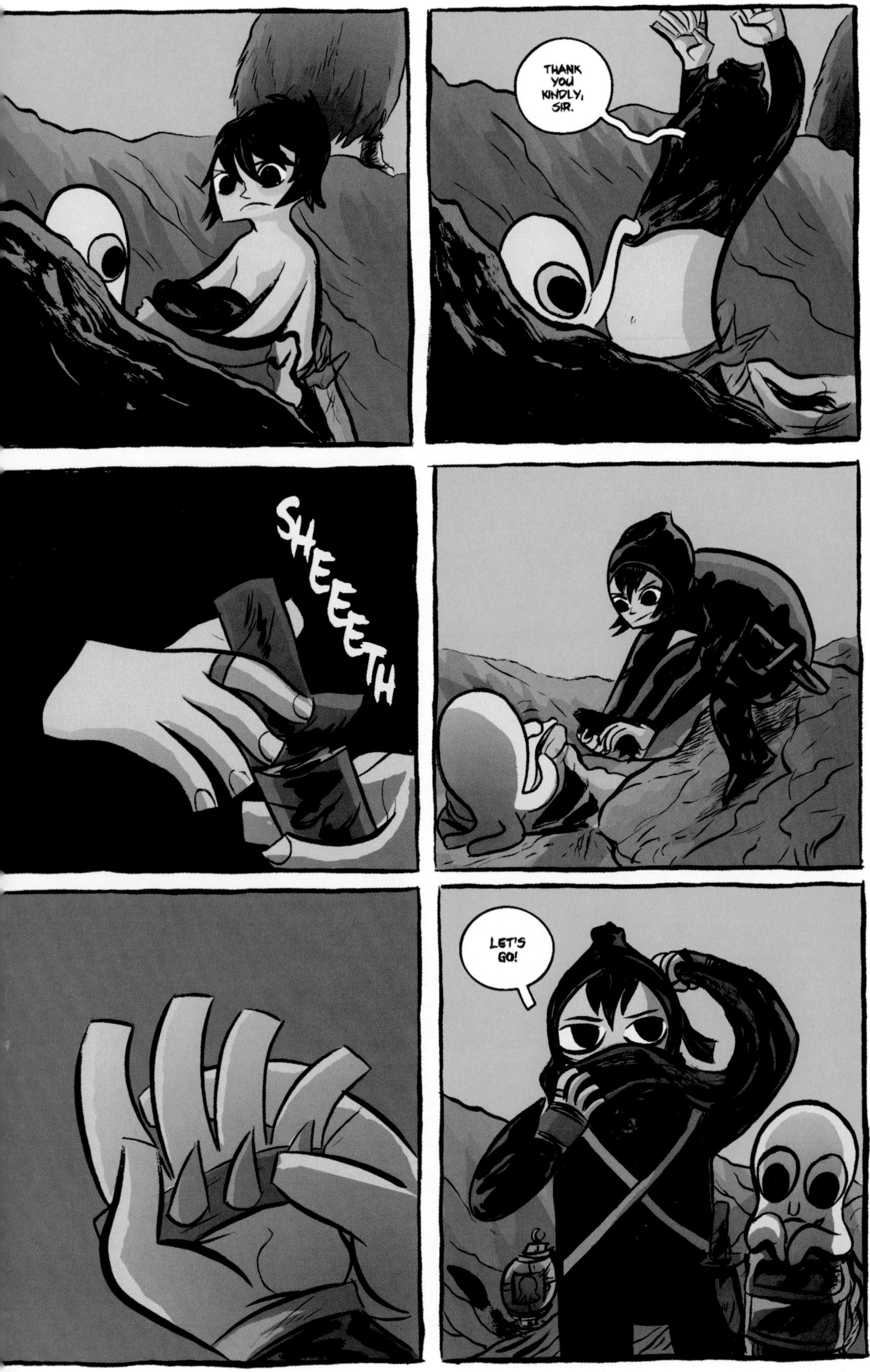
THANK YOU KINDLY, SIR.
SHEEEETH
LET'S GO!

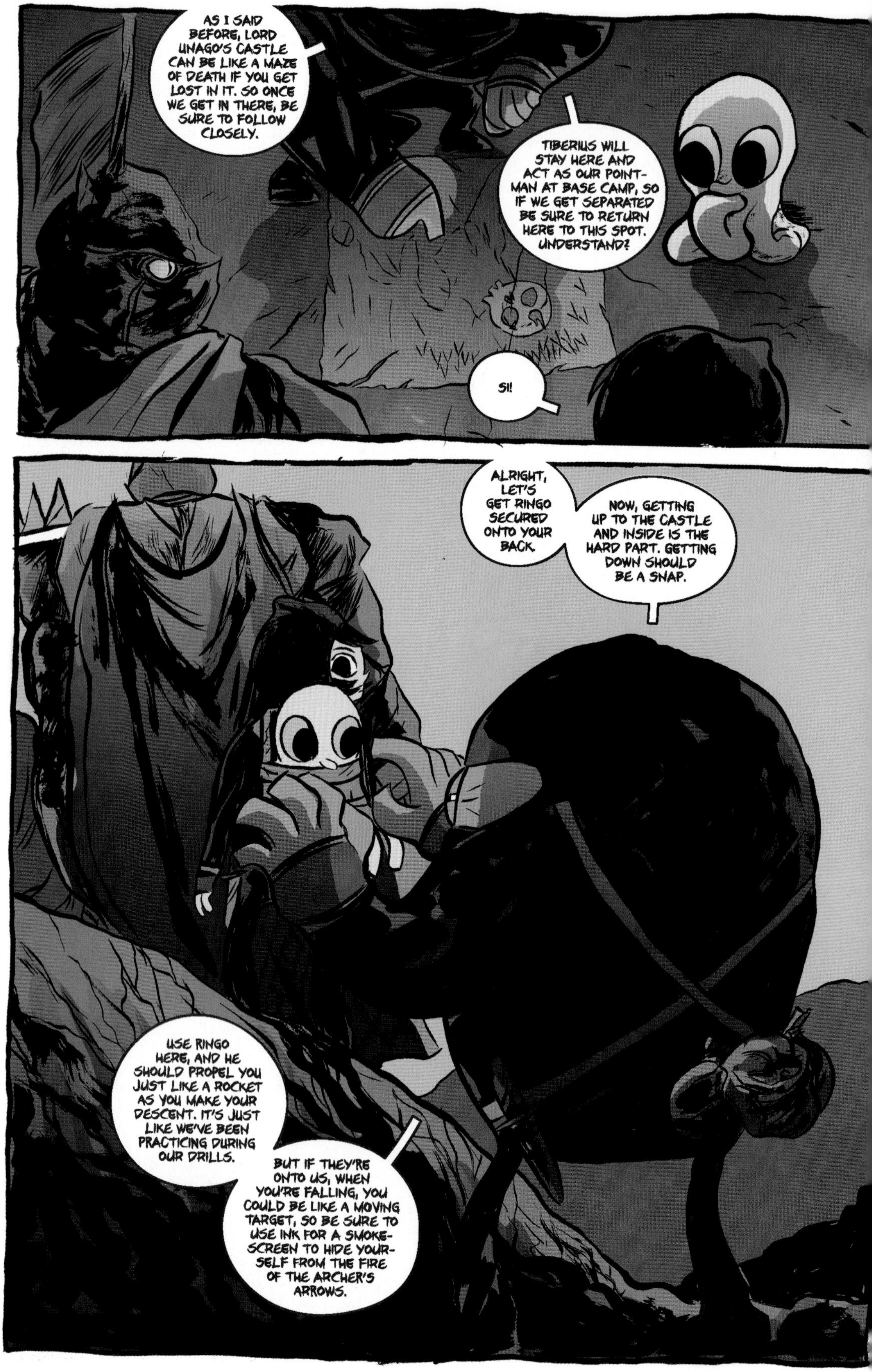
AS I SAID BEFORE, LORD UNAGO'S CASTLE CAN BE LIKE A MAZE OF DEATH IF YOU GET LOST IN IT. SO ONCE WE GET IN THERE, BE SURE TO FOLLOW CLOSELY.
TIBERIUS WILL STAY HERE AND ACT AS OUR POINT-MAN AT BASE CAMP, SO IF WE GET SEPARATED BE SURE TO RETURN HERE TO THIS SPOT. UNDERSTAND?
SI!
ALRIGHT, LET'S GET RINGO SECURED ONTO YOUR BACK.
NOW, GETTING UP TO THE CASTLE AND INSIDE IS THE HARD PART. GETTING DOWN SHOULD BE A SNAP.
USE RINGO HERE, AND HE SHOULD PROPEL YOU JUST LIKE A ROCKET AS YOU MAKE YOUR DESCENT. IT'S JUST LIKE WE'VE BEEN PRACTICING DURING OUR DRILLS.
BUT IF THEY'RE ONTO US, WHEN YOU'RE FALLING, YOU COULD BE LIKE A MOVING TARGET, SO BE SURE TO USE INK FOR A SMOKE-SCREEN TO HIDE YOUR-SELF FROM THE FIRE OF THE ARCHER'S ARROWS.

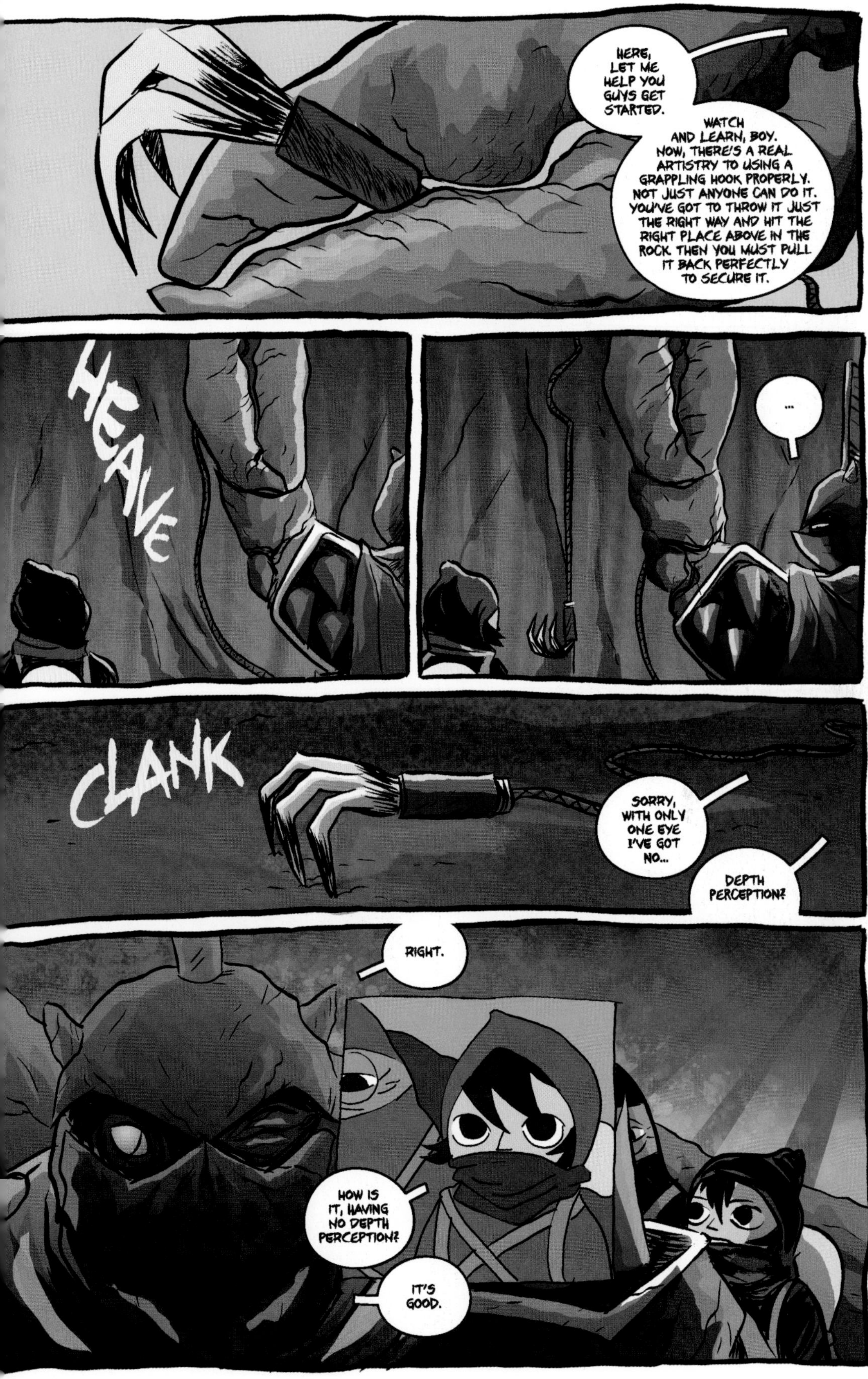
HERE, LET ME HELP YOU GUYS GET STARTED.
WATCH AND LEARN, BOY. NOW, THERE'S A REAL ARTISTRY TO USING A GRAPPLING HOOK PROPERLY. NOT JUST ANYONE CAN DO IT. YOU'VE GOT TO THROW IT JUST THE RIGHT WAY AND HIT THE RIGHT PLACE ABOVE IN THE ROCK THEN YOU MUST PULL IT BACK PERFECTLY TO SECURE IT.
HEAVE
...
CLANK
SORRY, WITH ONLY ONE EYE I'VE GOT NO...
DEPTH PERCEPTION?
RIGHT.
HOW IS IT, HAVING NO DEPTH PERCEPTION?
IT'S GOOD.

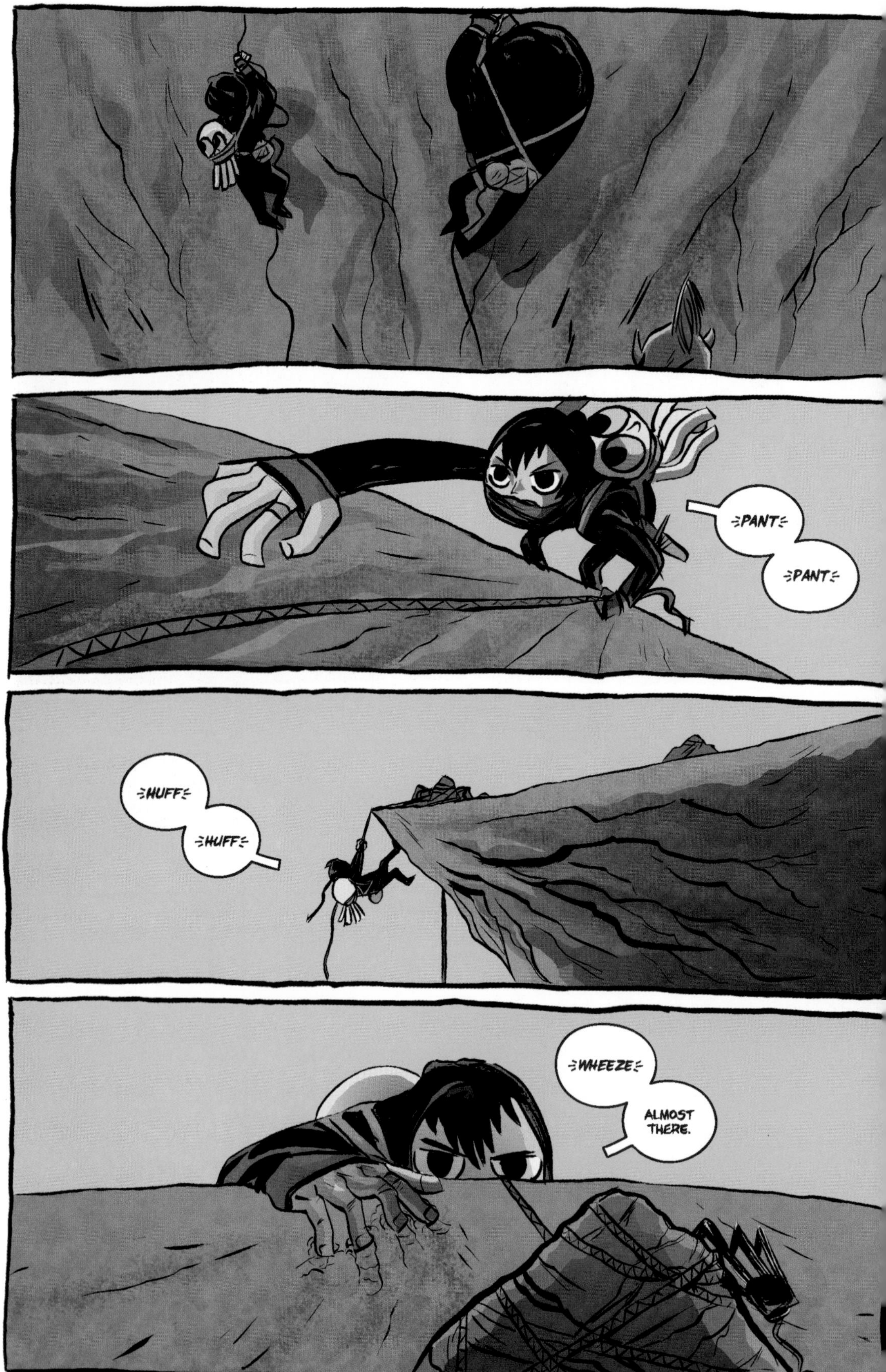

PANT
PANT
HUFF
HUFF
WHEEZE
ALMOST THERE.

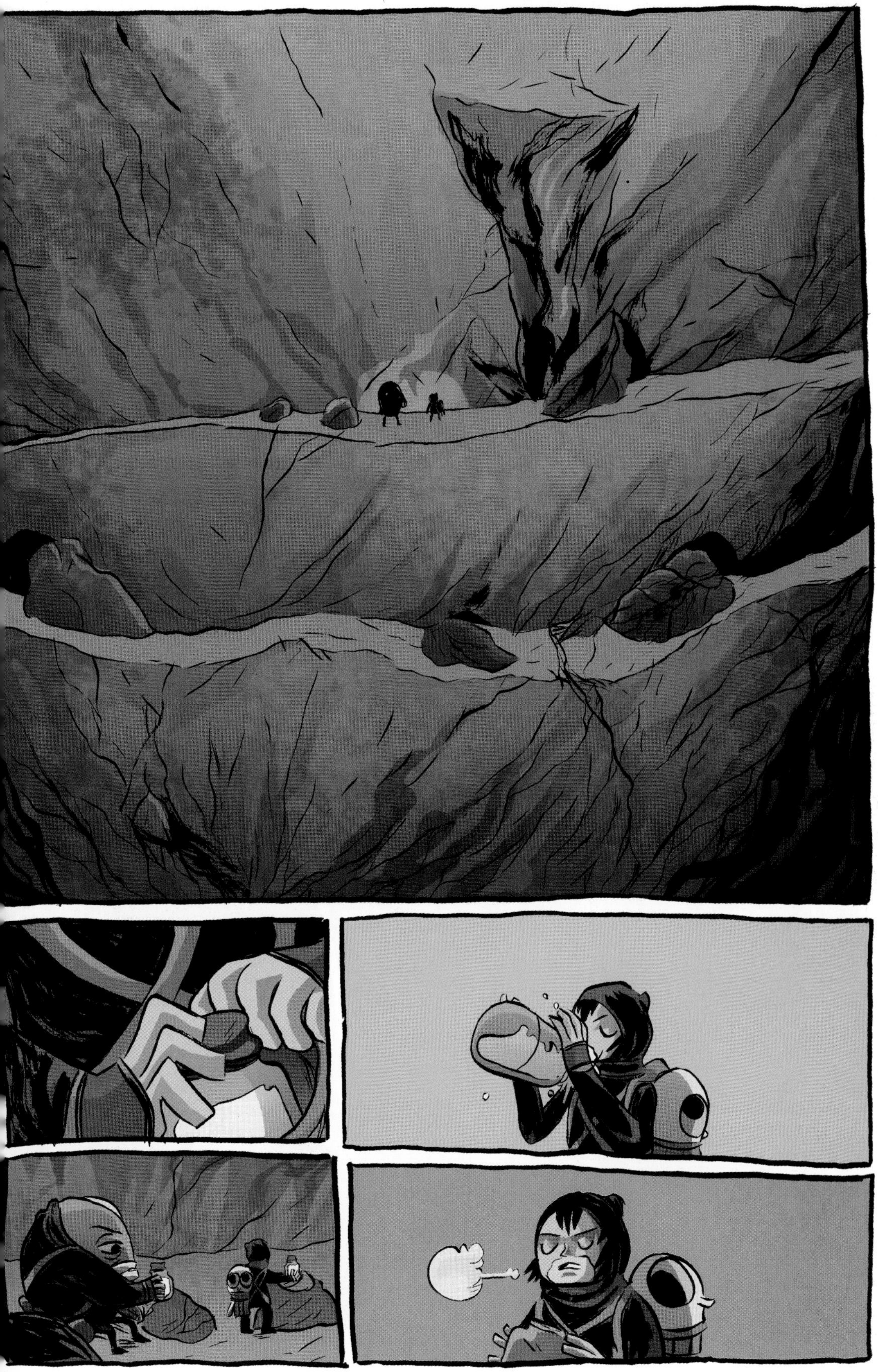

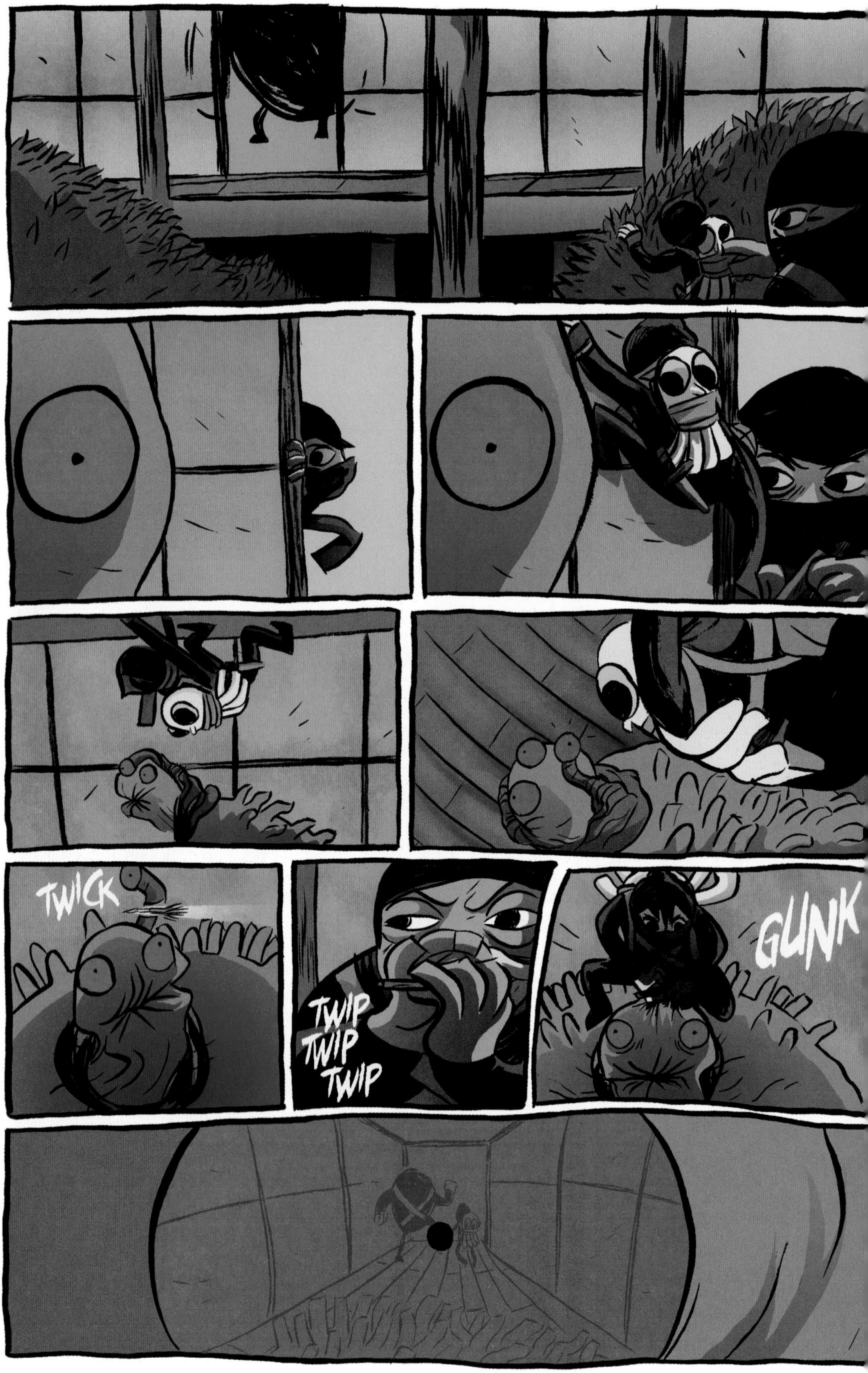
TWICK
TWIP
TWIP
TWIP
GUNK

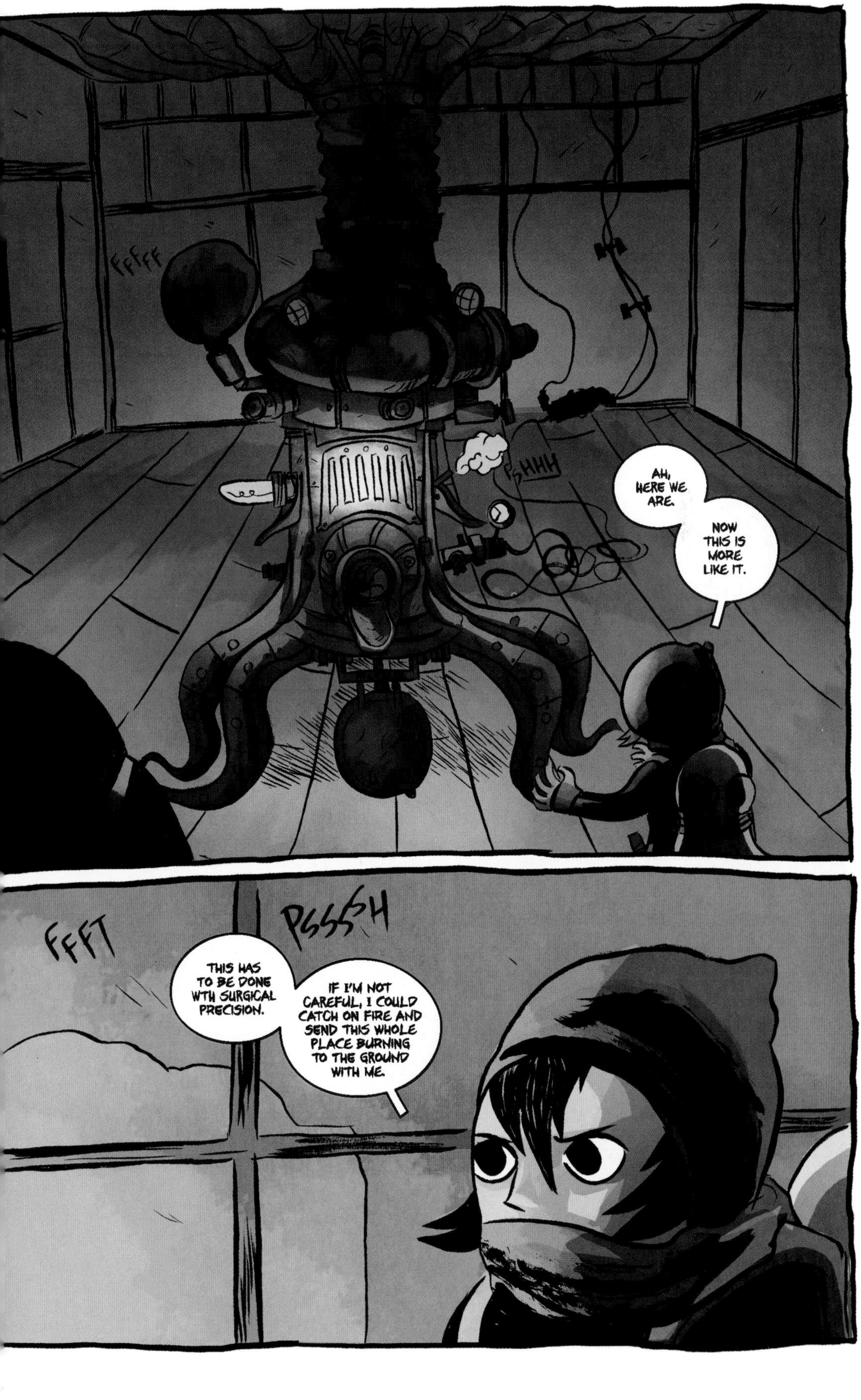
FFFFF
PSHHH
AH, HERE WE ARE.
NOW THIS IS MORE LIKE IT.
FFFT
PSSSH
THIS HAS TO BE DONE WTH SURGICAL PRECISION.
IF I'M NOT CAREFUL, I COULD CATCH ON FIRE AND SEND THIS WHOLE PLACE BURNING TO THE GROUND WITH ME.

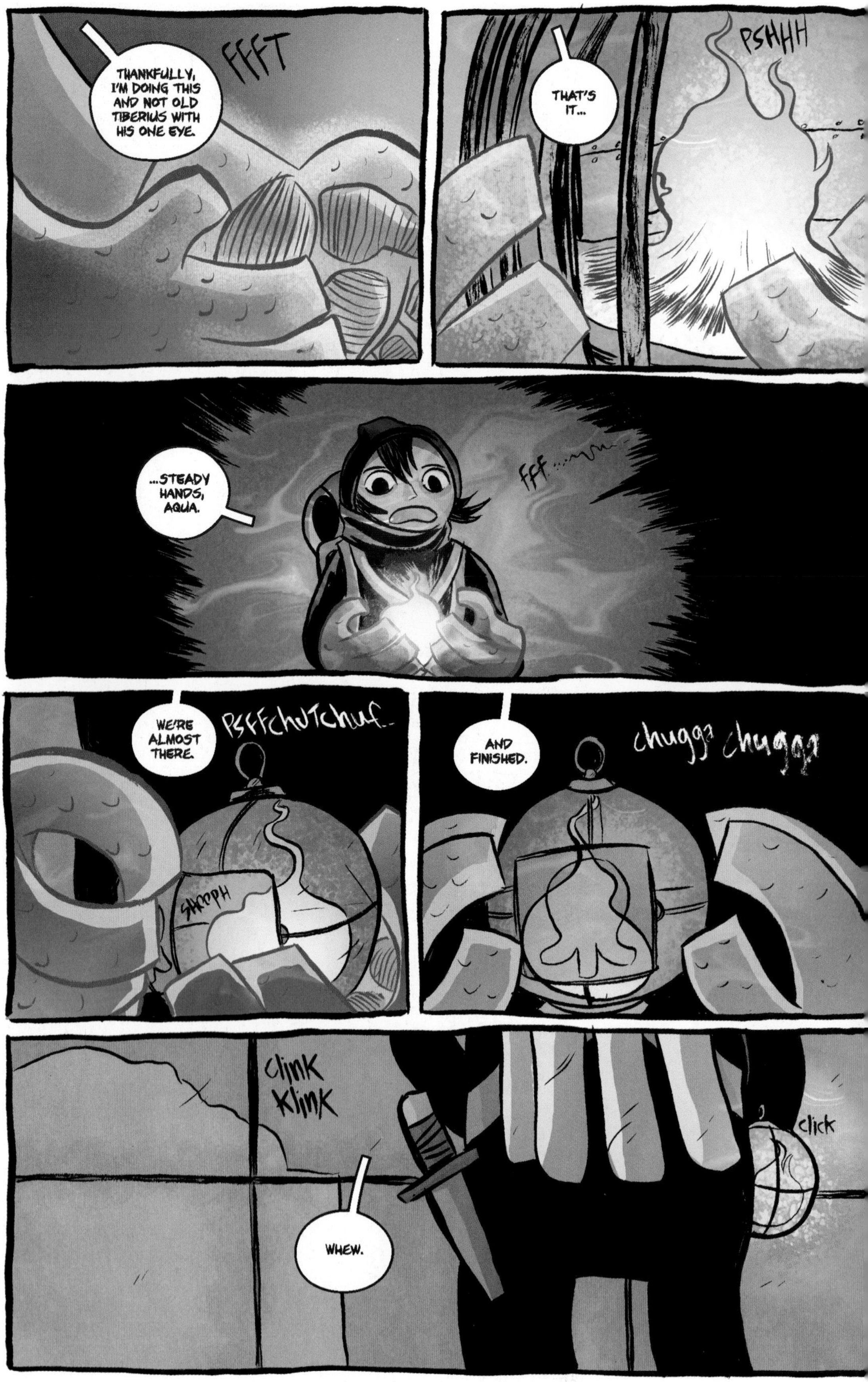
THANKFULLY, I'M DOING THIS AND NOT OLD TIBERIUS WITH HIS ONE EYE.
FFFT
THAT'S IT...
PSHHH
...STEADY HANDS, AQUA.
FFF.......
WE'RE ALMOST THERE.
PSFFCHUTCHUF..
SHOOPH
AND FINISHED.
chugga chugga
clink
Klink
click
WHEW.

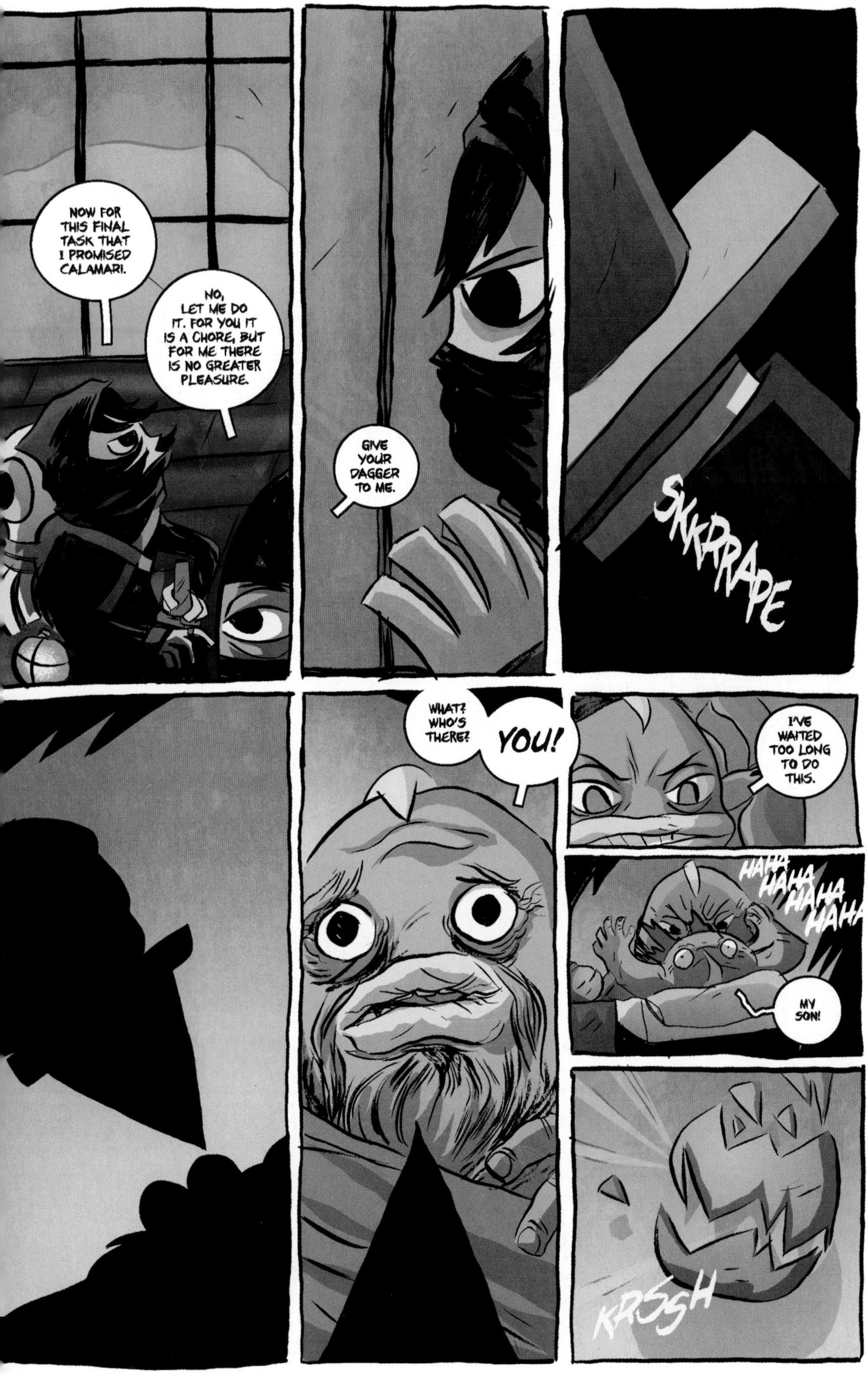
NOW FOR THIS FINAL TASK THAT I PROMISED CALAMARI.
NO, LET ME DO IT. FOR YOU IT IS A CHORE, BUT FOR ME THERE IS NO GREATER PLEASURE.
GIVE YOUR DAGGER TO ME.
SKKRRAPE
WHAT? WHO'S THERE?
YOU!
I'VE WAITED TOO LONG TO DO THIS.
HAHA HAHA HAHA HAHA
MY SON!
KRSSH

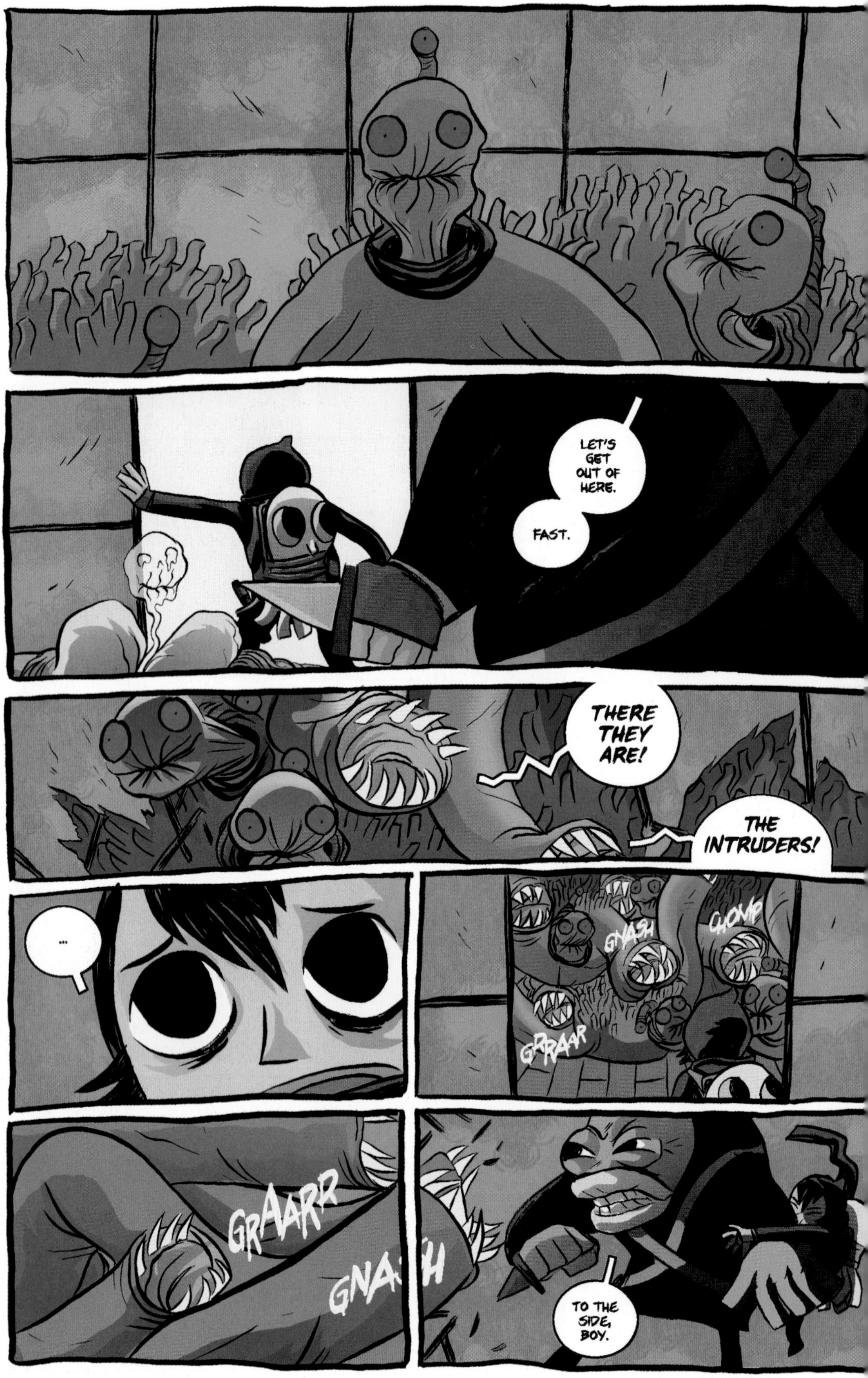
LET'S GET OUT OF HERE.
FAST.
THERE THEY ARE!
THE INTRUDERS!
...
GNASH
CHOMP
GRRAAR
GRAARR
GNASH
TO THE SIDE, BOY.

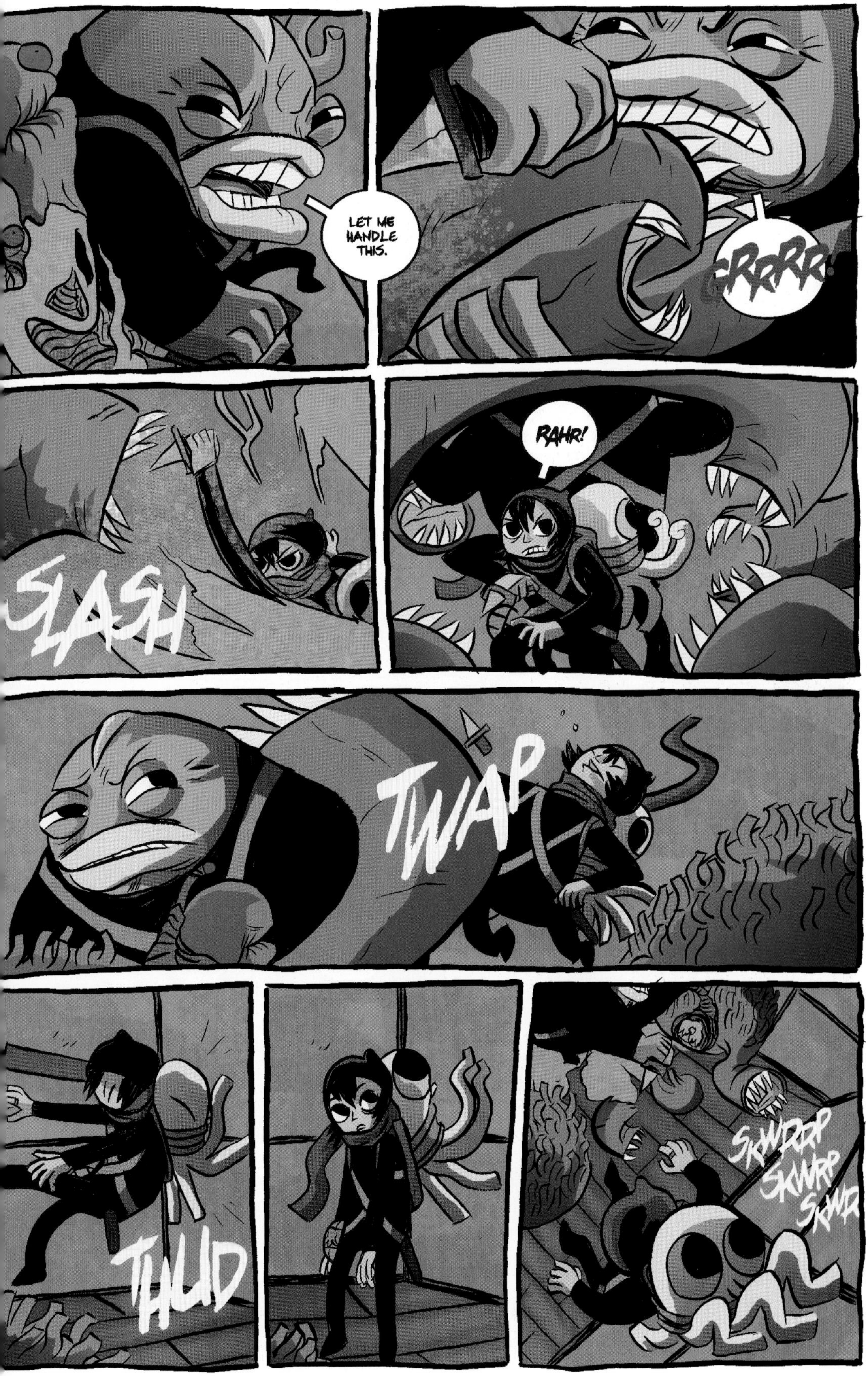
LET ME HANDLE THIS.
GRRRR!
SLASH
RAHR!
TWAP
THUD
SKWRRP
SKWRP
SKWR

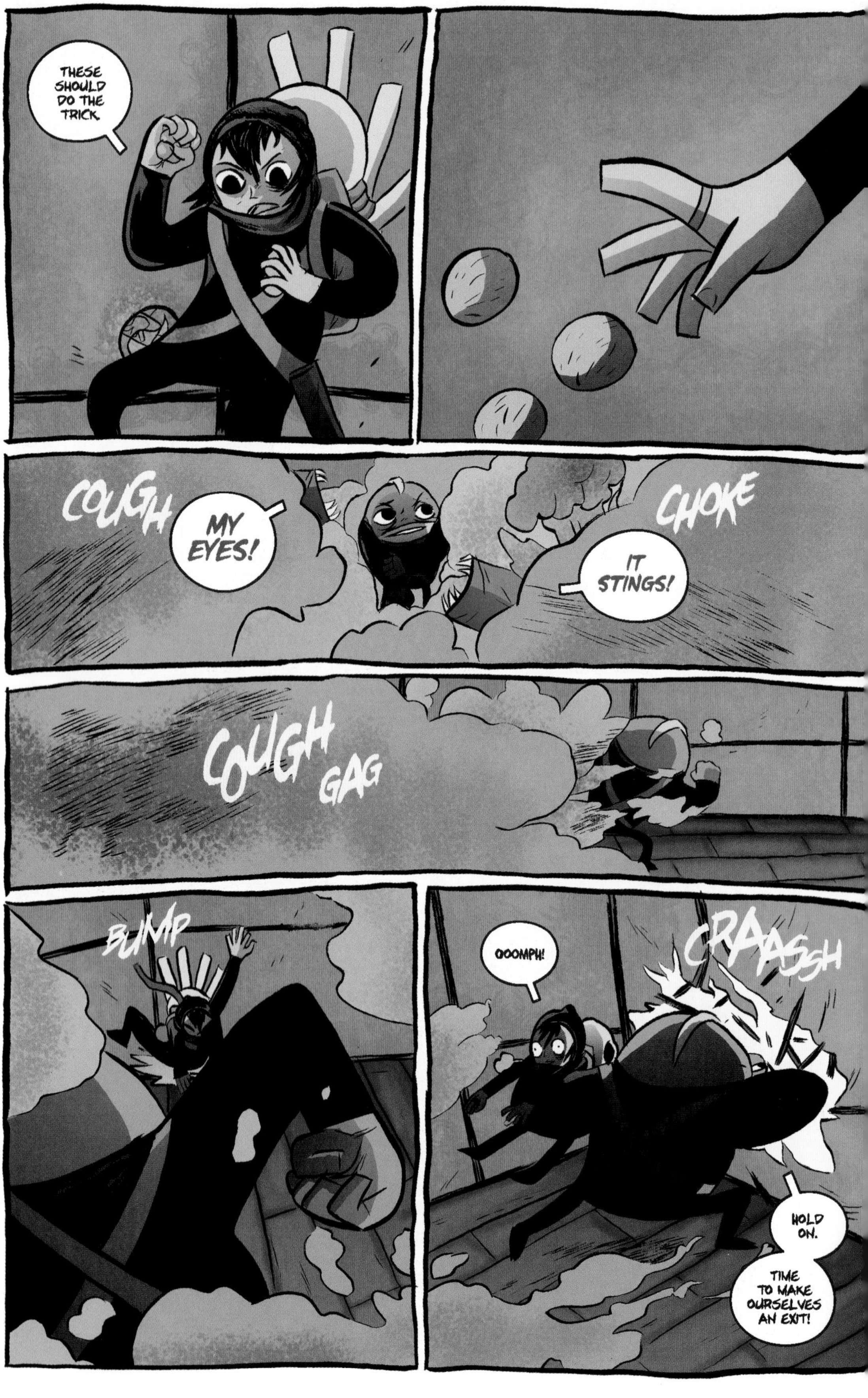
THESE SHOULD DO THE TRICK.
COUGH
MY EYES!
CHOKE
IT STINGS!
COUGH
GAG
BUMP
OOOMPH!
CRAASSH
HOLD ON.
TIME TO MAKE OURSELVES AN EXIT!

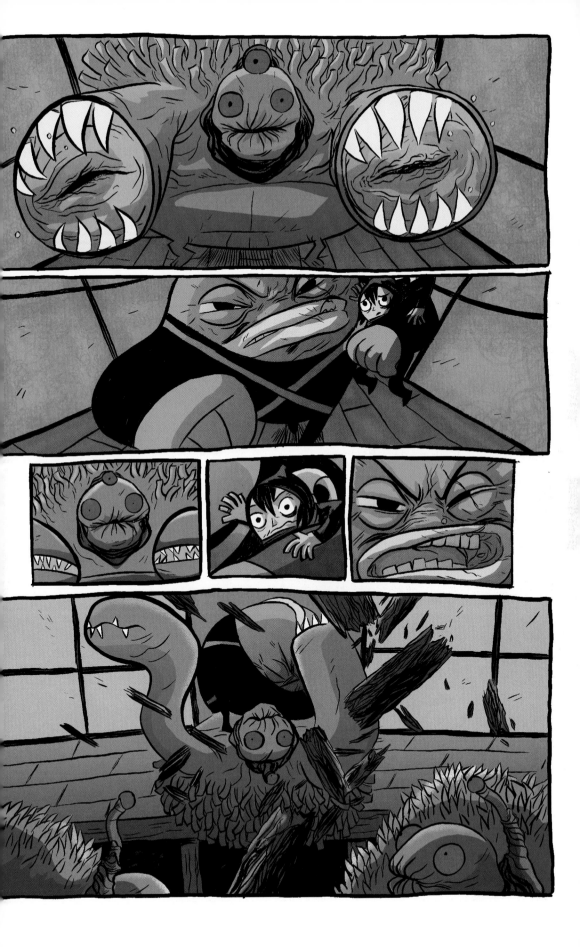

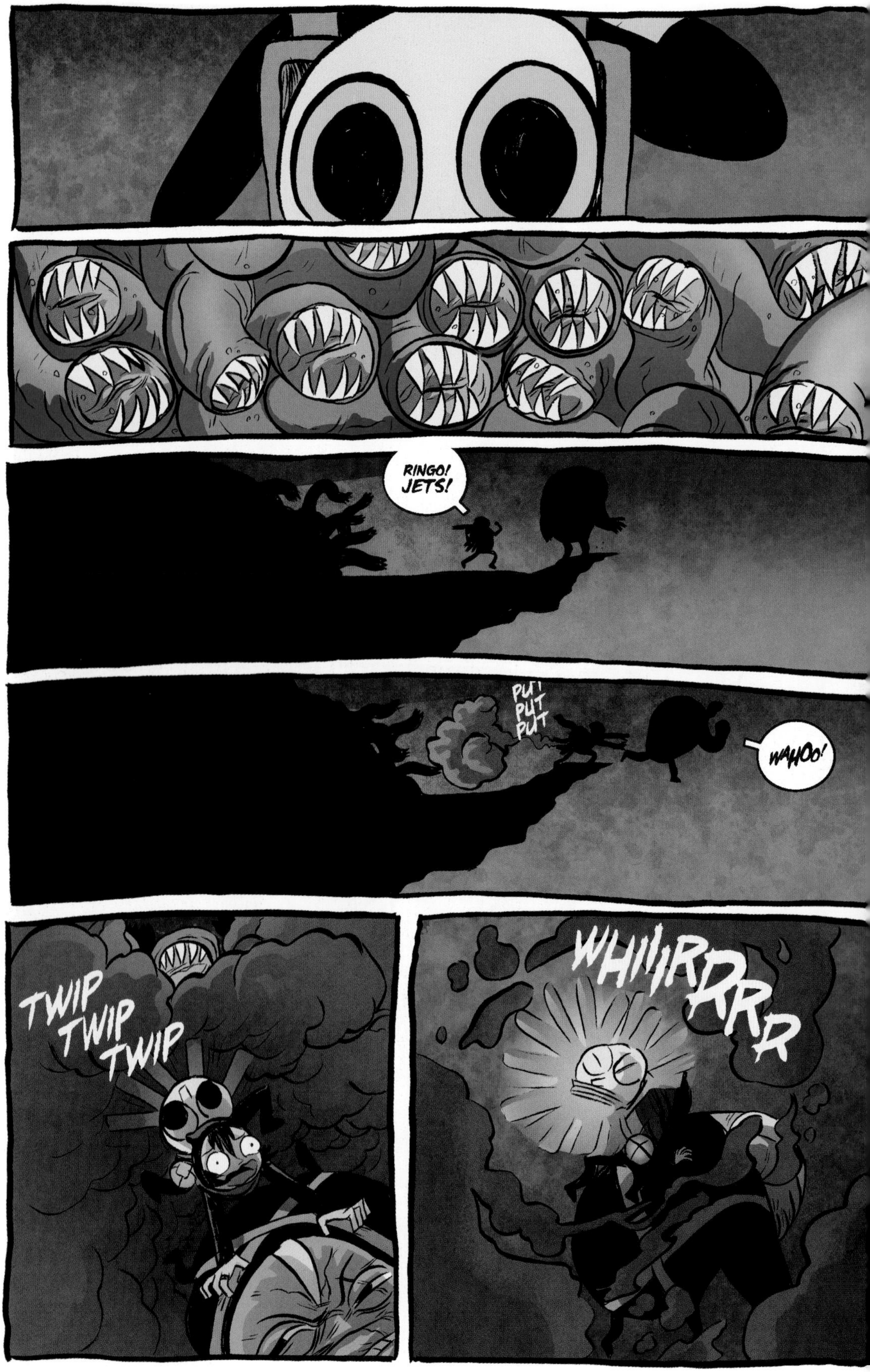
RINGO! JETS!
PUT PUT PUT
WAHOO!
TWIP TWIP TWIP
WHIIIRRRR

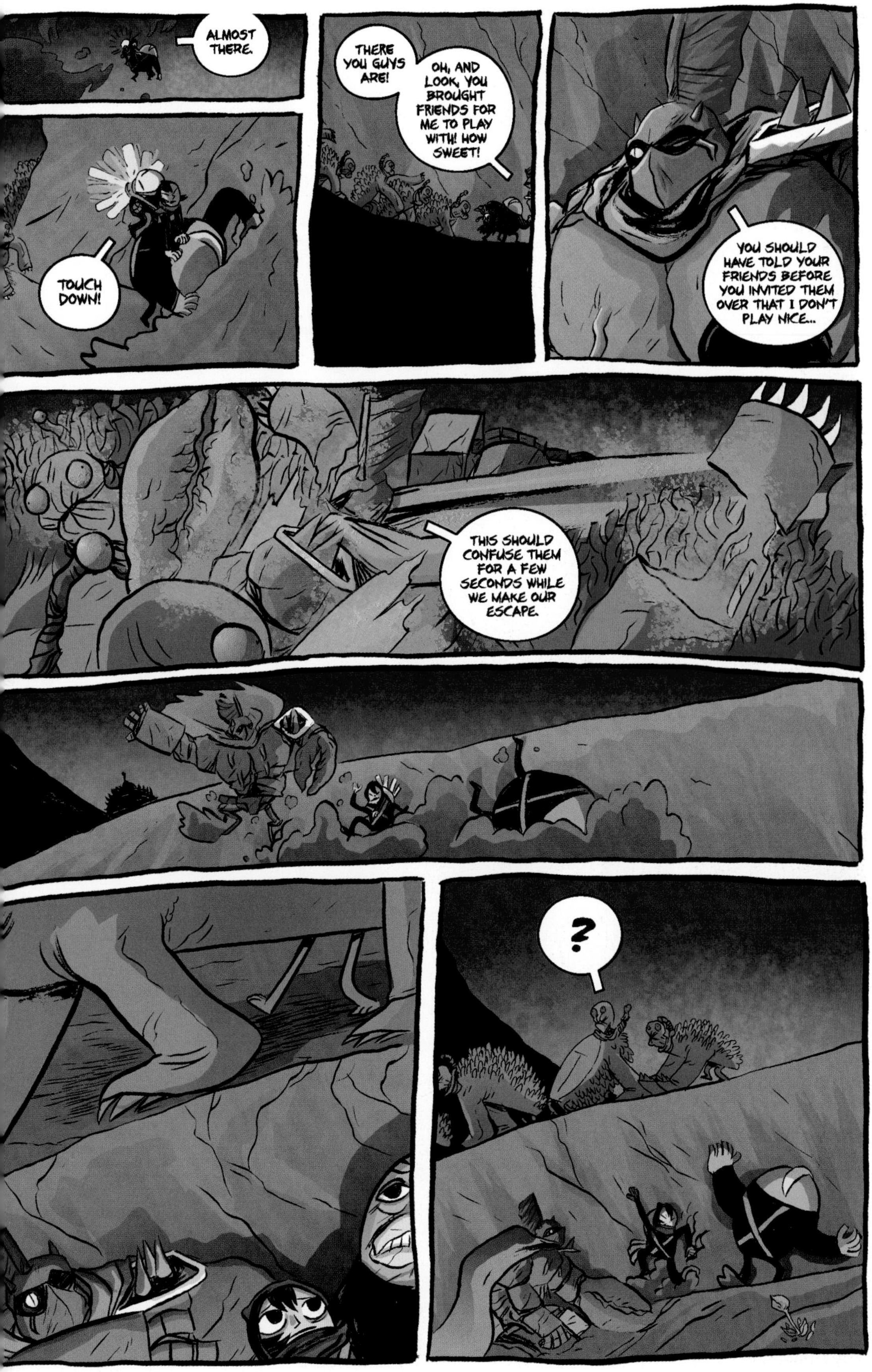
ALMOST THERE.
TOUCH DOWN!
THERE YOU GUYS ARE!
OH, AND LOOK, YOU BROUGHT FRIENDS FOR ME TO PLAY WITH! HOW SWEET!
YOU SHOULD HAVE TOLD YOUR FRIENDS BEFORE YOU INVITED THEM OVER THAT I DON'T PLAY NICE...
THIS SHOULD CONFUSE THEM FOR A FEW SECONDS WHILE WE MAKE OUR ESCAPE.
?

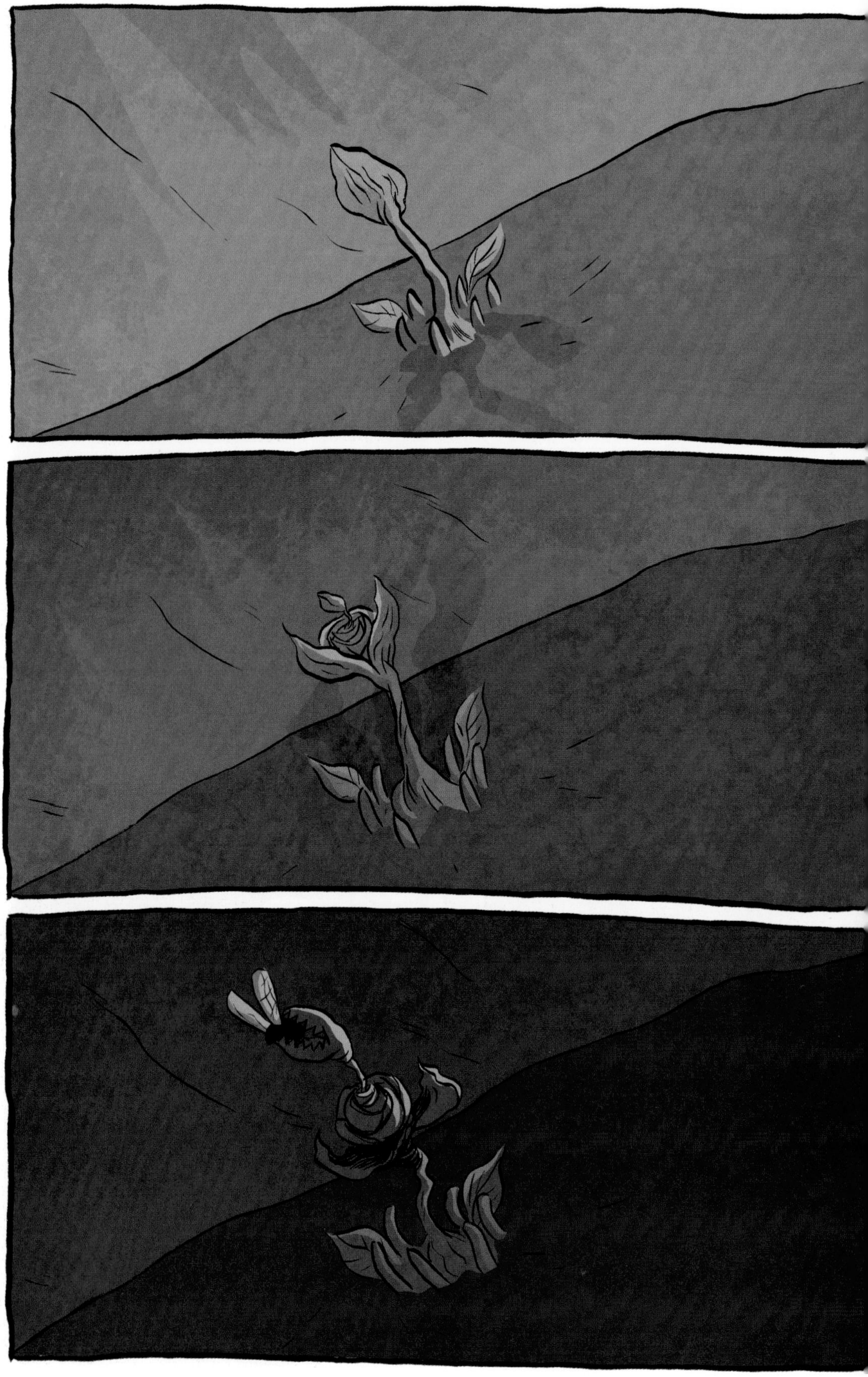

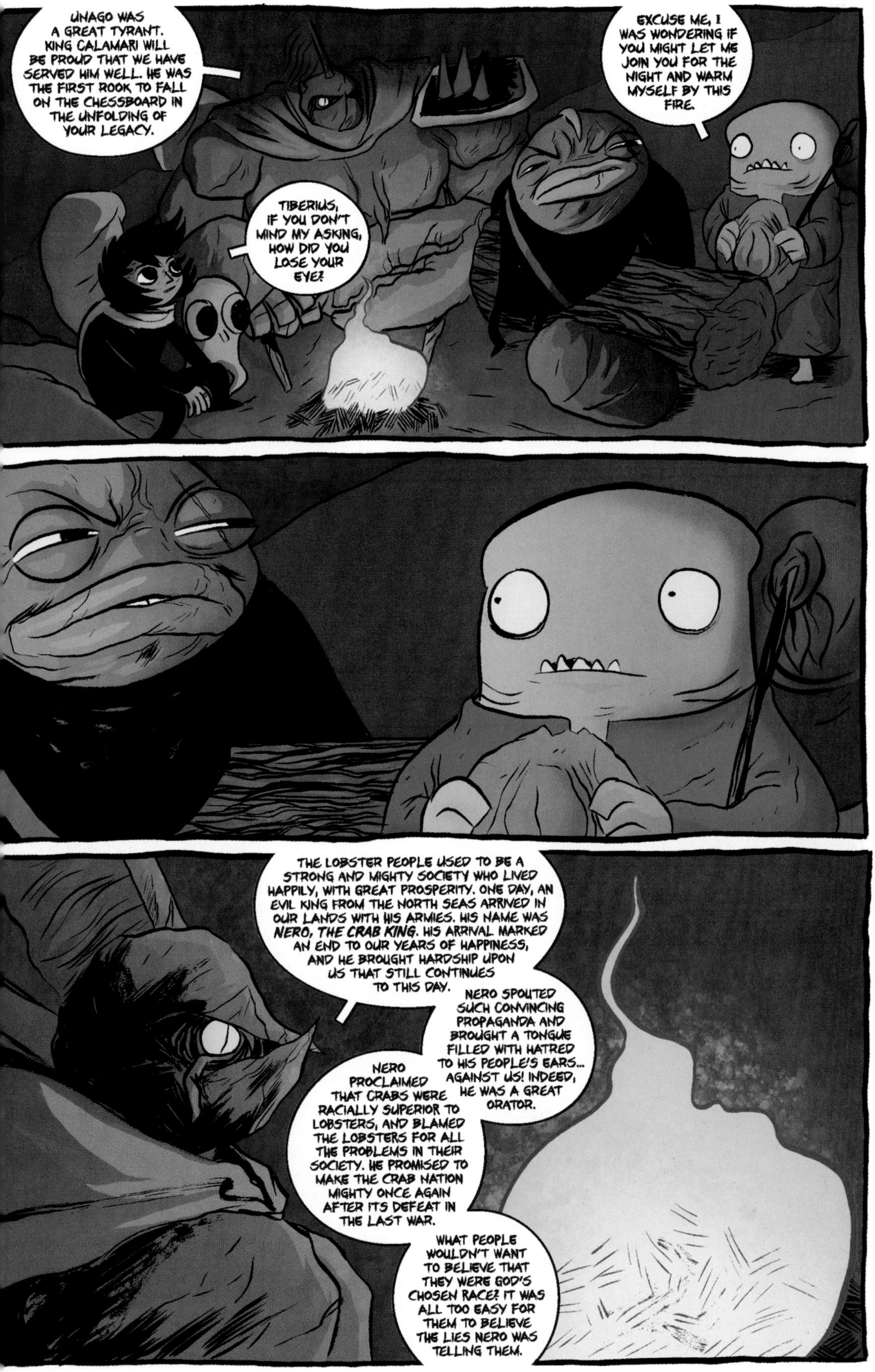
UNAGO WAS A GREAT TYRANT. KING CALAMARI WILL BE PROUD THAT WE HAVE SERVED HIM WELL. HE WAS THE FIRST ROOK TO FALL ON THE CHESSBOARD IN THE UNFOLDING OF YOUR LEGACY.
EXCUSE ME, I WAS WONDERING IF YOU MIGHT LET ME JOIN YOU FOR THE NIGHT AND WARM MYSELF BY THIS FIRE.
TIBERIUS, IF YOU DON'T MIND MY ASKING, HOW DID YOU LOSE YOUR EYE?
THE LOBSTER PEOPLE USED TO BE A STRONG AND MIGHTY SOCIETY WHO LIVED HAPPILY, WITH GREAT PROSPERITY. ONE DAY, AN EVIL KING FROM THE NORTH SEAS ARRIVED IN OUR LANDS WITH HIS ARMIES. HIS NAME WAS *NERO, THE CRAB KING*. HIS ARRIVAL MARKED AN END TO OUR YEARS OF HAPPINESS, AND HE BROUGHT HARDSHIP UPON US THAT STILL CONTINUES TO THIS DAY.
NERO SPOUTED SUCH CONVINCING PROPAGANDA AND BROUGHT A TONGUE FILLED WITH HATRED TO HIS PEOPLE'S EARS... AGAINST US! INDEED, HE WAS A GREAT ORATOR.
NERO PROCLAIMED THAT CRABS WERE RACIALLY SUPERIOR TO LOBSTERS, AND BLAMED THE LOBSTERS FOR ALL THE PROBLEMS IN THEIR SOCIETY. HE PROMISED TO MAKE THE CRAB NATION MIGHTY ONCE AGAIN AFTER ITS DEFEAT IN THE LAST WAR.
WHAT PEOPLE WOULDN'T WANT TO BELIEVE THAT THEY WERE GOD'S CHOSEN RACE? IT WAS ALL TOO EASY FOR THEM TO BELIEVE THE LIES NERO WAS TELLING THEM.

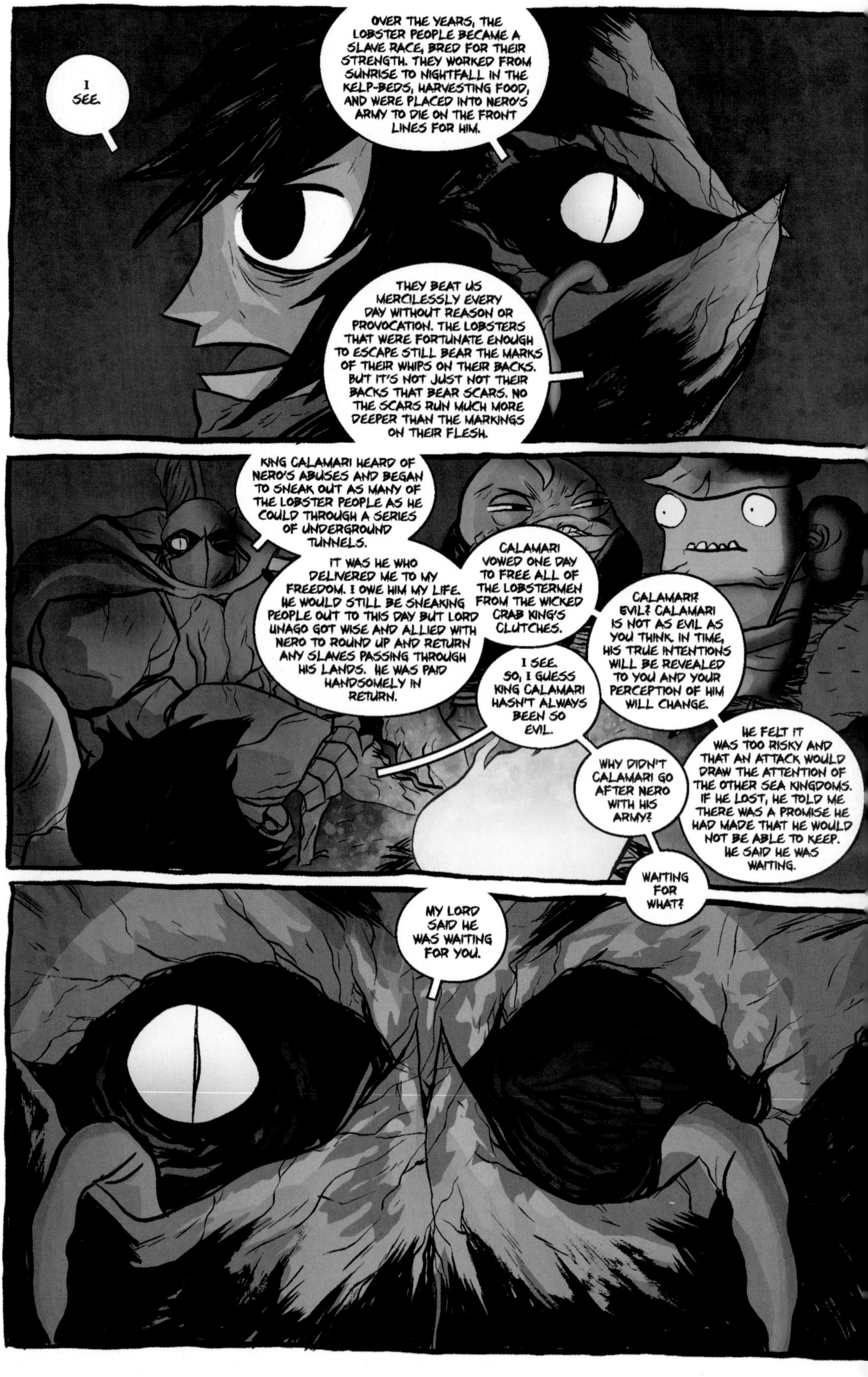
OVER THE YEARS, THE LOBSTER PEOPLE BECAME A SLAVE RACE, BRED FOR THEIR STRENGTH. THEY WORKED FROM SUNRISE TO NIGHTFALL IN THE KELP-BEDS, HARVESTING FOOD, AND WERE PLACED INTO NERO'S ARMY TO DIE ON THE FRONT LINES FOR HIM.
I SEE.
THEY BEAT US MERCILESSLY EVERY DAY WITHOUT REASON OR PROVOCATION. THE LOBSTERS THAT WERE FORTUNATE ENOUGH TO ESCAPE STILL BEAR THE MARKS OF THEIR WHIPS ON THEIR BACKS. BUT IT'S NOT JUST NOT THEIR BACKS THAT BEAR SCARS. NO THE SCARS RUN MUCH MORE DEEPER THAN THE MARKINGS ON THEIR FLESH.
KING CALAMARI HEARD OF NERO'S ABUSES AND BEGAN TO SNEAK OUT AS MANY OF THE LOBSTER PEOPLE AS HE COULD THROUGH A SERIES OF UNDERGROUND TUNNELS.
IT WAS HE WHO DELIVERED ME TO MY FREEDOM. I OWE HIM MY LIFE. HE WOULD STILL BE SNEAKING PEOPLE OUT TO THIS DAY BUT LORD UNAGO GOT WISE AND ALLIED WITH NERO TO ROUND UP AND RETURN ANY SLAVES PASSING THROUGH HIS LANDS. HE WAS PAID HANDSOMELY IN RETURN.
CALAMARI VOWED ONE DAY TO FREE ALL OF THE LOBSTERMEN FROM THE WICKED CRAB KING'S CLUTCHES.
I SEE. SO, I GUESS KING CALAMARI HASN'T ALWAYS BEEN SO EVIL.
CALAMARI? EVIL? CALAMARI IS NOT AS EVIL AS YOU THINK. IN TIME, HIS TRUE INTENTIONS WILL BE REVEALED TO YOU AND YOUR PERCEPTION OF HIM WILL CHANGE.
WHY DIDN'T CALAMARI GO AFTER NERO WITH HIS ARMY?
HE FELT IT WAS TOO RISKY AND THAT AN ATTACK WOULD DRAW THE ATTENTION OF THE OTHER SEA KINGDOMS. IF HE LOST, HE TOLD ME THERE WAS A PROMISE HE HAD MADE THAT HE WOULD NOT BE ABLE TO KEEP. HE SAID HE WAS WAITING.
WAITING FOR WHAT?
MY LORD SAID HE WAS WAITING FOR YOU.

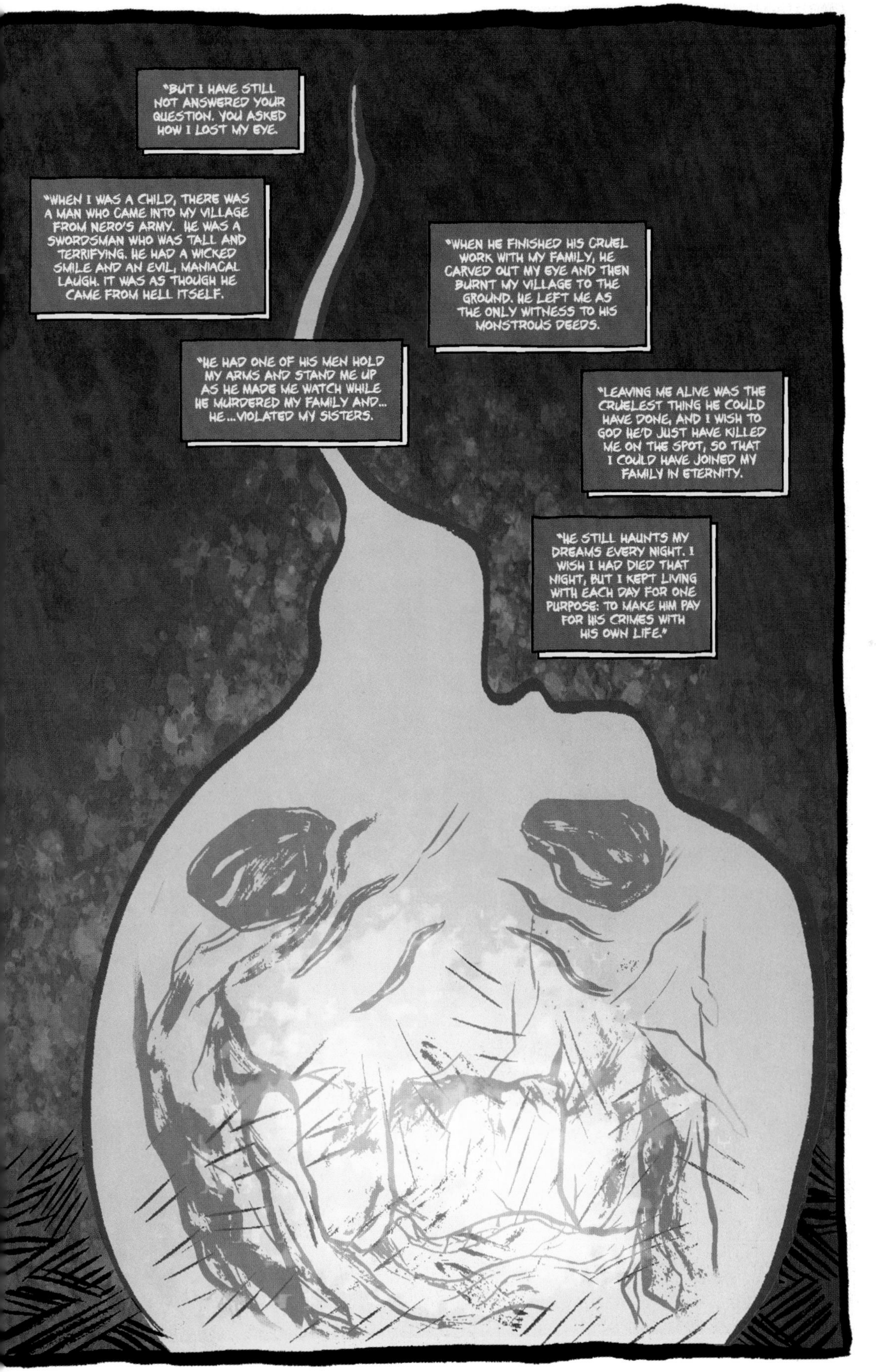
"BUT I HAVE STILL NOT ANSWERED YOUR QUESTION. YOU ASKED HOW I LOST MY EYE.
"WHEN I WAS A CHILD, THERE WAS A MAN WHO CAME INTO MY VILLAGE FROM NERO'S ARMY. HE WAS A SWORDSMAN WHO WAS TALL AND TERRIFYING. HE HAD A WICKED SMILE AND AN EVIL, MANIACAL LAUGH. IT WAS AS THOUGH HE CAME FROM HELL ITSELF.
"HE HAD ONE OF HIS MEN HOLD MY ARMS AND STAND ME UP AS HE MADE ME WATCH WHILE HE MURDERED MY FAMILY AND... HE...VIOLATED MY SISTERS.
"WHEN HE FINISHED HIS CRUEL WORK WITH MY FAMILY, HE CARVED OUT MY EYE AND THEN BURNT MY VILLAGE TO THE GROUND. HE LEFT ME AS THE ONLY WITNESS TO HIS MONSTROUS DEEDS.
"LEAVING ME ALIVE WAS THE CRUELEST THING HE COULD HAVE DONE, AND I WISH TO GOD HE'D JUST HAVE KILLED ME ON THE SPOT, SO THAT I COULD HAVE JOINED MY FAMILY IN ETERNITY.
"HE STILL HAUNTS MY DREAMS EVERY NIGHT. I WISH I HAD DIED THAT NIGHT, BUT I KEPT LIVING WITH EACH DAY FOR ONE PURPOSE: TO MAKE HIM PAY FOR HIS CRIMES WITH HIS OWN LIFE."

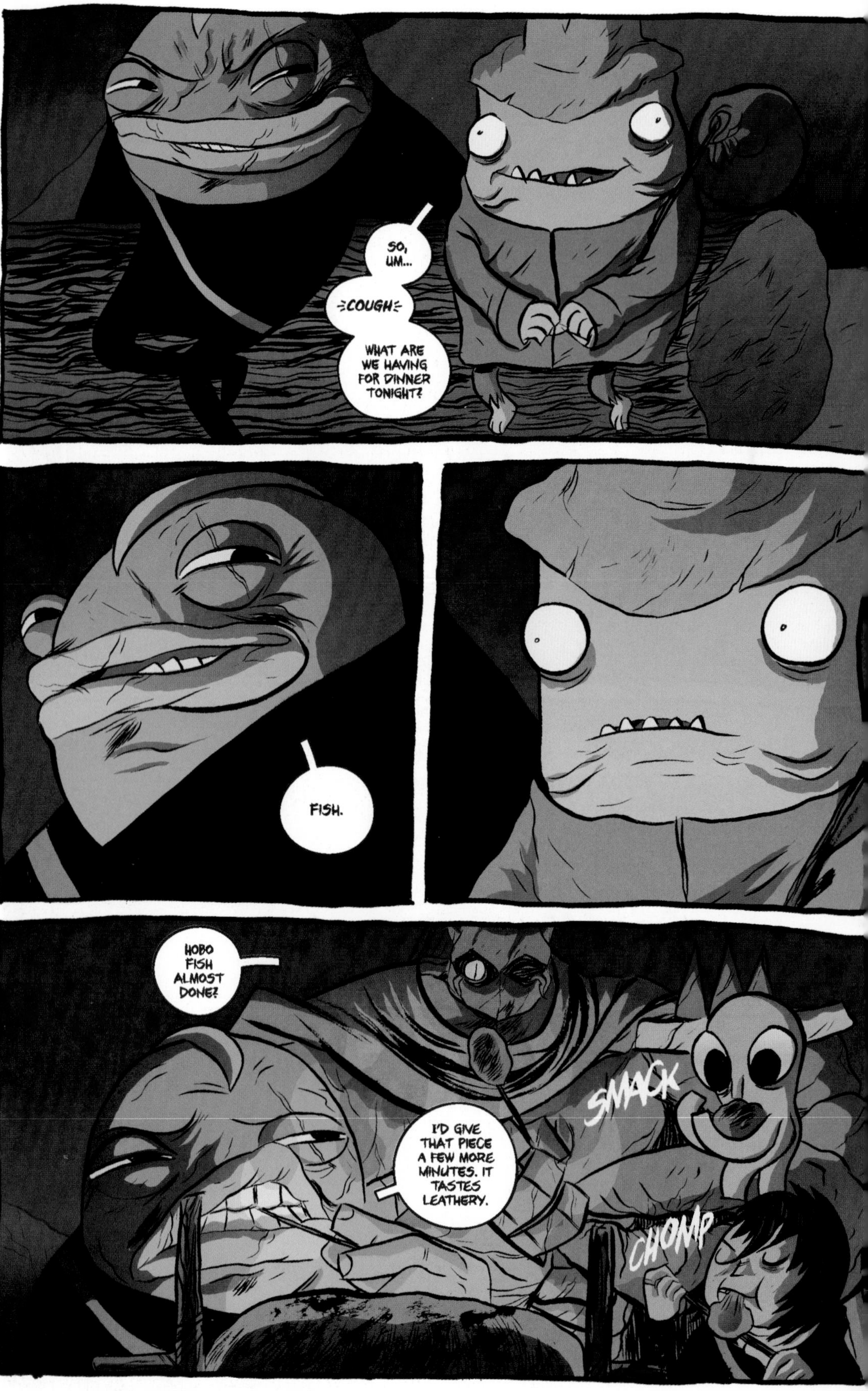
SO, UM...
COUGH
WHAT ARE WE HAVING FOR DINNER TONIGHT?
FISH.
HOBO FISH ALMOST DONE?
SMACK
I'D GIVE THAT PIECE A FEW MORE MINUTES. IT TASTES LEATHERY.
CHOMP

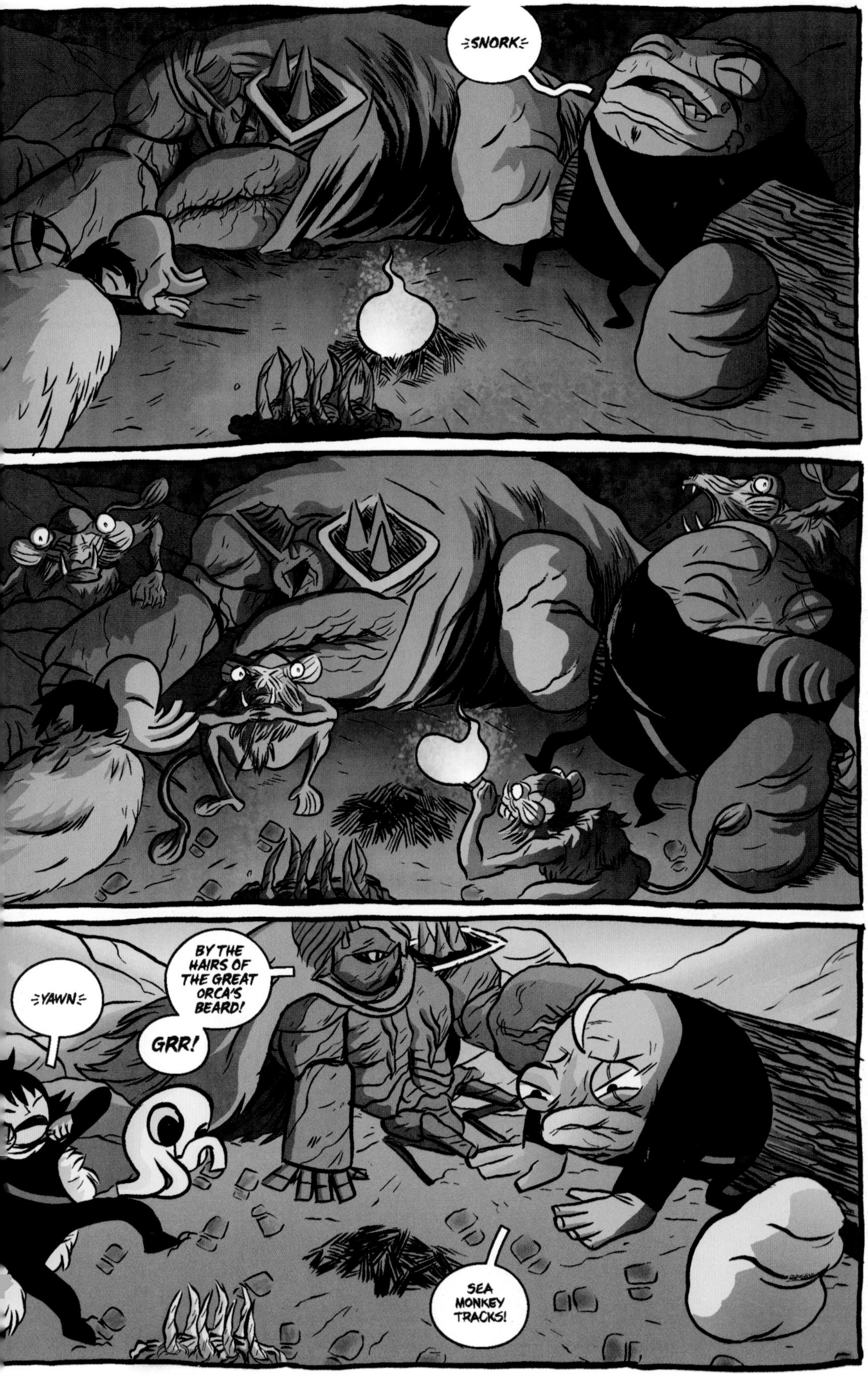
SNORK
YAWN
BY THE HAIRS OF THE GREAT ORCA'S BEARD!
GRR!
SEA MONKEY TRACKS!

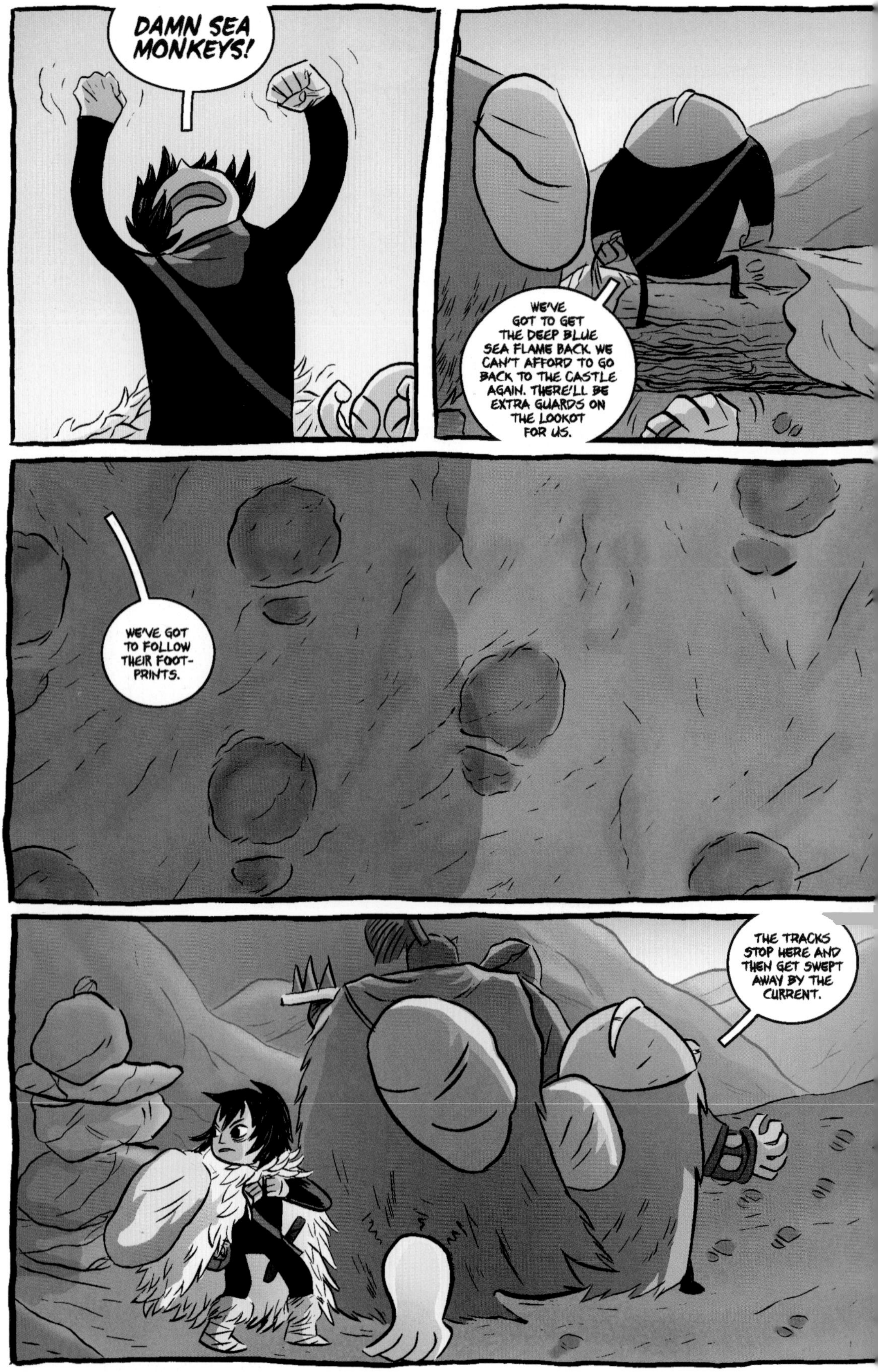
DAMN SEA MONKEYS!
WE'VE GOT TO GET THE DEEP BLUE SEA FLAME BACK. WE CAN'T AFFORD TO GO BACK TO THE CASTLE AGAIN. THERE'LL BE EXTRA GUARDS ON THE LOOKOT FOR US.
WE'VE GOT TO FOLLOW THEIR FOOT-PRINTS.
THE TRACKS STOP HERE AND THEN GET SWEPT AWAY BY THE CURRENT.

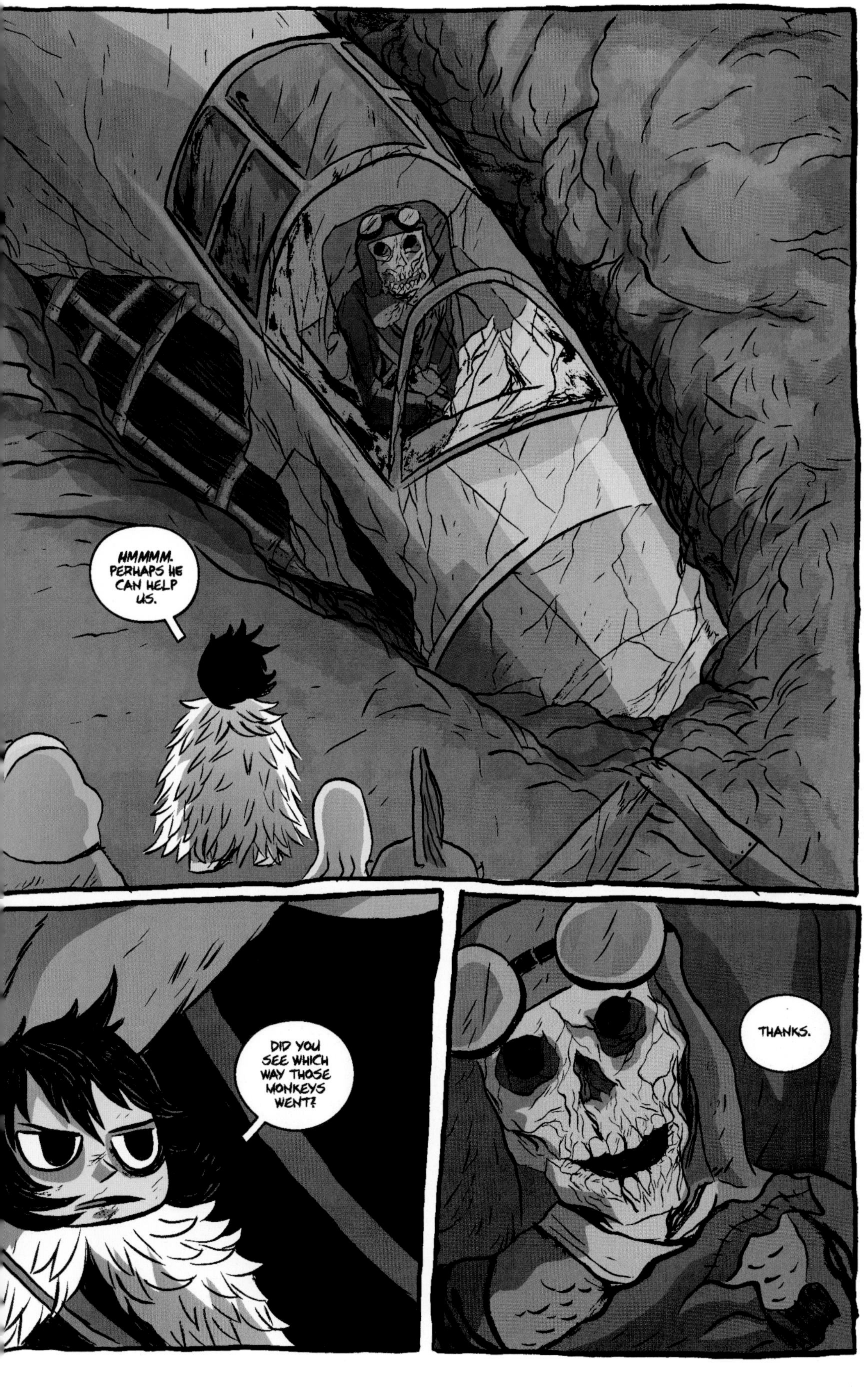
HMMMM. PERHAPS HE CAN HELP US.
DID YOU SEE WHICH WAY THOSE MONKEYS WENT?
THANKS.

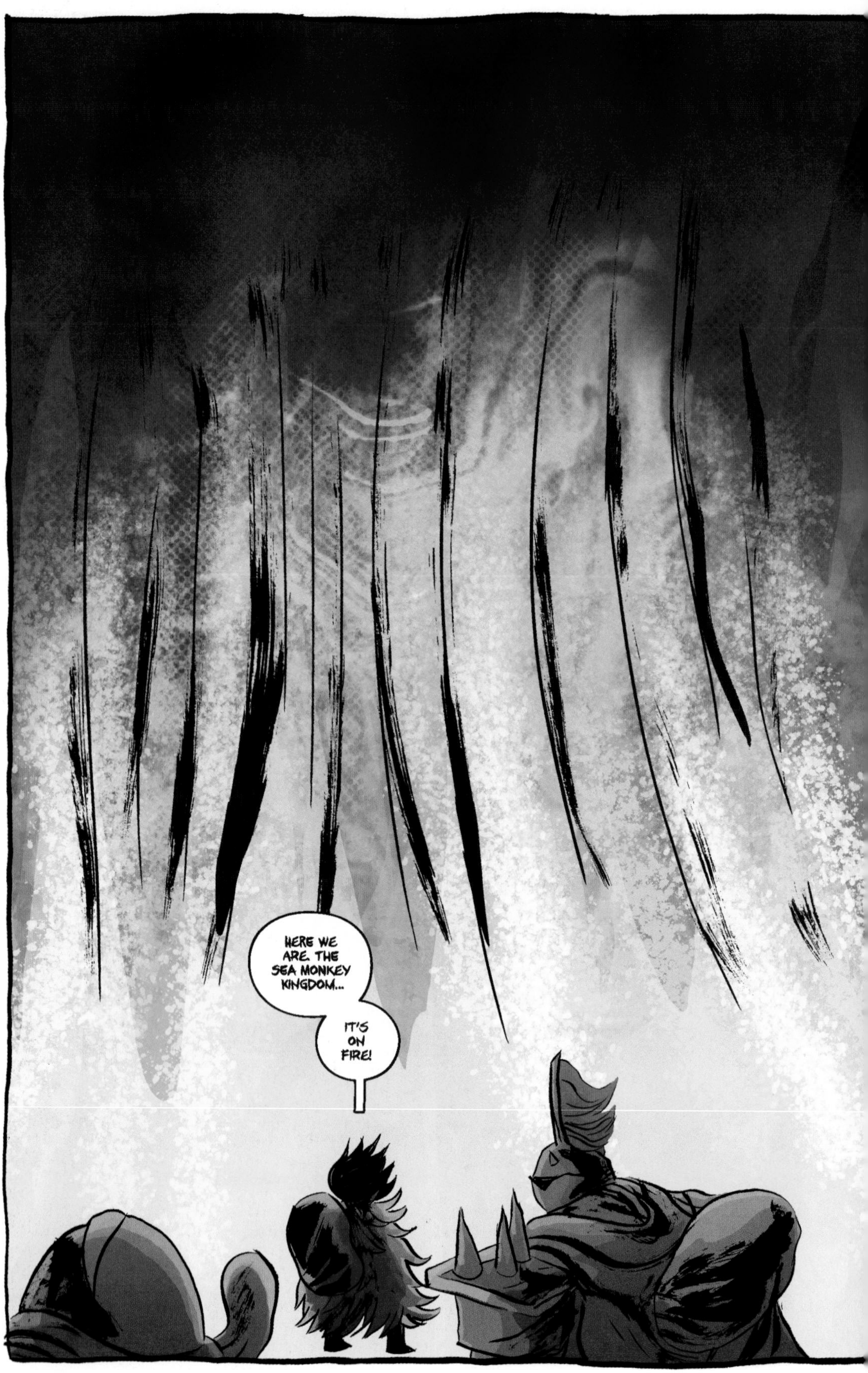
HERE WE ARE. THE SEA MONKEY KINGDOM...
IT'S ON FIRE!

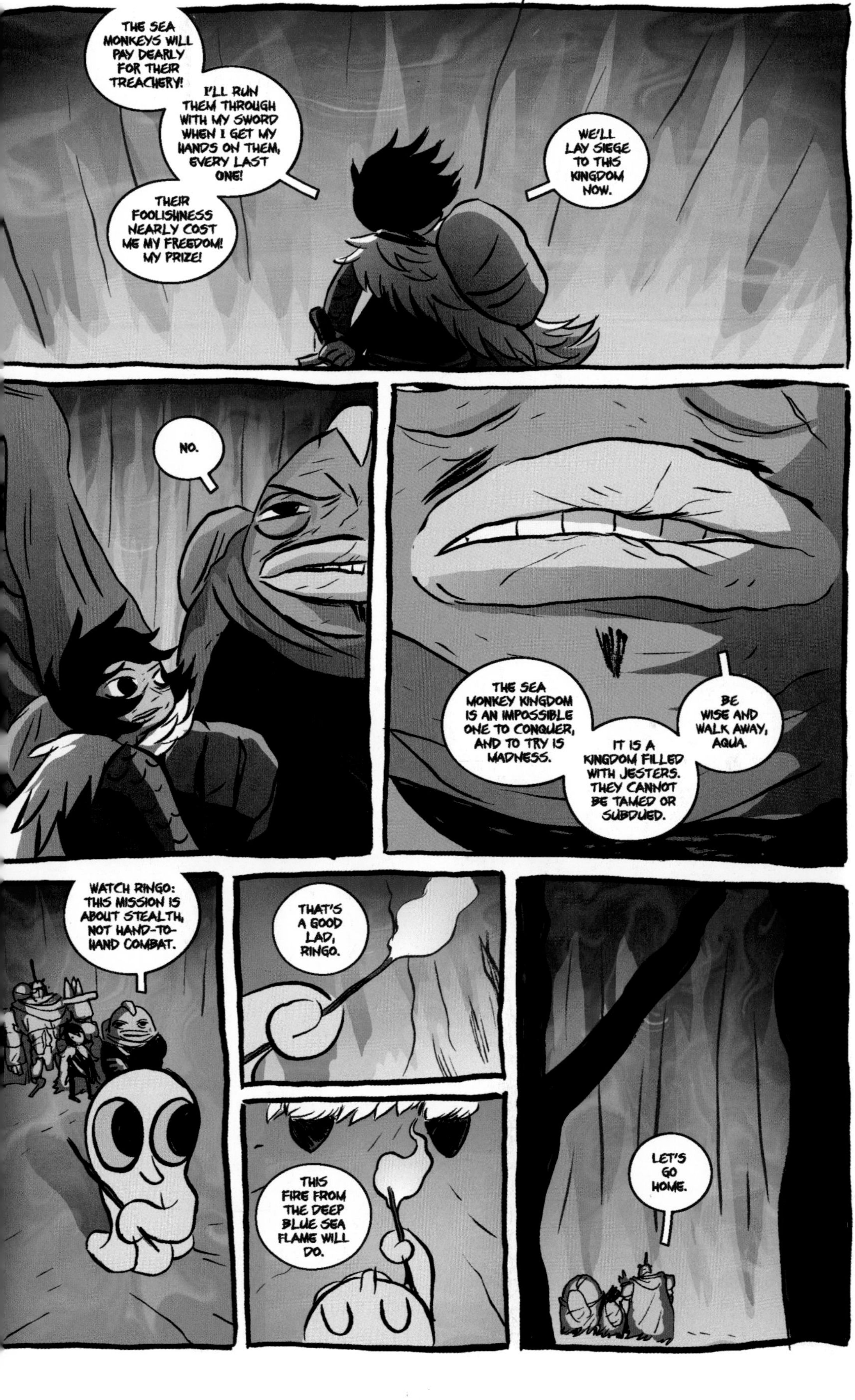
THE SEA MONKEYS WILL PAY DEARLY FOR THEIR TREACHERY!
I'LL RUN THEM THROUGH WITH MY SWORD WHEN I GET MY HANDS ON THEM, EVERY LAST ONE!
THEIR FOOLISHNESS NEARLY COST ME MY FREEDOM! MY PRIZE!
WE'LL LAY SIEGE TO THIS KINGDOM NOW.
NO.
THE SEA MONKEY KINGDOM IS AN IMPOSSIBLE ONE TO CONQUER, AND TO TRY IS MADNESS.
IT IS A KINGDOM FILLED WITH JESTERS. THEY CANNOT BE TAMED OR SUBDUED.
BE WISE AND WALK AWAY, AQUA.
WATCH RINGO: THIS MISSION IS ABOUT STEALTH, NOT HAND-TO-HAND COMBAT.
THAT'S A GOOD LAD, RINGO.
THIS FIRE FROM THE DEEP BLUE SEA FLAME WILL DO.
LET'S GO HOME.

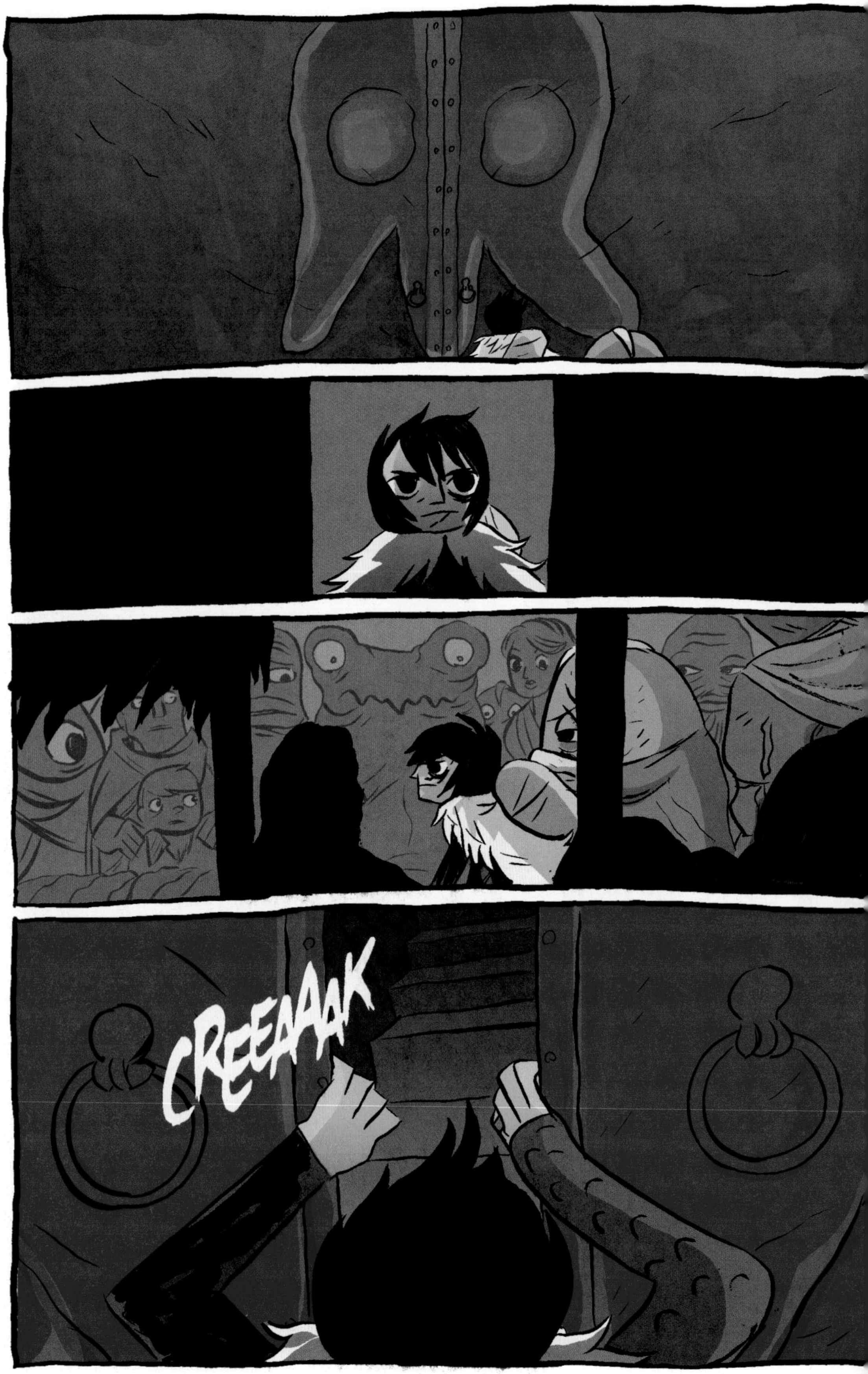
CREEAAAK

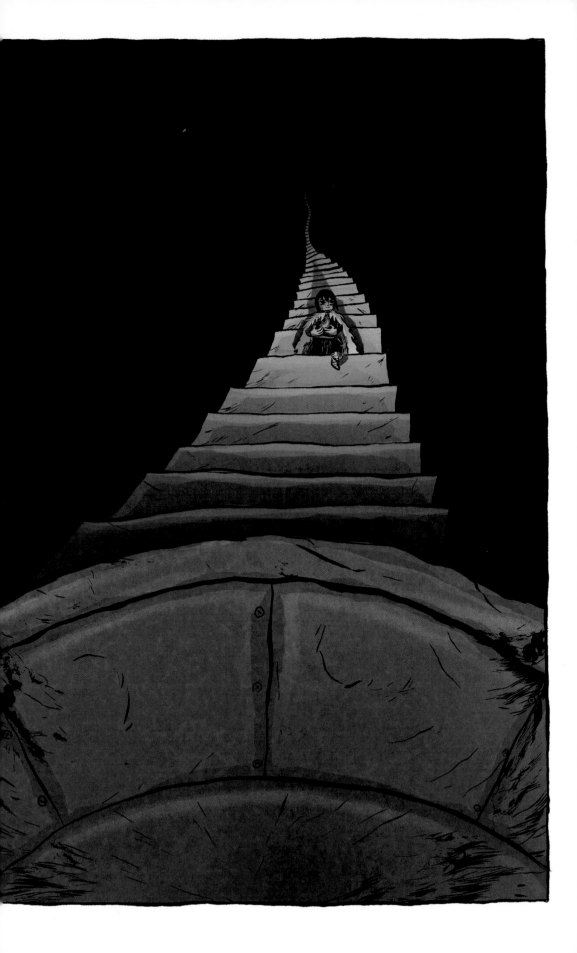

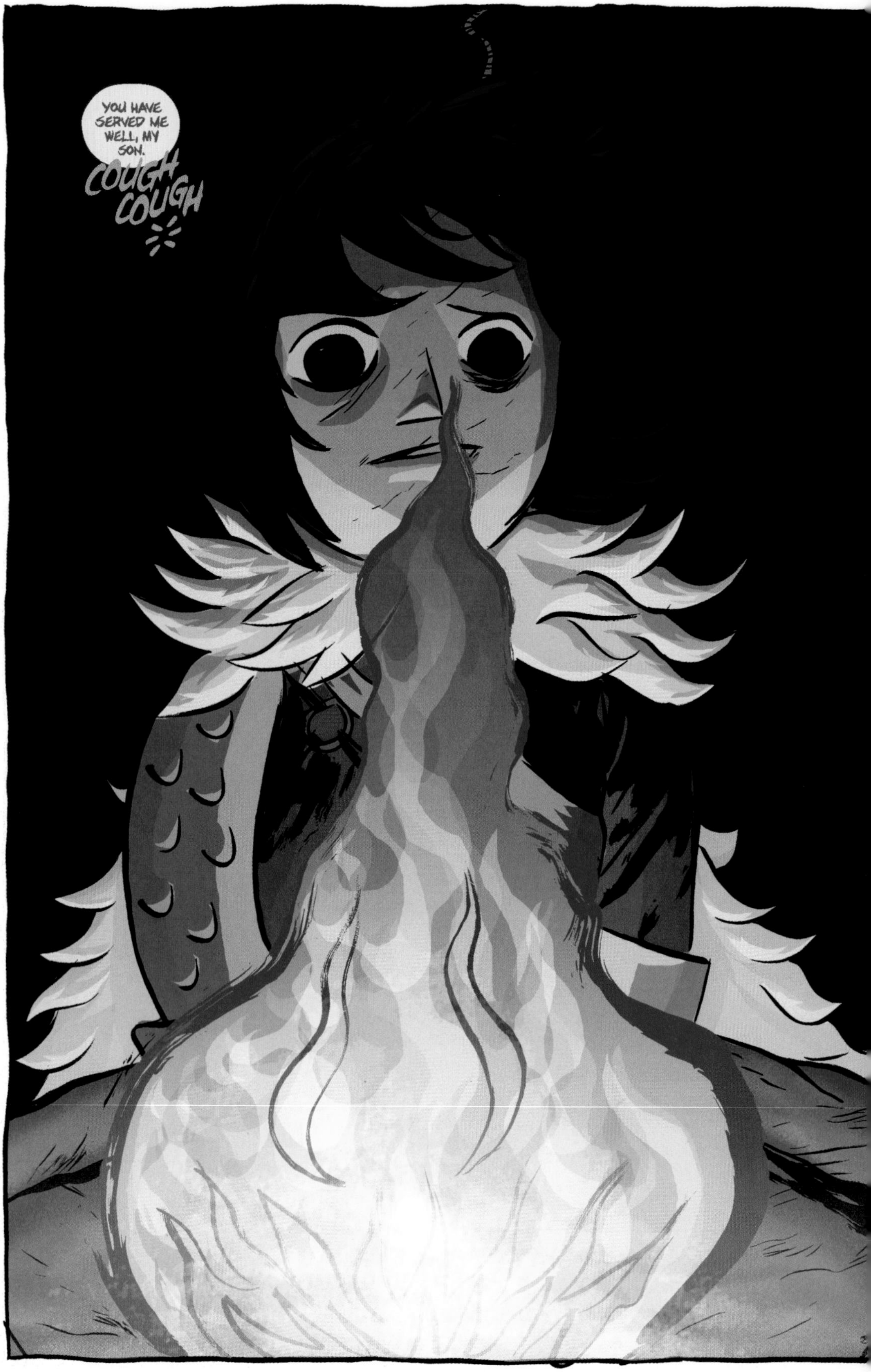

YOU HAVE SERVED ME WELL, MY SON.
COUGH COUGH

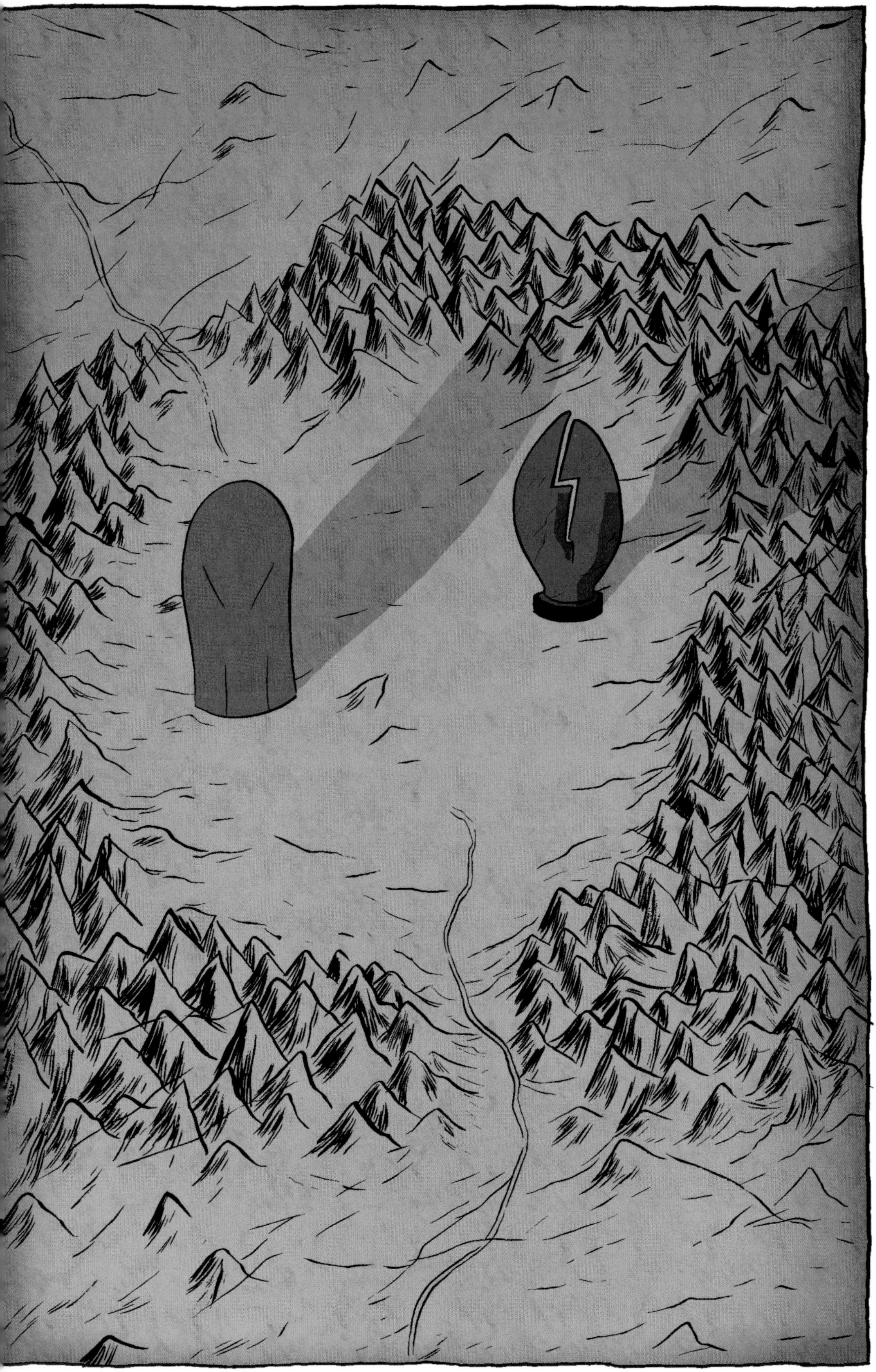

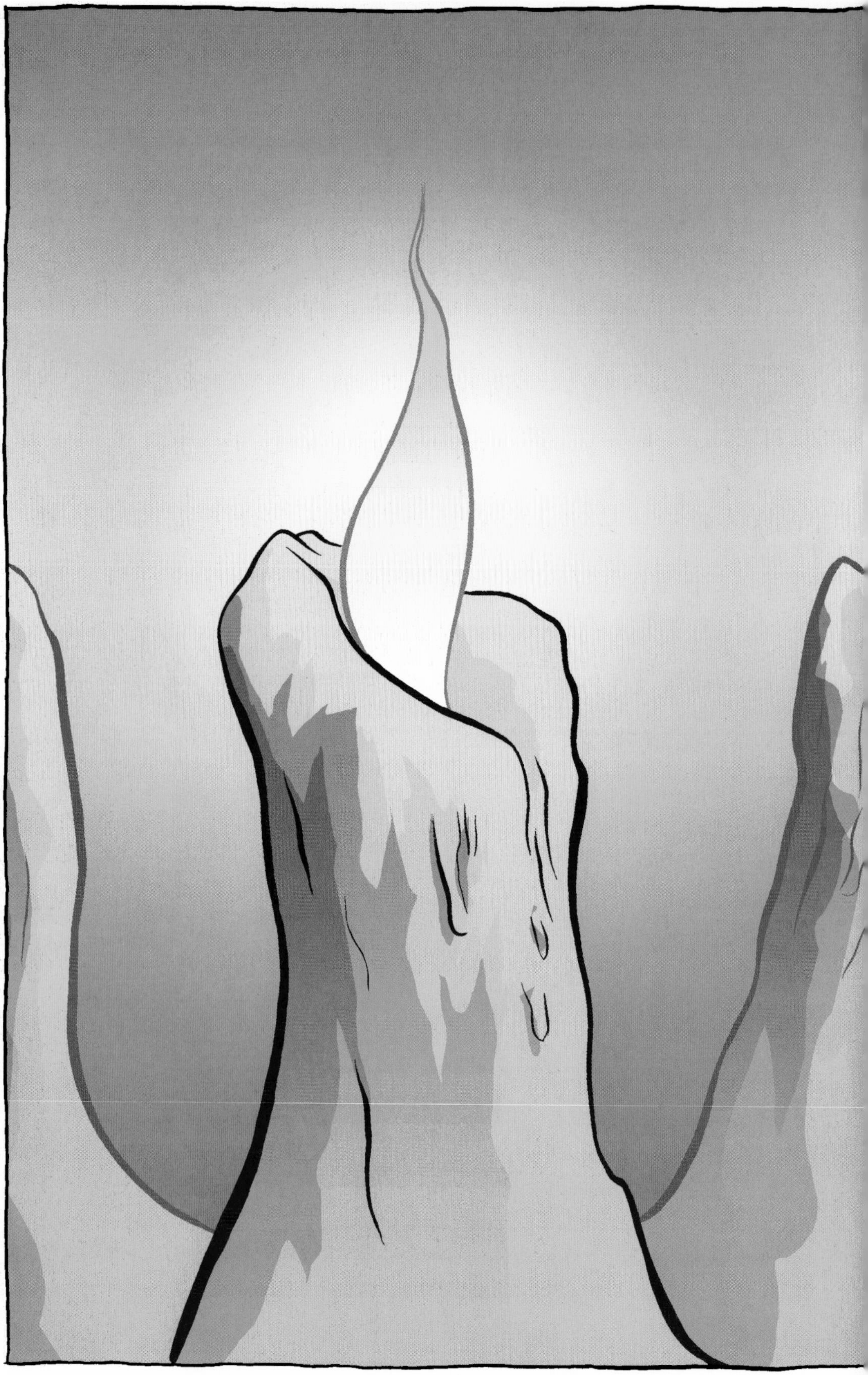

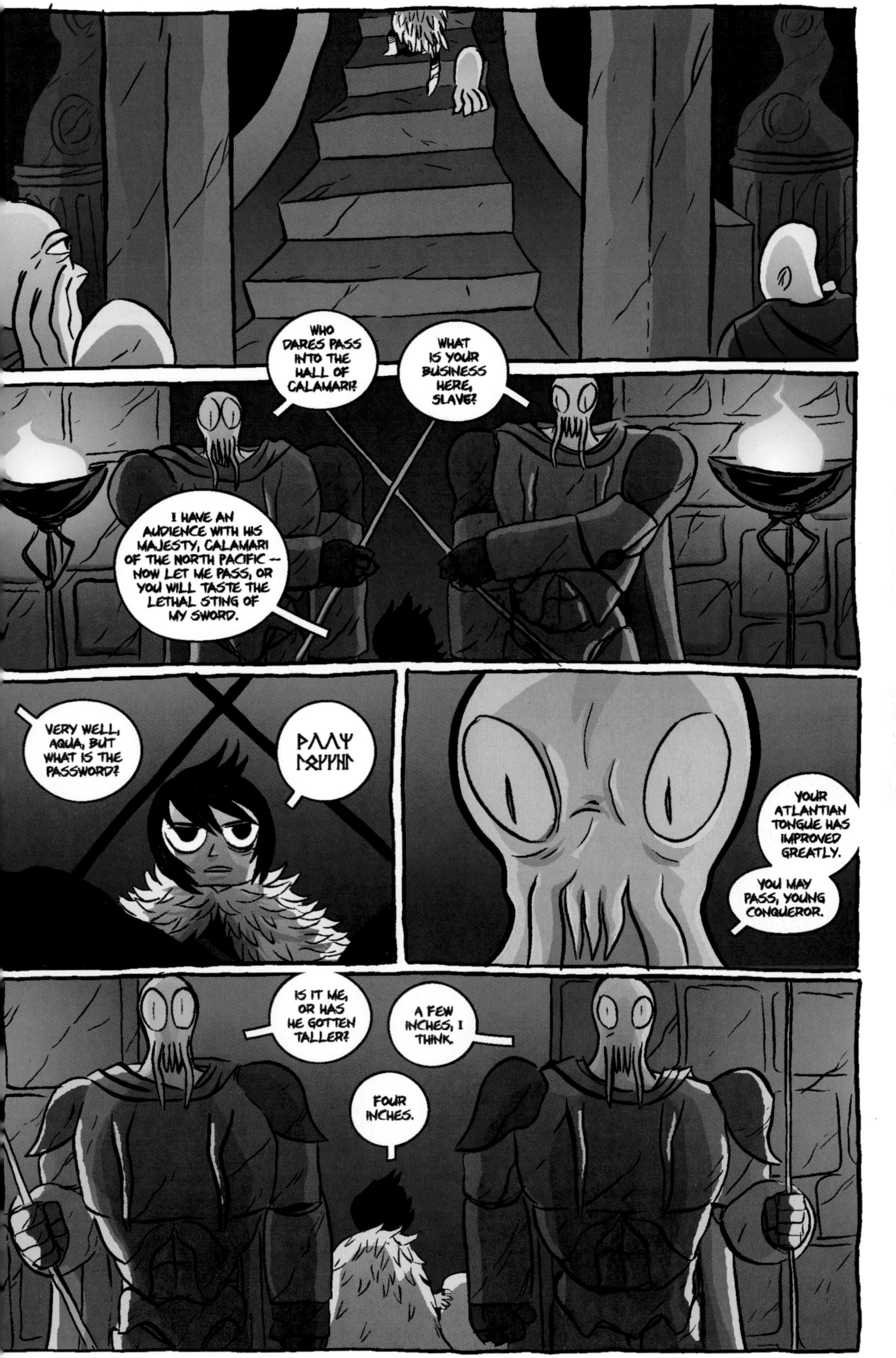
WHO DARES PASS INTO THE HALL OF CALAMARI?
WHAT IS YOUR BUSINESS HERE, SLAVE?
I HAVE AN AUDIENCE WITH HIS MAJESTY, CALAMARI OF THE NORTH PACIFIC -- NOW LET ME PASS, OR YOU WILL TASTE THE LETHAL STING OF MY SWORD.
VERY WELL, AQUA, BUT WHAT IS THE PASSWORD?
YOUR ATLANTIAN TONGUE HAS IMPROVED GREATLY.
YOU MAY PASS, YOUNG CONQUEROR.
IS IT ME, OR HAS HE GOTTEN TALLER?
A FEW INCHES, I THINK.
FOUR INCHES.

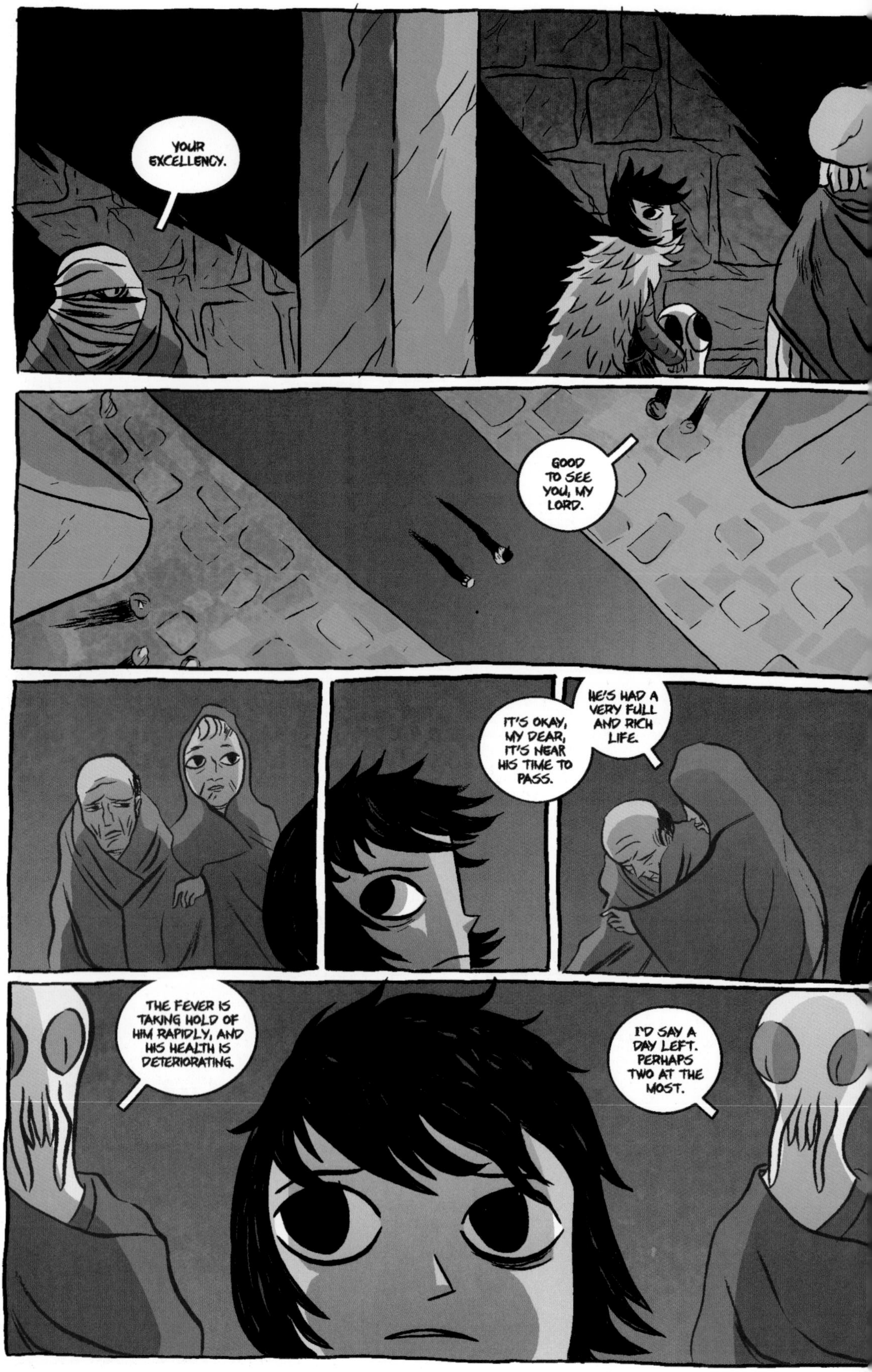
YOUR EXCELLENCY.
GOOD TO SEE YOU, MY LORD.
IT'S OKAY, MY DEAR, IT'S NEAR HIS TIME TO PASS.
HE'S HAD A VERY FULL AND RICH LIFE.
THE FEVER IS TAKING HOLD OF HIM RAPIDLY, AND HIS HEALTH IS DETERIORATING.
I'D SAY A DAY LEFT. PERHAPS TWO AT THE MOST.

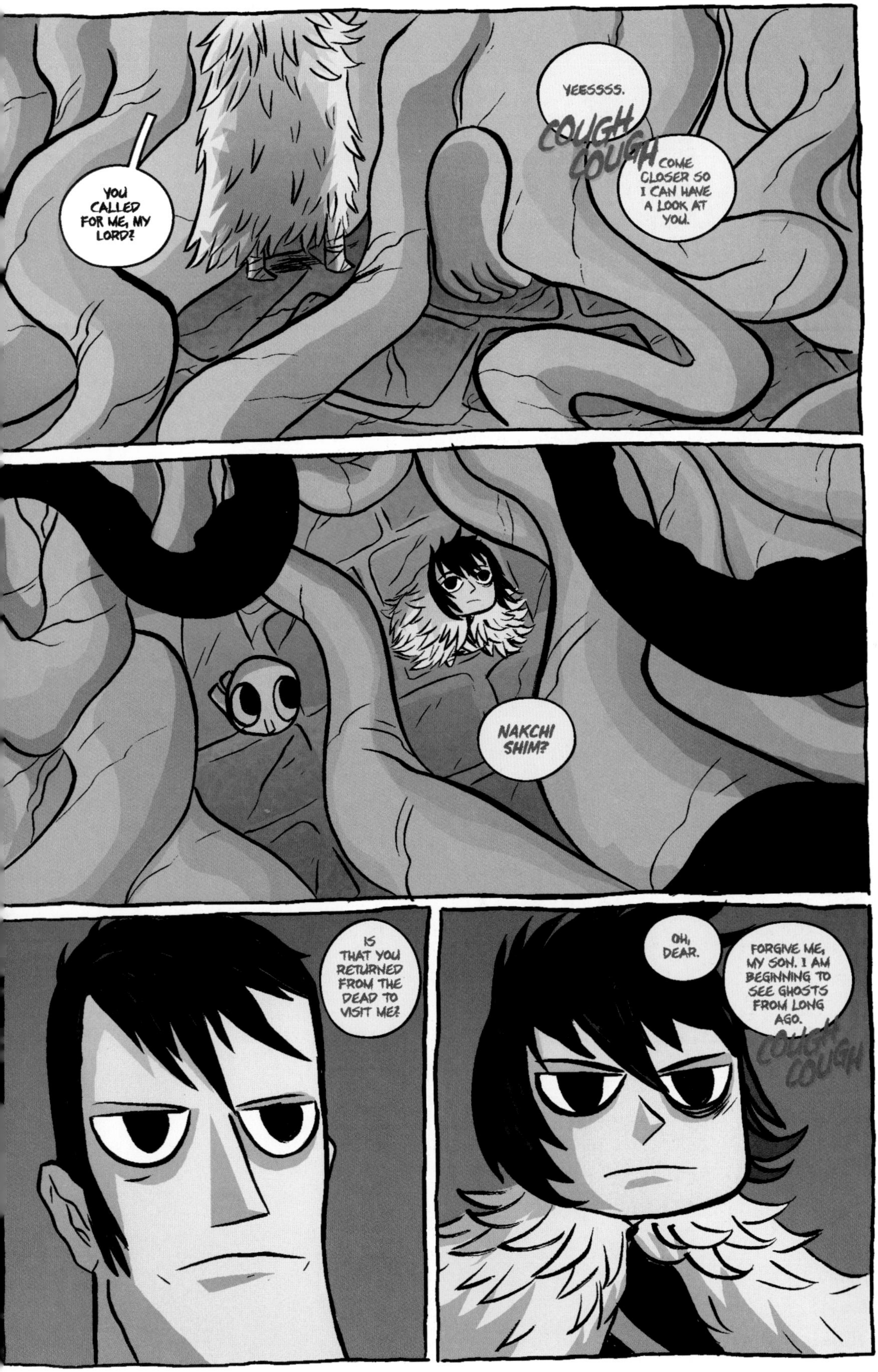
YOU CALLED FOR ME, MY LORD?
YEESSSS.
COUGH COUGH
COME CLOSER SO I CAN HAVE A LOOK AT YOU.
NAKCHI SHIM?
IS THAT YOU RETURNED FROM THE DEAD TO VISIT ME?
OH, DEAR.
FORGIVE ME, MY SON. I AM BEGINNING TO SEE GHOSTS FROM LONG AGO.
COUGH COUGH

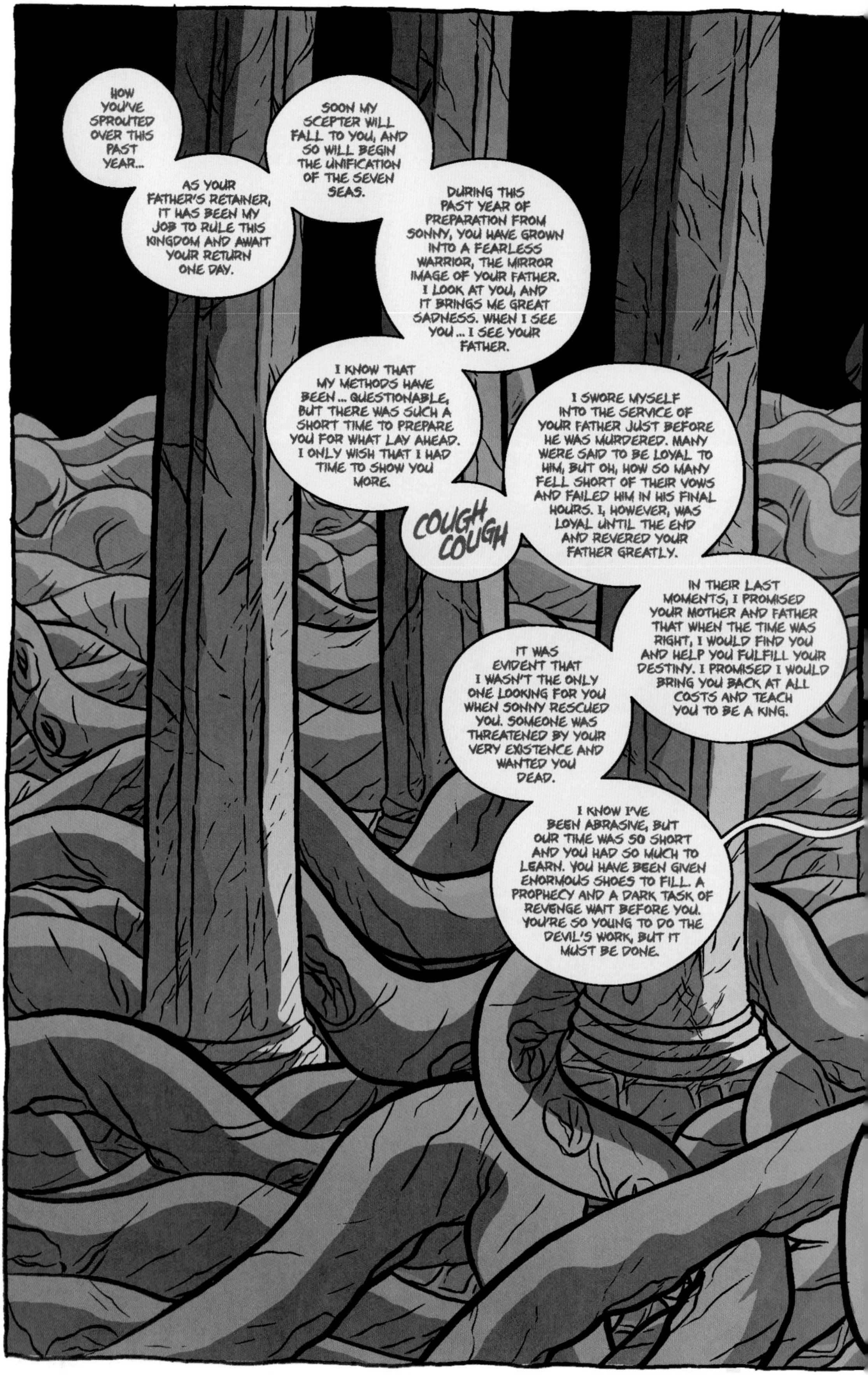
HOW YOU'VE SPROUTED OVER THIS PAST YEAR...
AS YOUR FATHER'S RETAINER, IT HAS BEEN MY JOB TO RULE THIS KINGDOM AND AWAIT YOUR RETURN ONE DAY.
SOON MY SCEPTER WILL FALL TO YOU, AND SO WILL BEGIN THE UNIFICATION OF THE SEVEN SEAS.
DURING THIS PAST YEAR OF PREPARATION FROM SONNY, YOU HAVE GROWN INTO A FEARLESS WARRIOR, THE MIRROR IMAGE OF YOUR FATHER. I LOOK AT YOU, AND IT BRINGS ME GREAT SADNESS. WHEN I SEE YOU ... I SEE YOUR FATHER.
I KNOW THAT MY METHODS HAVE BEEN ... QUESTIONABLE, BUT THERE WAS SUCH A SHORT TIME TO PREPARE YOU FOR WHAT LAY AHEAD. I ONLY WISH THAT I HAD TIME TO SHOW YOU MORE.
COUGH COUGH
I SWORE MYSELF INTO THE SERVICE OF YOUR FATHER JUST BEFORE HE WAS MURDERED. MANY WERE SAID TO BE LOYAL TO HIM, BUT OH, HOW SO MANY FELL SHORT OF THEIR VOWS AND FAILED HIM IN HIS FINAL HOURS. I, HOWEVER, WAS LOYAL UNTIL THE END AND REVERED YOUR FATHER GREATLY.
IN THEIR LAST MOMENTS, I PROMISED YOUR MOTHER AND FATHER THAT WHEN THE TIME WAS RIGHT, I WOULD FIND YOU AND HELP YOU FULFILL YOUR DESTINY. I PROMISED I WOULD BRING YOU BACK AT ALL COSTS AND TEACH YOU TO BE A KING.
IT WAS EVIDENT THAT I WASN'T THE ONLY ONE LOOKING FOR YOU WHEN SONNY RESCUED YOU. SOMEONE WAS THREATENED BY YOUR VERY EXISTENCE AND WANTED YOU DEAD.
I KNOW I'VE BEEN ABRASIVE, BUT OUR TIME WAS SO SHORT AND YOU HAD SO MUCH TO LEARN. YOU HAVE BEEN GIVEN ENORMOUS SHOES TO FILL. A PROPHECY AND A DARK TASK OF REVENGE WAIT BEFORE YOU. YOU'RE SO YOUNG TO DO THE DEVIL'S WORK, BUT IT MUST BE DONE.

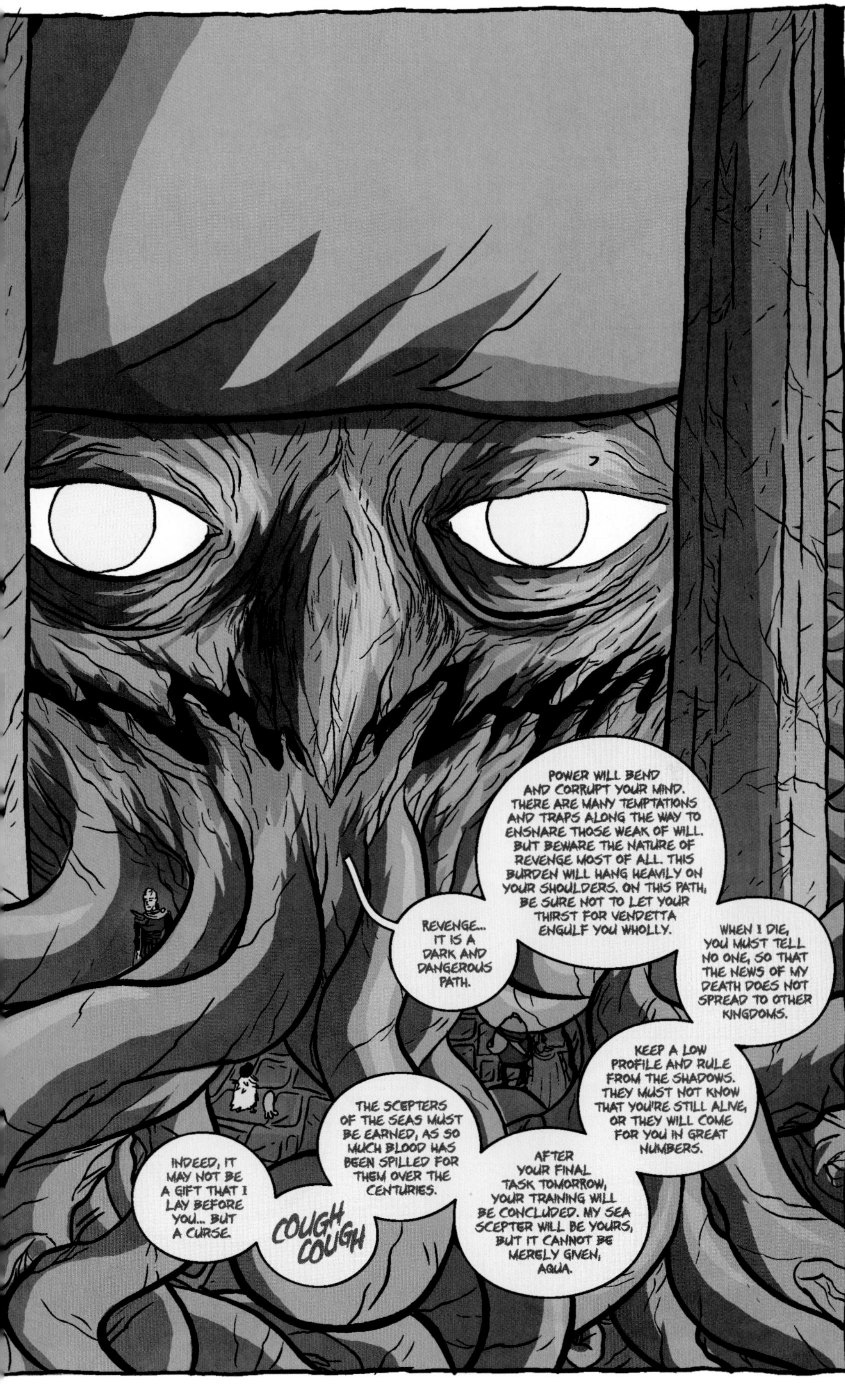

REVENGE... IT IS A DARK AND DANGEROUS PATH.
POWER WILL BEND AND CORRUPT YOUR MIND. THERE ARE MANY TEMPTATIONS AND TRAPS ALONG THE WAY TO ENSNARE THOSE WEAK OF WILL. BUT BEWARE THE NATURE OF REVENGE MOST OF ALL. THIS BURDEN WILL HANG HEAVILY ON YOUR SHOULDERS. ON THIS PATH, BE SURE NOT TO LET YOUR THIRST FOR VENDETTA ENGULF YOU WHOLLY.
WHEN I DIE, YOU MUST TELL NO ONE, SO THAT THE NEWS OF MY DEATH DOES NOT SPREAD TO OTHER KINGDOMS.
KEEP A LOW PROFILE AND RULE FROM THE SHADOWS. THEY MUST NOT KNOW THAT YOU'RE STILL ALIVE, OR THEY WILL COME FOR YOU IN GREAT NUMBERS.
AFTER YOUR FINAL TASK TOMORROW, YOUR TRAINING WILL BE CONCLUDED. MY SEA SCEPTER WILL BE YOURS, BUT IT CANNOT BE MERELY GIVEN, AQUA.
THE SCEPTERS OF THE SEAS MUST BE EARNED, AS SO MUCH BLOOD HAS BEEN SPILLED FOR THEM OVER THE CENTURIES.
COUGH COUGH
INDEED, IT MAY NOT BE A GIFT THAT I LAY BEFORE YOU... BUT A CURSE.

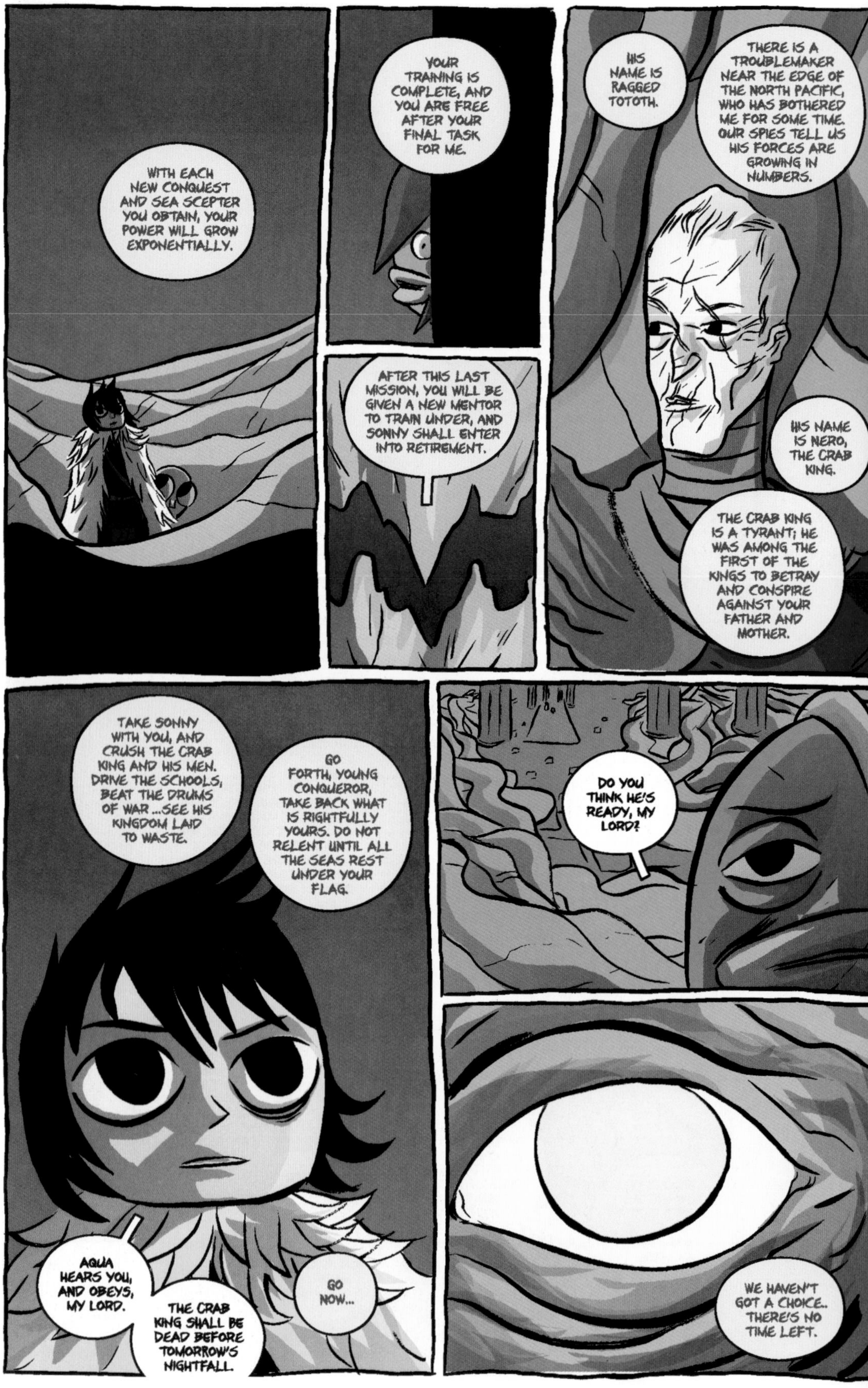

WITH EACH NEW CONQUEST AND SEA SCEPTER YOU OBTAIN, YOUR POWER WILL GROW EXPONENTIALLY.
YOUR TRAINING IS COMPLETE, AND YOU ARE FREE AFTER YOUR FINAL TASK FOR ME.
AFTER THIS LAST MISSION, YOU WILL BE GIVEN A NEW MENTOR TO TRAIN UNDER, AND SONNY SHALL ENTER INTO RETIREMENT.
THERE IS A TROUBLEMAKER NEAR THE EDGE OF THE NORTH PACIFIC, WHO HAS BOTHERED ME FOR SOME TIME. OUR SPIES TELL US HIS FORCES ARE GROWING IN NUMBERS.
HIS NAME IS RAGGED TOTOTH.
HIS NAME IS NERO, THE CRAB KING.
THE CRAB KING IS A TYRANT; HE WAS AMONG THE FIRST OF THE KINGS TO BETRAY AND CONSPIRE AGAINST YOUR FATHER AND MOTHER.
TAKE SONNY WITH YOU, AND CRUSH THE CRAB KING AND HIS MEN. DRIVE THE SCHOOLS, BEAT THE DRUMS OF WAR ...SEE HIS KINGDOM LAID TO WASTE.
GO FORTH, YOUNG CONQUEROR, TAKE BACK WHAT IS RIGHTFULLY YOURS. DO NOT RELENT UNTIL ALL THE SEAS REST UNDER YOUR FLAG.
AQUA HEARS YOU, AND OBEYS, MY LORD.
THE CRAB KING SHALL BE DEAD BEFORE TOMORROW'S NIGHTFALL.
GO NOW...
DO YOU THINK HE'S READY, MY LORD?
WE HAVEN'T GOT A CHOICE.. THERE'S NO TIME LEFT.

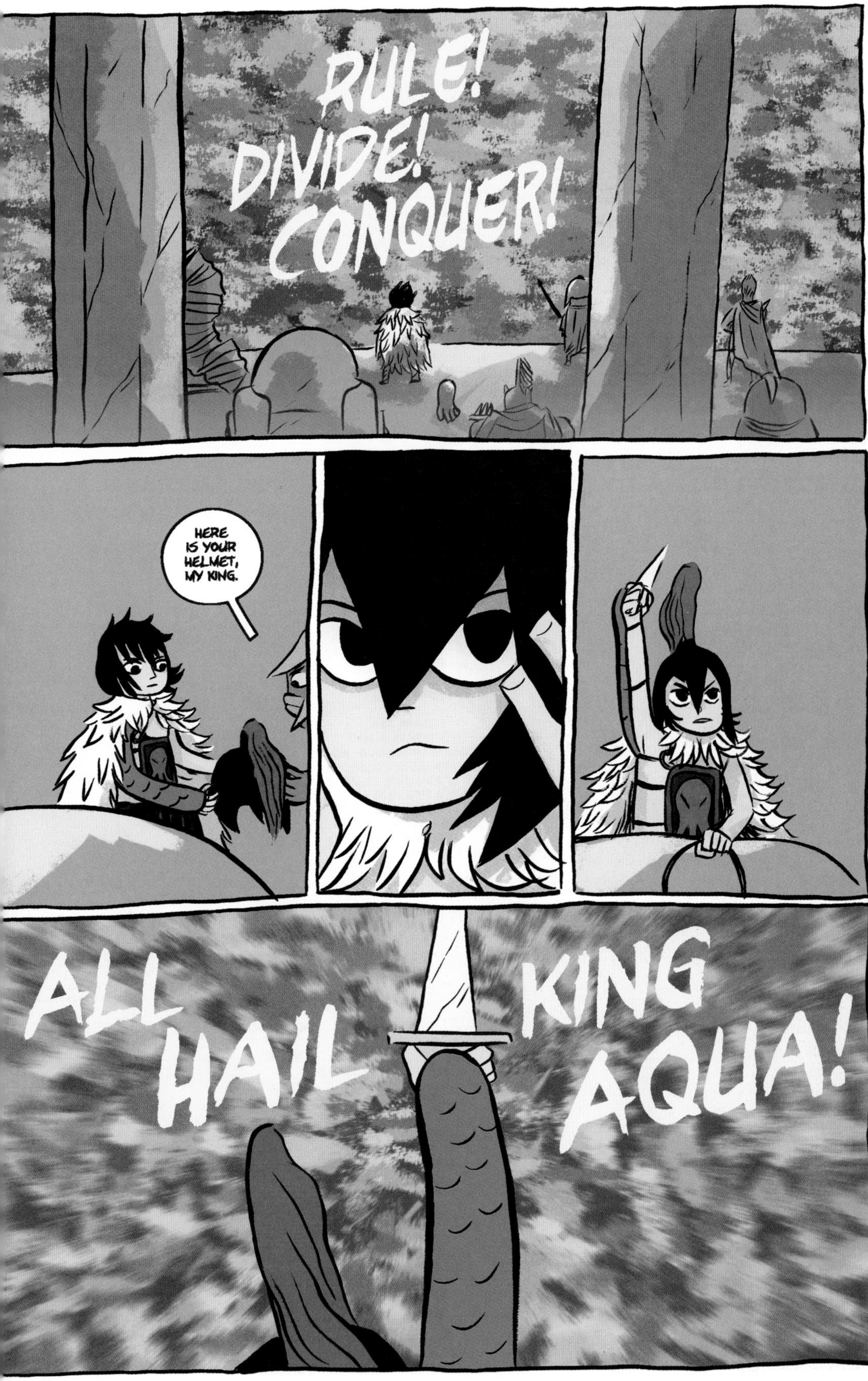
RULE! DIVIDE! CONQUER!
HERE IS YOUR HELMET, MY KING.
ALL HAIL KING AQUA!

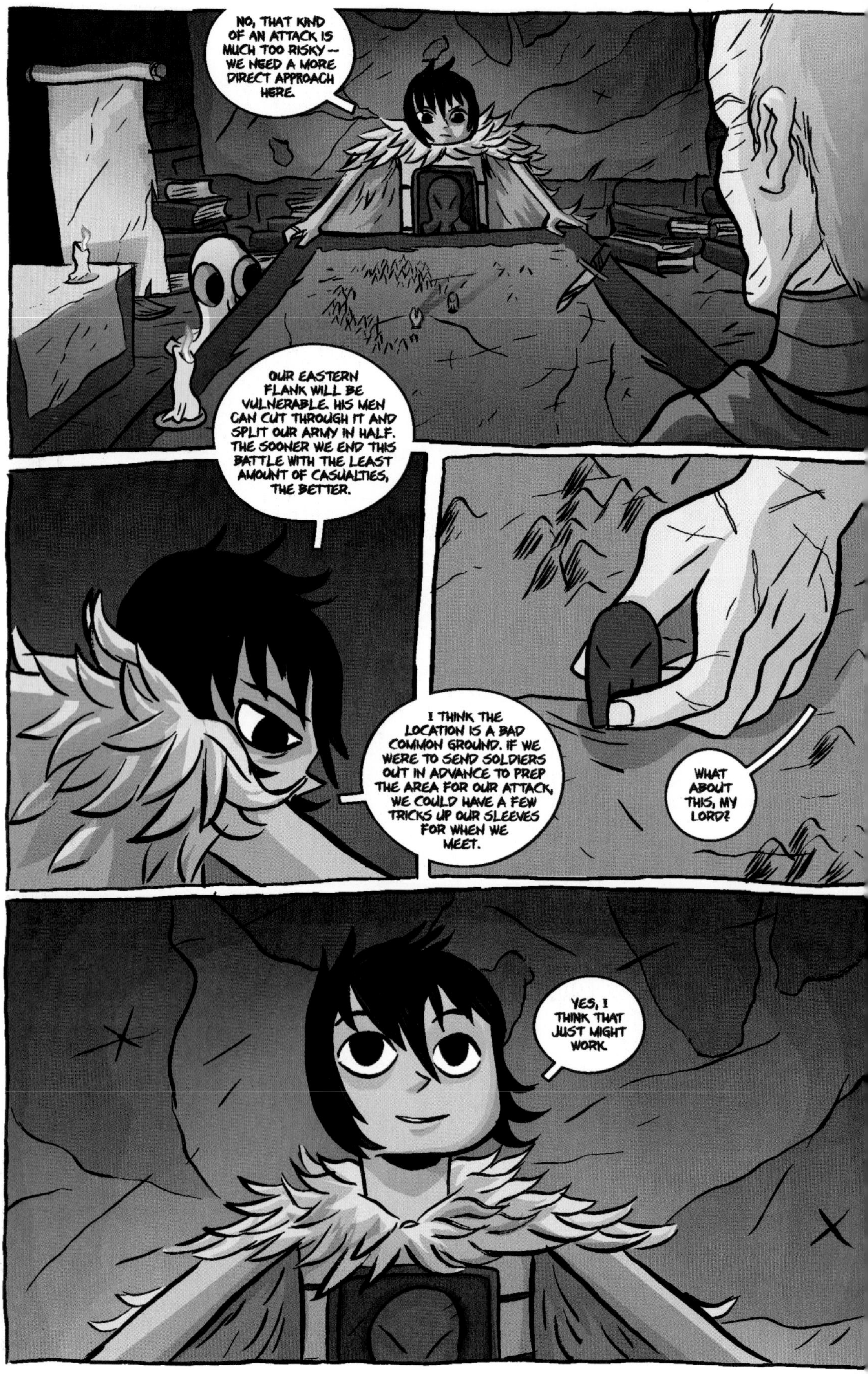
NO, THAT KIND OF AN ATTACK IS MUCH TOO RISKY -- WE NEED A MORE DIRECT APPROACH HERE.
OUR EASTERN FLANK WILL BE VULNERABLE. HIS MEN CAN CUT THROUGH IT AND SPLIT OUR ARMY IN HALF. THE SOONER WE END THIS BATTLE WITH THE LEAST AMOUNT OF CASUALTIES, THE BETTER.
I THINK THE LOCATION IS A BAD COMMON GROUND. IF WE WERE TO SEND SOLDIERS OUT IN ADVANCE TO PREP THE AREA FOR OUR ATTACK, WE COULD HAVE A FEW TRICKS UP OUR SLEEVES FOR WHEN WE MEET.
WHAT ABOUT THIS, MY LORD?
YES, I THINK THAT JUST MIGHT WORK.

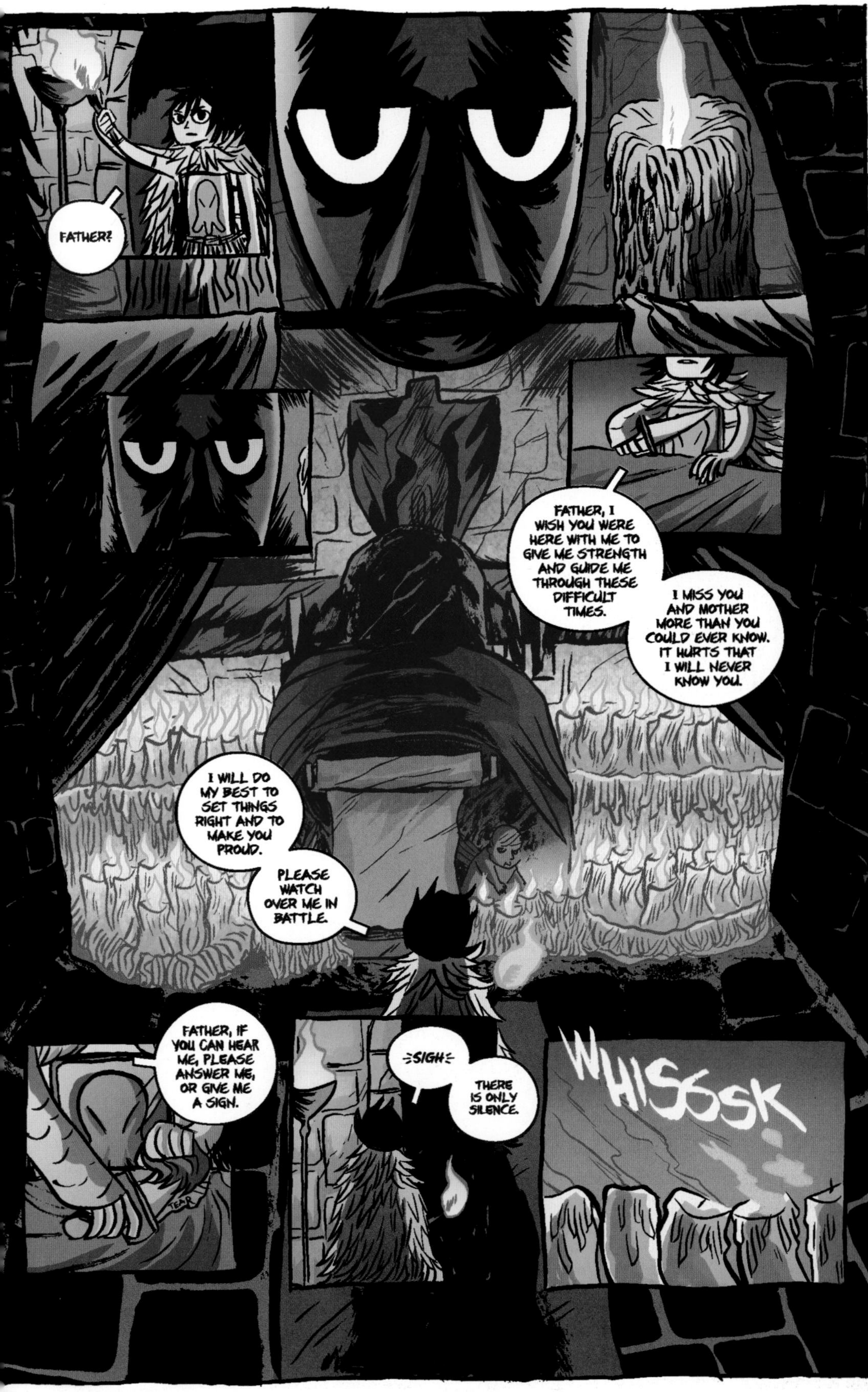
FATHER?
FATHER, I WISH YOU WERE HERE WITH ME TO GIVE ME STRENGTH AND GUIDE ME THROUGH THESE DIFFICULT TIMES.
I MISS YOU AND MOTHER MORE THAN YOU COULD EVER KNOW. IT HURTS THAT I WILL NEVER KNOW YOU.
I WILL DO MY BEST TO SET THINGS RIGHT AND TO MAKE YOU PROUD.
PLEASE WATCH OVER ME IN BATTLE.
FATHER, IF YOU CAN HEAR ME, PLEASE ANSWER ME, OR GIVE ME A SIGN.
TEAR
SIGH
THERE IS ONLY SILENCE.
WHISSSK

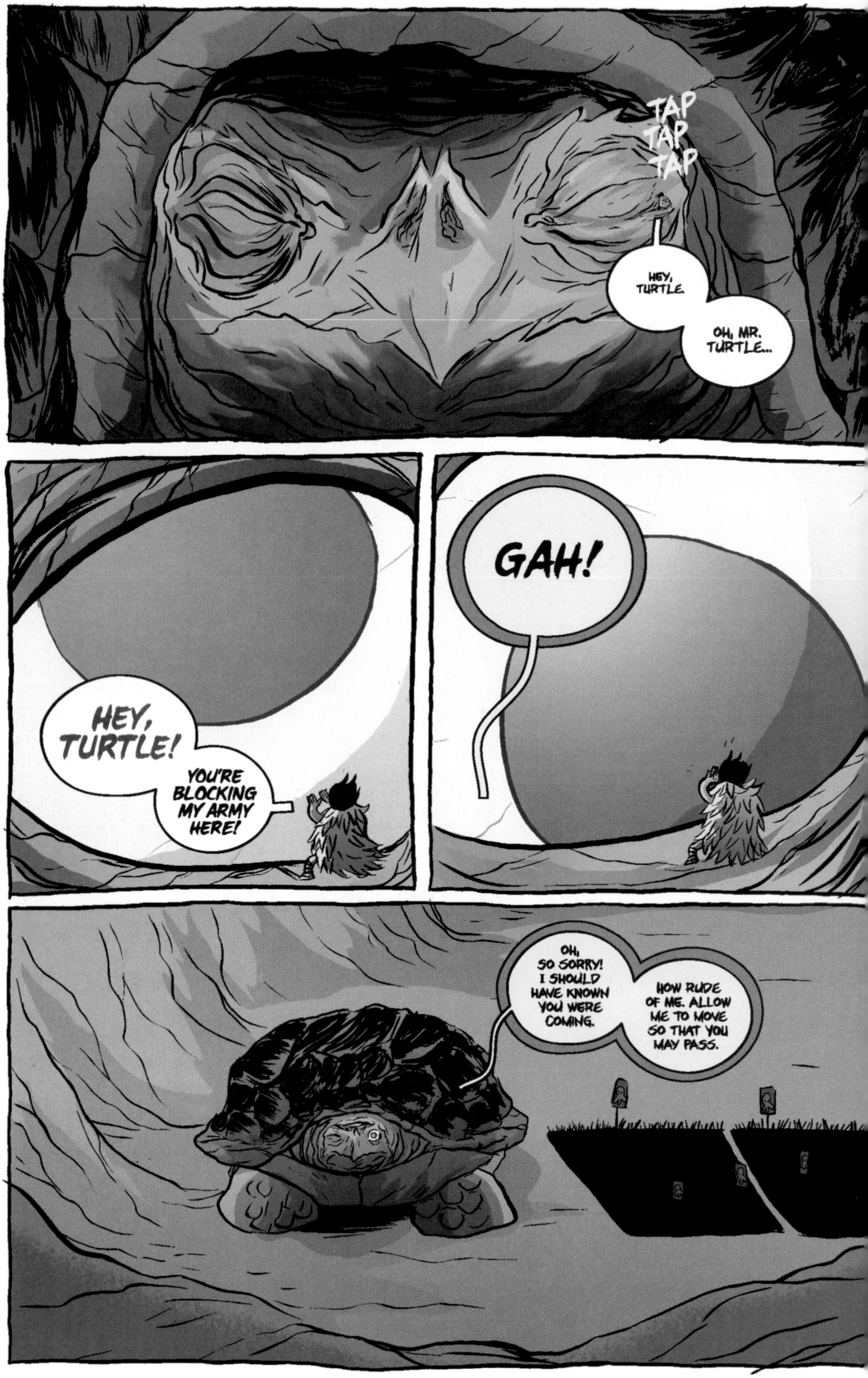
TAP
TAP
TAP
HEY, TURTLE.
OH, MR. TURTLE...
HEY, TURTLE!
YOU'RE BLOCKING MY ARMY HERE!
GAH!
OH, SO SORRY! I SHOULD HAVE KNOWN YOU WERE COMING.
HOW RUDE OF ME. ALLOW ME TO MOVE SO THAT YOU MAY PASS.

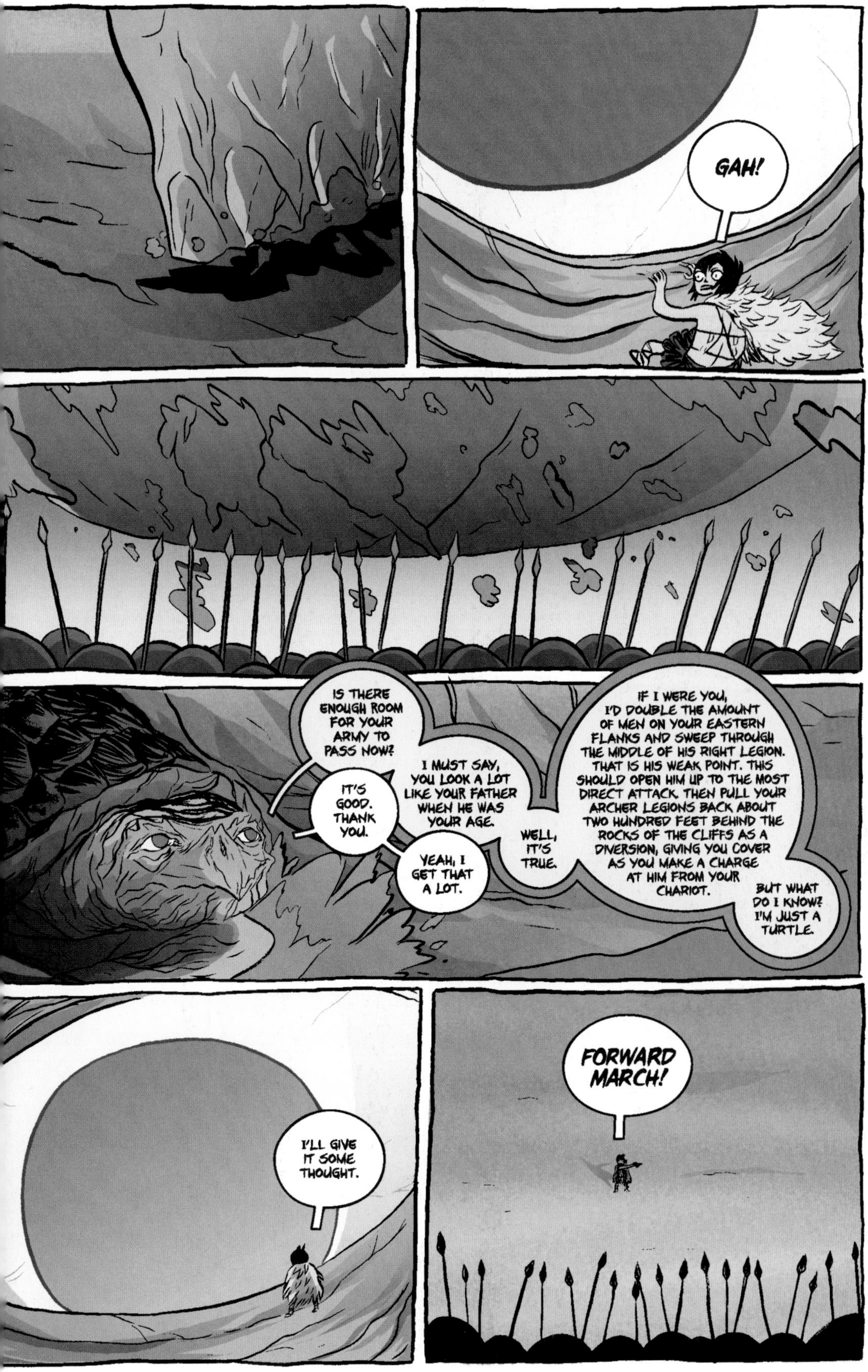
GAH!
IS THERE ENOUGH ROOM FOR YOUR ARMY TO PASS NOW?
IT'S GOOD. THANK YOU.
I MUST SAY, YOU LOOK A LOT LIKE YOUR FATHER WHEN HE WAS YOUR AGE.
YEAH, I GET THAT A LOT.
WELL, IT'S TRUE.
IF I WERE YOU, I'D DOUBLE THE AMOUNT OF MEN ON YOUR EASTERN FLANKS AND SWEEP THROUGH THE MIDDLE OF HIS RIGHT LEGION. THAT IS HIS WEAK POINT. THIS SHOULD OPEN HIM UP TO THE MOST DIRECT ATTACK. THEN PULL YOUR ARCHER LEGIONS BACK ABOUT TWO HUNDRED FEET BEHIND THE ROCKS OF THE CLIFFS AS A DIVERSION, GIVING YOU COVER AS YOU MAKE A CHARGE AT HIM FROM YOUR CHARIOT.
BUT WHAT DO I KNOW? I'M JUST A TURTLE.
I'LL GIVE IT SOME THOUGHT.
FORWARD MARCH!

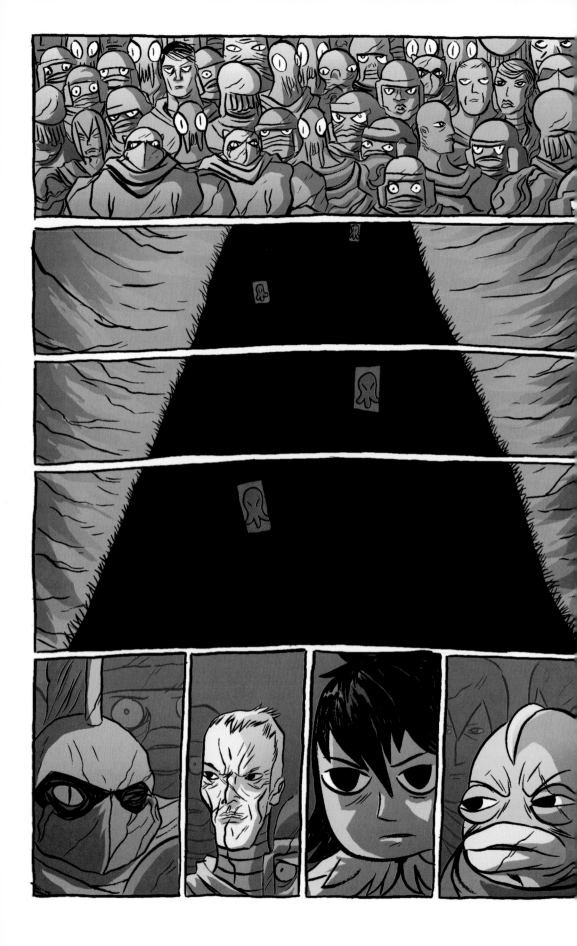

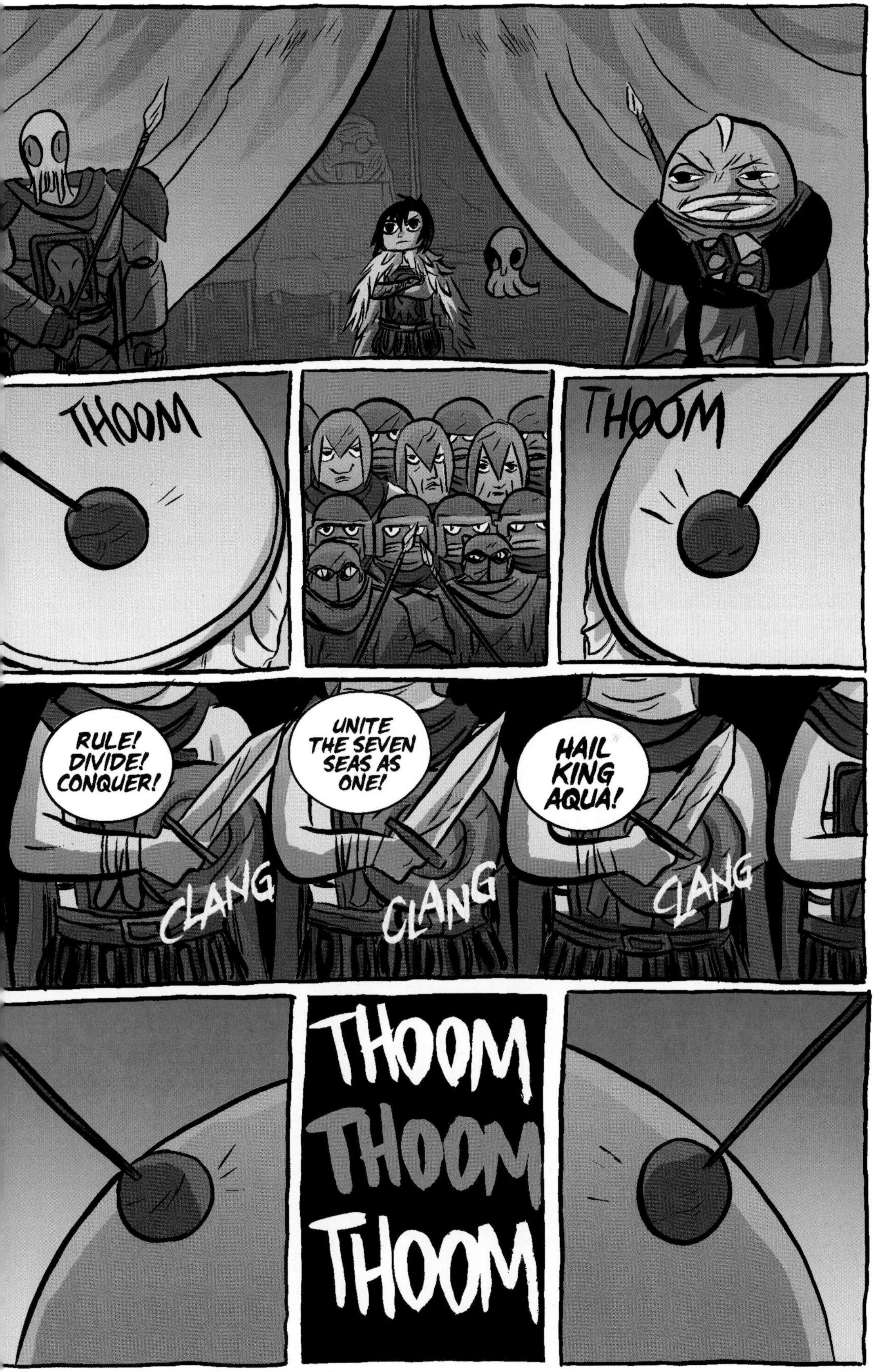
THOOM
THOOM
RULE! DIVIDE! CONQUER!
UNITE THE SEVEN SEAS AS ONE!
HAIL KING AQUA!
CLANG
CLANG
CLANG
THOOM
THOOM
THOOM

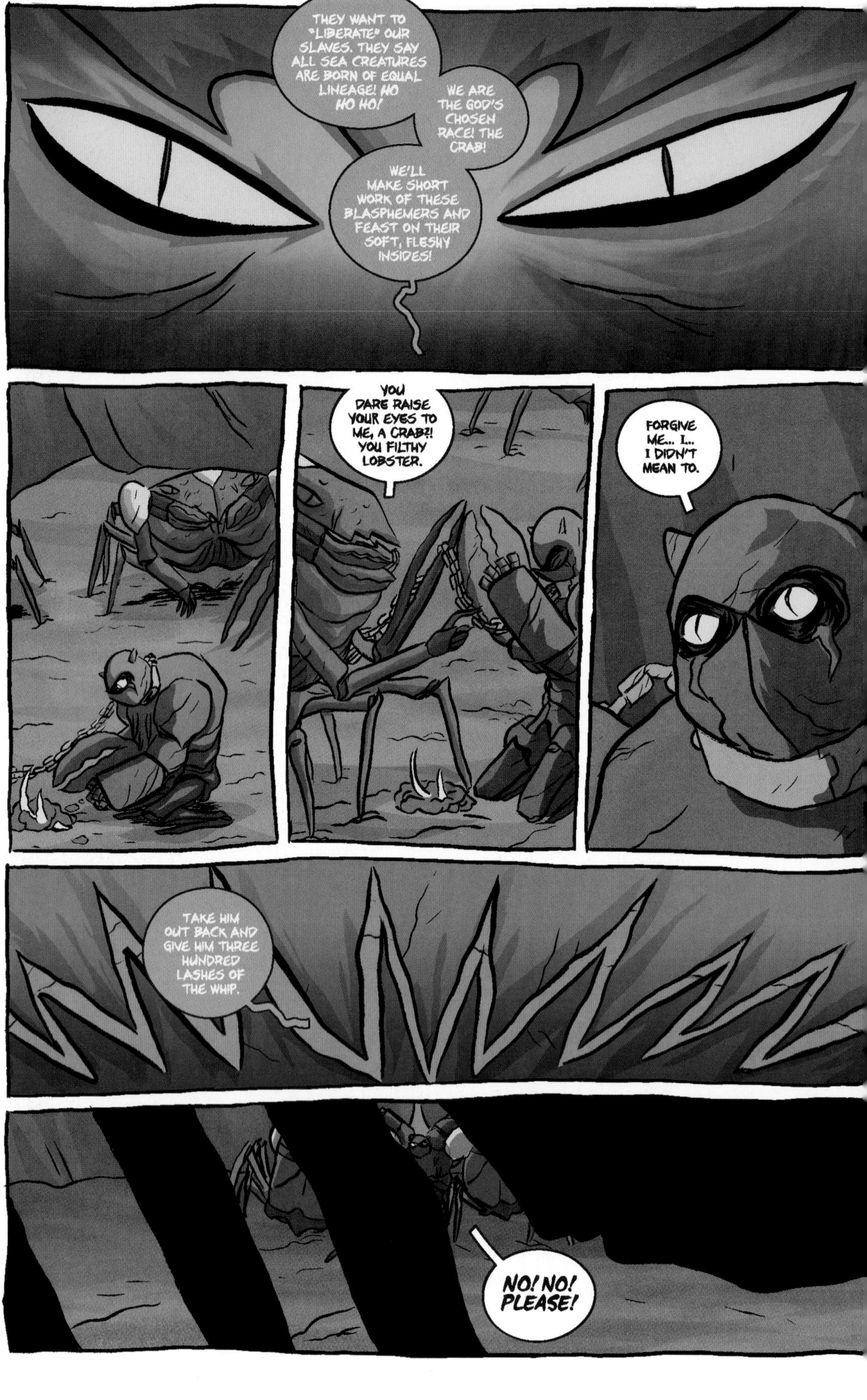
THEY WANT TO "LIBERATE" OUR SLAVES. THEY SAY ALL SEA CREATURES ARE BORN OF EQUAL LINEAGE! HO HO HO!
WE ARE THE GOD'S CHOSEN RACE! THE CRAB!
WE'LL MAKE SHORT WORK OF THESE BLASPHEMERS AND FEAST ON THEIR SOFT, FLESHY INSIDES!
YOU DARE RAISE YOUR EYES TO ME, A CRABZ?! YOU FILTHY LOBSTER.
FORGIVE ME... I... I DIDN'T MEAN TO.
TAKE HIM OUT BACK AND GIVE HIM THREE HUNDRED LASHES OF THE WHIP.
NO! NO! PLEASE!

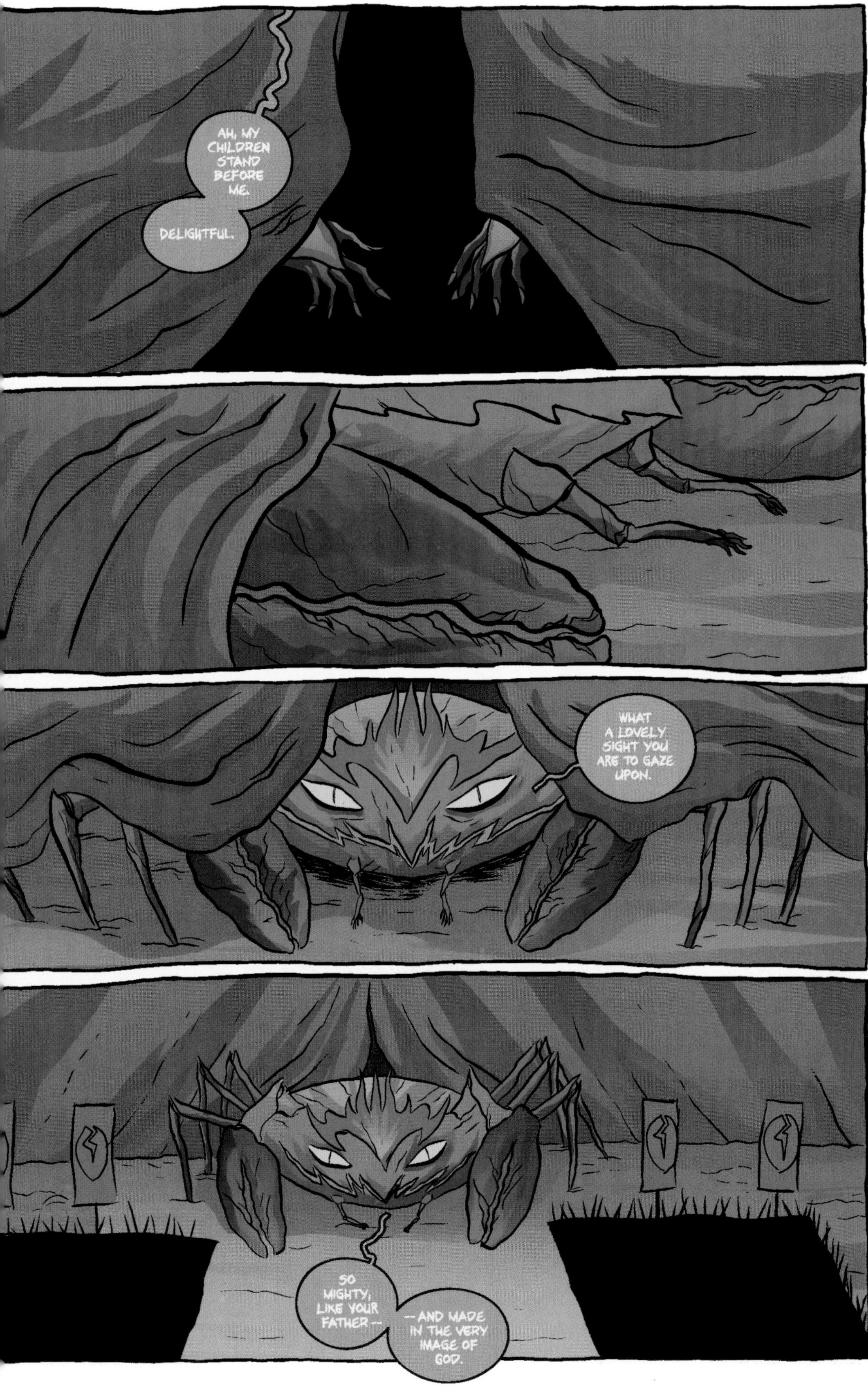
AH, MY CHILDREN STAND BEFORE ME.
DELIGHTFUL.
WHAT A LOVELY SIGHT YOU ARE TO GAZE UPON.
SO MIGHTY, LIKE YOUR FATHER--
--AND MADE IN THE VERY IMAGE OF GOD.

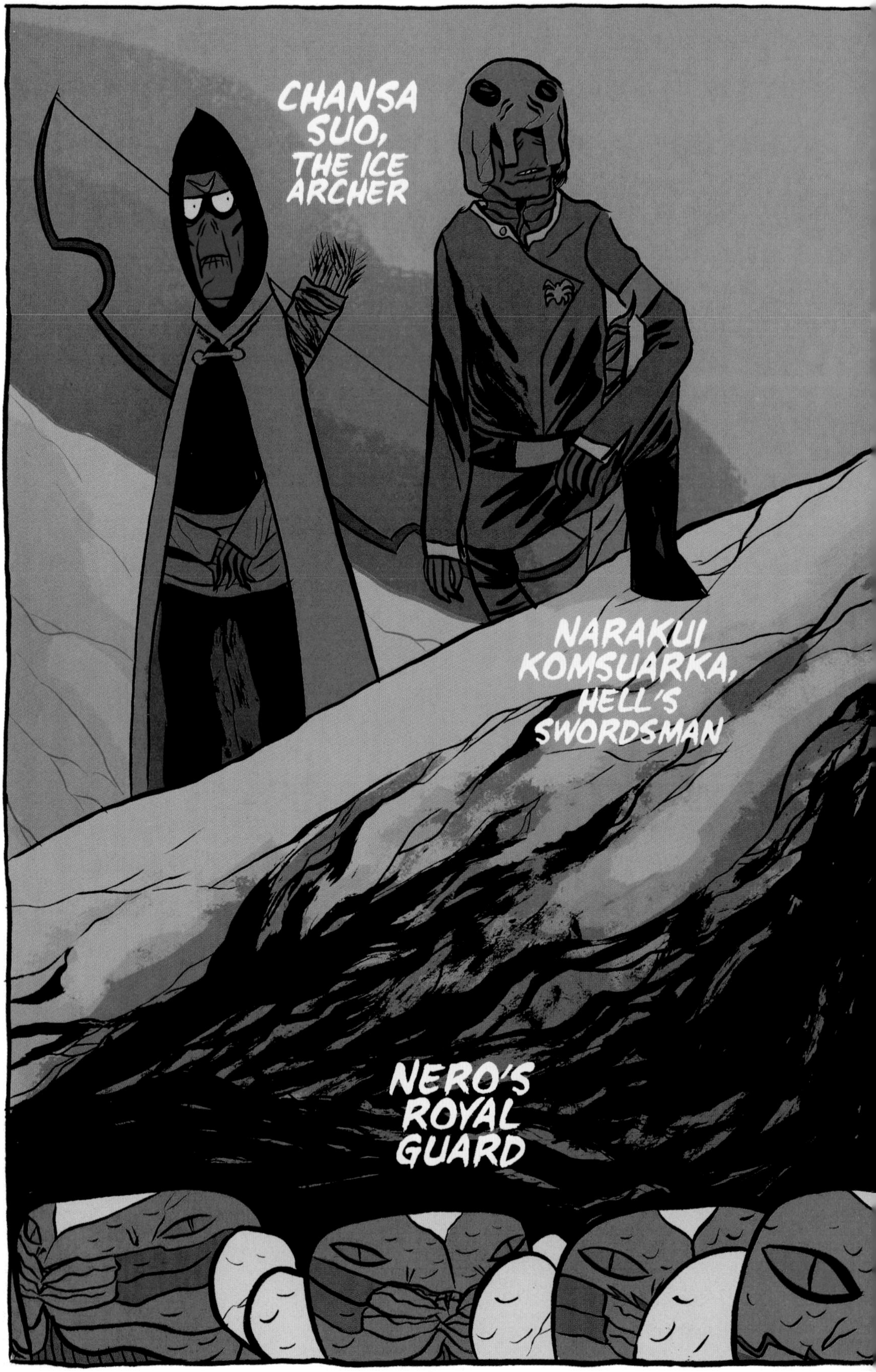
CHANSA SUO, THE ICE ARCHER
NARAKUI KOMSUARKA, HELL'S SWORDSMAN
NERO'S ROYAL GUARD

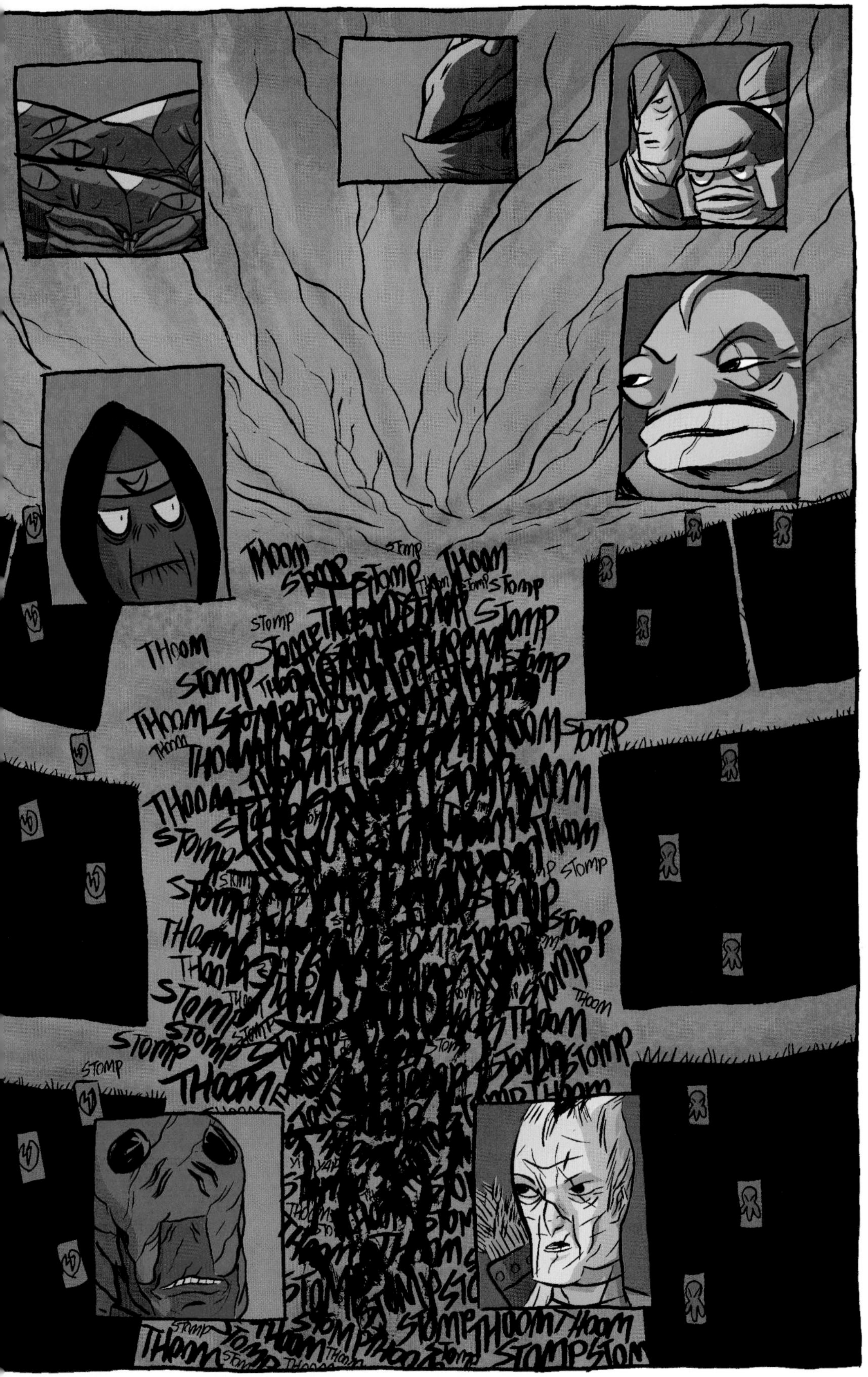
THOOM
STOMP
THOOM
STOMP
STOMP
THOOM
STOMP
THOOM
STOMP
THOOM
STOMP
THOOM
STOMP
STOMP
THOOM
THOOM
STOMP
STOMP
THOOM
STOMP
THOOM
STOMP
THOOM
STOMP

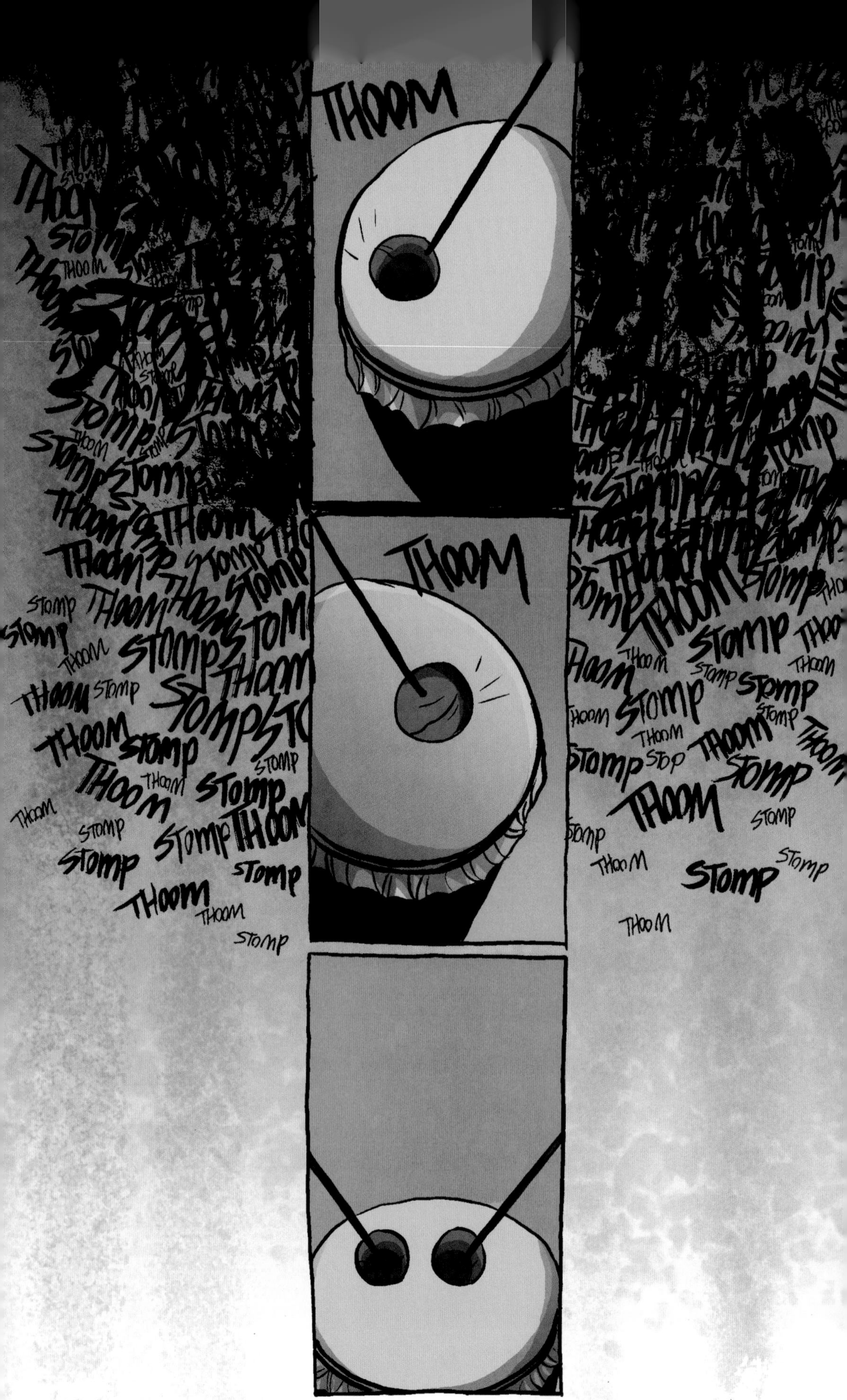
THOOM
THOOM
STOMP
THOOM
STOMP
THOOM

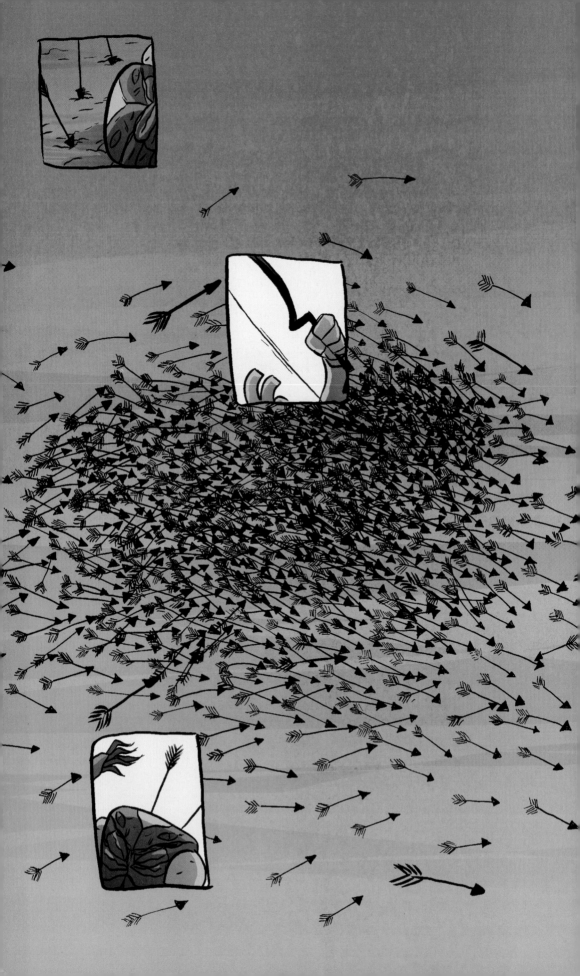

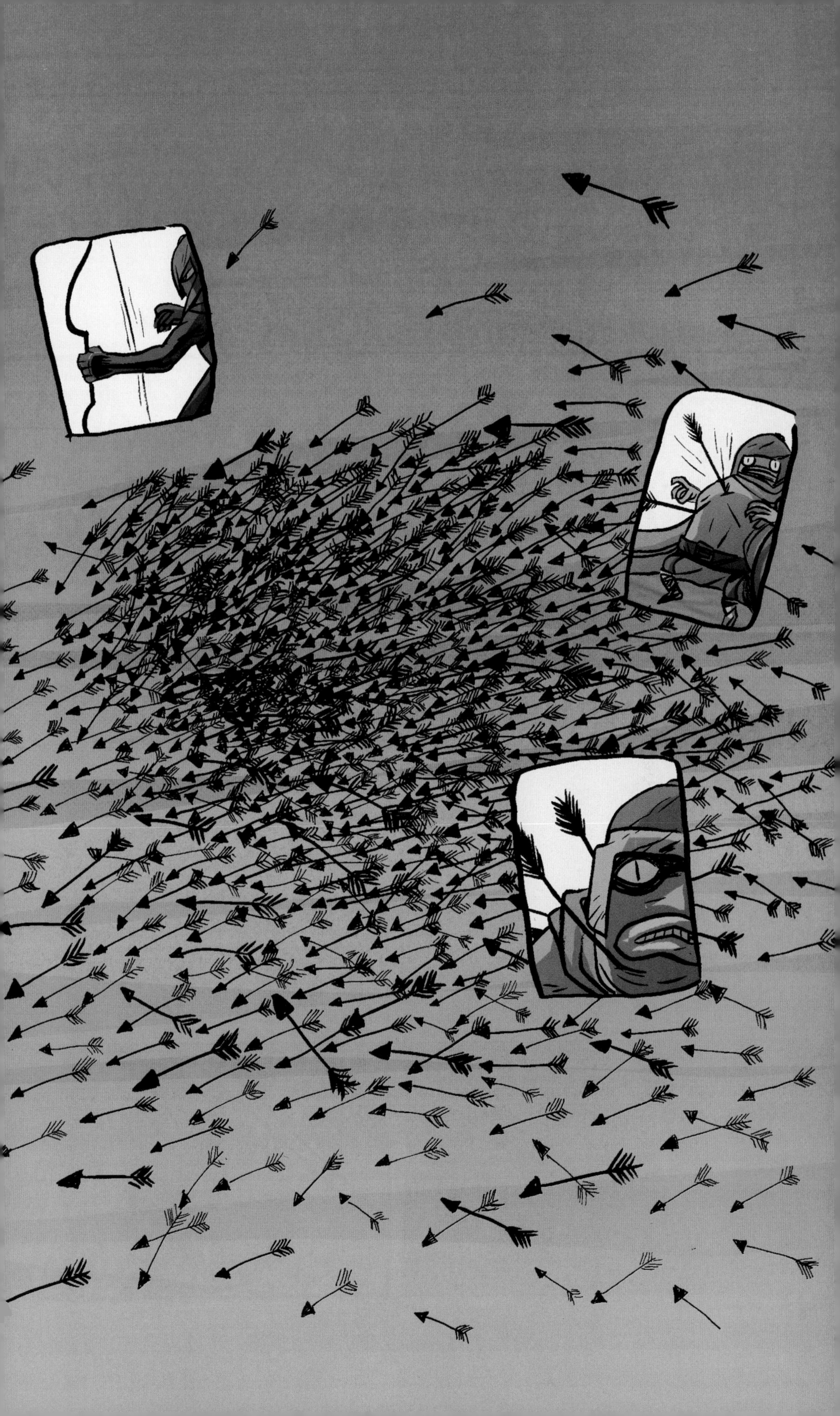

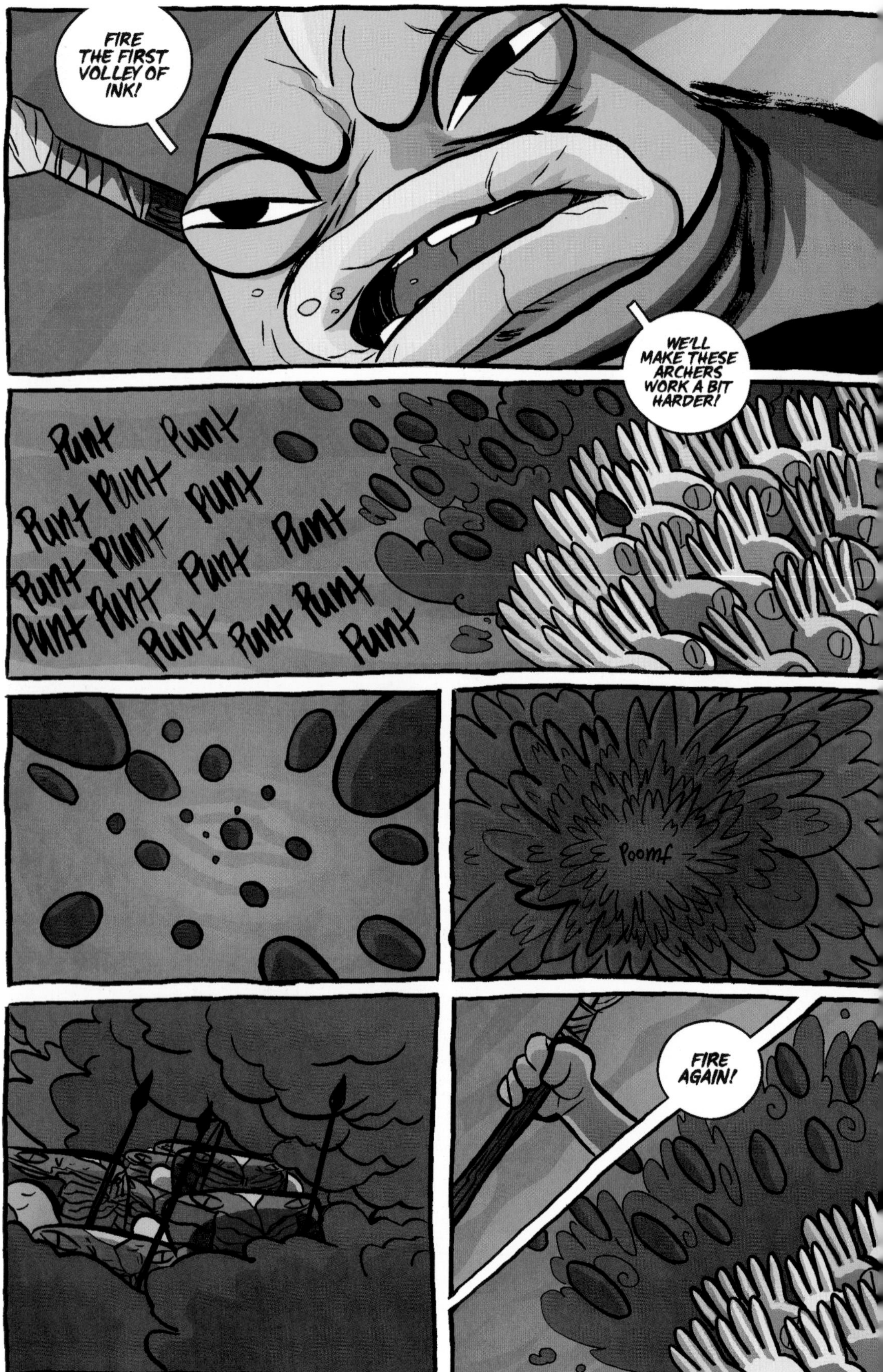
FIRE THE FIRST VOLLEY OF INK!
WE'LL MAKE THESE ARCHERS WORK A BIT HARDER!
Punt Punt Punt Punt Punt Punt Punt Punt Punt Punt Punt Punt Punt Punt Punt Punt Punt Punt
Poomf
FIRE AGAIN!

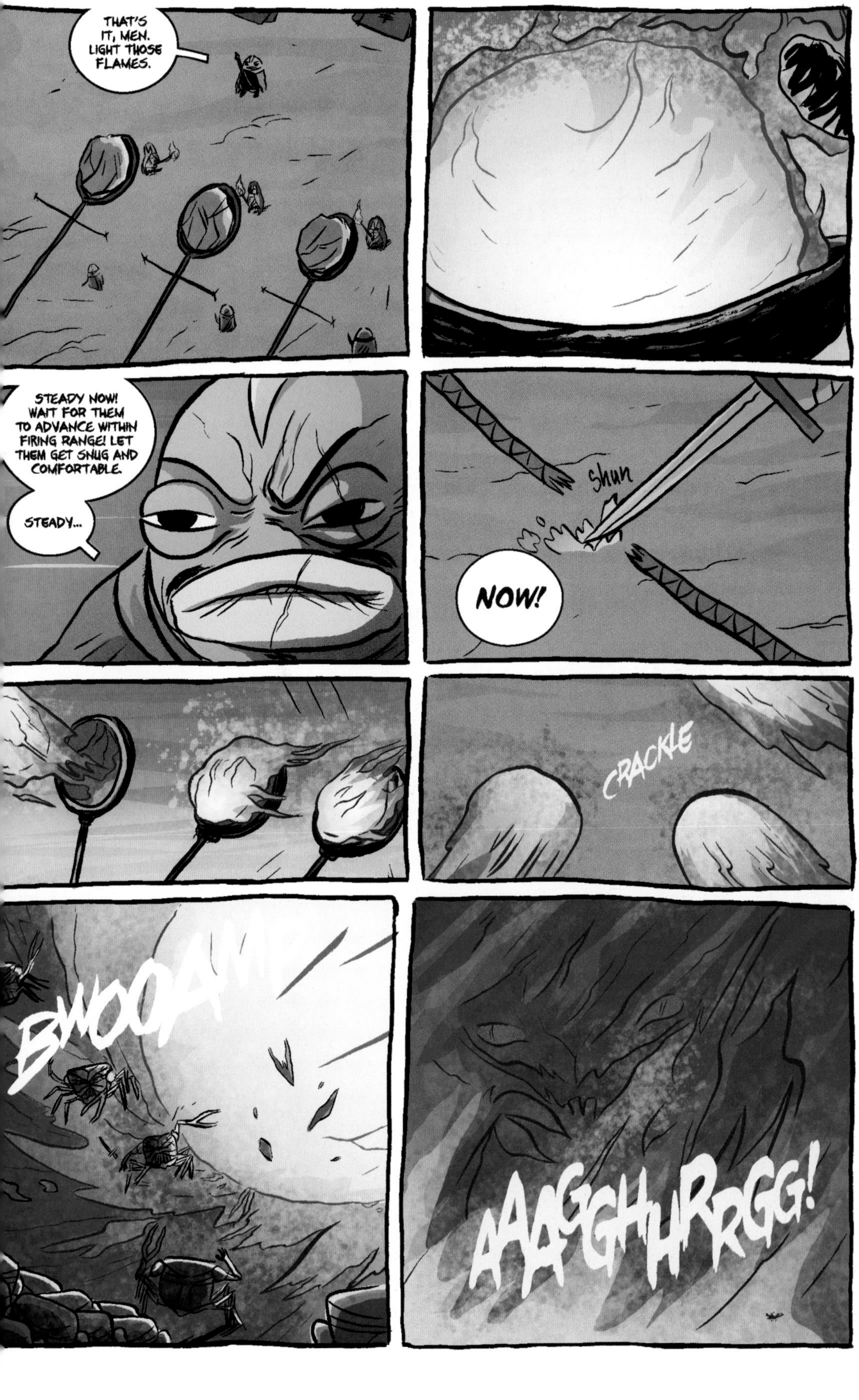
THAT'S IT, MEN. LIGHT THOSE FLAMES.
STEADY NOW! WAIT FOR THEM TO ADVANCE WITHIN FIRING RANGE! LET THEM GET SNUG AND COMFORTABLE.
STEADY...
Shun
NOW!
CRACKLE
AAAGHURRGG!

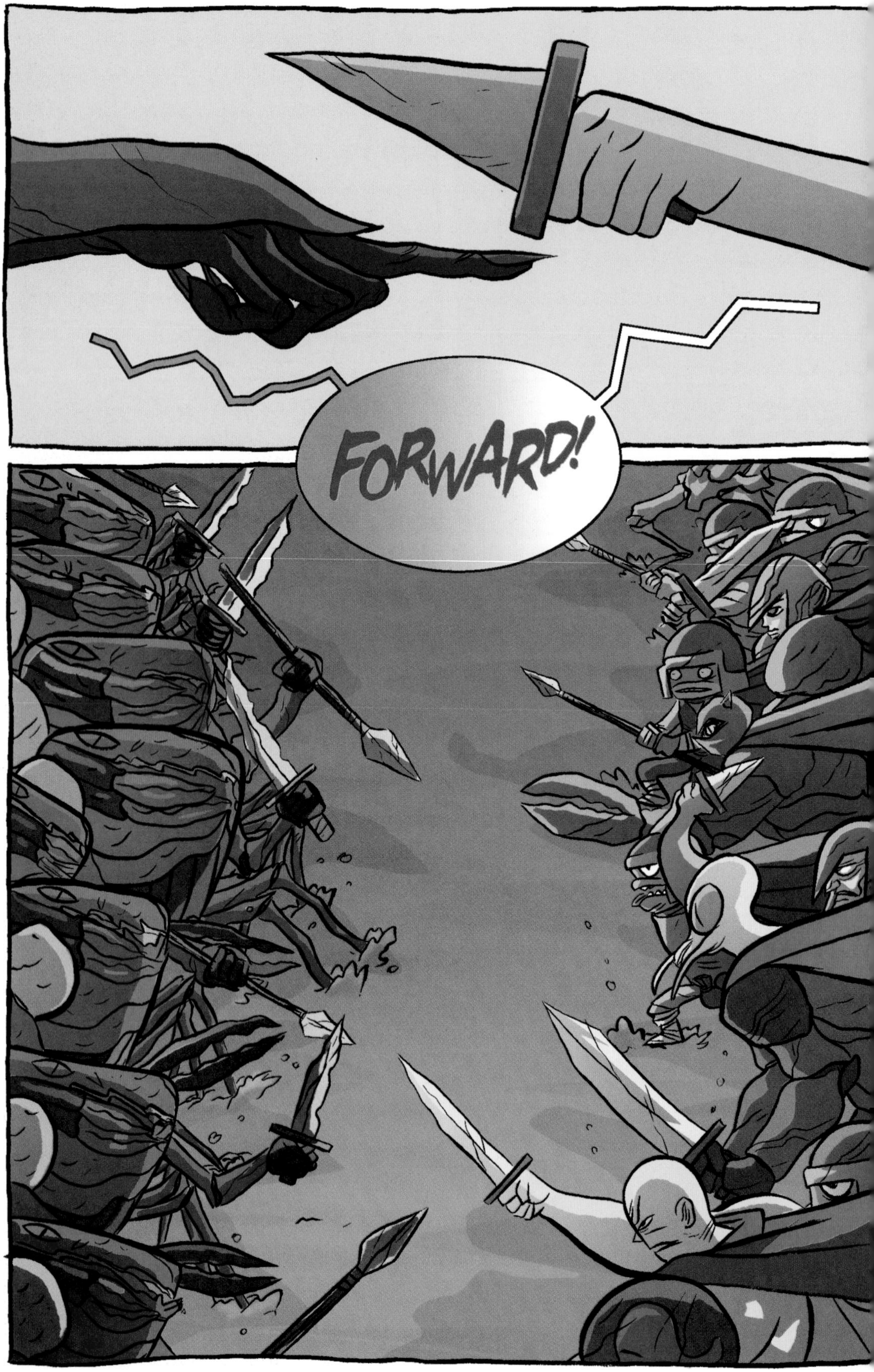
FORWARD!

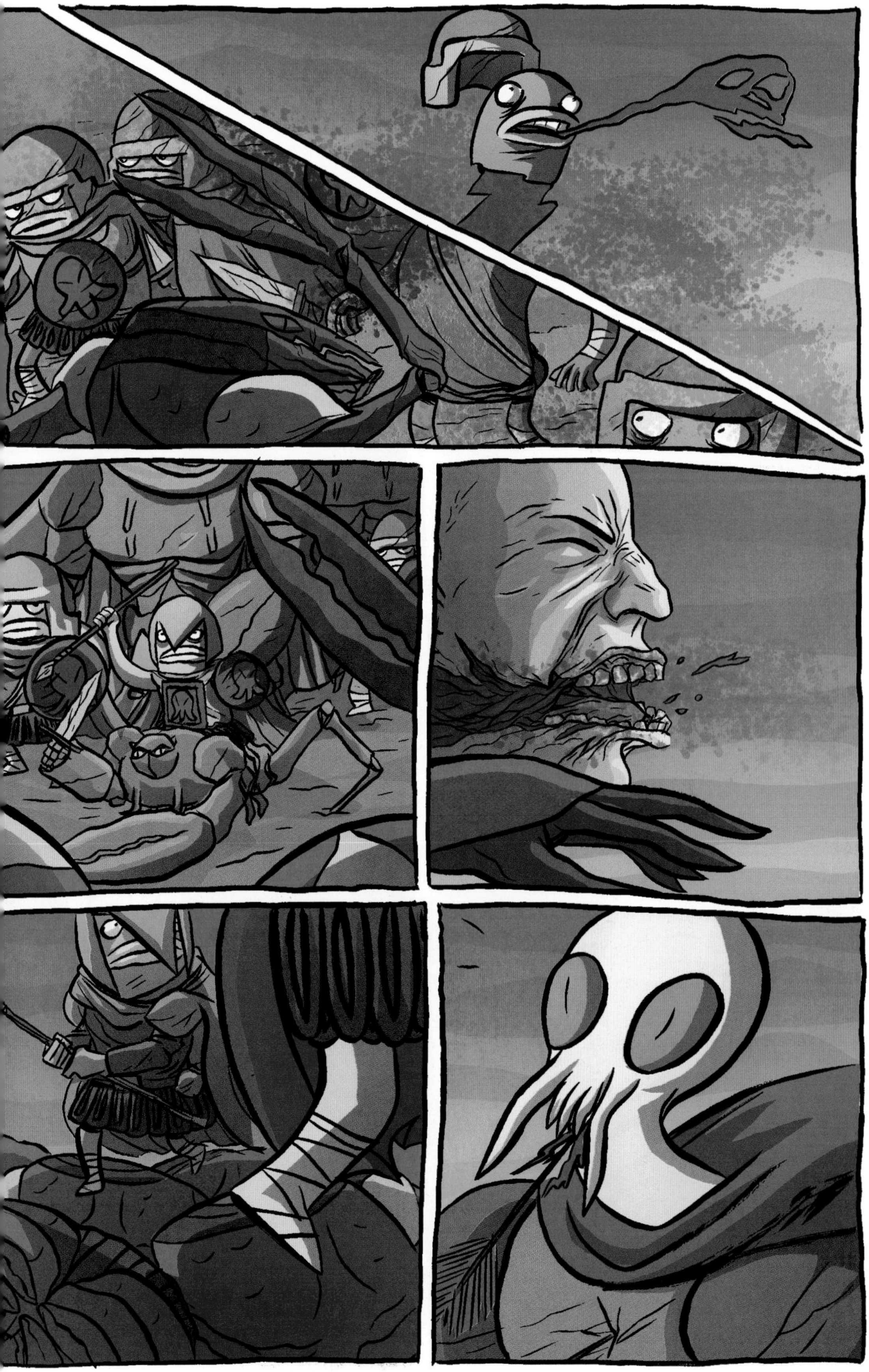

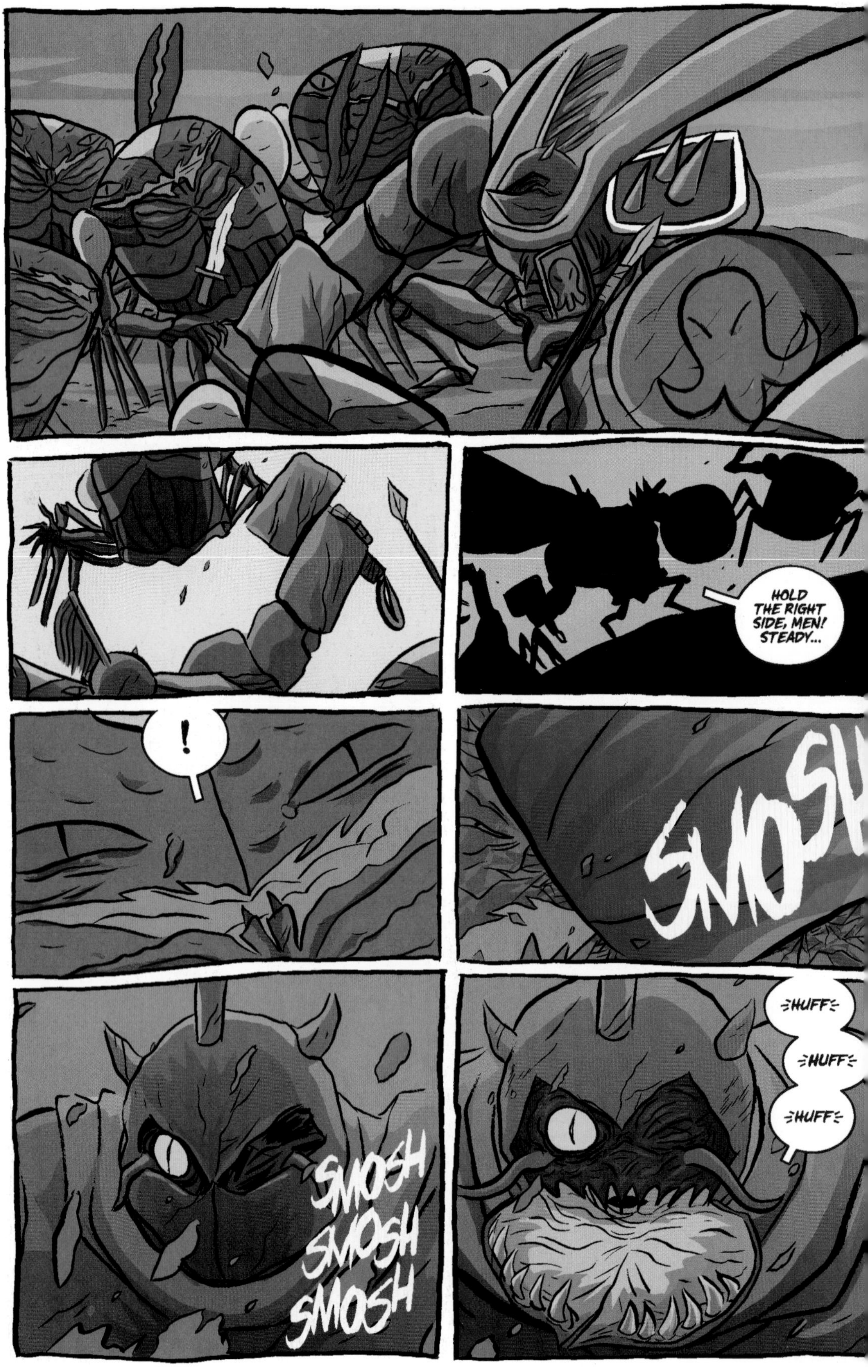
HOLD THE RIGHT SIDE, MEN! STEADY...
!
SMOSH
SMOSH
SMOSH
SMOSH
HUFF
HUFF
HUFF

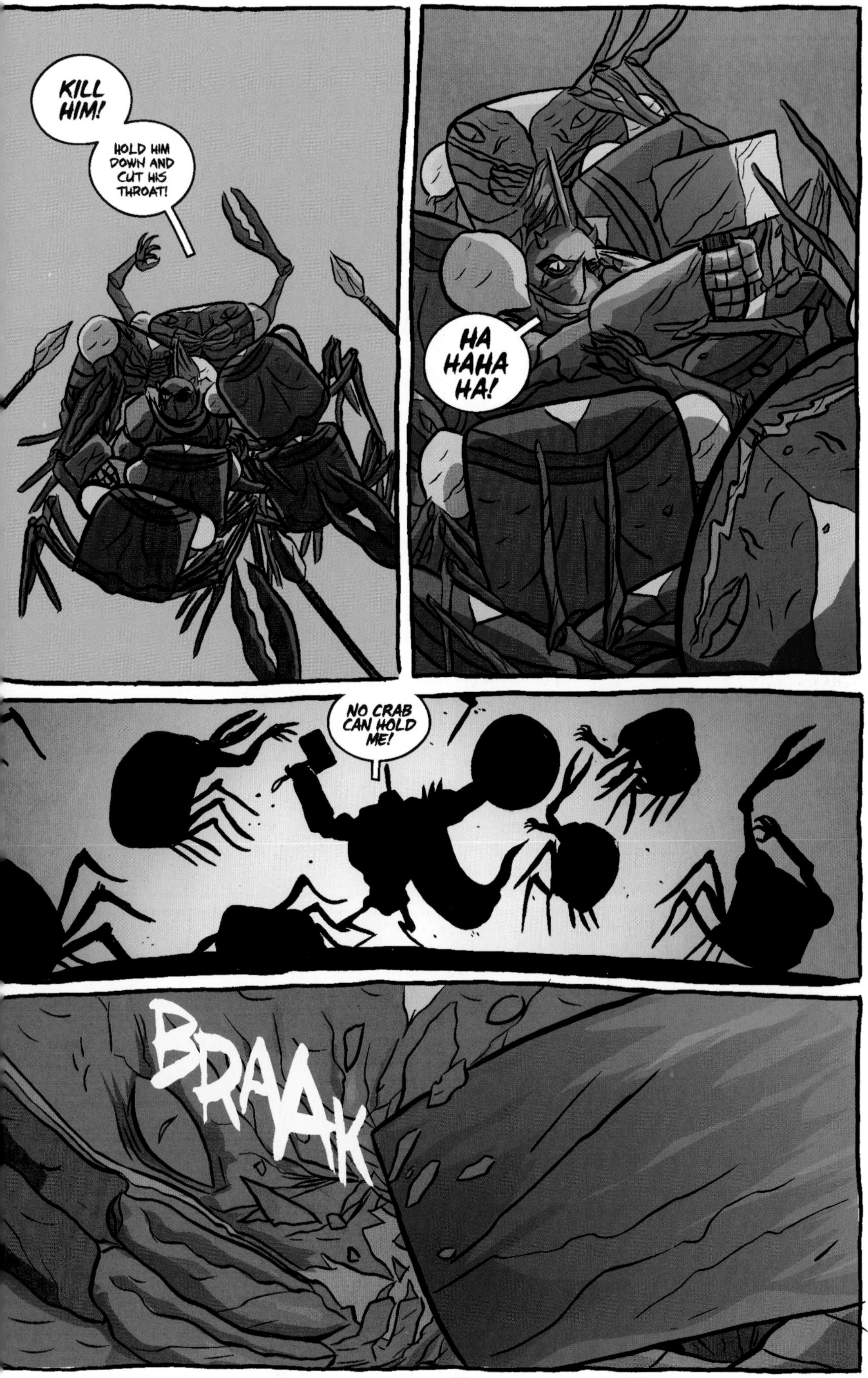
KILL HIM!
HOLD HIM DOWN AND CUT HIS THROAT!
HA HAHA HA!
NO CRAB CAN HOLD ME!
BRAAAK

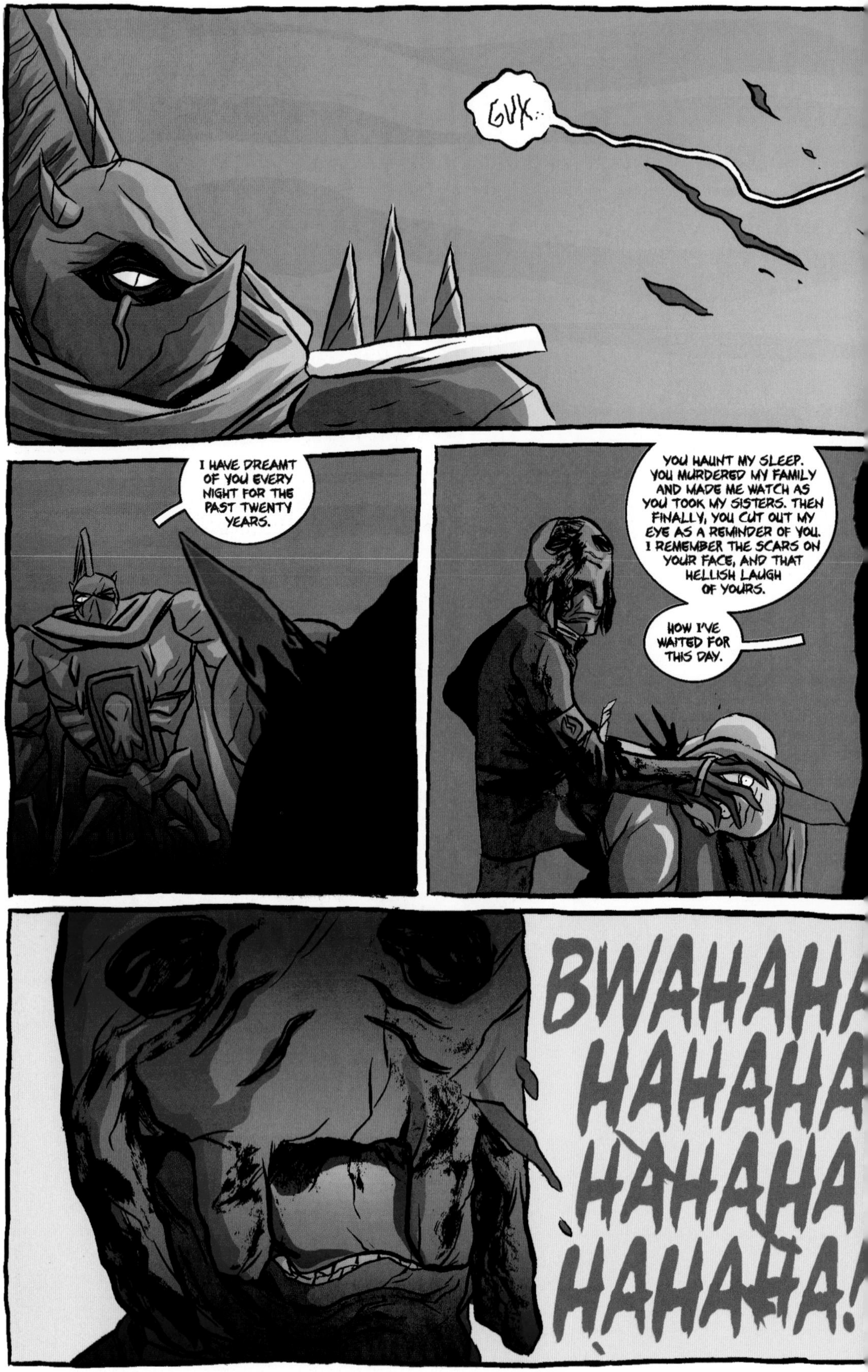
GUK..
I HAVE DREAMT OF YOU EVERY NIGHT FOR THE PAST TWENTY YEARS.
YOU HAUNT MY SLEEP. YOU MURDERED MY FAMILY AND MADE ME WATCH AS YOU TOOK MY SISTERS. THEN FINALLY, YOU CUT OUT MY EYE AS A REMINDER OF YOU. I REMEMBER THE SCARS ON YOUR FACE, AND THAT HELLISH LAUGH OF YOURS.
HOW I'VE WAITED FOR THIS DAY.
BWAHAHA HAHAHA HAHAHA HAHAHA!

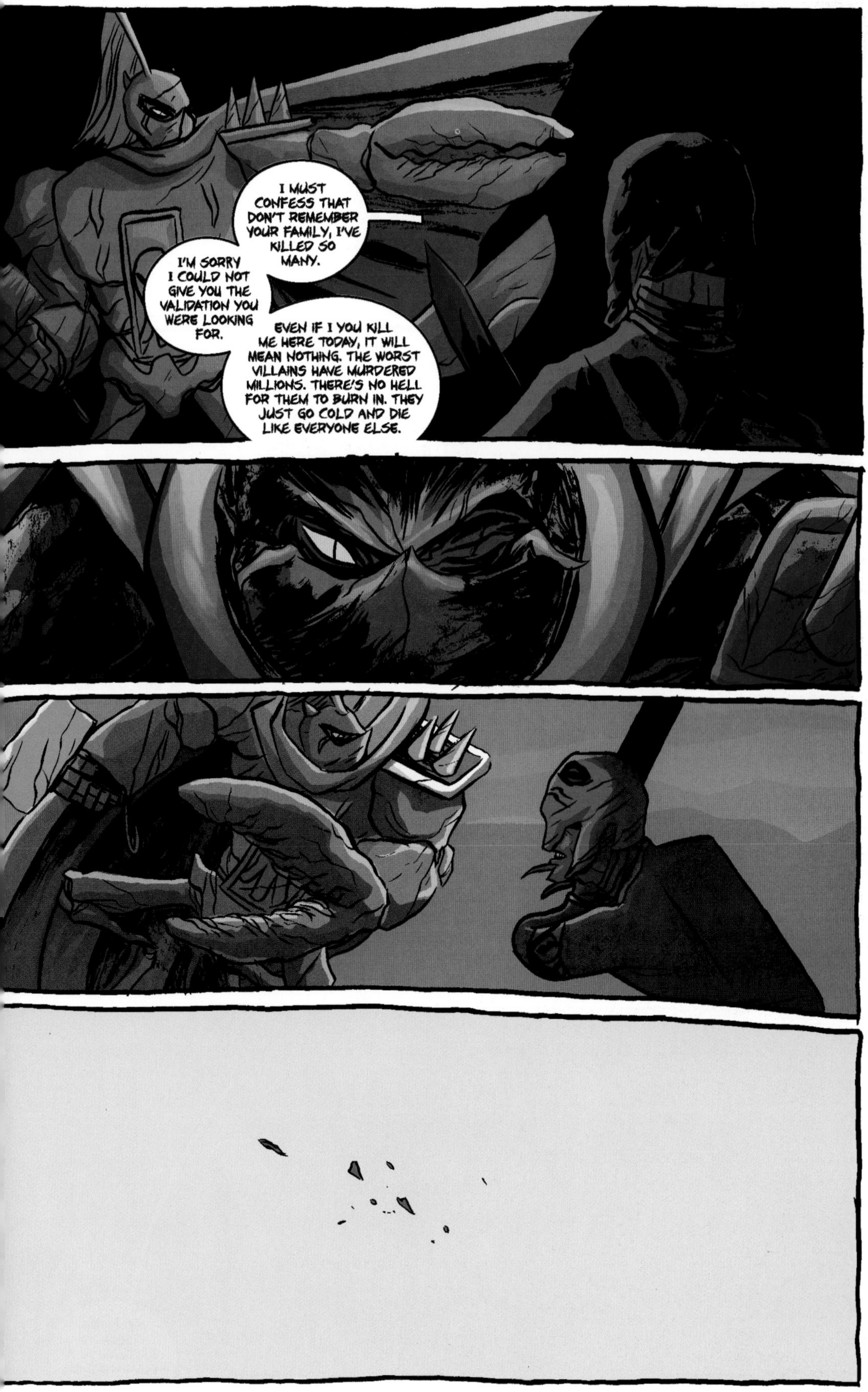
I MUST CONFESS THAT DON'T REMEMBER YOUR FAMILY, I'VE KILLED SO MANY.
I'M SORRY I COULD NOT GIVE YOU THE VALIDATION YOU WERE LOOKING FOR.
EVEN IF I YOU KILL ME HERE TODAY, IT WILL MEAN NOTHING. THE WORST VILLAINS HAVE MURDERED MILLIONS. THERE'S NO HELL FOR THEM TO BURN IN. THEY JUST GO COLD AND DIE LIKE EVERYONE ELSE.

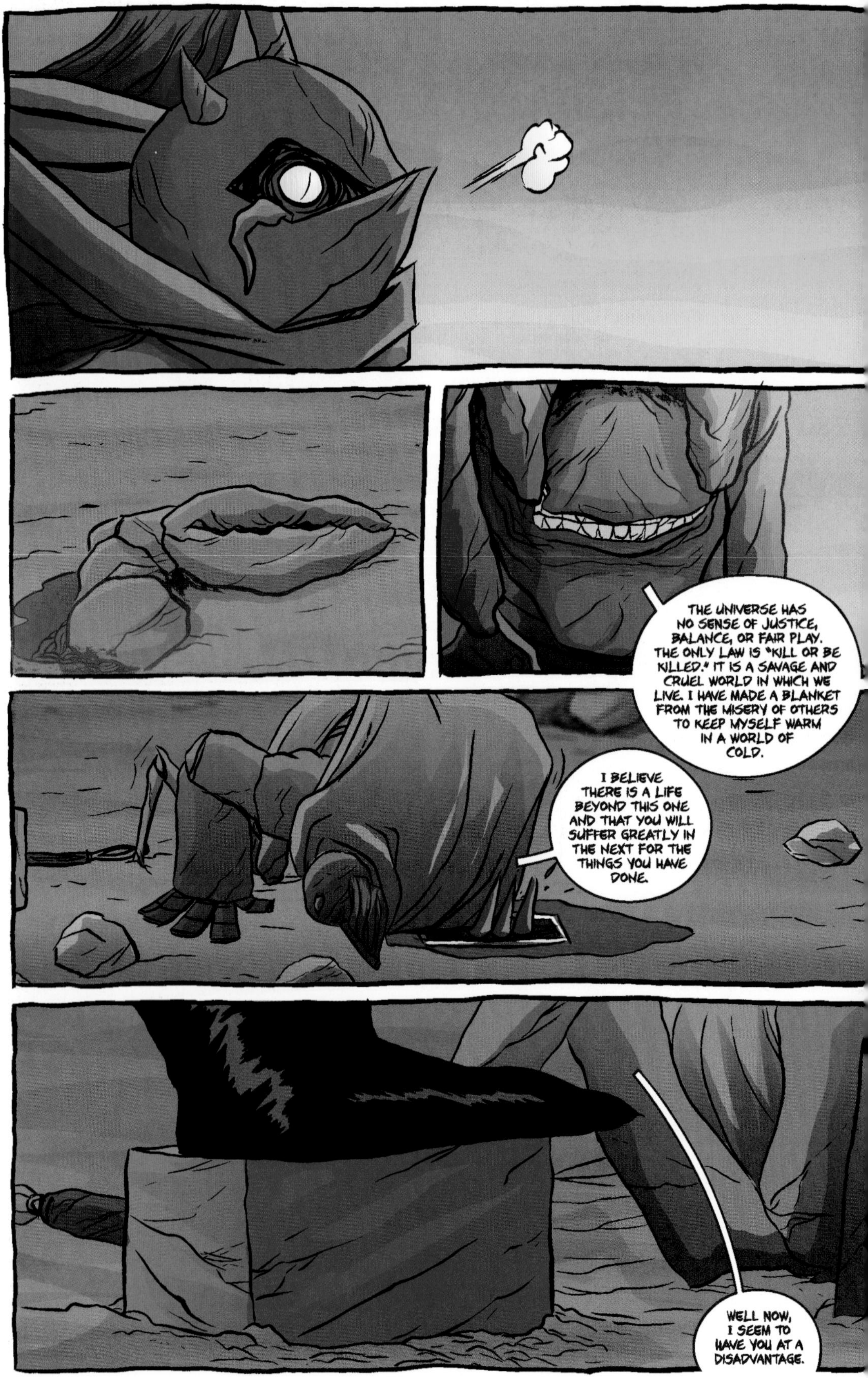
THE UNIVERSE HAS NO SENSE OF JUSTICE, BALANCE, OR FAIR PLAY. THE ONLY LAW IS "KILL OR BE KILLED." IT IS A SAVAGE AND CRUEL WORLD IN WHICH WE LIVE. I HAVE MADE A BLANKET FROM THE MISERY OF OTHERS TO KEEP MYSELF WARM IN A WORLD OF COLD.
I BELIEVE THERE IS A LIFE BEYOND THIS ONE AND THAT YOU WILL SUFFER GREATLY IN THE NEXT FOR THE THINGS YOU HAVE DONE.
WELL NOW, I SEEM TO HAVE YOU AT A DISADVANTAGE.

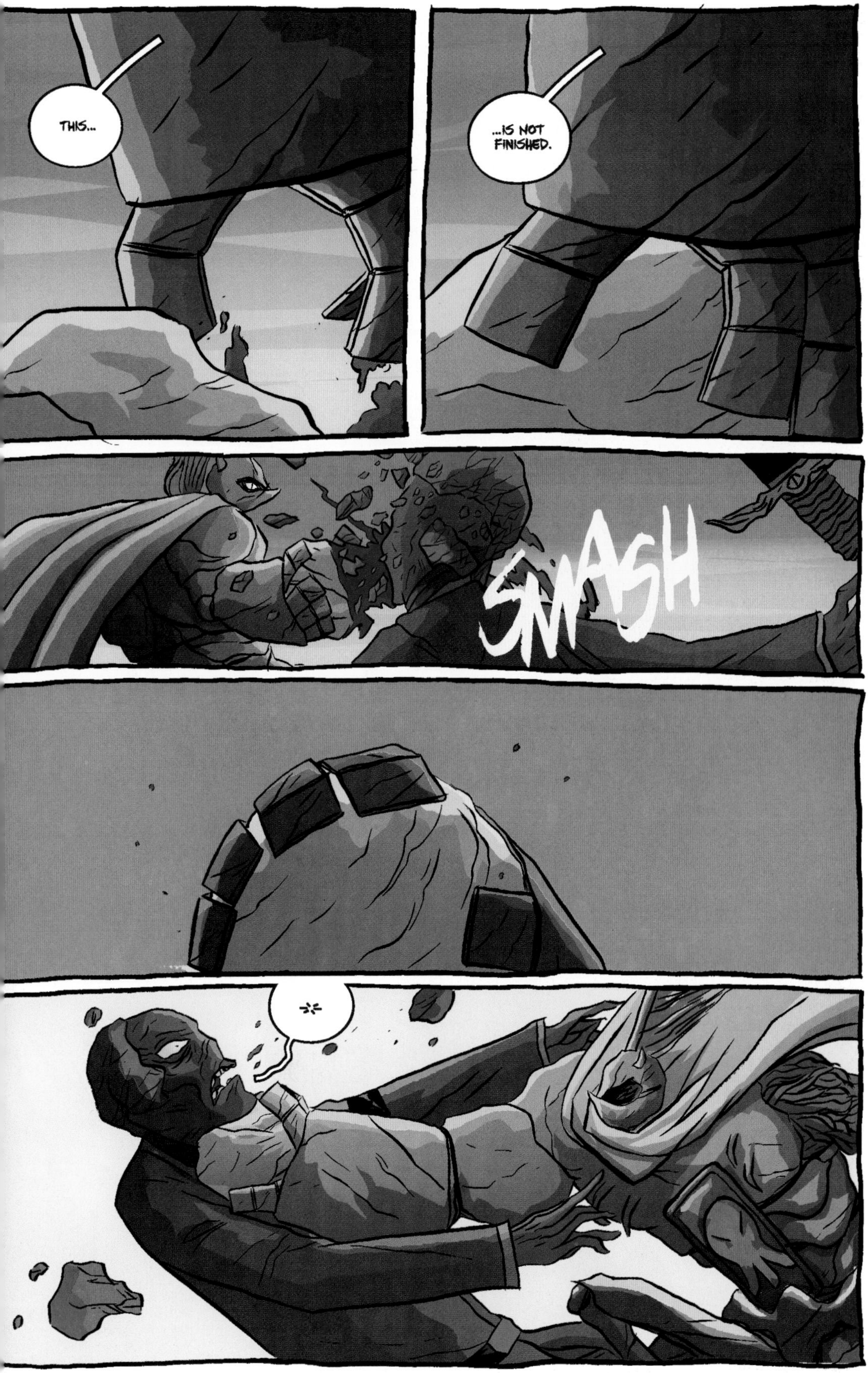
THIS...
...IS NOT FINISHED.
SMASH

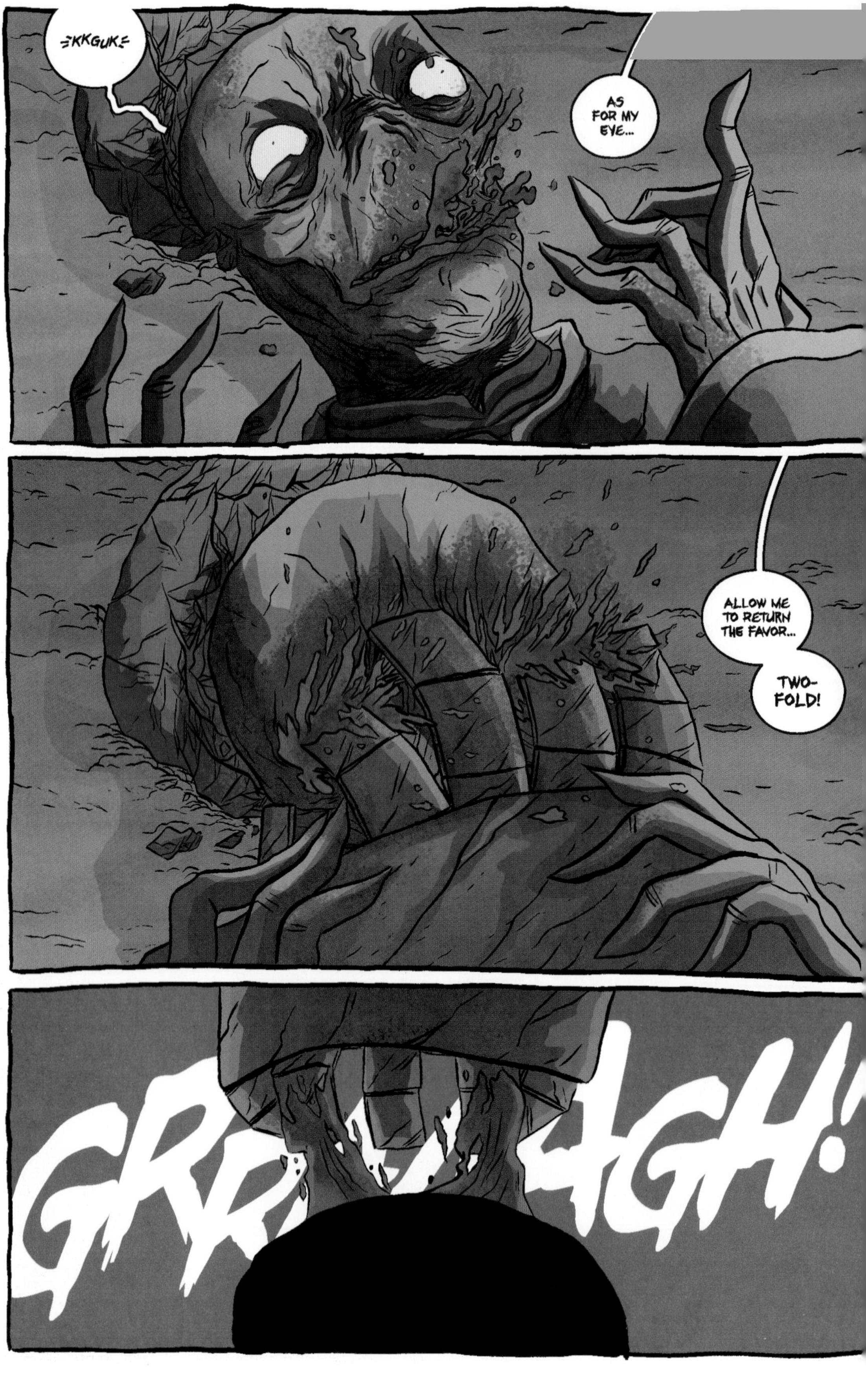
=KKGUK=
AS FOR MY EYE...
ALLOW ME TO RETURN THE FAVOR...
TWO-FOLD!
GRR...AGH!

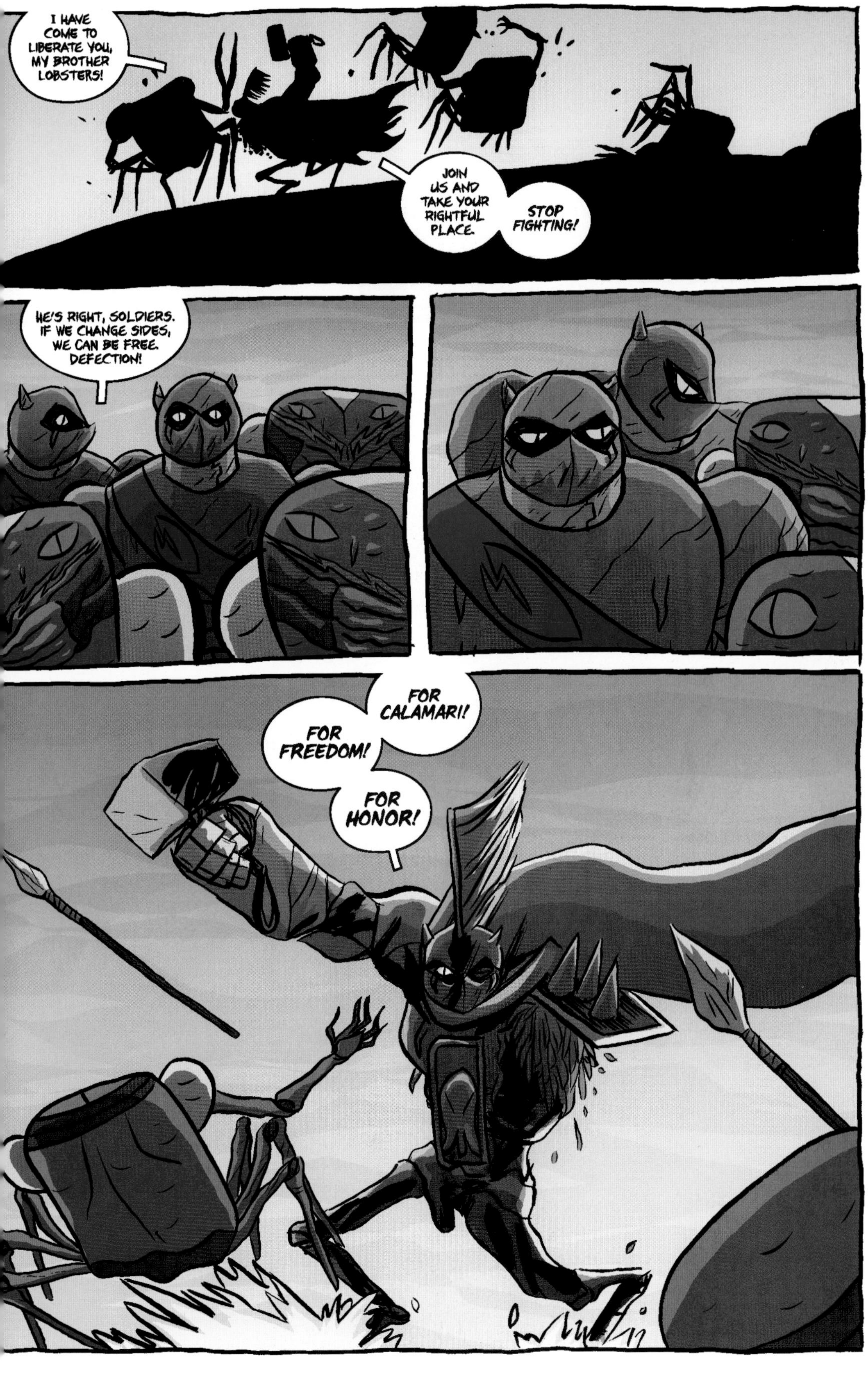
I HAVE COME TO LIBERATE YOU, MY BROTHER LOBSTERS!
JOIN US AND TAKE YOUR RIGHTFUL PLACE.
STOP FIGHTING!
HE'S RIGHT, SOLDIERS. IF WE CHANGE SIDES, WE CAN BE FREE. DEFECTION!
FOR CALAMARI!
FOR FREEDOM!
FOR HONOR!

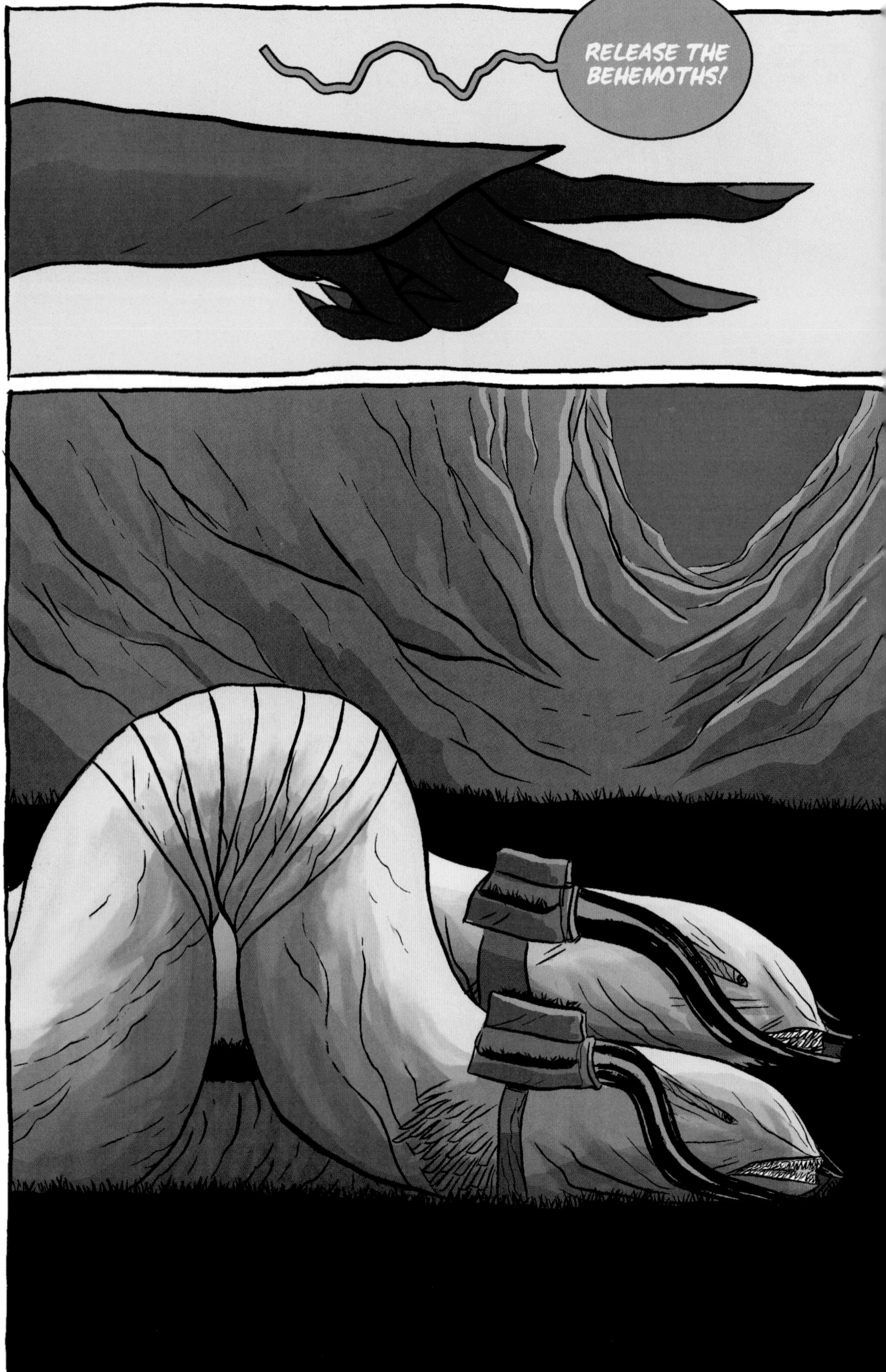
RELEASE THE BEHEMOTHS!

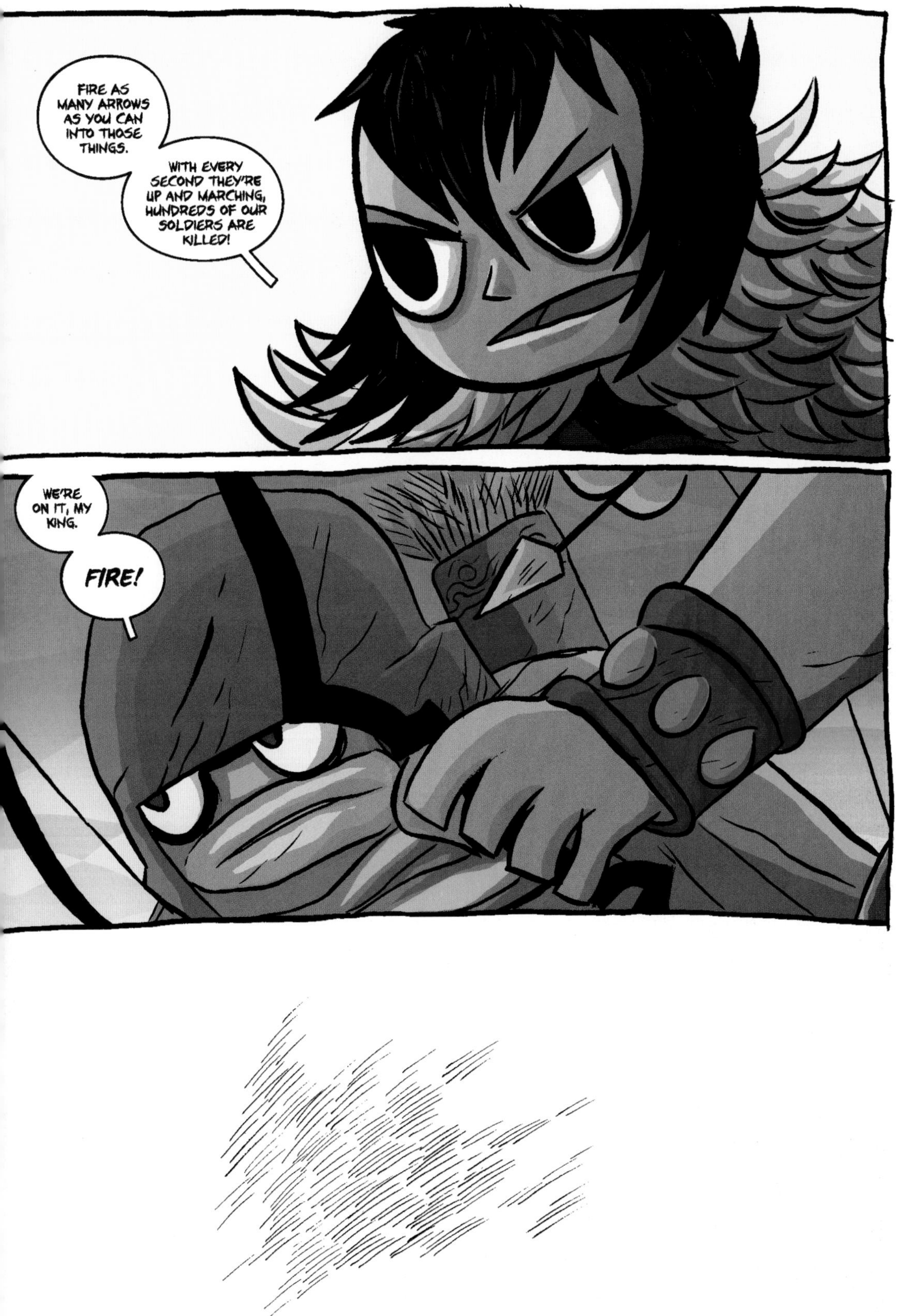
FIRE AS MANY ARROWS AS YOU CAN INTO THOSE THINGS.
WITH EVERY SECOND THEY'RE UP AND MARCHING, HUNDREDS OF OUR SOLDIERS ARE KILLED!
WE'RE ON IT, MY KING.
FIRE!

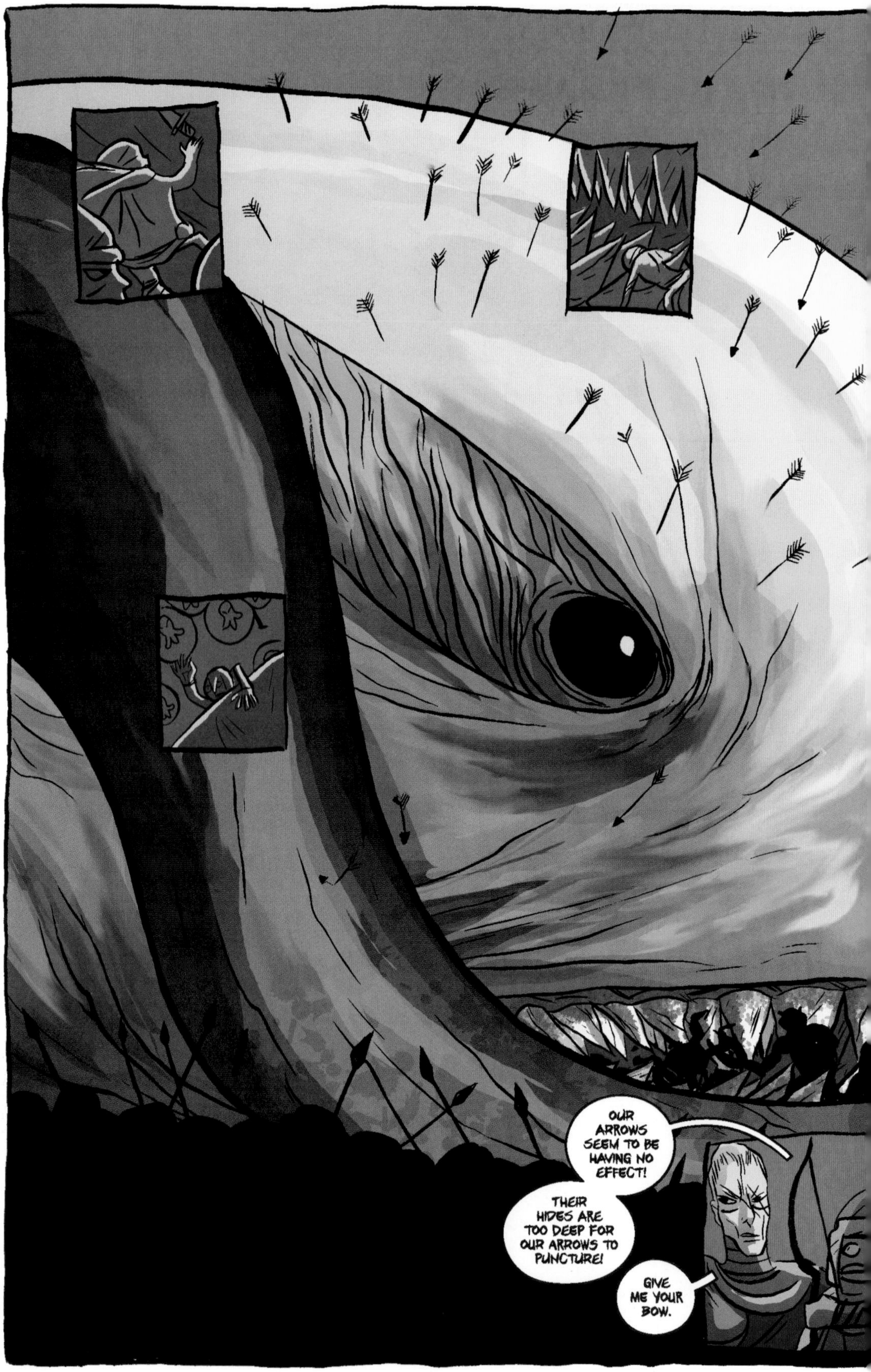
OUR ARROWS SEEM TO BE HAVING NO EFFECT!
THEIR HIDES ARE TOO DEEP FOR OUR ARROWS TO PUNCTURE!
GIVE ME YOUR BOW.

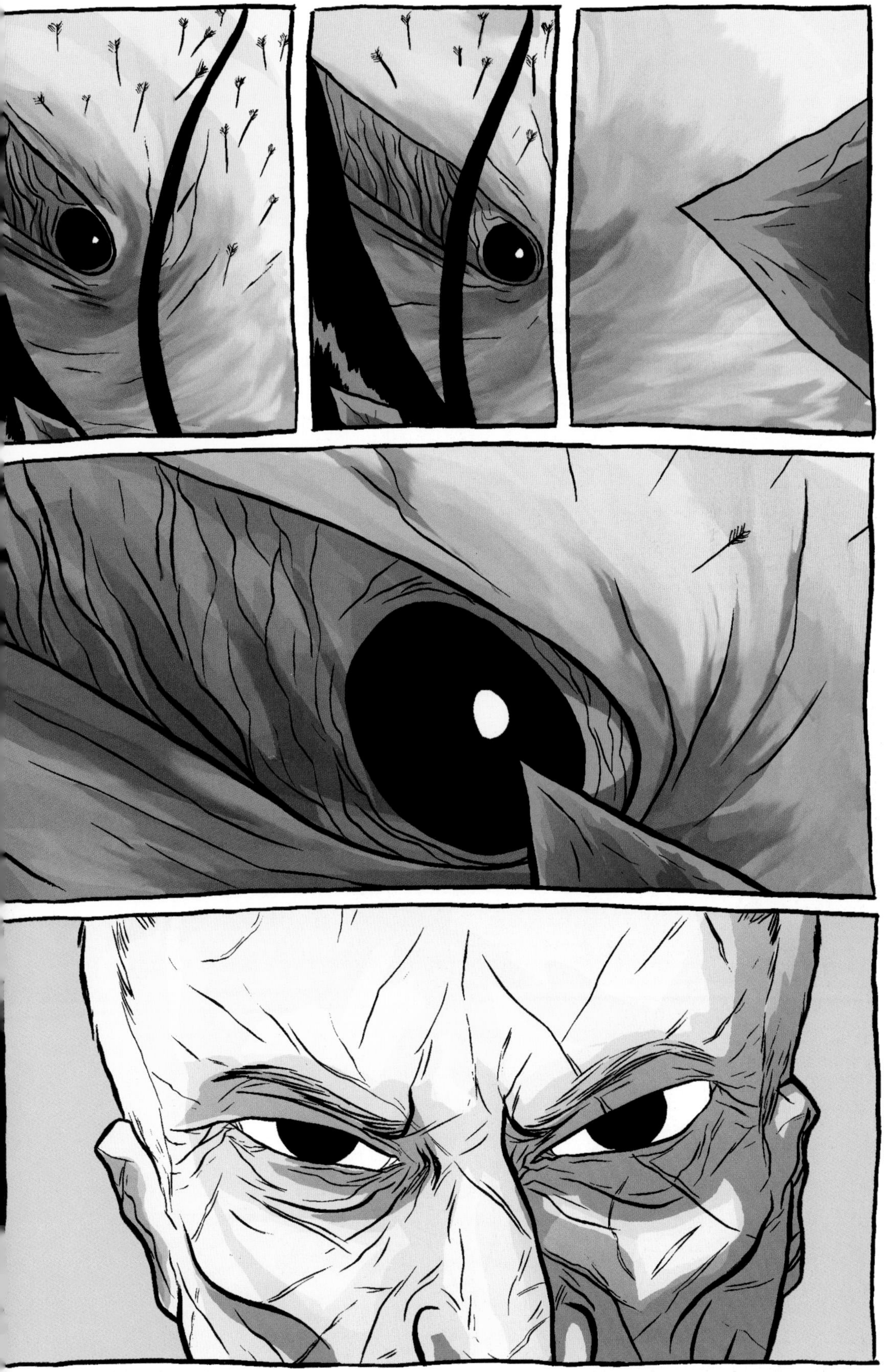

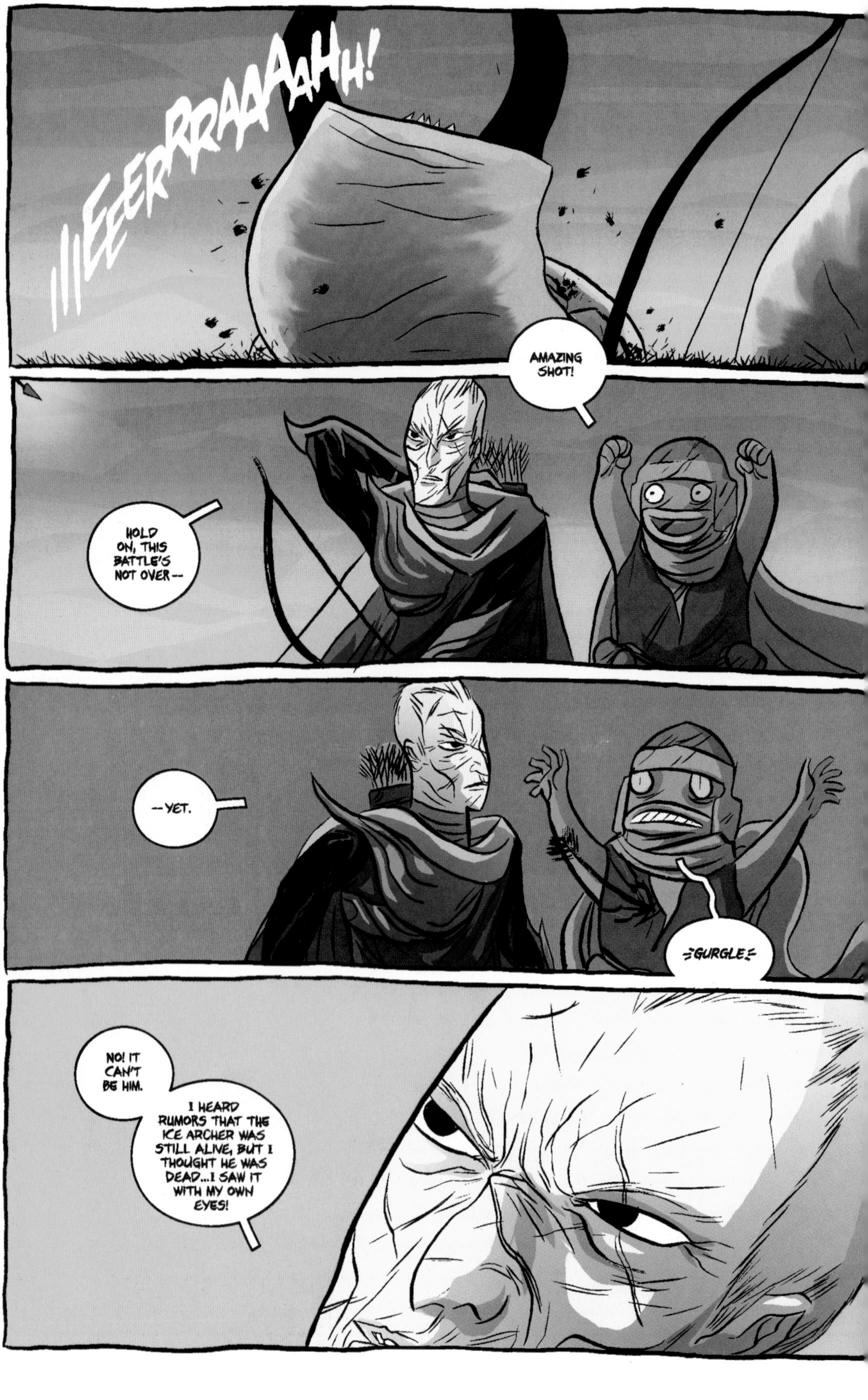

IIIEEERRRAAAAHH!
AMAZING SHOT!
HOLD ON, THIS BATTLE'S NOT OVER--
--YET.
=GURGLE=
NO! IT CAN'T BE HIM.
I HEARD RUMORS THAT THE ICE ARCHER WAS STILL ALIVE, BUT I THOUGHT HE WAS DEAD...I SAW IT WITH MY OWN EYES!

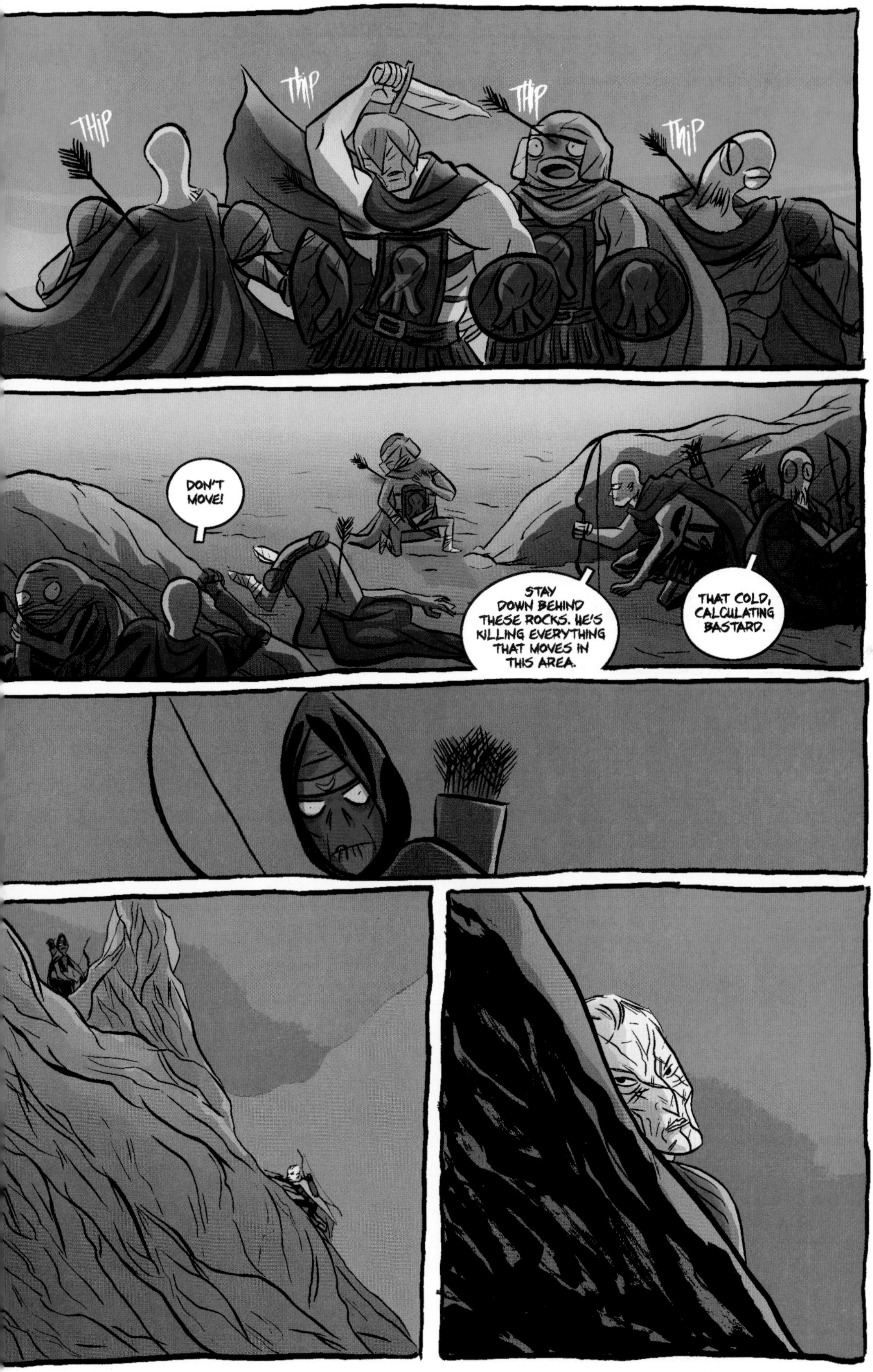
THIP
THIP
THIP
THIP
DON'T MOVE!
STAY DOWN BEHIND THESE ROCKS. HE'S KILLING EVERYTHING THAT MOVES IN THIS AREA.
THAT COLD, CALCULATING BASTARD.

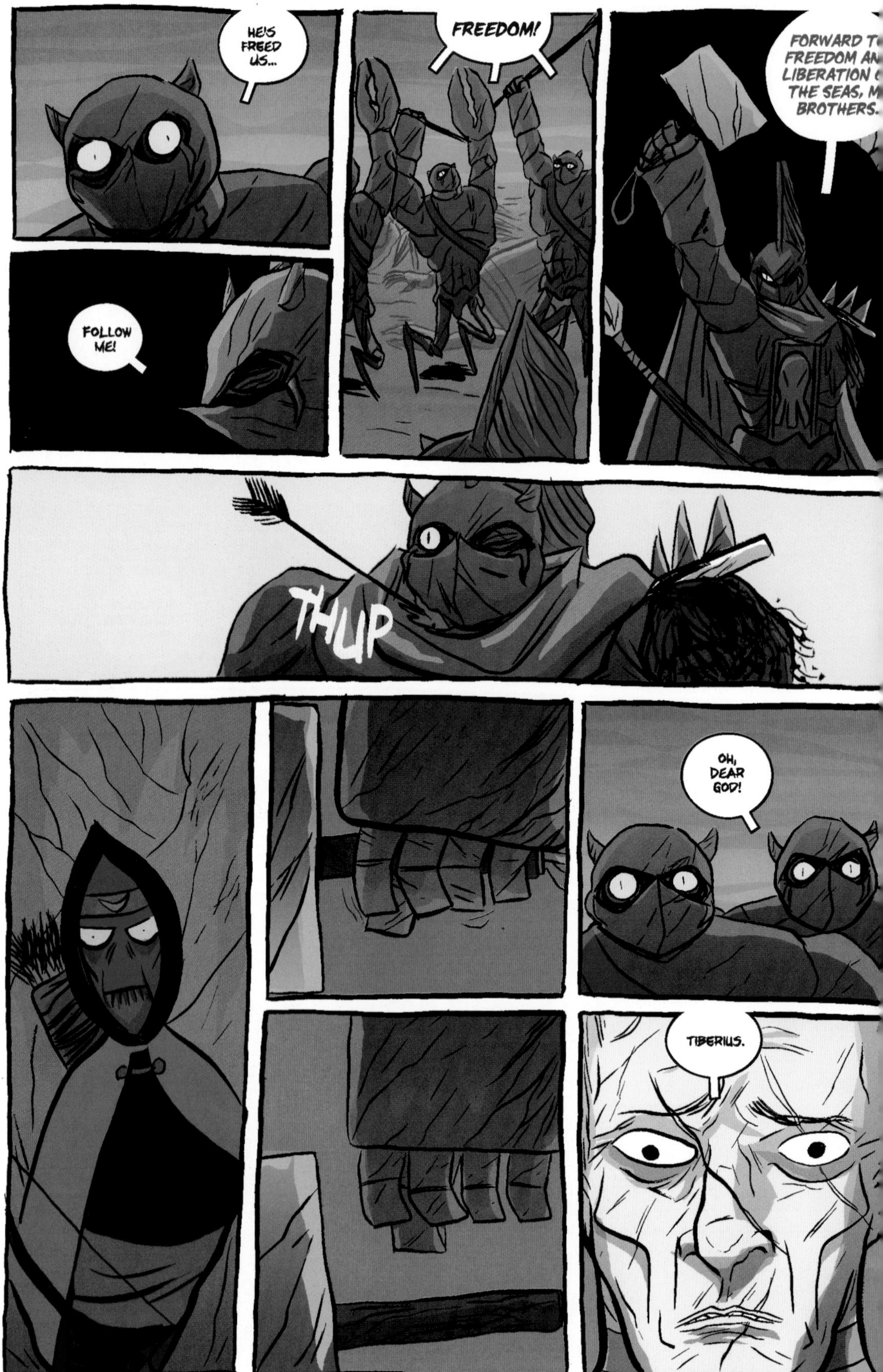
HE'S FREED US...
FOLLOW ME!
FREEDOM!
FORWARD T FREEDOM AN LIBERATION THE SEAS, M BROTHERS.
THUP
OH, DEAR GOD!
TIBERIUS.

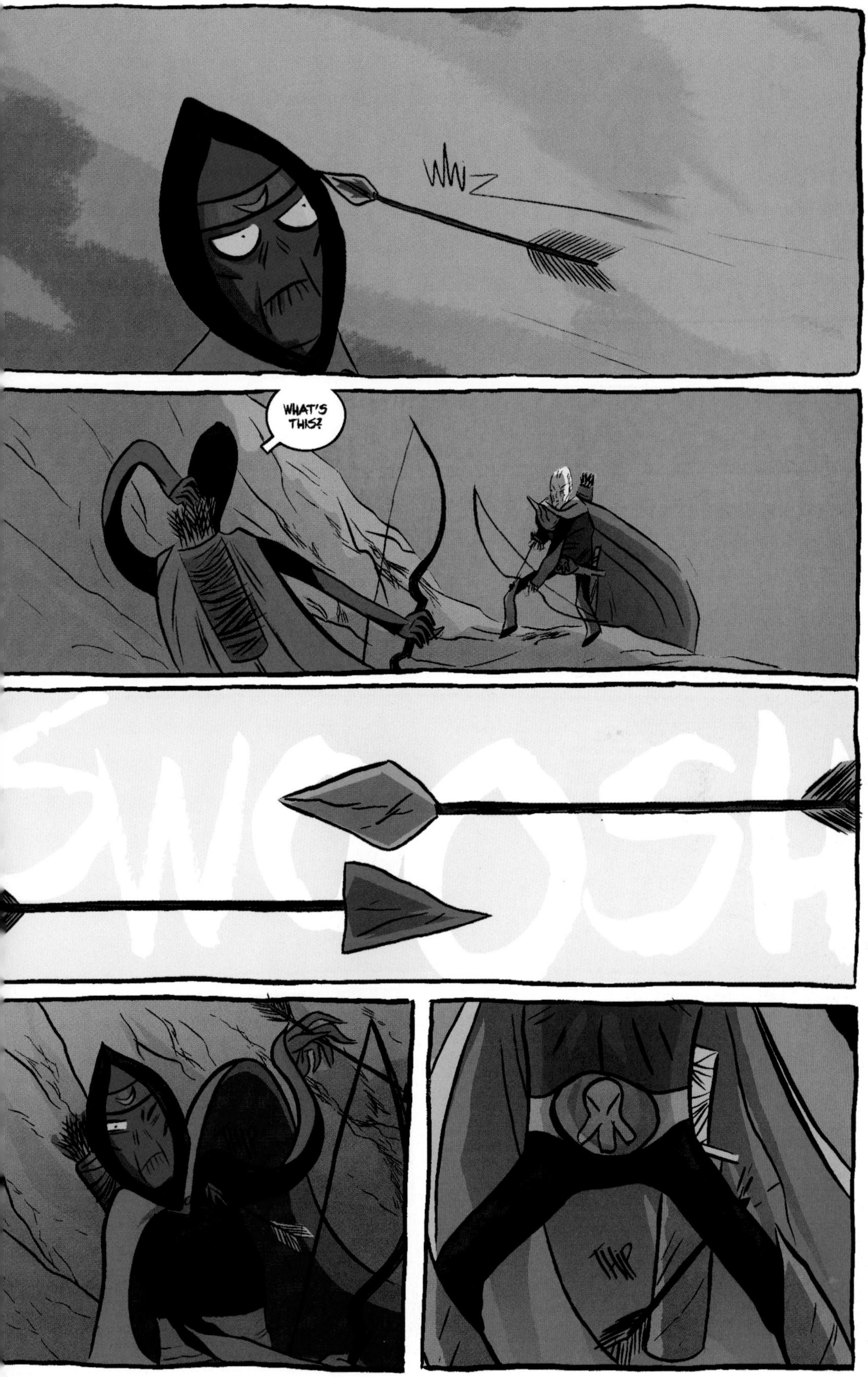
WHIZ
WHAT'S THIS?
SWOOSH
THIP

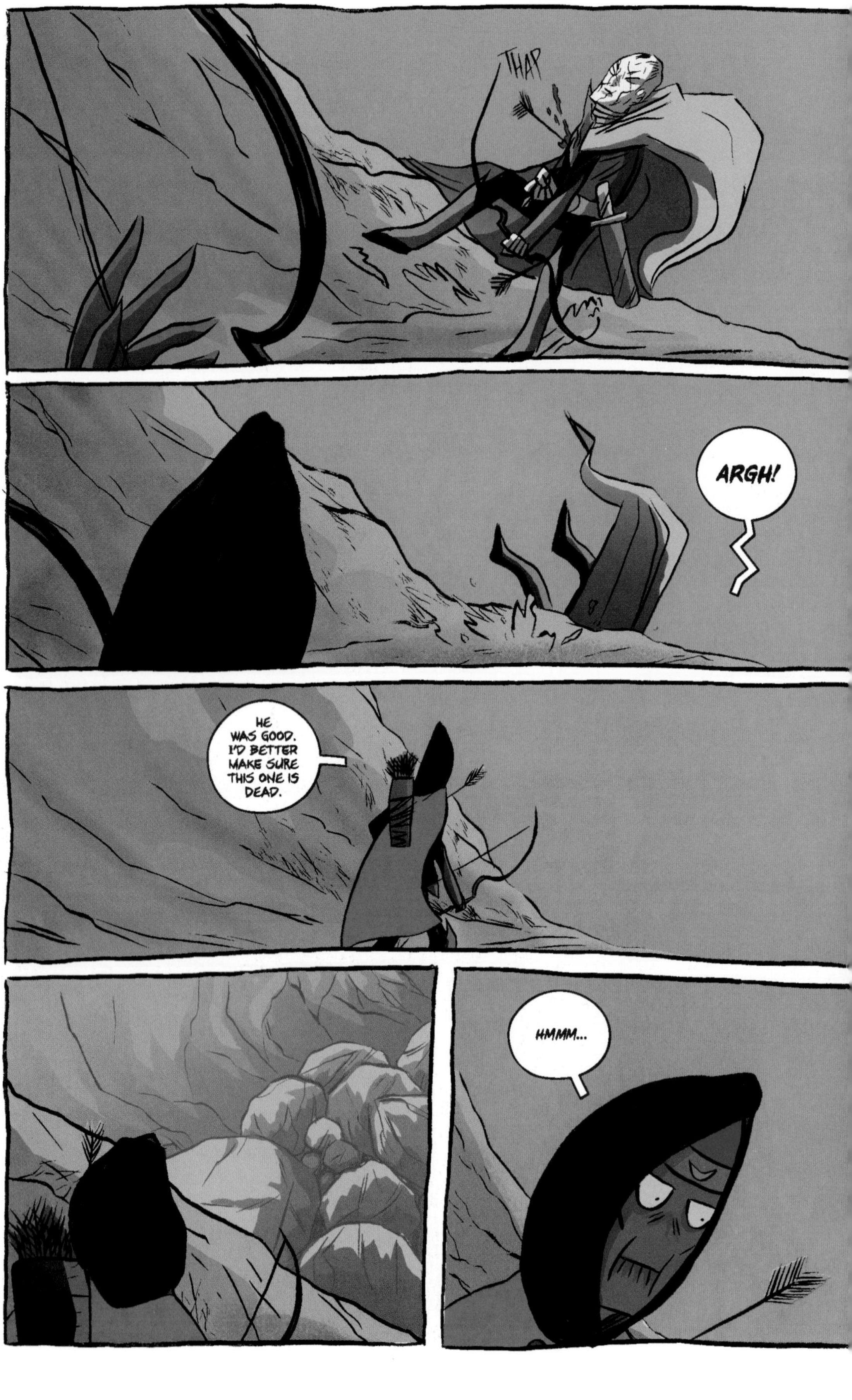
THAP
ARGH!
HE WAS GOOD. I'D BETTER MAKE SURE THIS ONE IS DEAD.
HMMM...

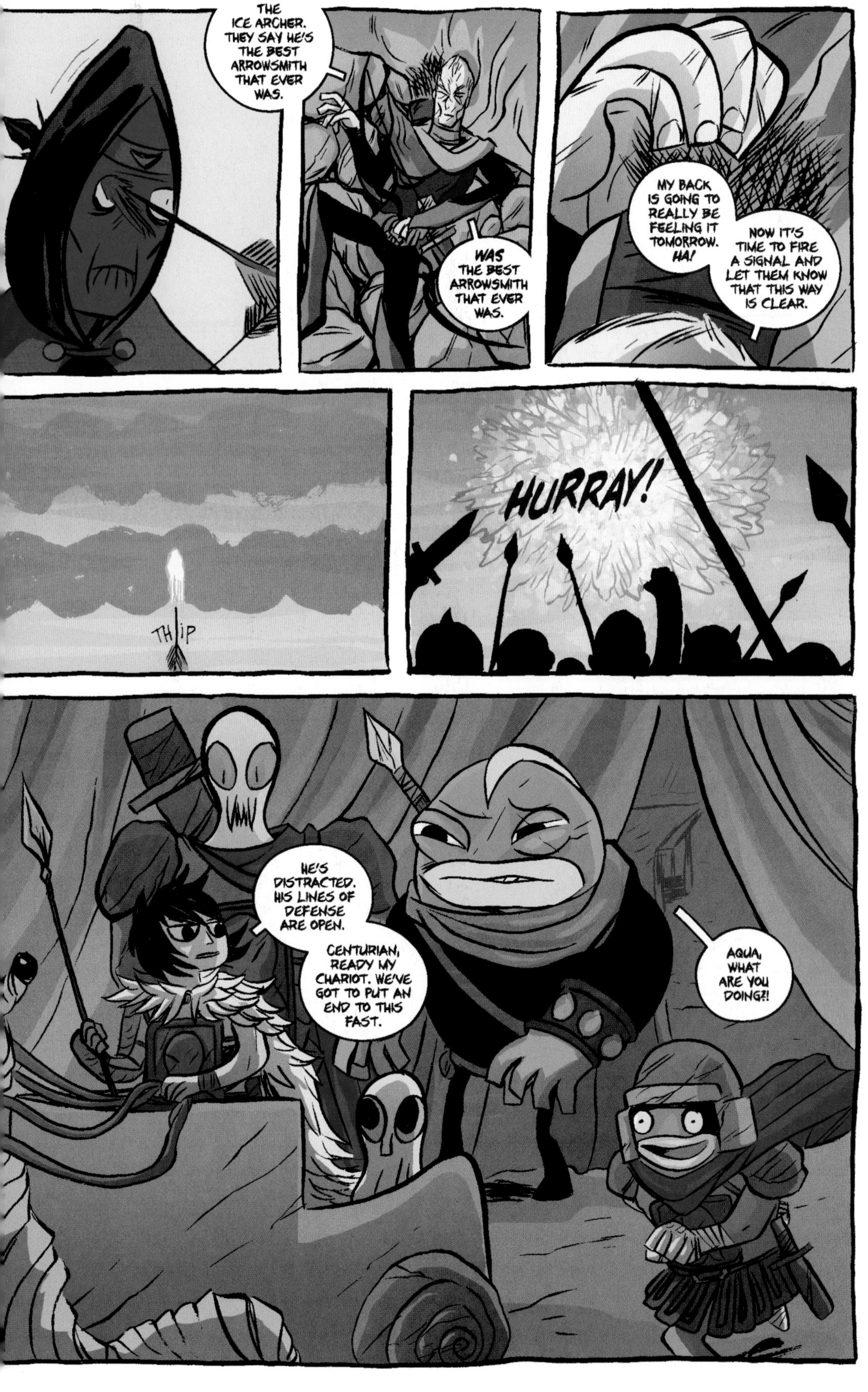
THE ICE ARCHER. THEY SAY HE'S THE BEST ARROWSMITH THAT EVER WAS.
WAS THE BEST ARROWSMITH THAT EVER WAS.
MY BACK IS GOING TO REALLY BE FEELING IT TOMORROW. HA!
NOW IT'S TIME TO FIRE A SIGNAL AND LET THEM KNOW THAT THIS WAY IS CLEAR.
THWIP
HURRAY!
HE'S DISTRACTED. HIS LINES OF DEFENSE ARE OPEN.
CENTURIAN, READY MY CHARIOT. WE'VE GOT TO PUT AN END TO THIS FAST.
AQUA, WHAT ARE YOU DOING?!

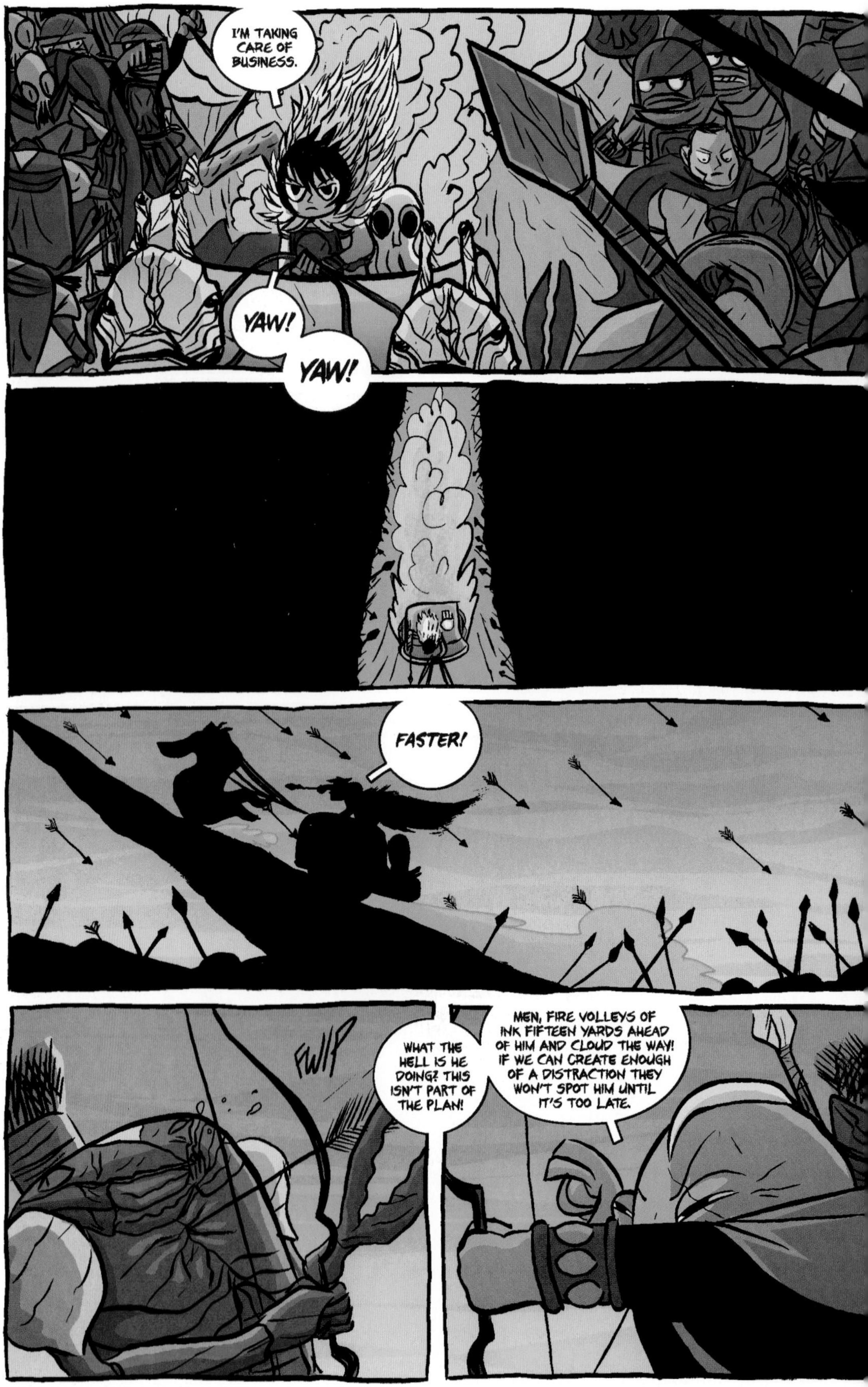
I'M TAKING CARE OF BUSINESS.
YAW!
YAW!
FASTER!
FWIP
WHAT THE HELL IS HE DOING? THIS ISN'T PART OF THE PLAN!
MEN, FIRE VOLLEYS OF INK FIFTEEN YARDS AHEAD OF HIM AND CLOUD THE WAY! IF WE CAN CREATE ENOUGH OF A DISTRACTION THEY WON'T SPOT HIM UNTIL IT'S TOO LATE.

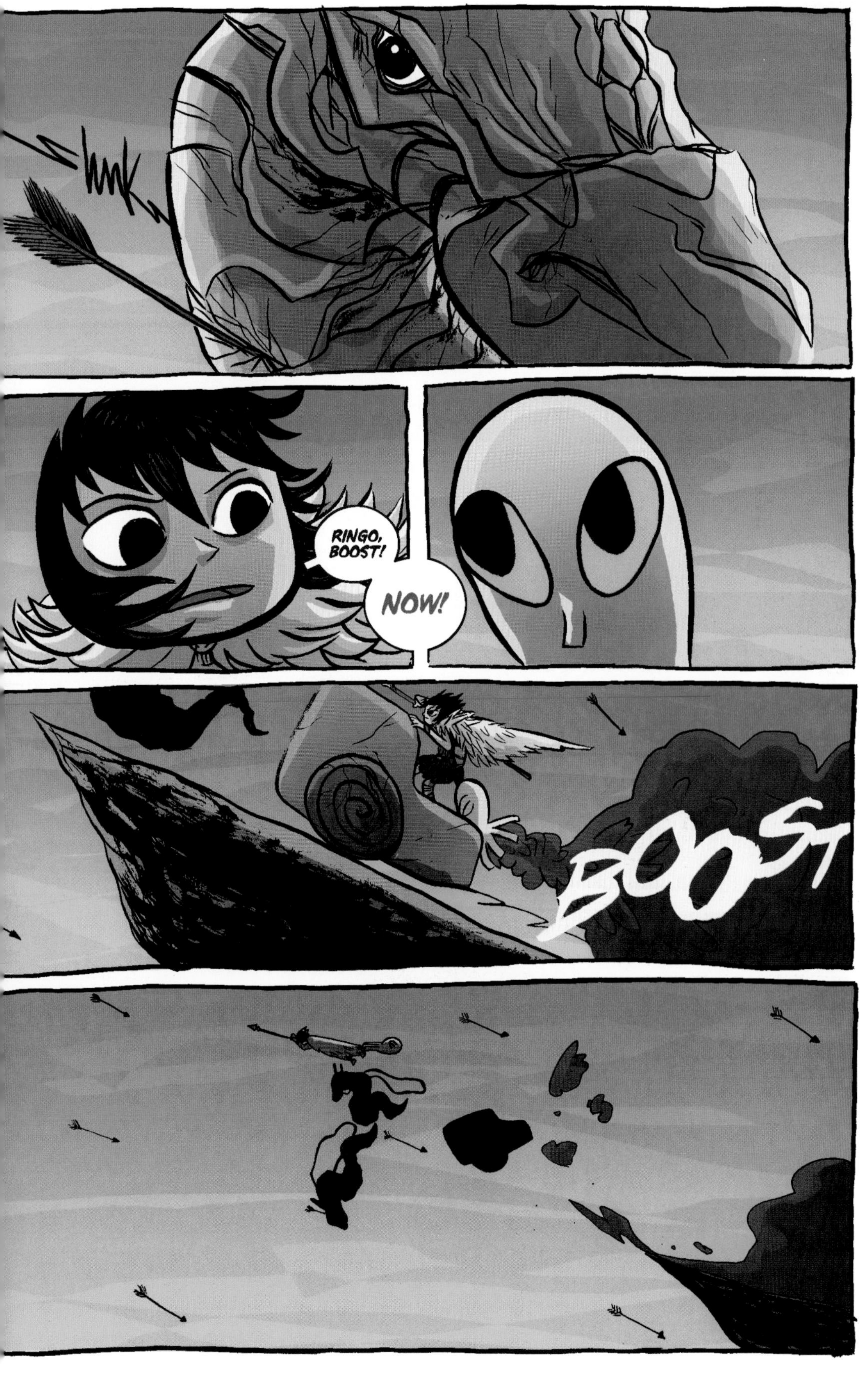
SHUNK
RINGO, BOOST!
NOW!
BOOST

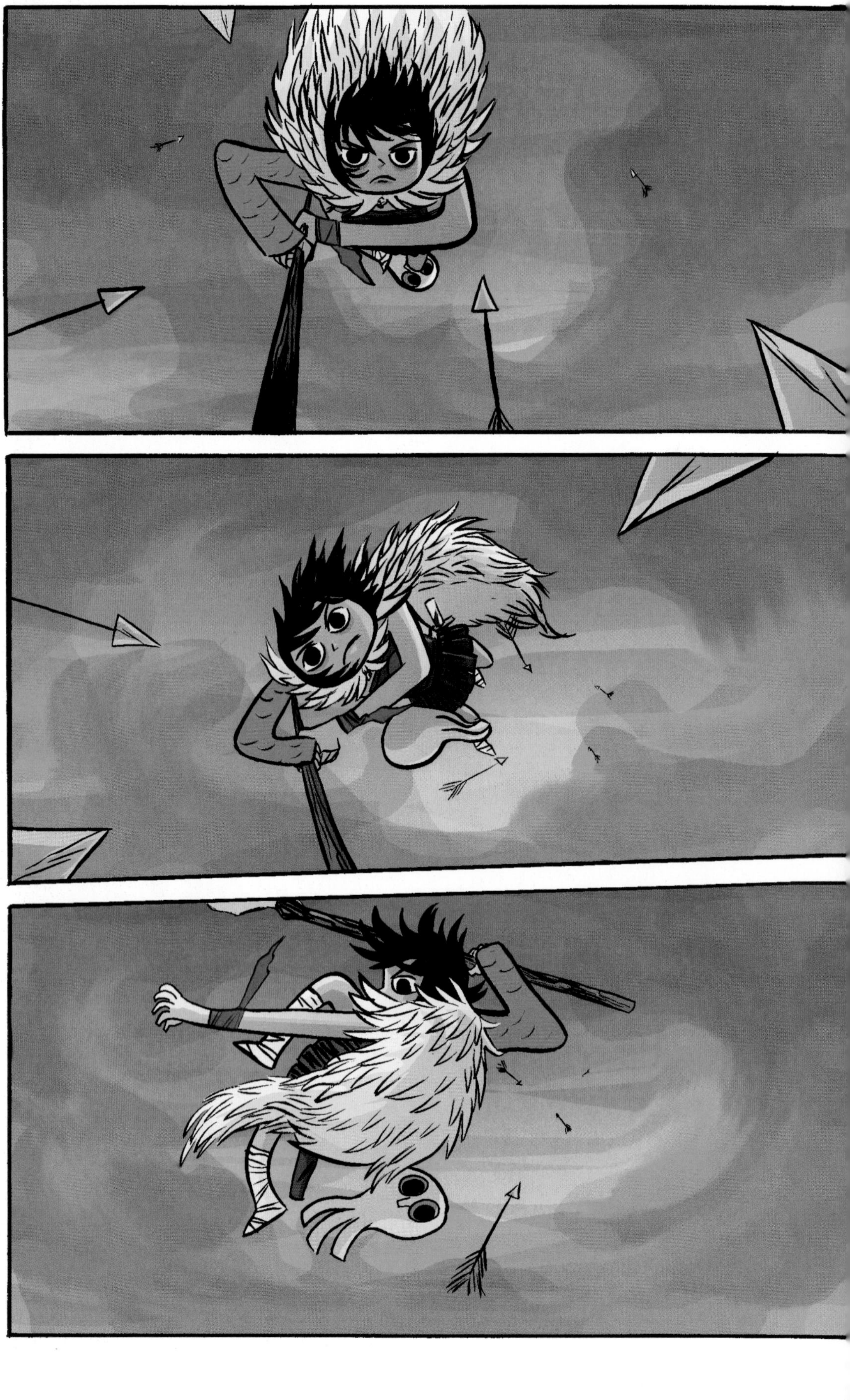

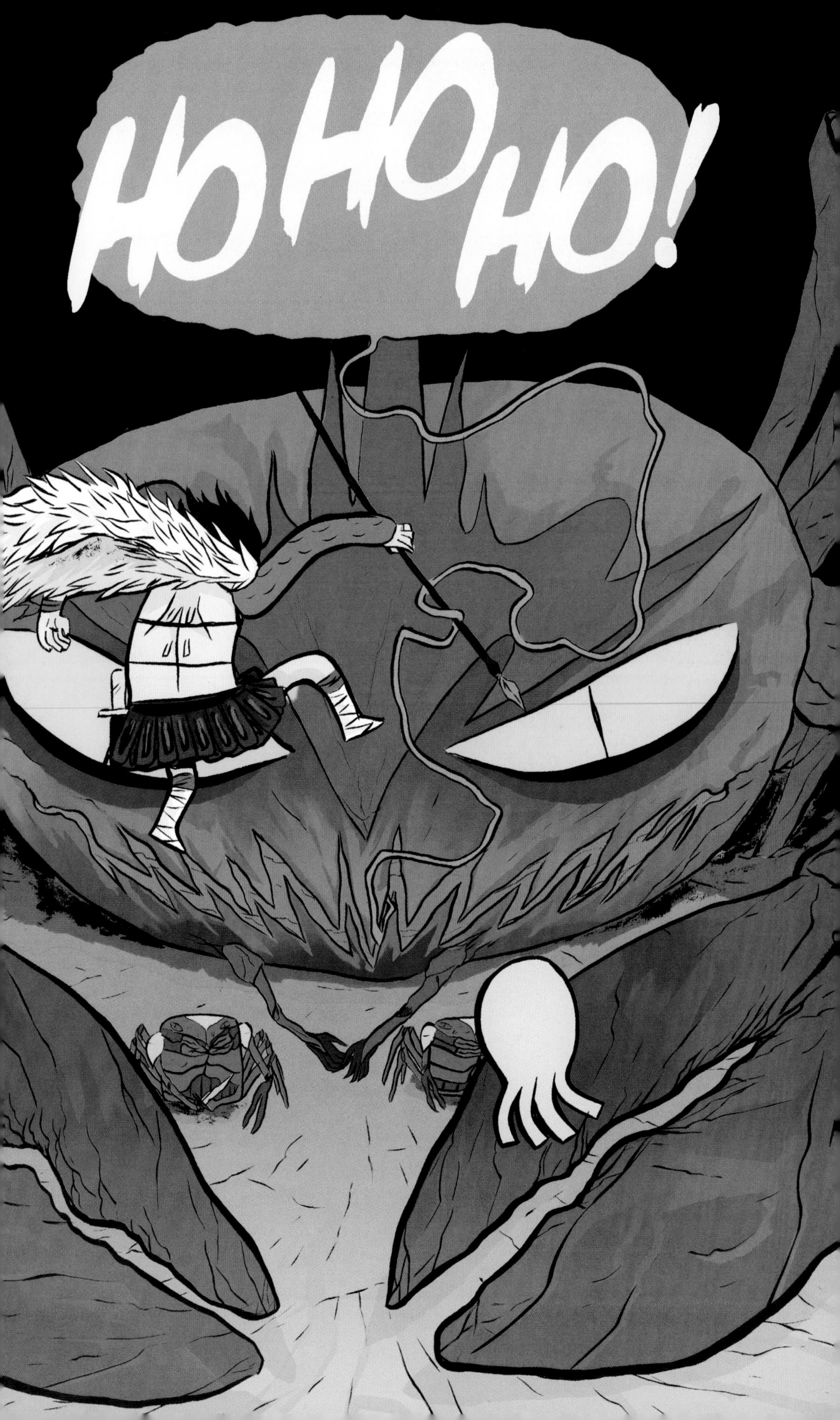
HO HO HO HO!

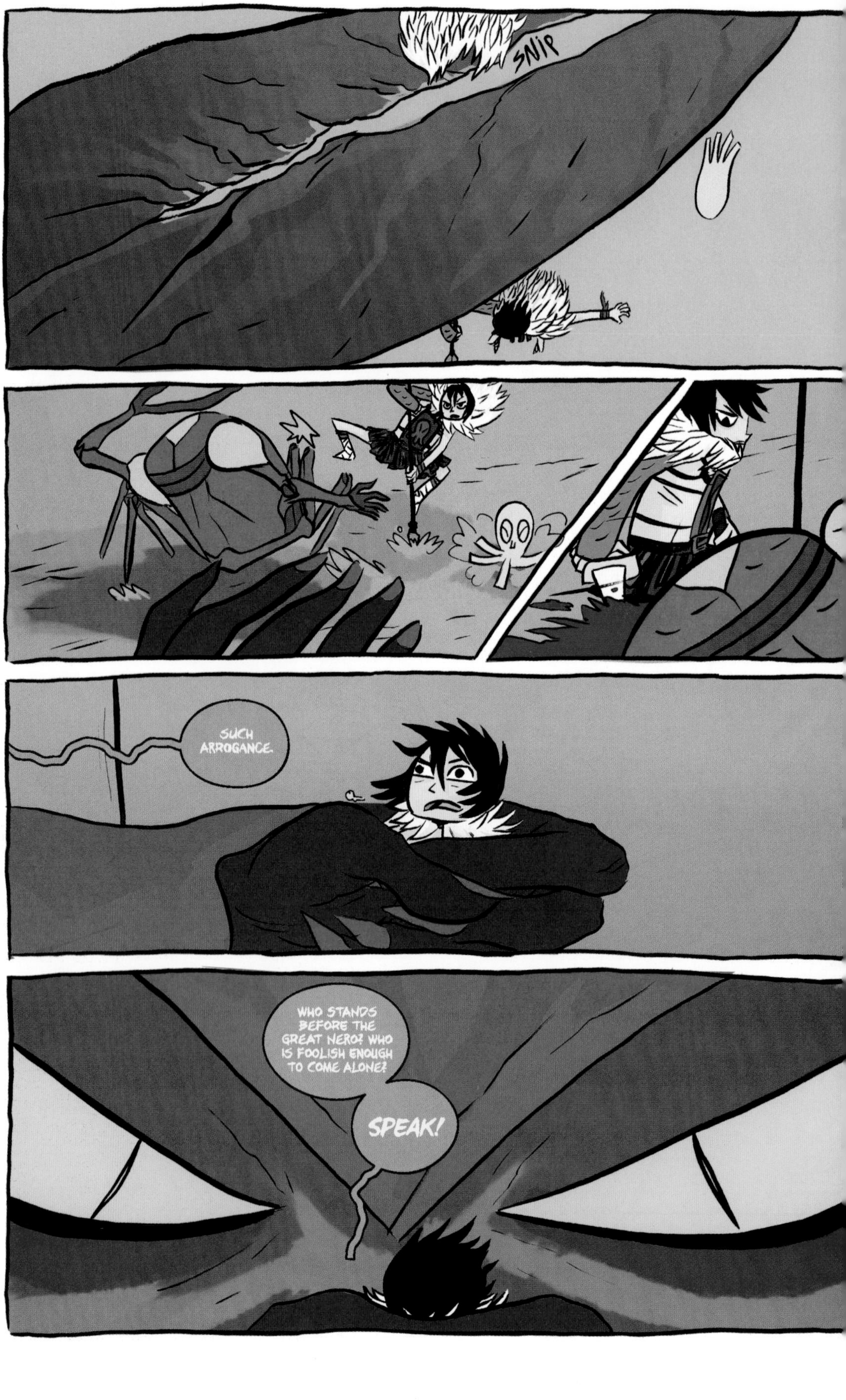
SNIP
SUCH ARROGANCE.
WHO STANDS BEFORE THE GREAT NERO? WHO IS FOOLISH ENOUGH TO COME ALONE?
SPEAK!

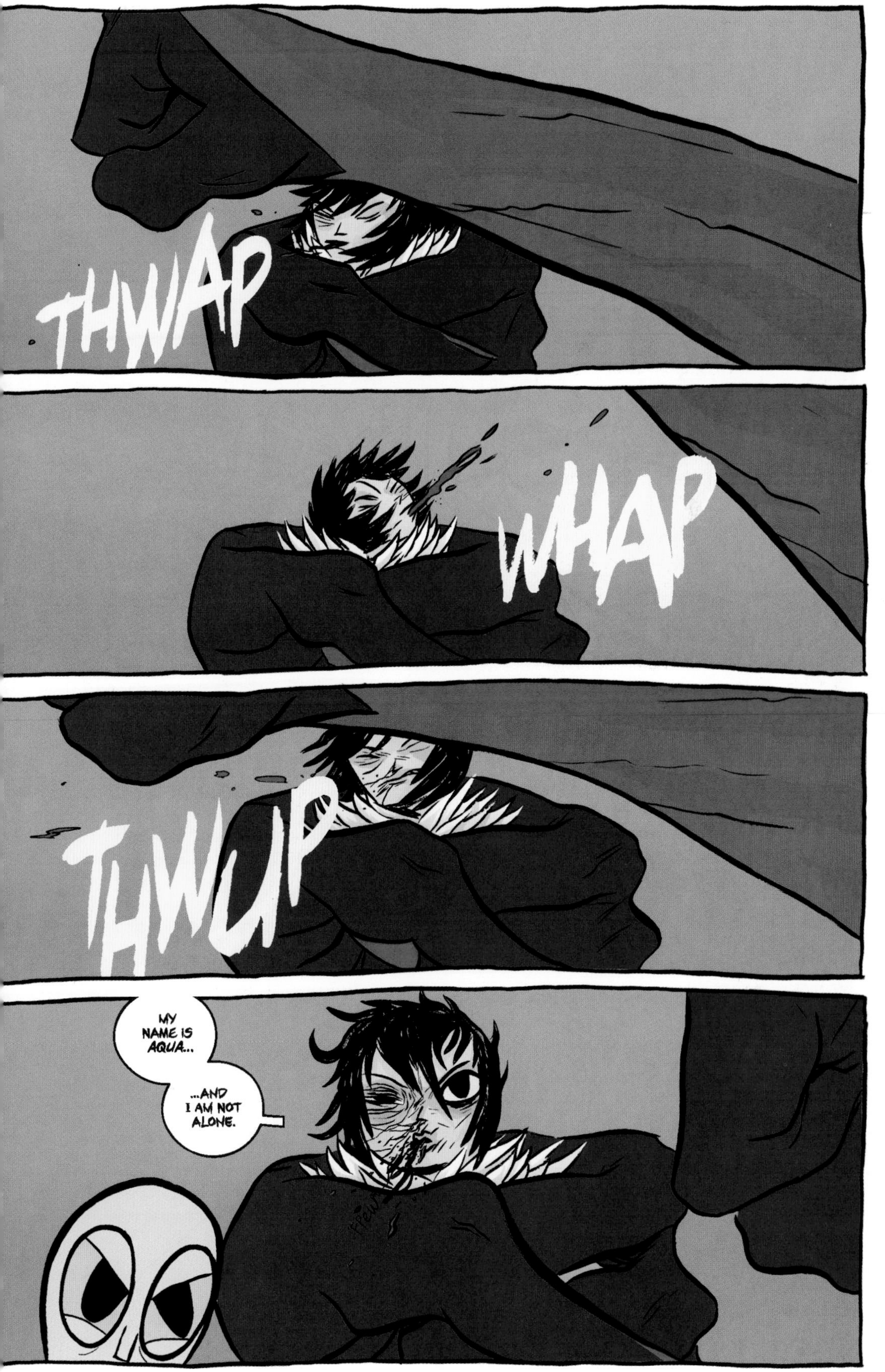
THWAP
WHAP
THWUP
MY NAME IS AQUA...
...AND I AM NOT ALONE.

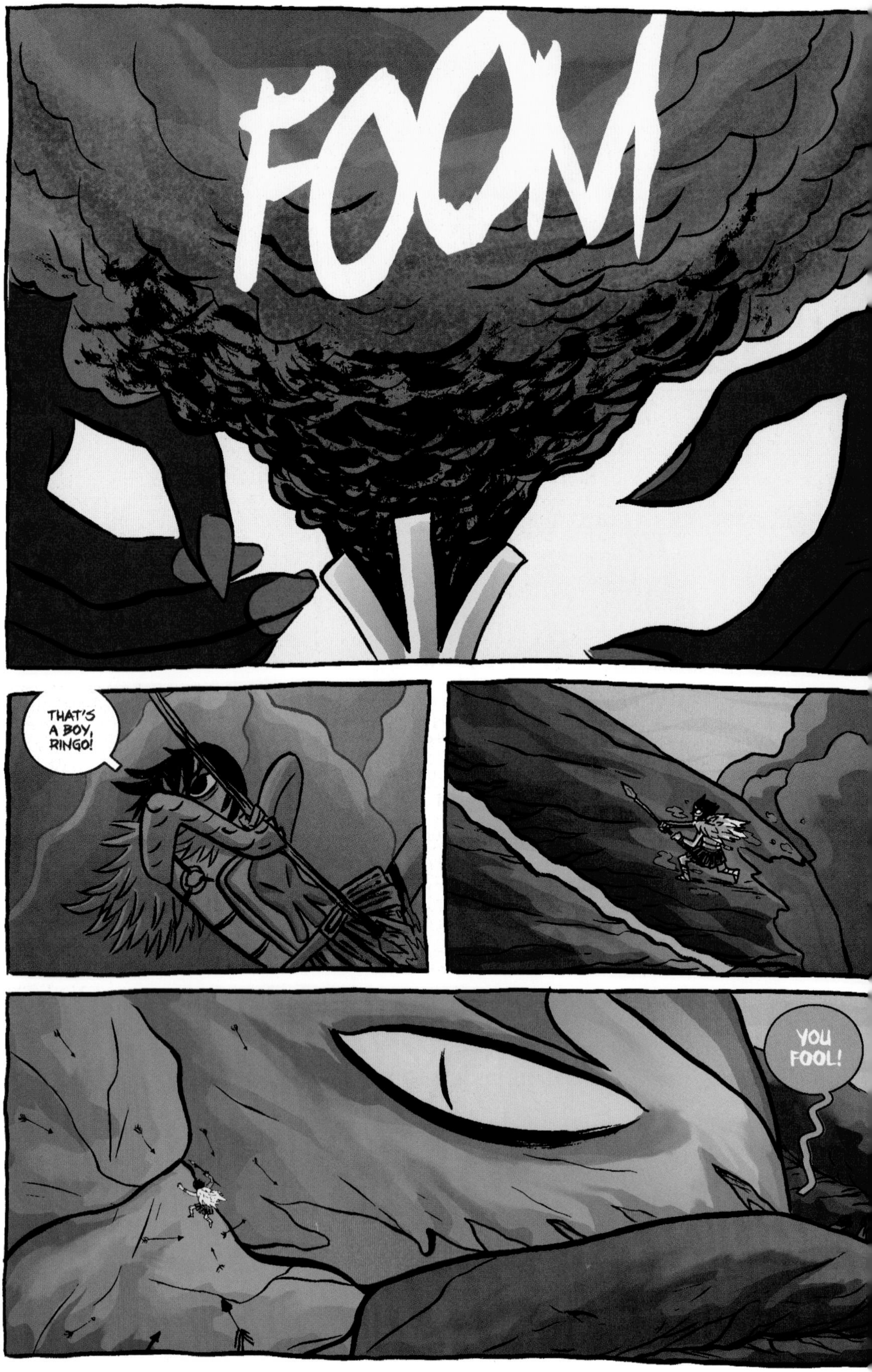
FOOM
THAT'S A BOY, RINGO!
YOU FOOL!

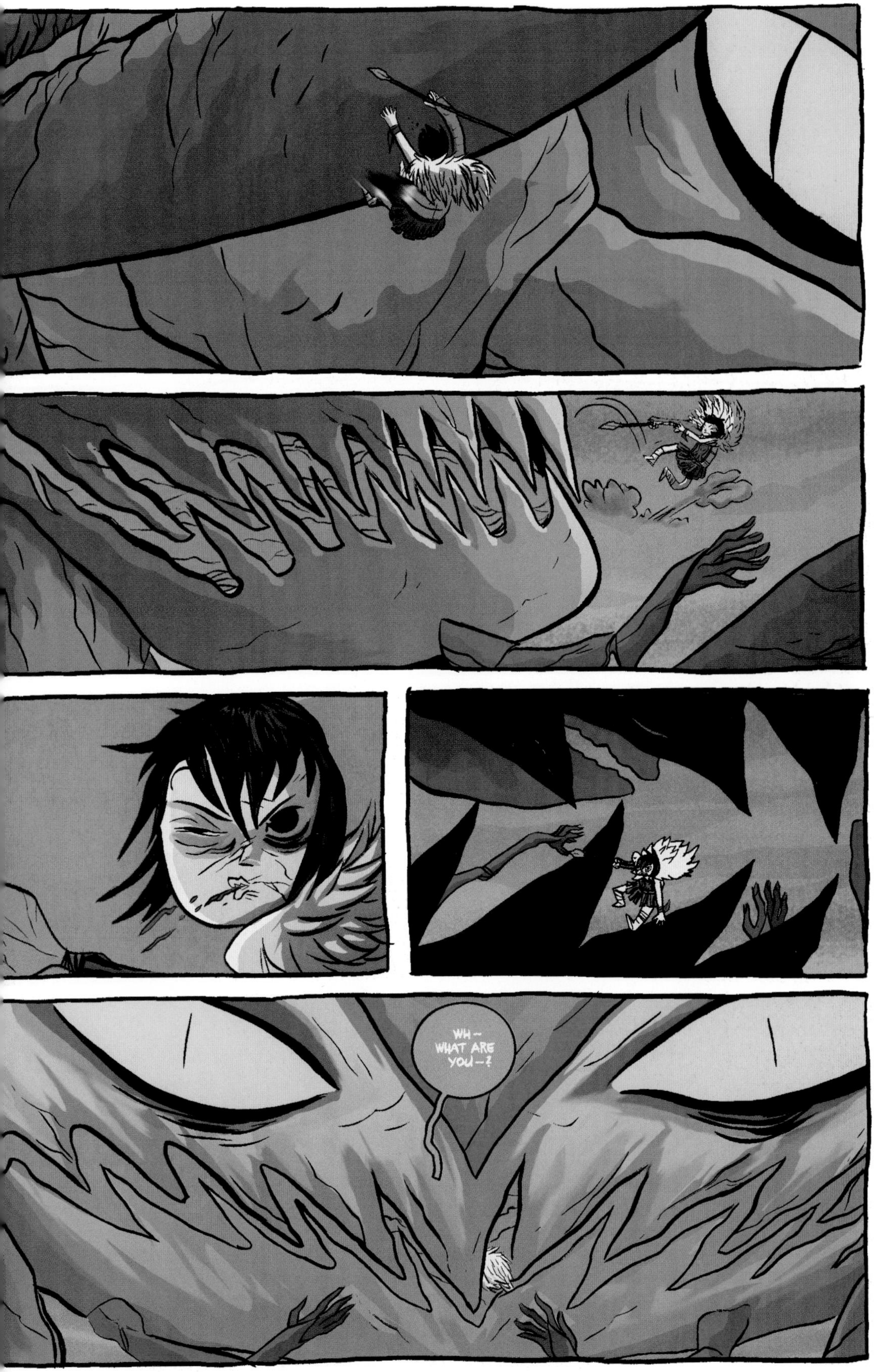
WH--
WHAT ARE
YOU--?

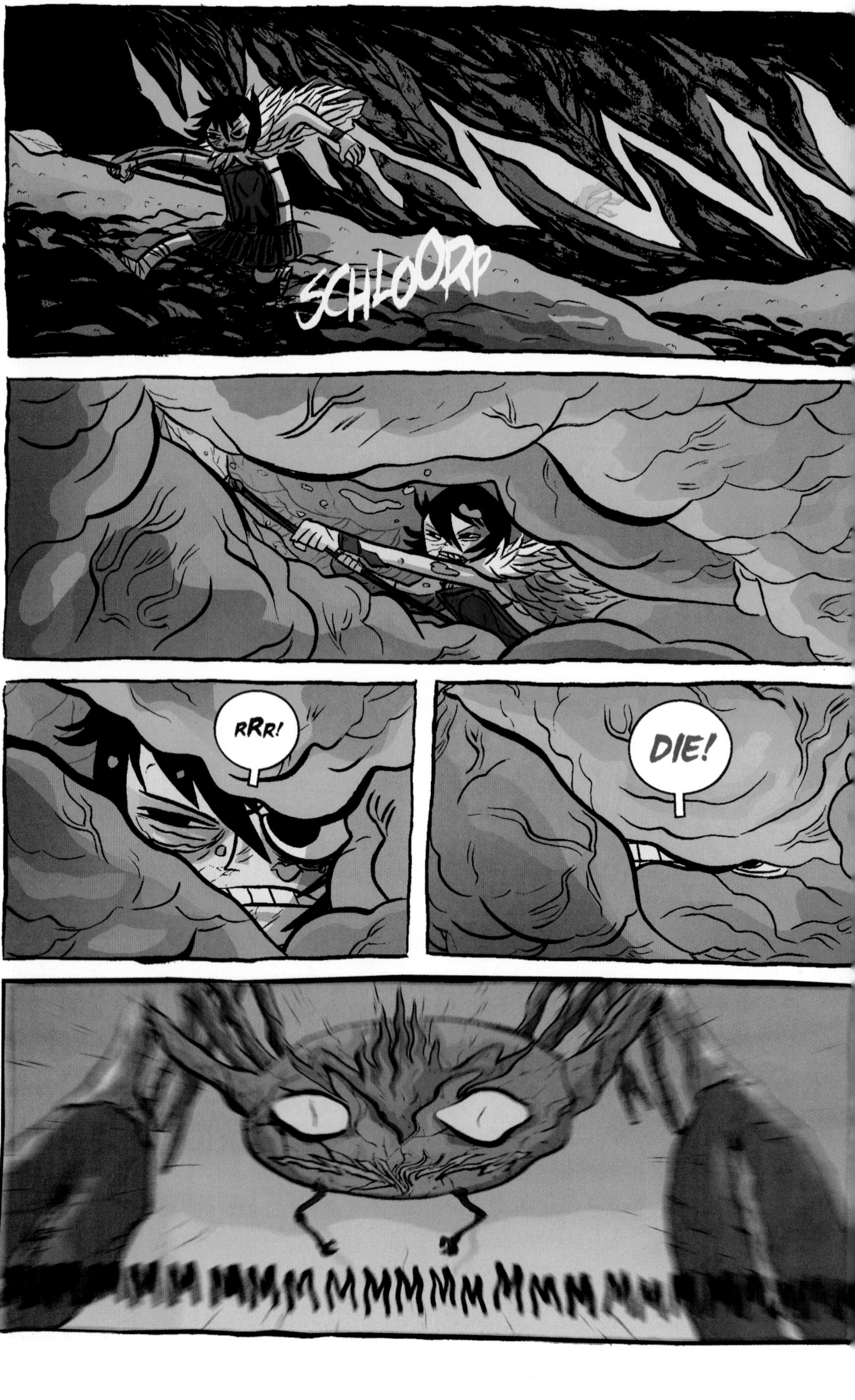
SCHLOORP
RRR!
DIE!
MMMMMMMMMMMMMMMMMMMM

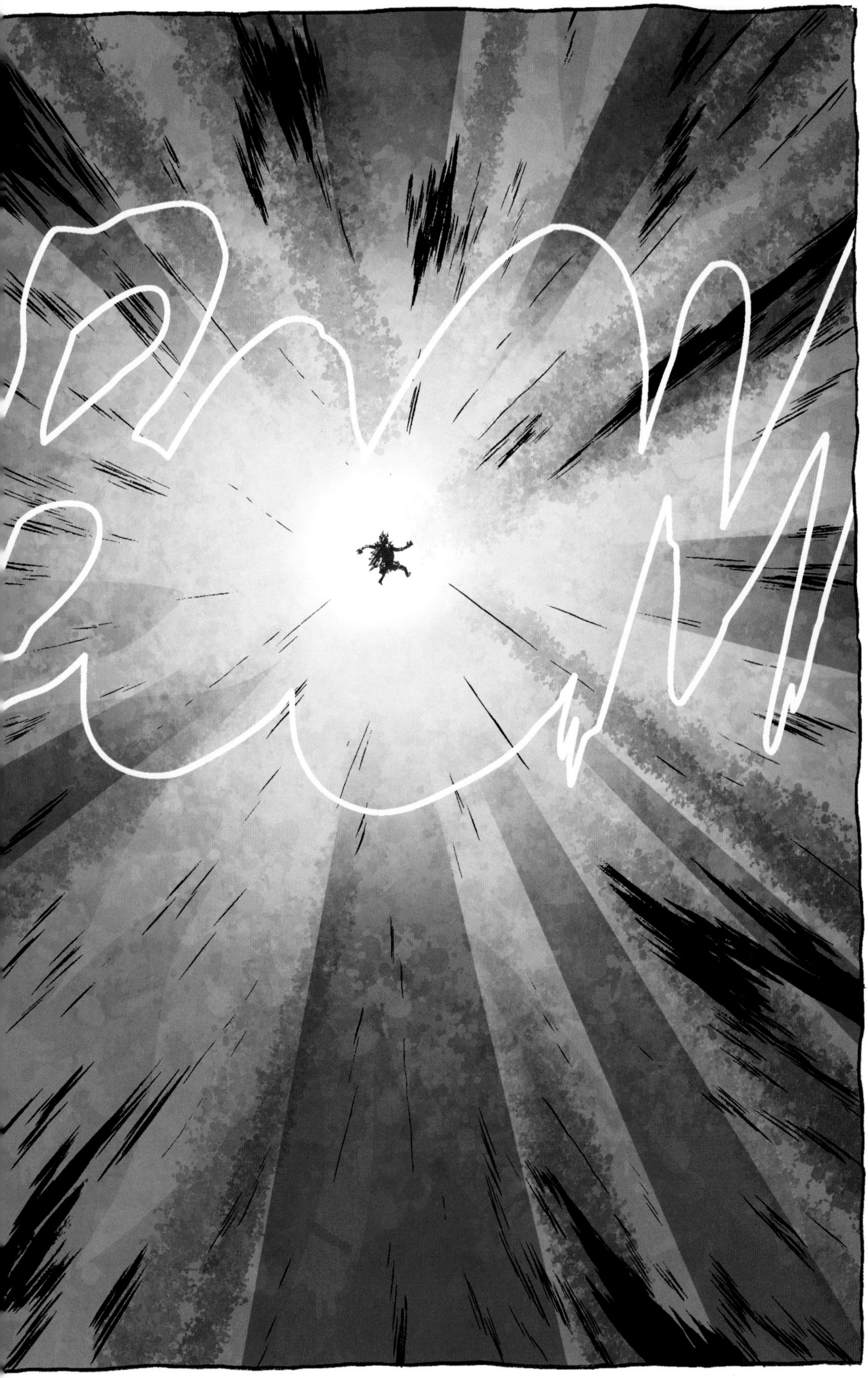

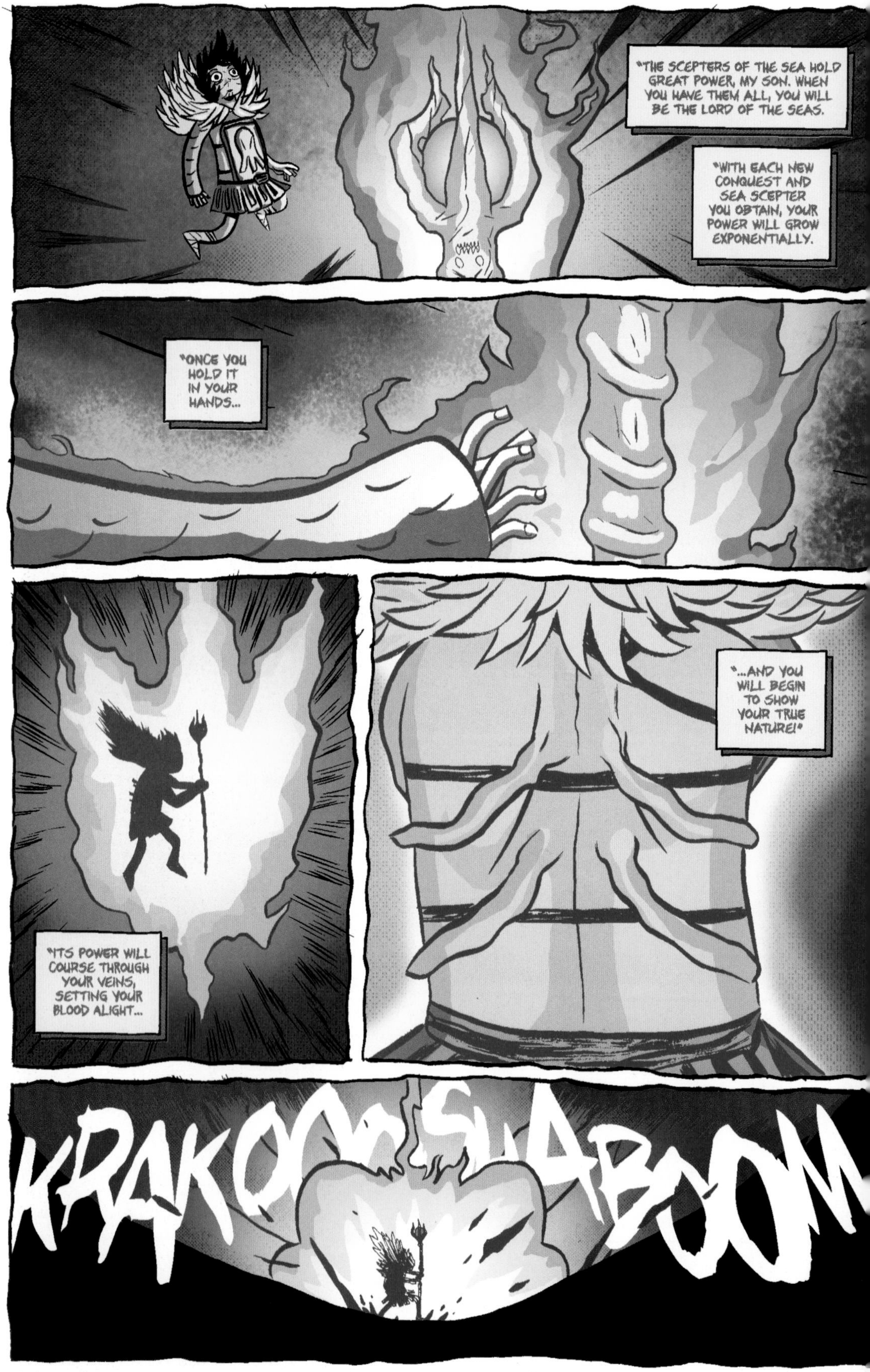
"THE SCEPTERS OF THE SEA HOLD GREAT POWER, MY SON. WHEN YOU HAVE THEM ALL, YOU WILL BE THE LORD OF THE SEAS.
"WITH EACH NEW CONQUEST AND SEA SCEPTER YOU OBTAIN, YOUR POWER WILL GROW EXPONENTIALLY.
"ONCE YOU HOLD IT IN YOUR HANDS...
"ITS POWER WILL COURSE THROUGH YOUR VEINS, SETTING YOUR BLOOD ALIGHT...
"...AND YOU WILL BEGIN TO SHOW YOUR TRUE NATURE!"
KRAKOOSHABOOM

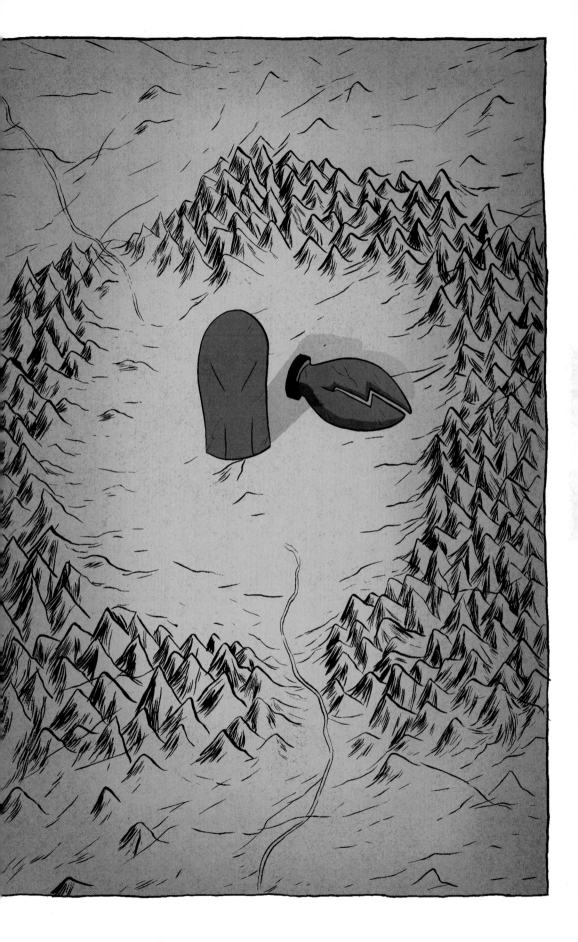

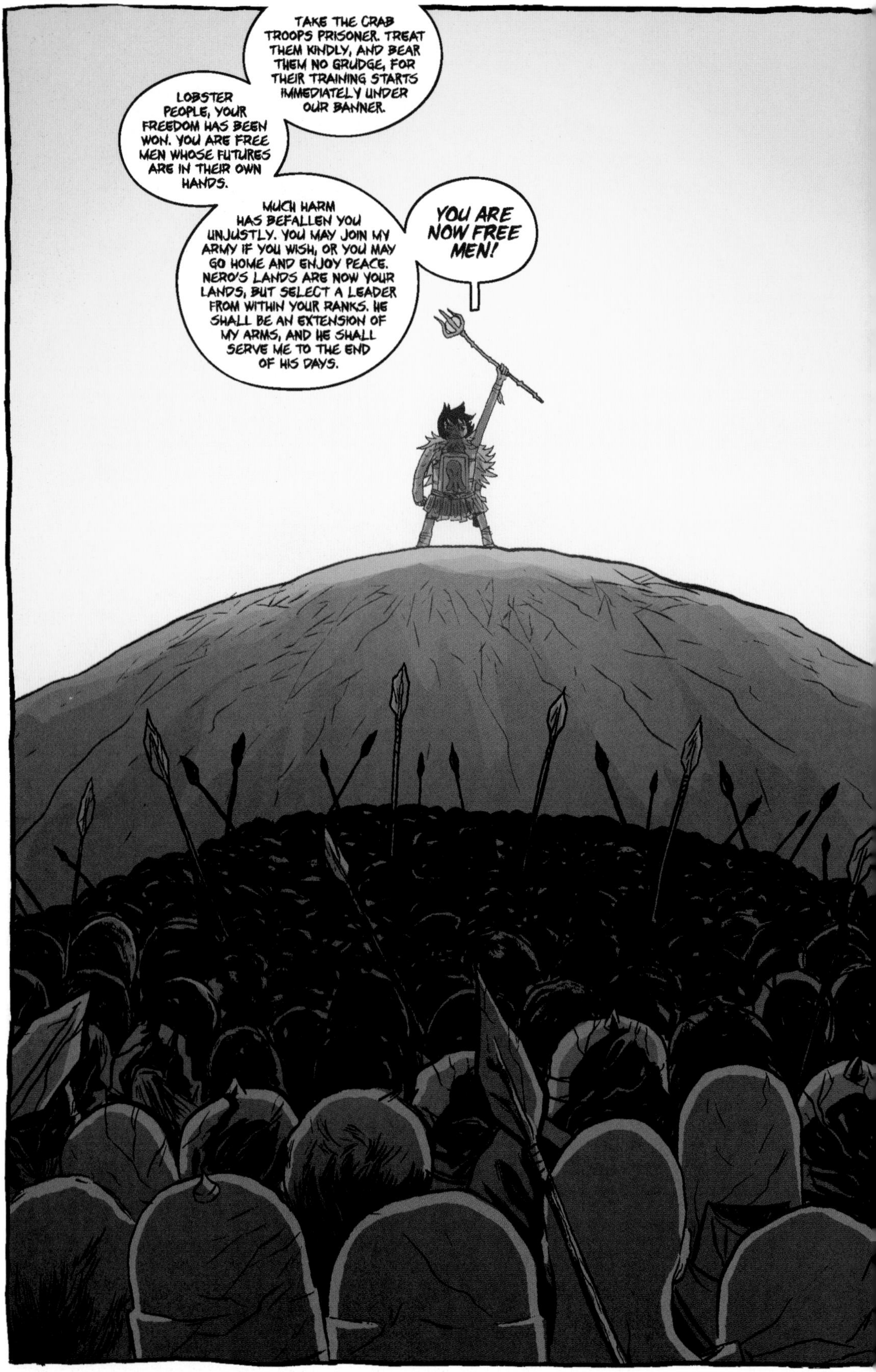
TAKE THE CRAB TROOPS PRISONER. TREAT THEM KINDLY, AND BEAR THEM NO GRUDGE, FOR THEIR TRAINING STARTS IMMEDIATELY UNDER OUR BANNER.
LOBSTER PEOPLE, YOUR FREEDOM HAS BEEN WON. YOU ARE FREE MEN WHOSE FUTURES ARE IN THEIR OWN HANDS.
MUCH HARM HAS BEFALLEN YOU UNJUSTLY. YOU MAY JOIN MY ARMY IF YOU WISH, OR YOU MAY GO HOME AND ENJOY PEACE. NERO'S LANDS ARE NOW YOUR LANDS, BUT SELECT A LEADER FROM WITHIN YOUR RANKS. HE SHALL BE AN EXTENSION OF MY ARMS, AND HE SHALL SERVE ME TO THE END OF HIS DAYS.
YOU ARE NOW FREE MEN!

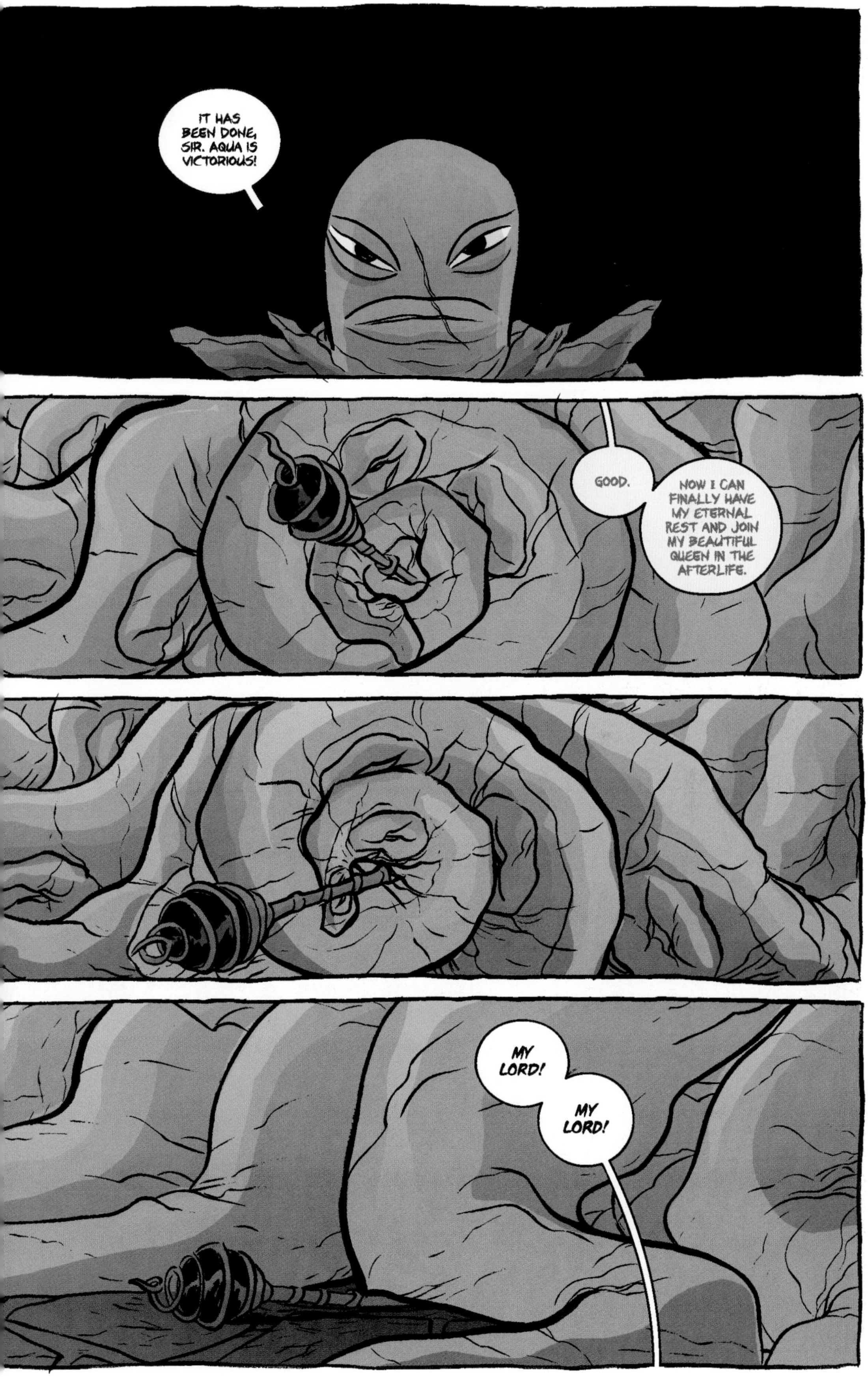
IT HAS BEEN DONE, SIR. AQUA IS VICTORIOUS!
GOOD.
NOW I CAN FINALLY HAVE MY ETERNAL REST AND JOIN MY BEAUTIFUL QUEEN IN THE AFTERLIFE.
MY LORD!
MY LORD!

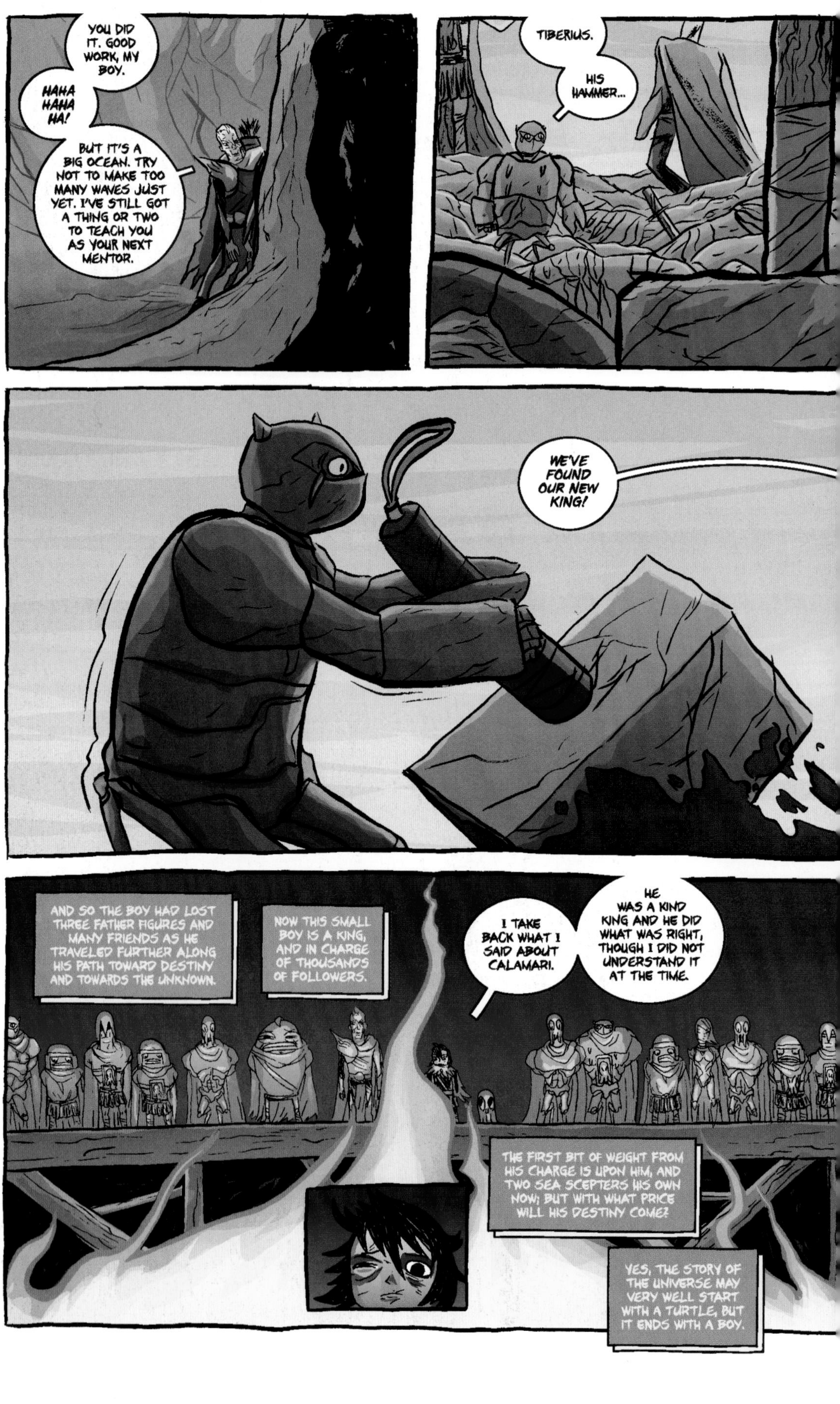
YOU DID IT. GOOD WORK, MY BOY.
HAHA HAHA HA!
BUT IT'S A BIG OCEAN. TRY NOT TO MAKE TOO MANY WAVES JUST YET. I'VE STILL GOT A THING OR TWO TO TEACH YOU AS YOUR NEXT MENTOR.
TIBERIUS.
HIS HAMMER...
WE'VE FOUND OUR NEW KING!
AND SO THE BOY HAD LOST THREE FATHER FIGURES AND MANY FRIENDS AS HE TRAVELED FURTHER ALONG HIS PATH TOWARD DESTINY AND TOWARDS THE UNKNOWN.
NOW THIS SMALL BOY IS A KING, AND IN CHARGE OF THOUSANDS OF FOLLOWERS.
I TAKE BACK WHAT I SAID ABOUT CALAMARI.
HE WAS A KIND KING AND HE DID WHAT WAS RIGHT, THOUGH I DID NOT UNDERSTAND IT AT THE TIME.
THE FIRST BIT OF WEIGHT FROM HIS CHARGE IS UPON HIM, AND TWO SEA SCEPTERS HIS OWN NOW; BUT WITH WHAT PRICE WILL HIS DESTINY COME?
YES, THE STORY OF THE UNIVERSE MAY VERY WELL START WITH A TURTLE, BUT IT ENDS WITH A BOY.

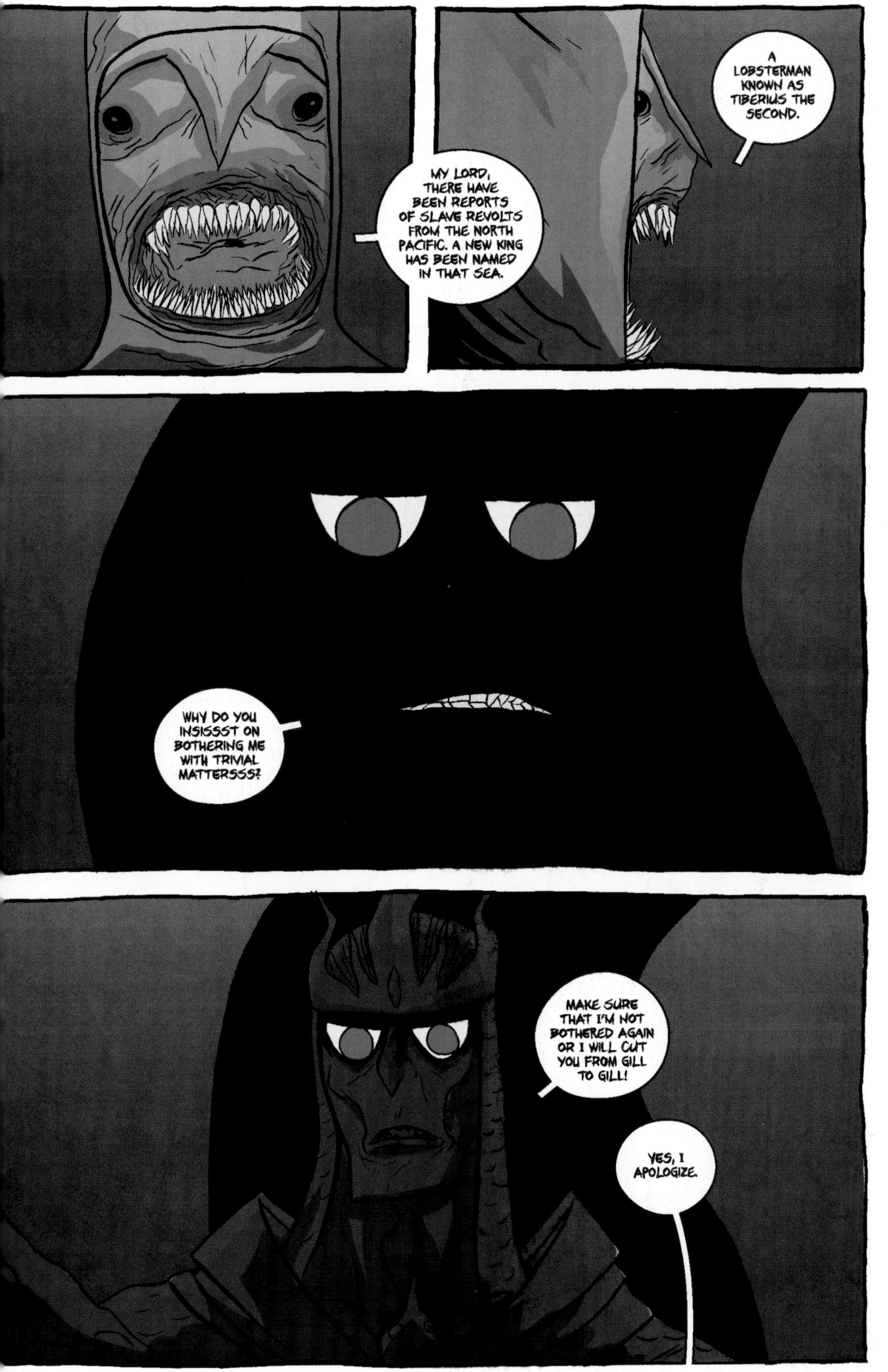
MY LORD, THERE HAVE BEEN REPORTS OF SLAVE REVOLTS FROM THE NORTH PACIFIC. A NEW KING HAS BEEN NAMED IN THAT SEA.
A LOBSTERMAN KNOWN AS TIBERIUS THE SECOND.
WHY DO YOU INSISSST ON BOTHERING ME WITH TRIVIAL MATTERSSS?
MAKE SURE THAT I'M NOT BOTHERED AGAIN OR I WILL CUT YOU FROM GILL TO GILL!
YES, I APOLOGIZE.

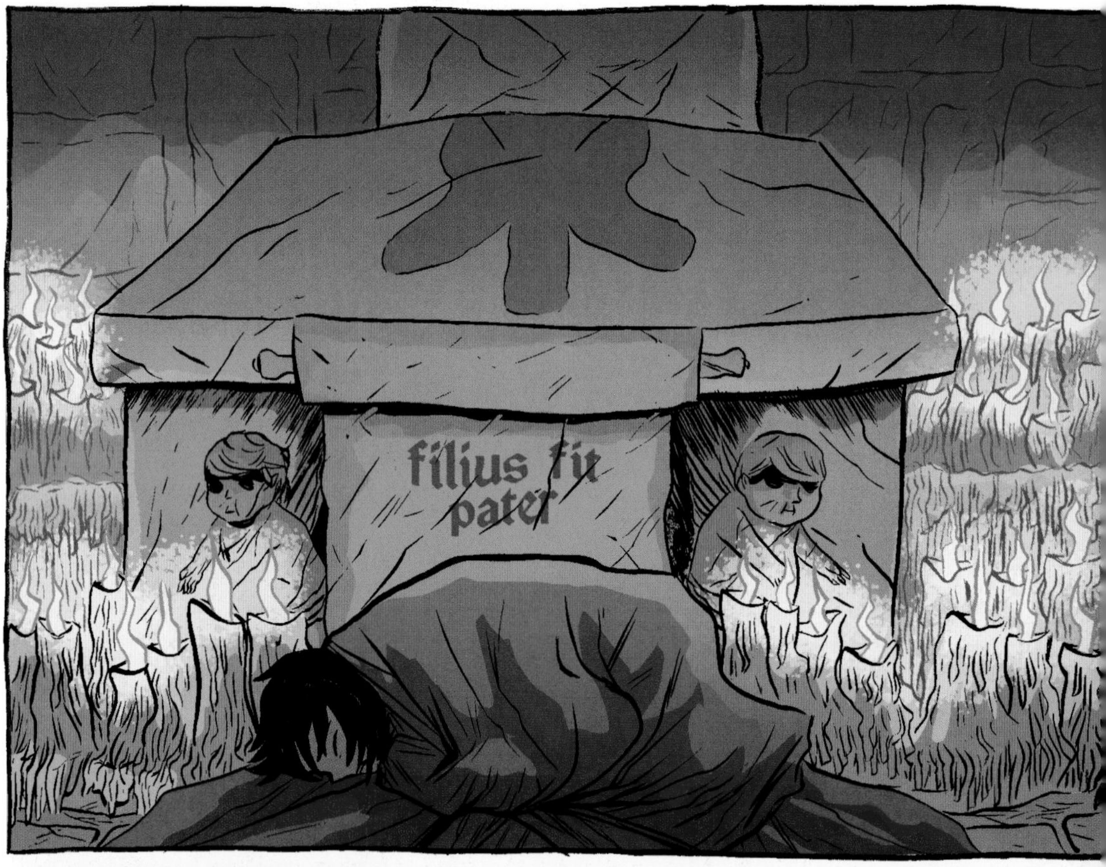
filius fit
pater

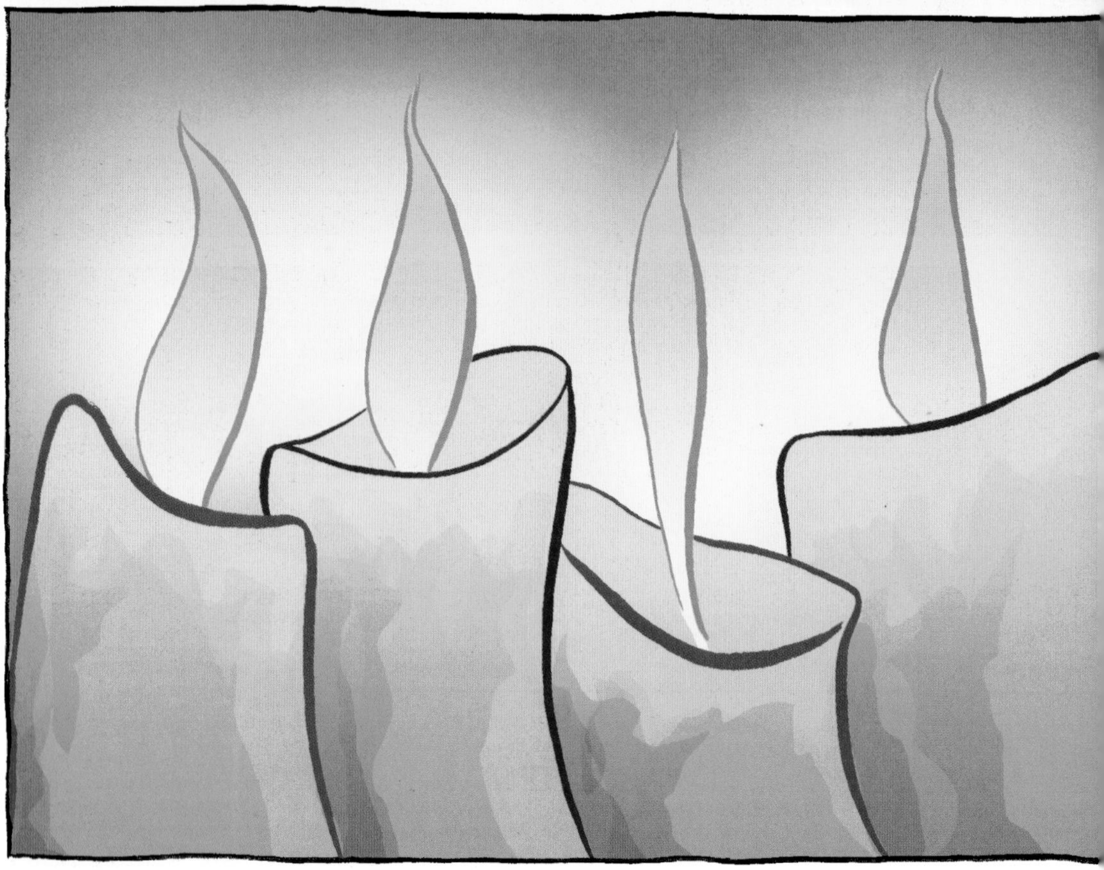

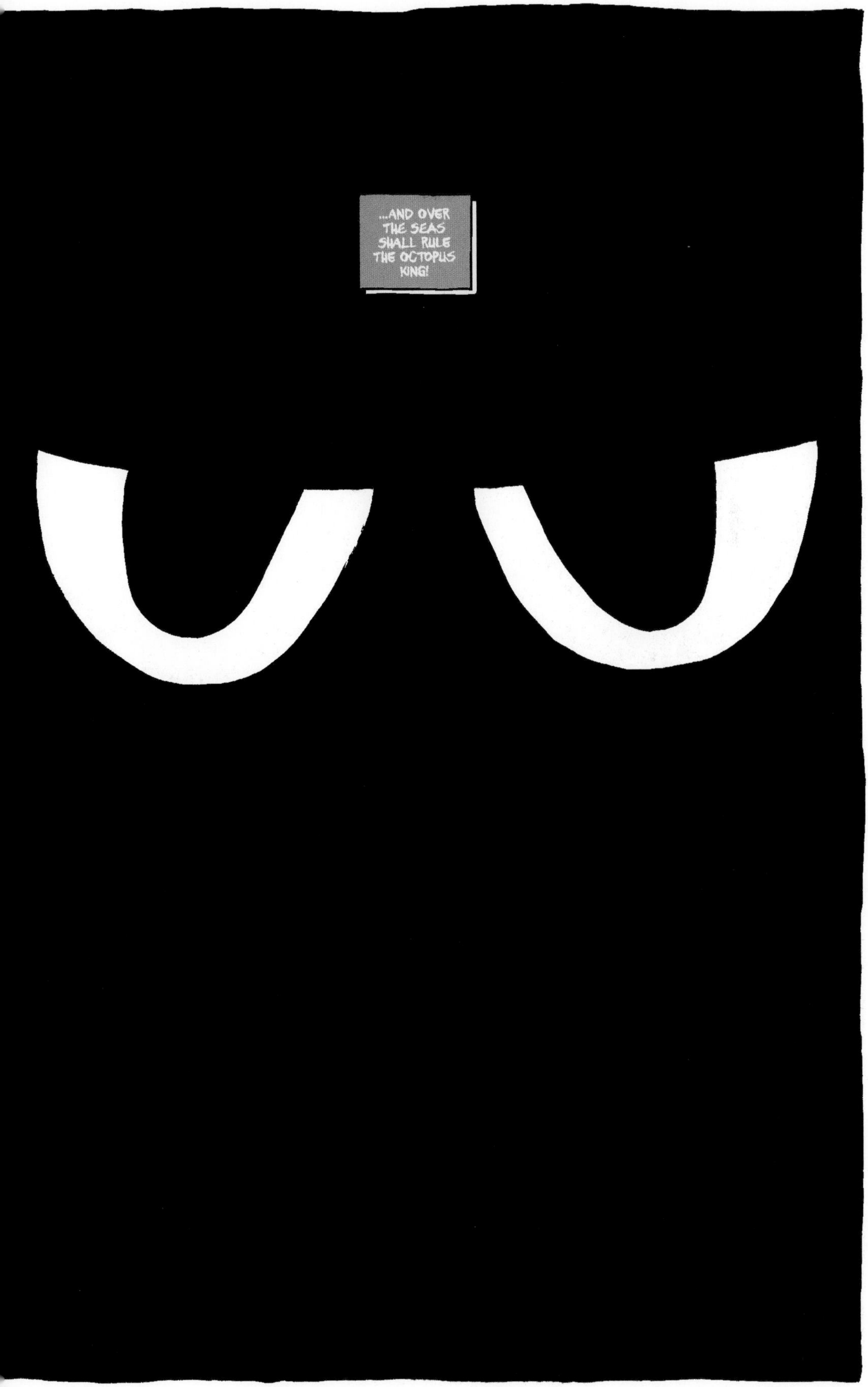
...AND OVER THE SEAS SHALL RULE THE OCTOPUS KING!

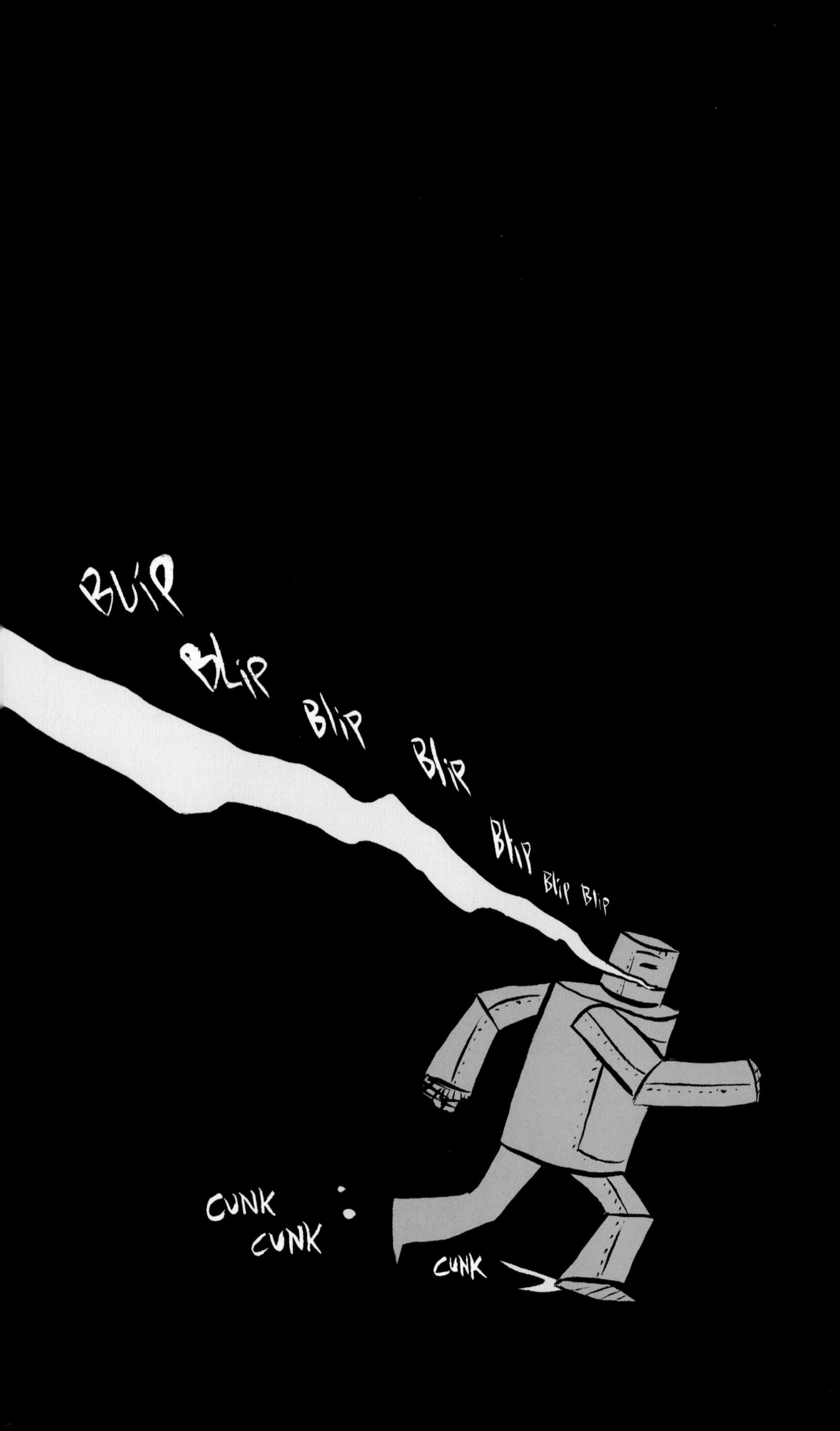
BLIP
BLIP
Blip
Blip
Blip
Blip Blip
CUNK
CUNK
CUNK

BIOGRAPHIES AND THANKS

MARK ANDREW SMITH

Aqua Leung, while looking very simple and elegant, was a hard book to create but it's also something that I'm very proud of on all levels and it's something I will always be very proud of on all levels. *Aqua Leung* is a book that I think years from now people will unearth and be blown away by. Movie deals will roll in and millions and millions of dollars will be made from the franchise. We'll all be dead of course, Paul and I, dying broke and miserable old slags filled with spite and contempt for the world, after starving in the name of our art! I know this  stuff, that's how it works. Look at Shrek and what happened to the guy who created him.

But hey it's going to happen eventually. If people want to appreciate us while we're still around that's even better. Let's raise our glasses and toast to that! I hope it's the latter.

I'm glad we survived it.

—Mark Andrew Smith
South Korea, 2008

Mark Andrew Smith is the writer of *The Amazing Joy Buzzards* from Image Comics. He is also the co-editor of the *PopGun* Anthology. *Aqua Leung* is his first full color book. Look for a lot more work from him this upcoming year.

Mark would like to thank his family: His Dad, Yvonne, and his brothers Neal, Cooper, and Benjamin, who he owes the world to.

He would also like to thank Dan Hipp, who created *The Amazing Joy Buzzards* with him and started with him in comics. A very big thank you is due to Jim Mahfood and Scott Morse for getting him excited about comics again and teaching him just what comics are capable of. A special thanks is due to Joe Keatinge, D.J. Kirkbride, Cassandra Pasley, and Justin Robinson. Special thanks to Jeff Kelly, the *Satellite Soda* Crew, Cheeks, Guy Davis, Mike Mignola, Dave Crosland, Mike Huddleston, James Kochalka, Count Chocula, the letters M & S, and Rick Cortes.

Mark would like to thank Erik Larsen, Eric Stephenson, and Image Comics for their continued belief and support

A VERY special thanks to Paul Maybury, Russ Lowery for colors that really made the pages come to life, Thomas Mauer, and Steven Finch—his letters are the voices of the characters.

PAUL MAYBURY

Paul Maybury is an award winning artist currently living in Austin, Texas. Born in 1982 in Boston, MA, Paul grew up with a love for modern art, graffiti and comics. In 1996, Paul began a career as a muralist contributing to over 45 works of art before leaving painting to pursue comics in 2001. Since then Paul has popped up in several anthologies and back up stories leading up to the release of his first full length graphic novel *Aqua Leung*. It should also be noted that Paul learned how to use a brush on this very book, and is quite embarrassed by the early  pages. In between making his dreams come true as a comic book artist and to pay rent, Paul has served you coffee, wrapped your cheese, sold you music and DVDs, cleaned up your streets and drawn those goofy grocery store chalkboards you enjoy. Paul is currently working on his next solo graphic novel titled *Party Bear*. He can be found at http://www.paulmaybury.com.

"First off, thanks to my mother Silvia and my father Paul for supporting what I've always wanted to do with myself. My girlfriend Cassandra and her parents for putting up with years of Aqua Leung talk. My friends, Ben, Melissa, Danny, Pontman, Jeni Flakes, Jen and Jess the super twins, and Chrissy.

"A special thanks to the people that were supportive of me before I was "that dude that drew *Aqua Leung*," Dan Goldman, Joe Keatinge and the rest of Image, Nikki Cook, Dino and the rest of my ACT-I-VATE family, Jarrod Decosta, Chris Piers, Robert Kirkman, Mike Oeming (I owe both Mike and Robert lunch in the future) ,Jimi Hazel, Niel Vokes, Sergio Aragones, Jim Mahfood, Ron at Comicopia, Ms.Bilal, Rich Gasbarro, Ed McGuiness, Ivan Brandon, Jon Malin, Tak Toyoshima and the DIG, Erin and Ben at NEC, Greg T., Ken Knudtsen, Thobeka Rigmaiden, Dean Trippe, Dick Hyacinth, Chris Arrant (for being one of the first to cover me), Steve Goldman, Jeff Newelt, Michael Deforgeo, David Hopkins and FBR, Kate McInnes and Tarwin Stroh-Spijer the master webdesigners, B. Clay Moore, Stan Sakai, Bob Dahlstrom, Chris Chua, Kimo, Ed Foster, Frank Espinosa, Heidi MacDonald, Jacque Fabrizi, Javier Hernandez, Alberto Ruiz, Khary Randolph, Kyle Scroggins, Mark Englert, Jeffrey Brown, Jacque Fabrizi, Michael Todd (even if you're an ass), Chris Pitzer, Robert Friis, Sean "Cheeks" Galloway and Jonboy, Danimation, Benito and 200Nate, Jeremy Dale, Dash Martin, Jen Lee, Terry Stevens and the rest of Penciljack.com, Jacob Baake. Mark, D.J., Steven, Thomas for working so hard on this book. A special thanks to Russ for putting up with me messing with the colors contantly to get it just the way I saw it in my head.

"If I forgot your name, I'm sorry, but this list is getting a little long!"

RUSS LOWERY

Russ Lowery is a comic book colorist in Louisville, KY. He is a boy among men and a god among atheists. He has no pets.

FONOGRAFIKS

Fonografiks is a studio specializing in digital lettering, graphic design, and pre-press production for comic books.

"Thanks to Benito, Nate, Ivan, Joe, Mark, and Paul for the breaks; Matt, Evin, and Dan for their patience; Joanne for the extra pair of eyes; and Sarah for nagging us into buying that first Mac."

D.J. KIRKBRIDE

D.J. Kirkbride has stories published in *PopGvun Vol. 1* and *The Dead Walk Again!* zombie anthology. He's also a columnist and editor for thefootnote.net, which he encourages everyone to take a look at next time they're on the interwebs. He'd like to thank Mark Smith for giving him sneak peeks at cool books like *Aqua Leung*. Also, he has to thank his mom for-you know-giving birth to him.

CASSANDRA PASLEY

Cassandra has no previous experience in comics but she is a teacher, nanny, business manager and grammar/spelling enthusiast. She would like to thank Paul and Mark for giving her this great opportunity, her parents for letting her continue to live in their back bedroom, and Wheelock for forcing her to learn the writing skills that most people never need or use.

Cassandra can be reached at cpasley001@gmail.com.

THOMAS MAUER

Over the past few years Thomas Mauer has burst onto the scene, working as a writer, editor, letterer, designer, art director and production manager for publishers such as AAM/Markosia, Archaia Studios Press, Brain Scan Comics, Image Comics, Ronin Studios, Silent Devil, Spacedog/Vibe Magazine, Speakeasy Comics, Th3rd World Studios, Viper Comics, and Zenescope Entertainment. He currently acts as AAM/Markosia's and Silent Devil's production manager. His lettering credits include *Kong: King of Skull Island, Starship Troopers,* and  *The Boy Who Made Silence* for AAM/Markosia, *Thirteen Steps* for Desperado, *PopGun, Outlaw Territories, Next Issue Project,* and *The Surreal Adventures of Edgar Allan Poo Vol. 1* for Image as well as *Killer of Demons* for Viper, *Awakening* for Archaia, *Willow Creek* for Zenescope, and dozens more.

"I'd like to thank Mark & Paul, Christian Beranek, Phil Hester, Joe Keatinge, Andy Kuhn, Rich Johnston, Harry Markos, Scott Wegener, and Christopher Yost for the many great opportunities in the industry, and my family for keeping the faith."

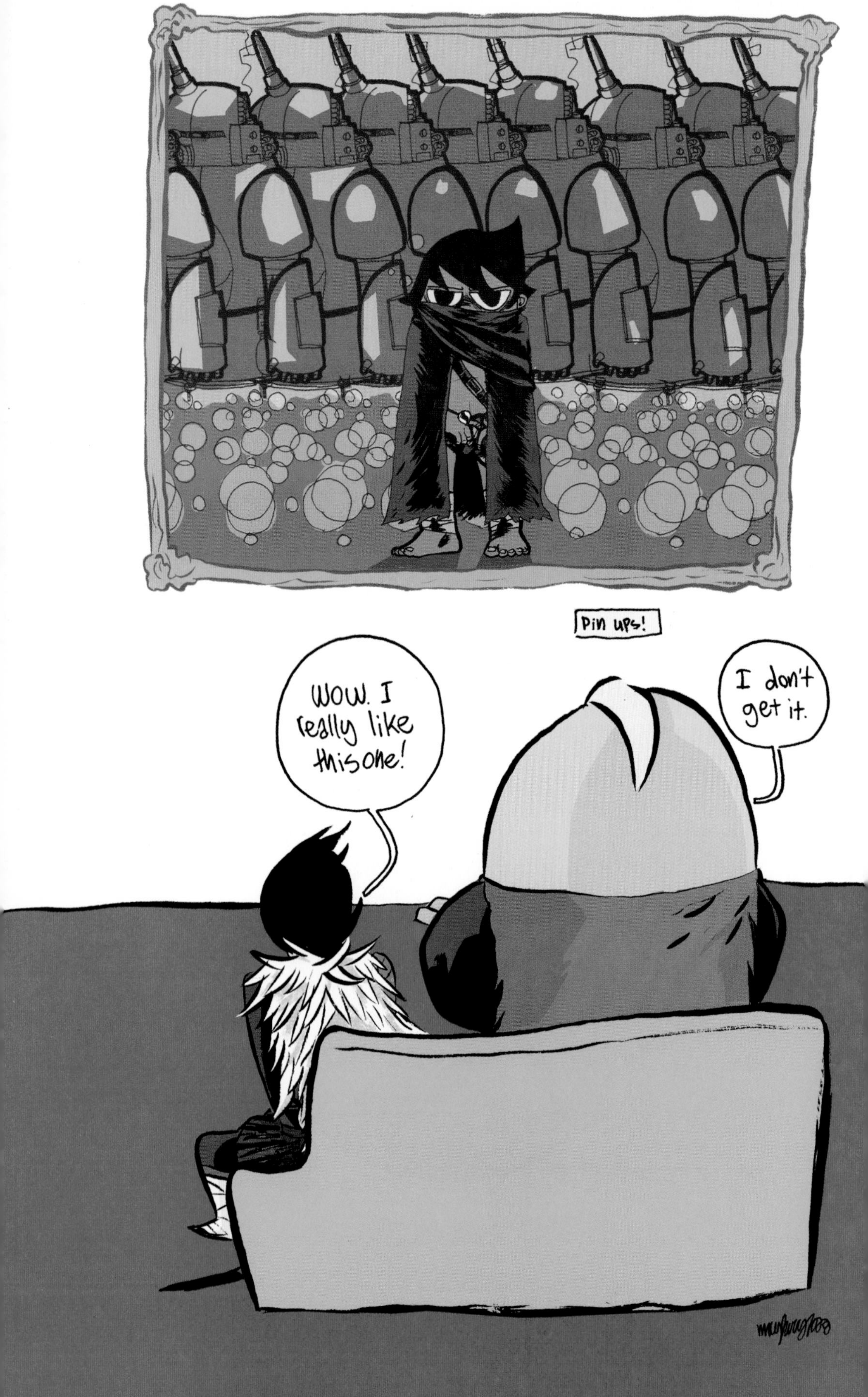
Pin ups!
Wow. I really like this one!
I don't get it.

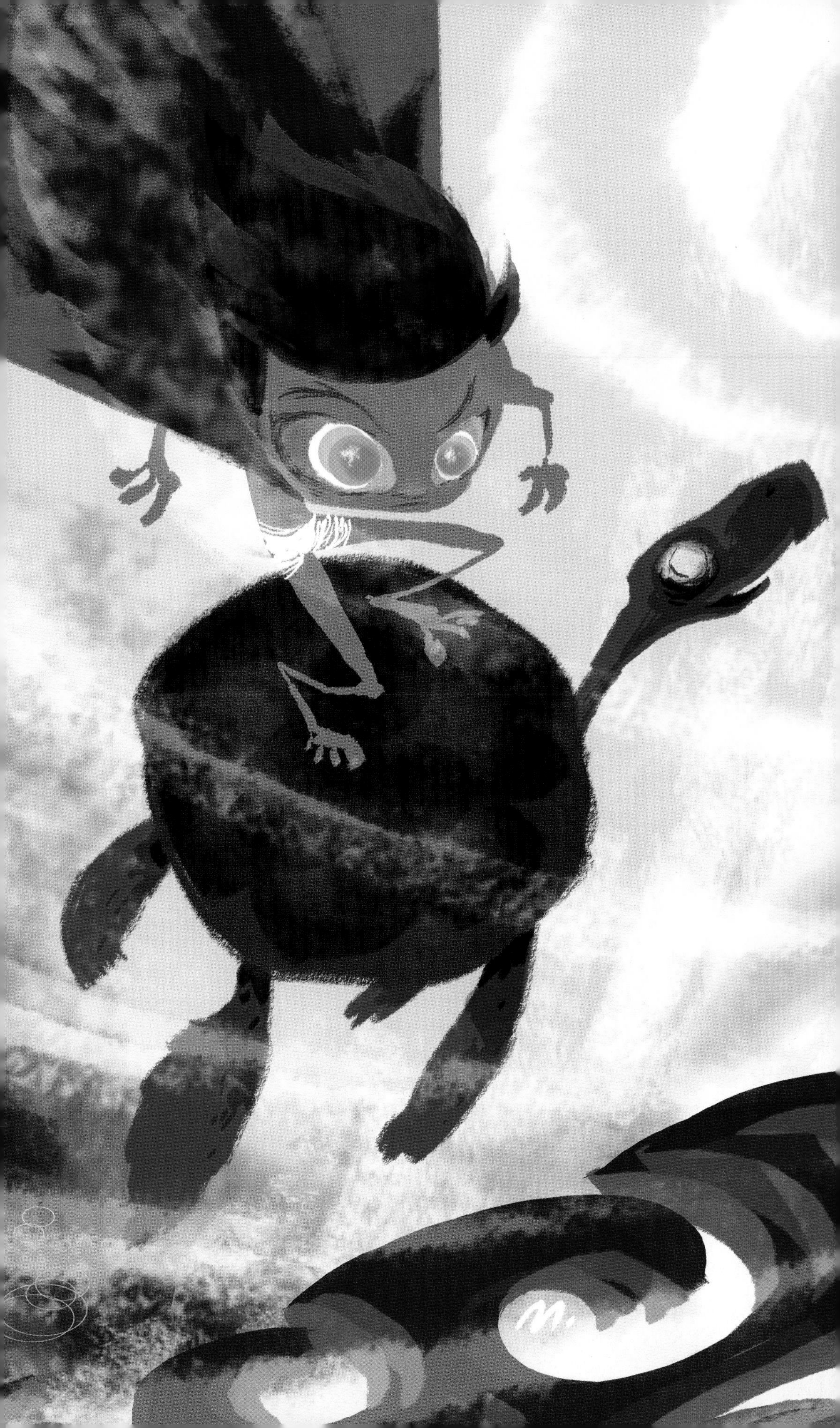

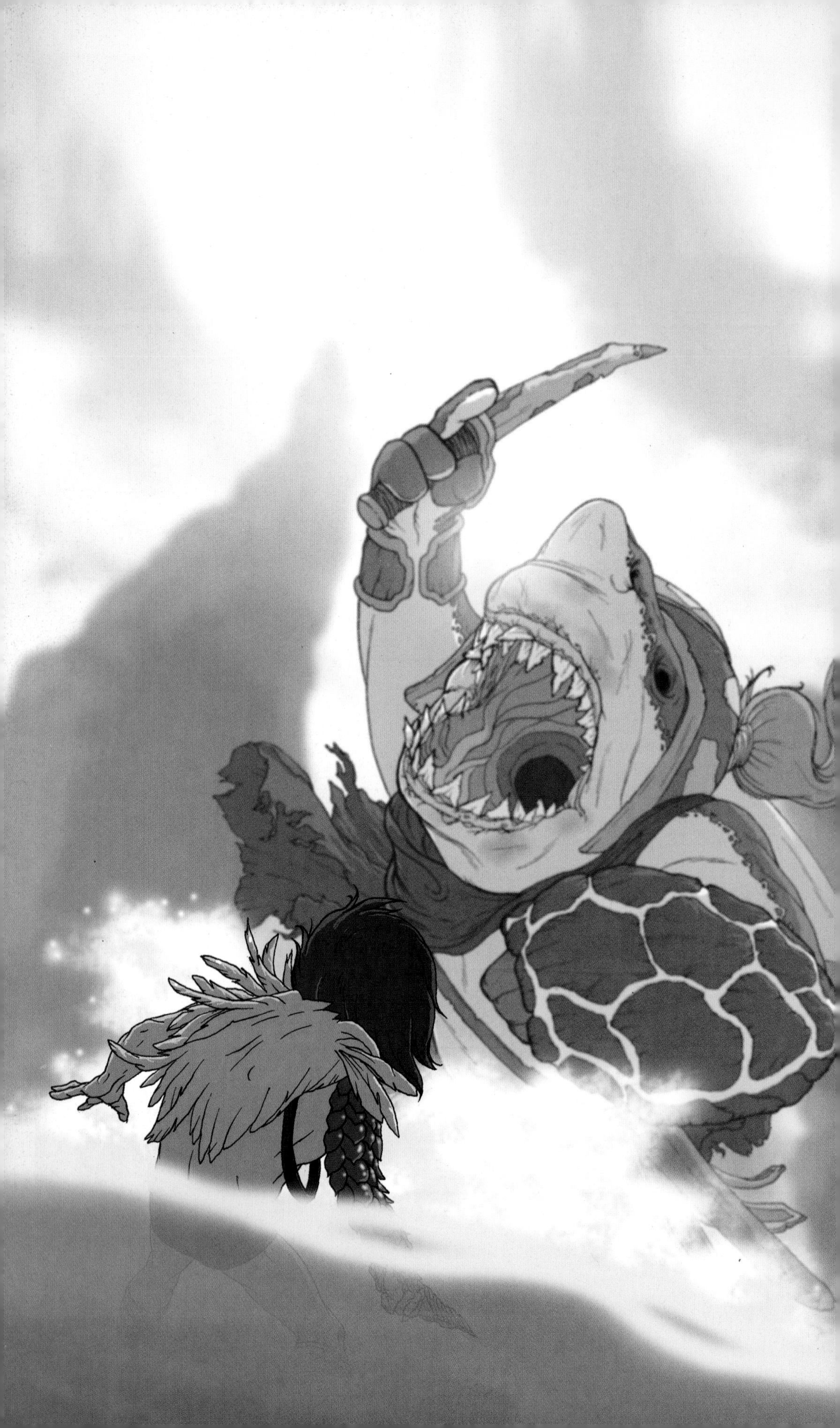

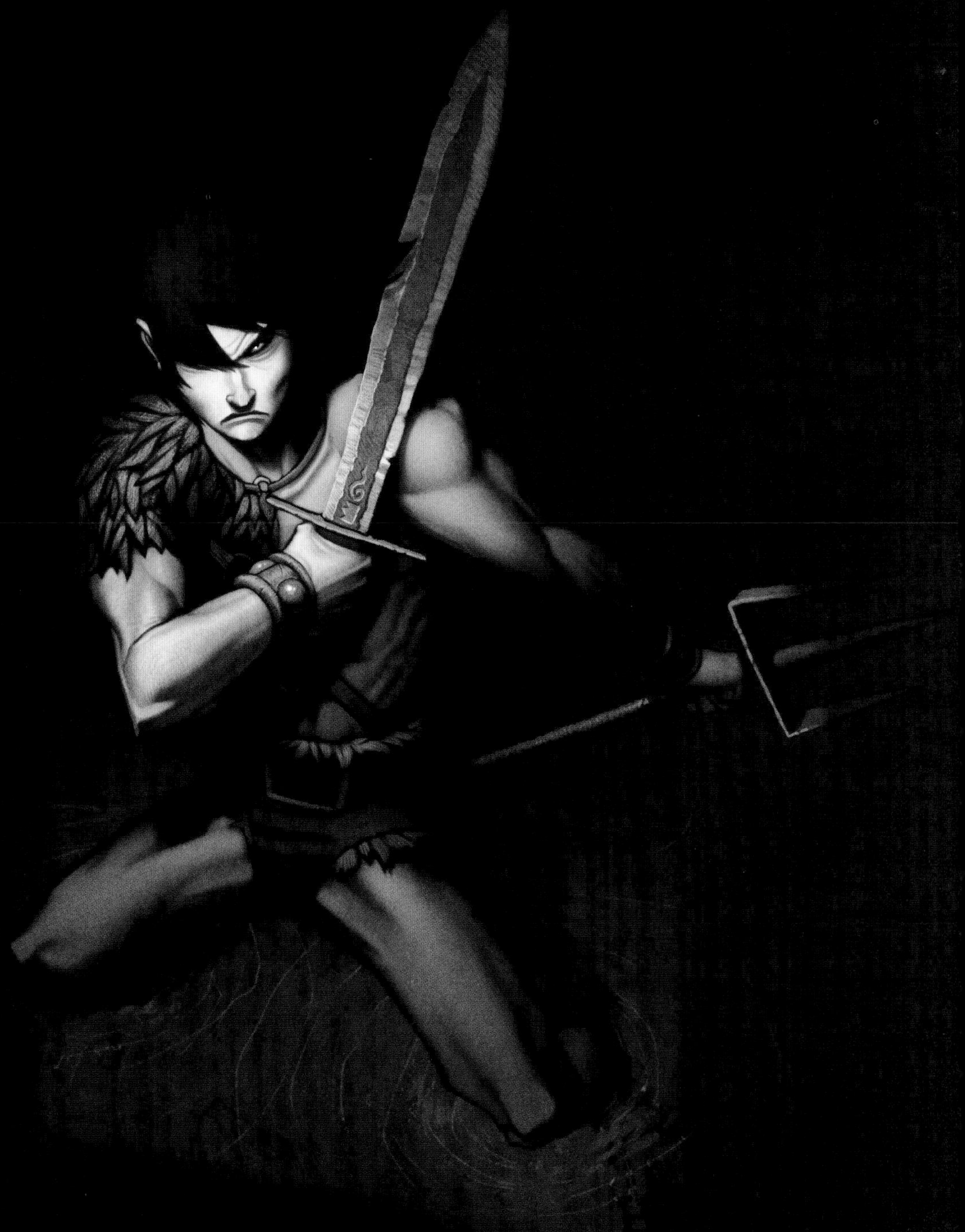

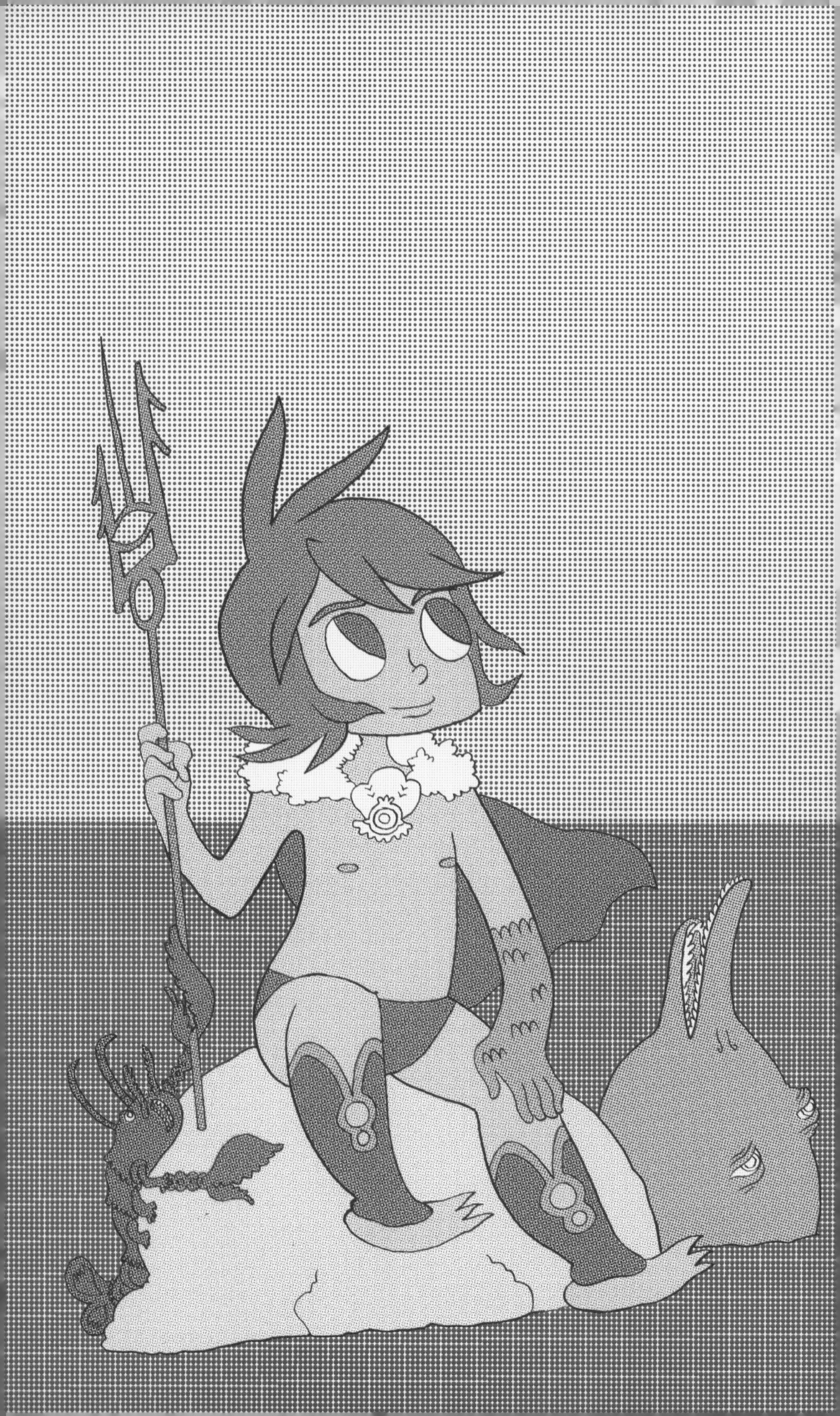

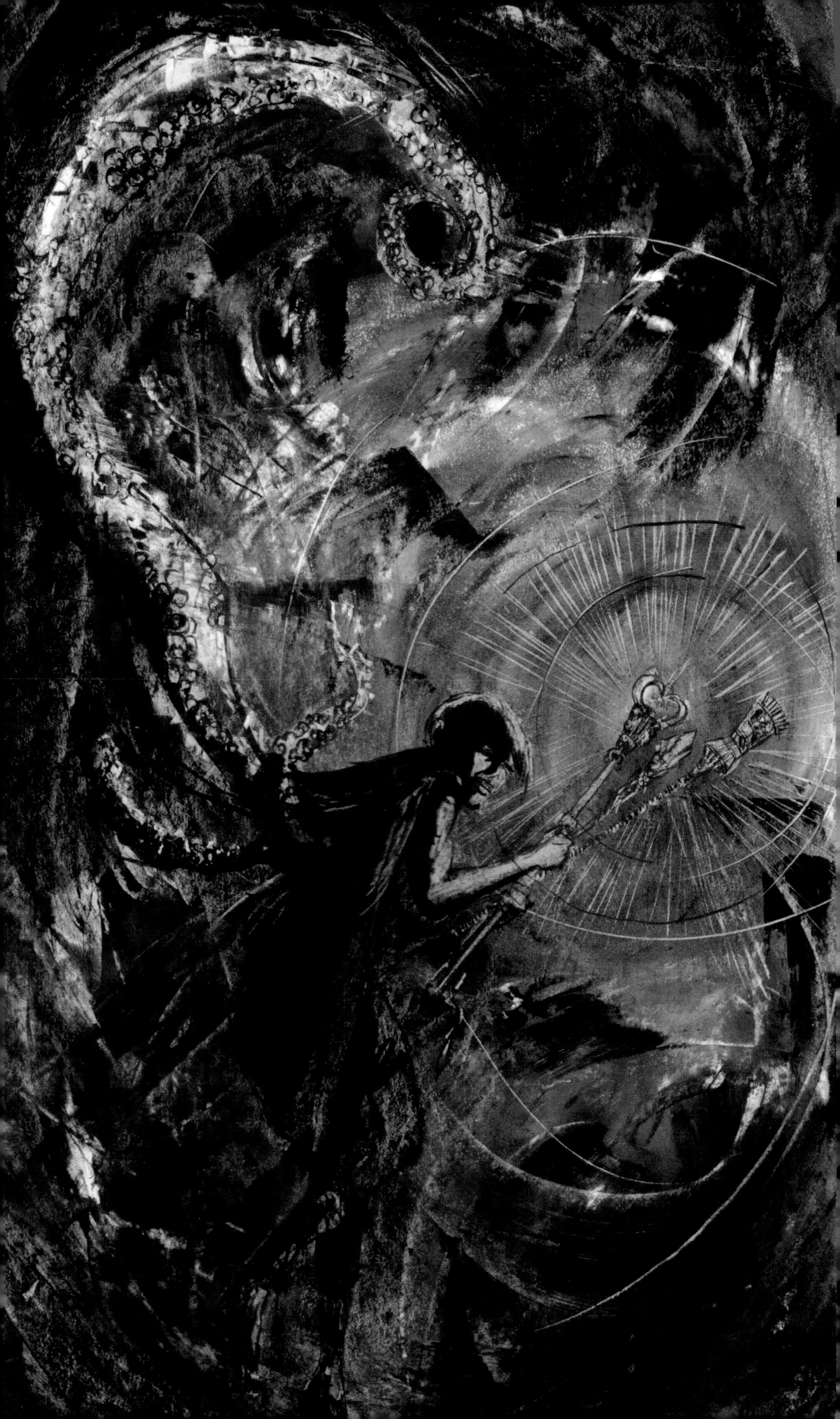

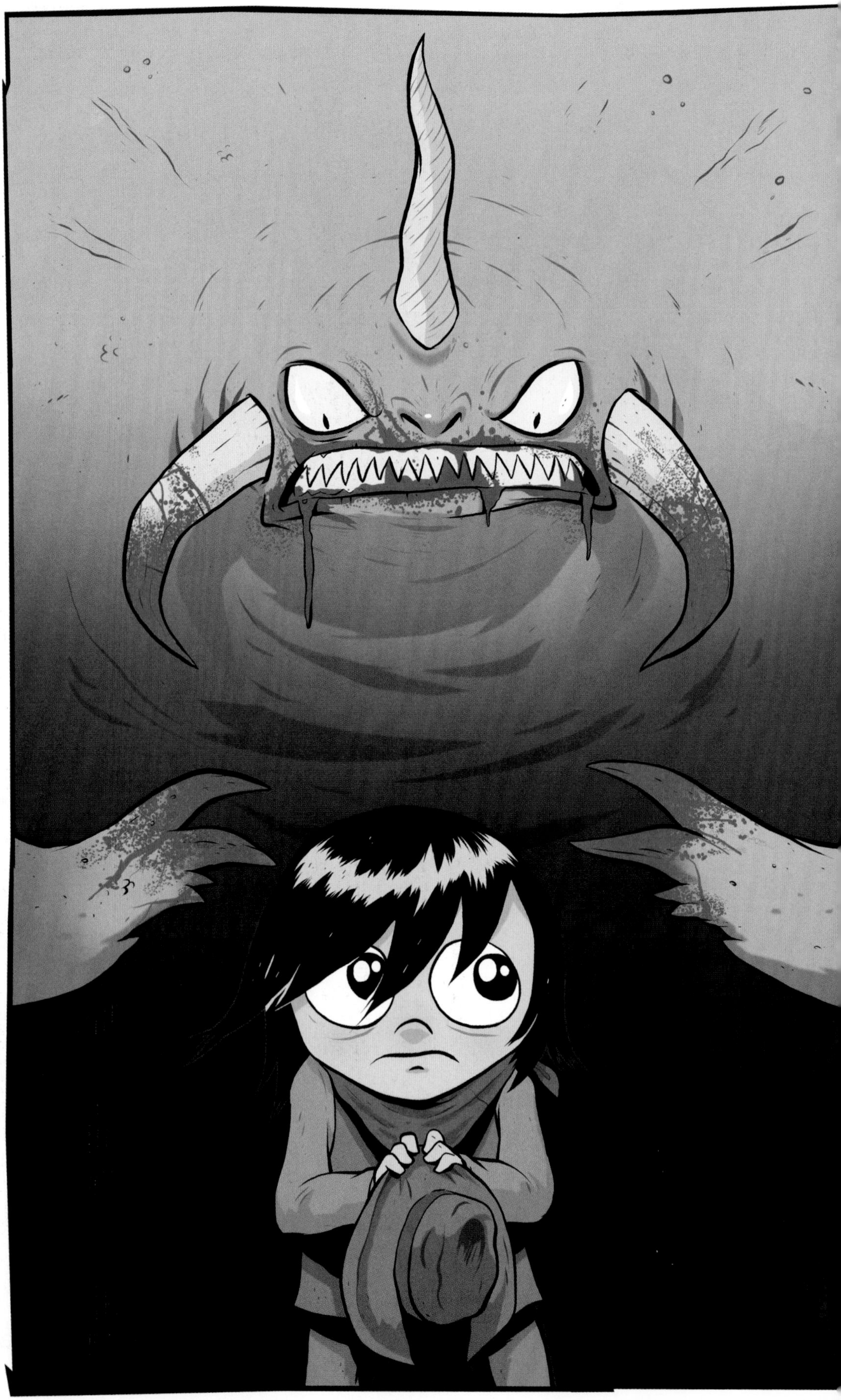

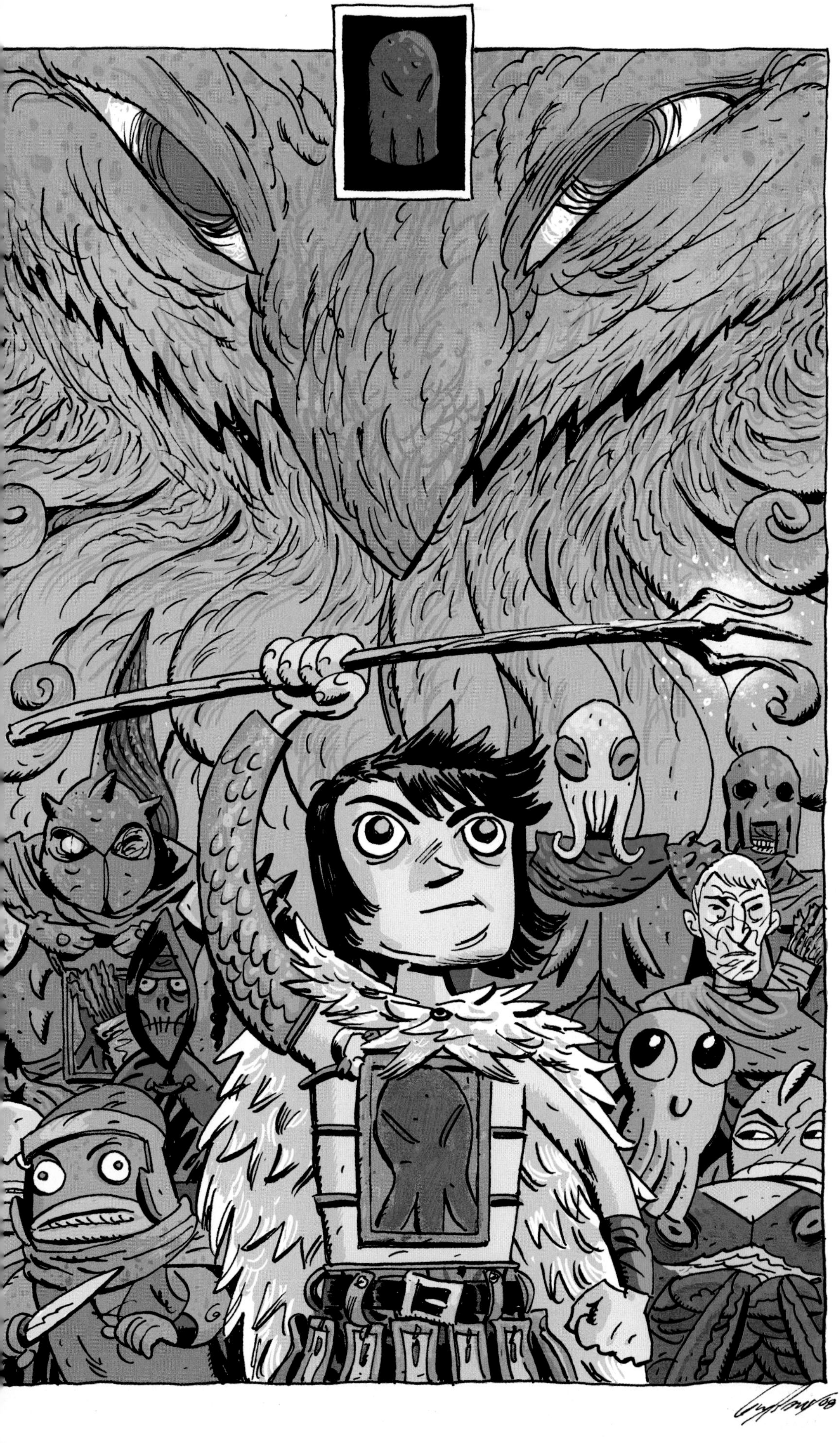

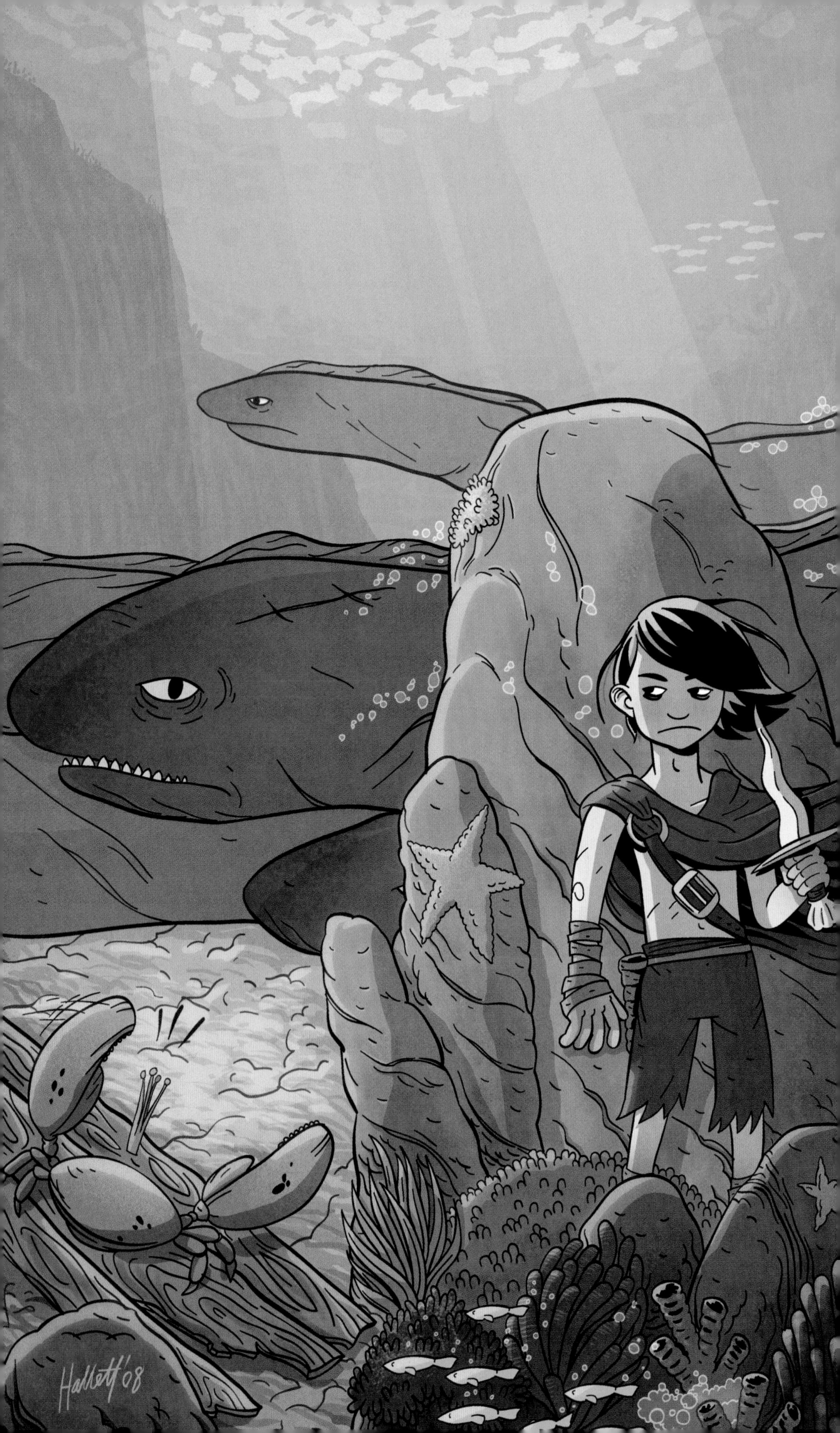
Hallett '08

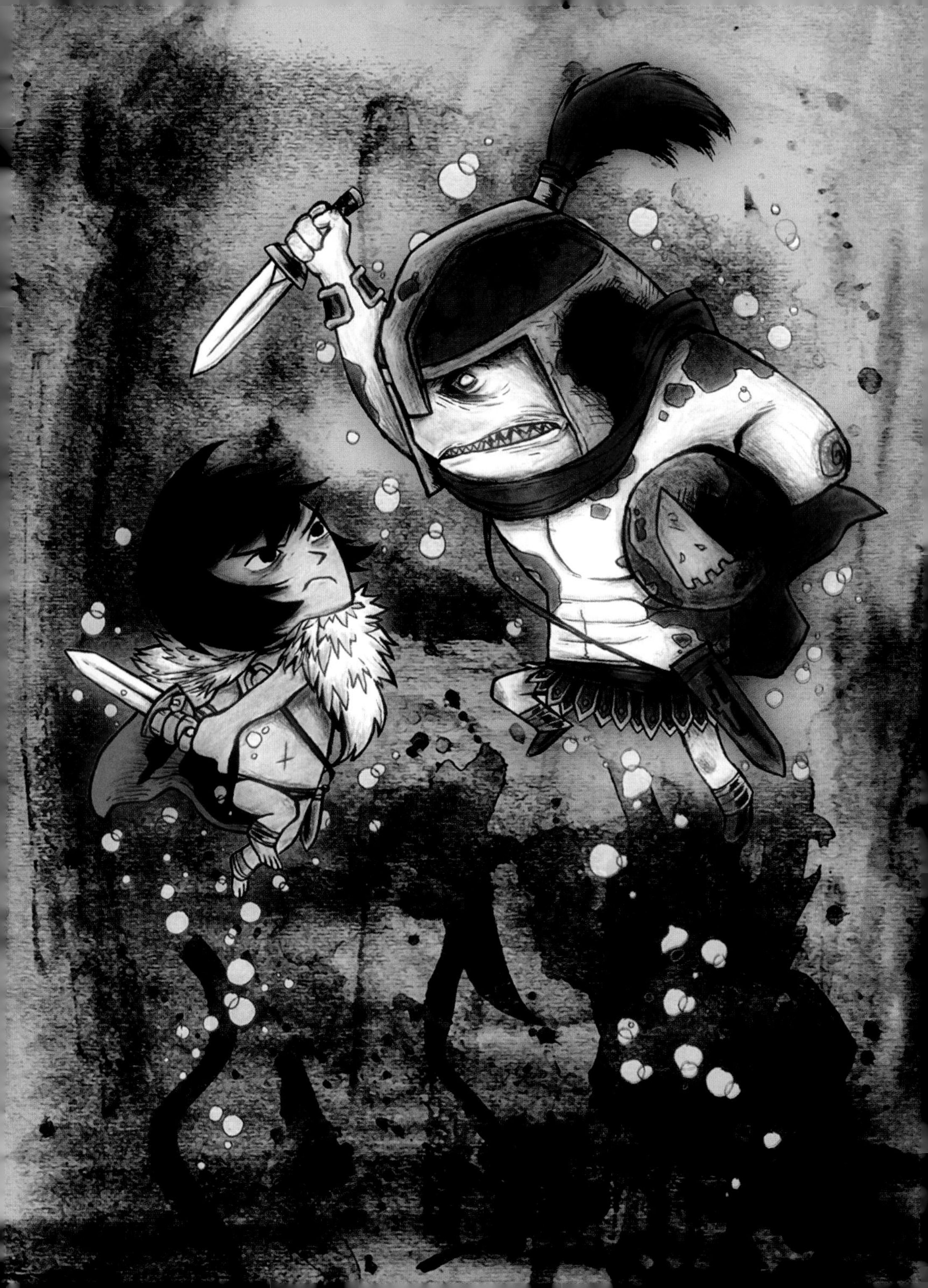

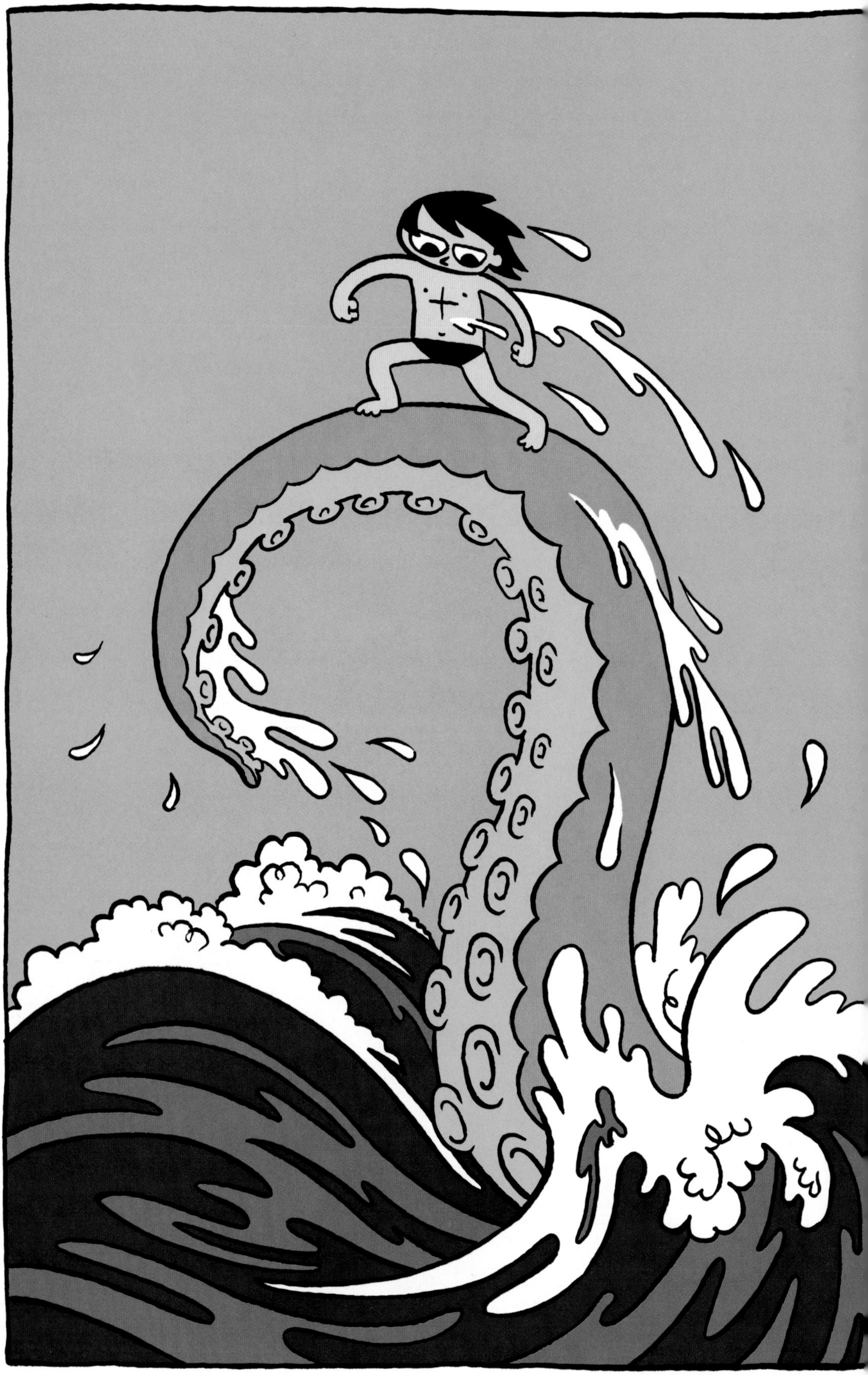

JAMES KOCHALK

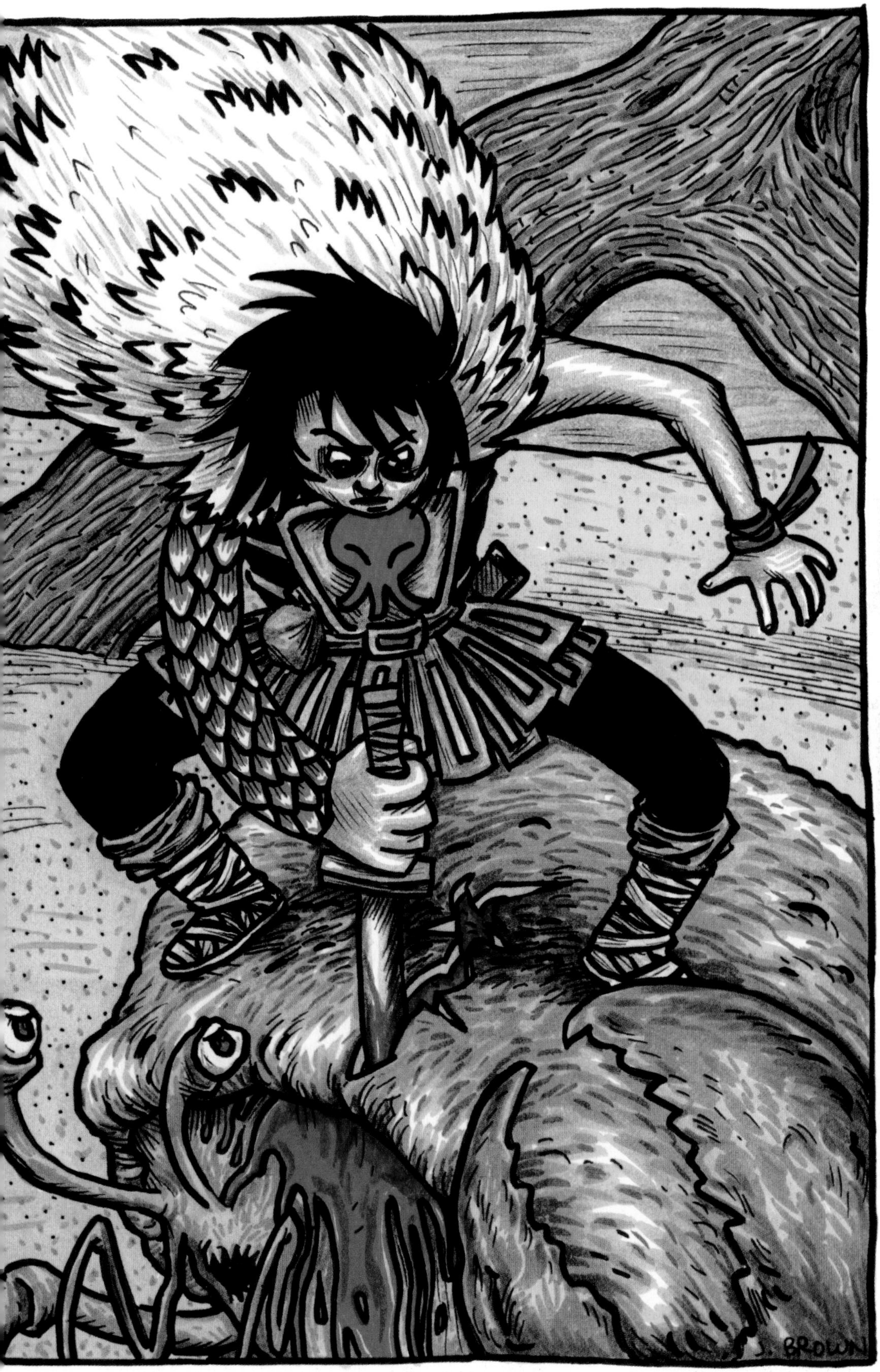
J. BROWN

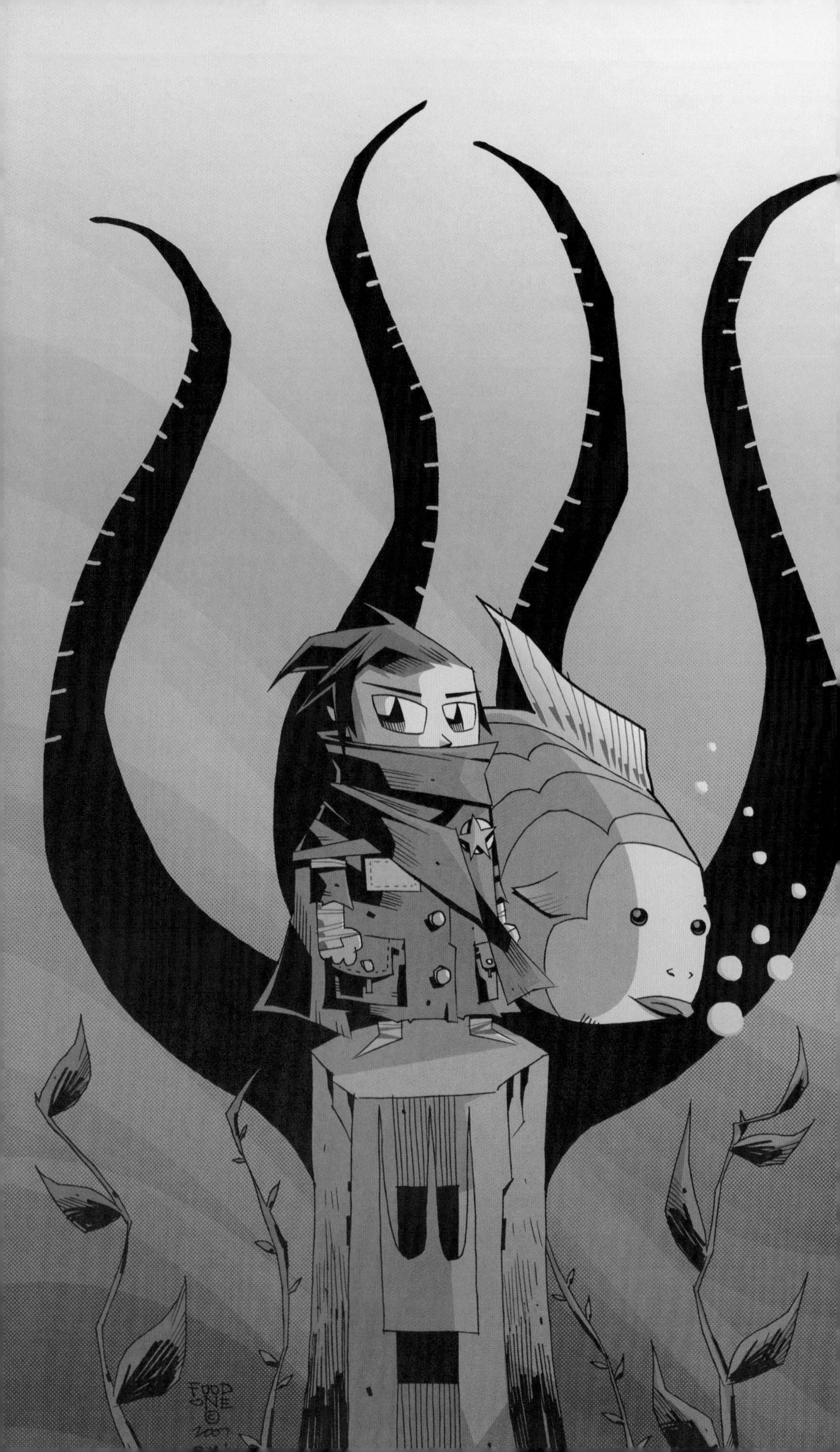
FOOD ONE © 2007

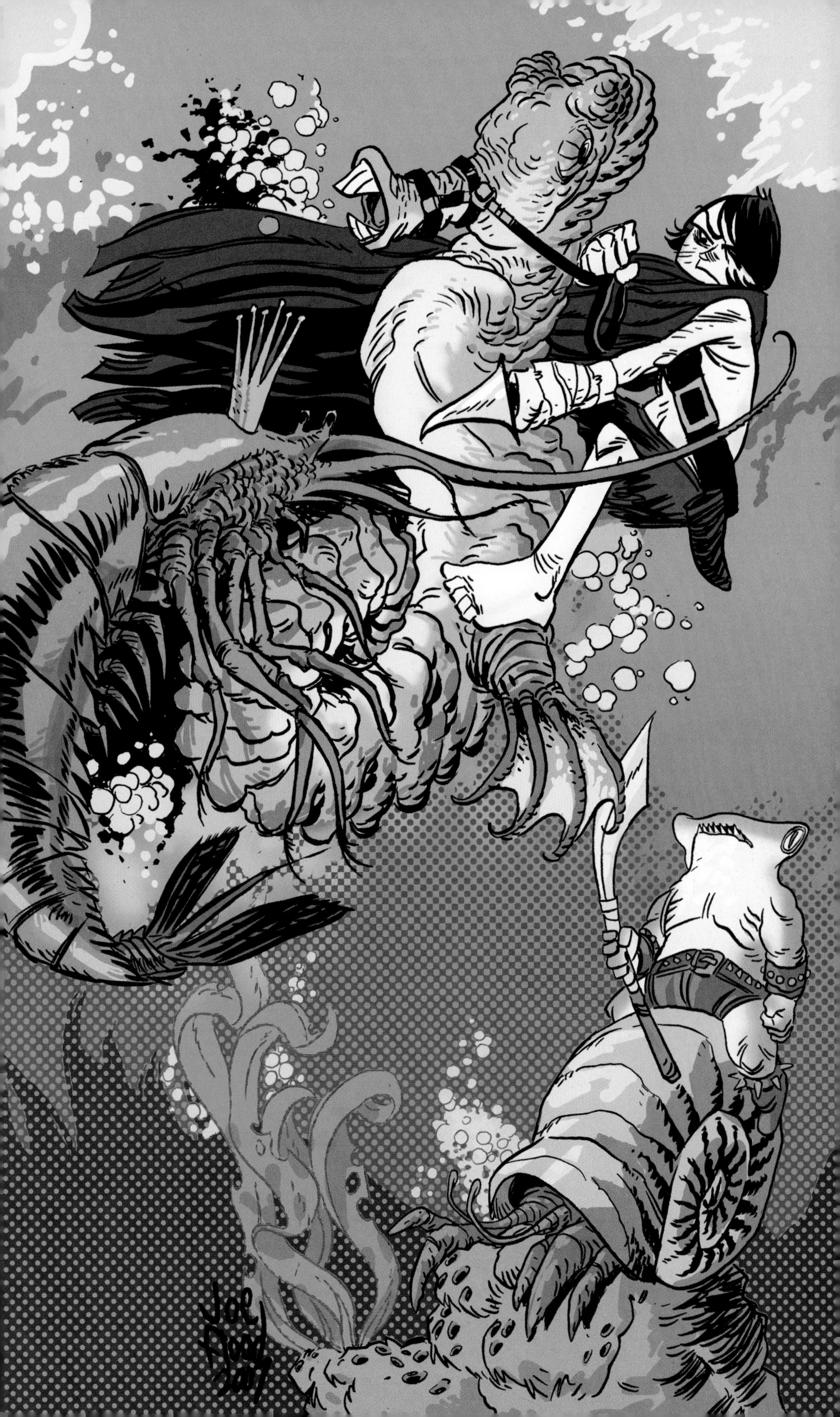

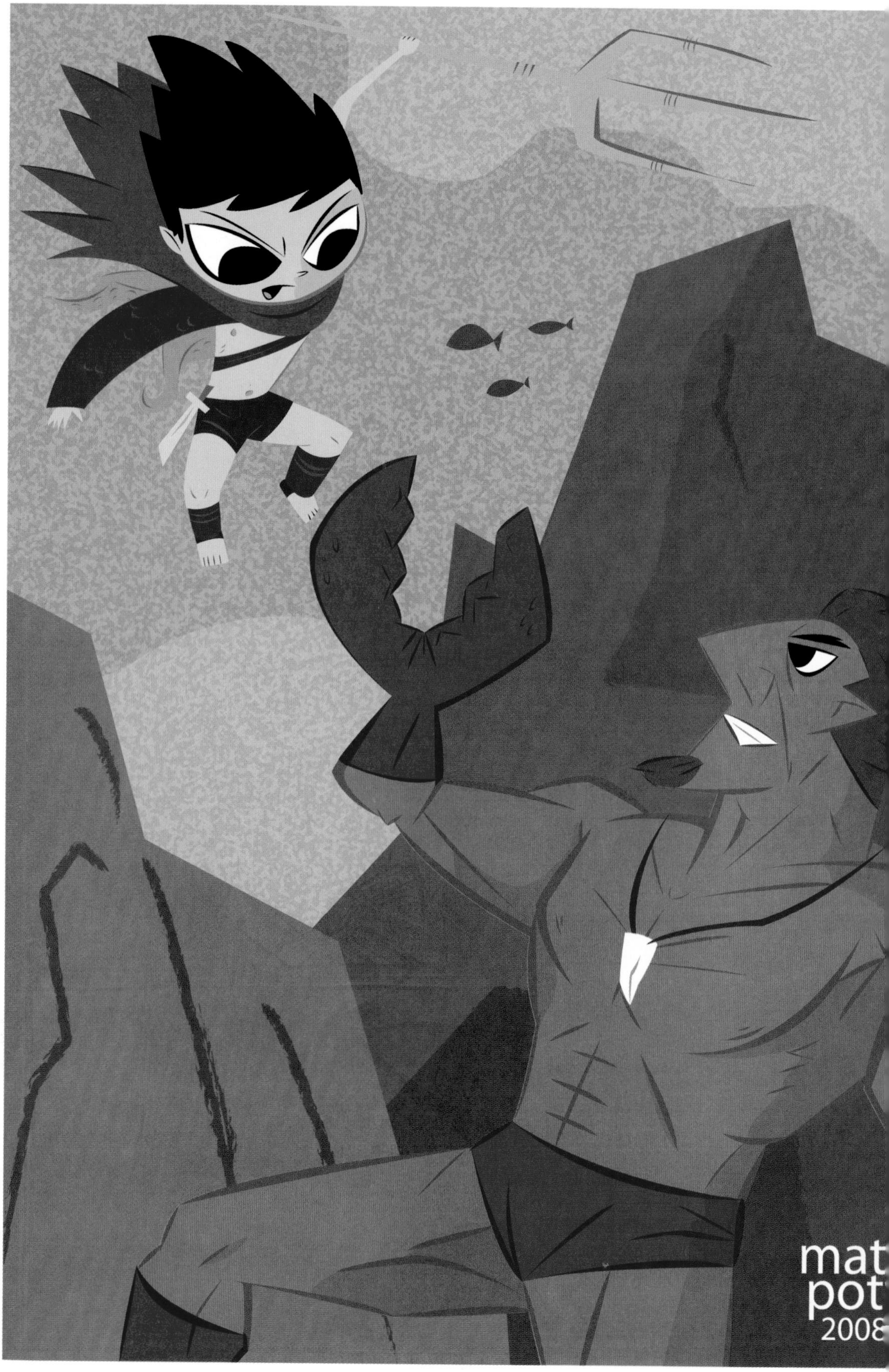
mat
pot
2008

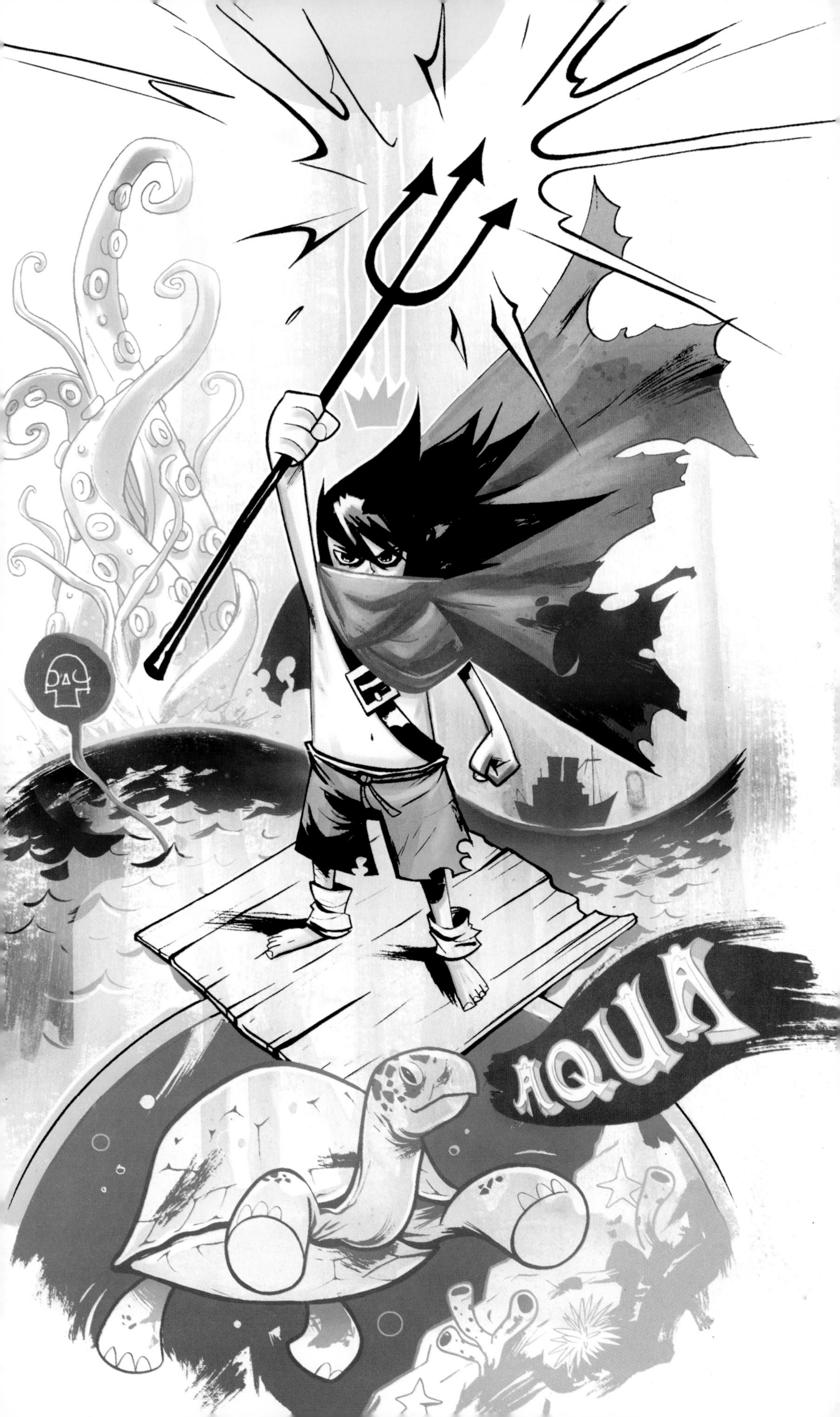
AQUA

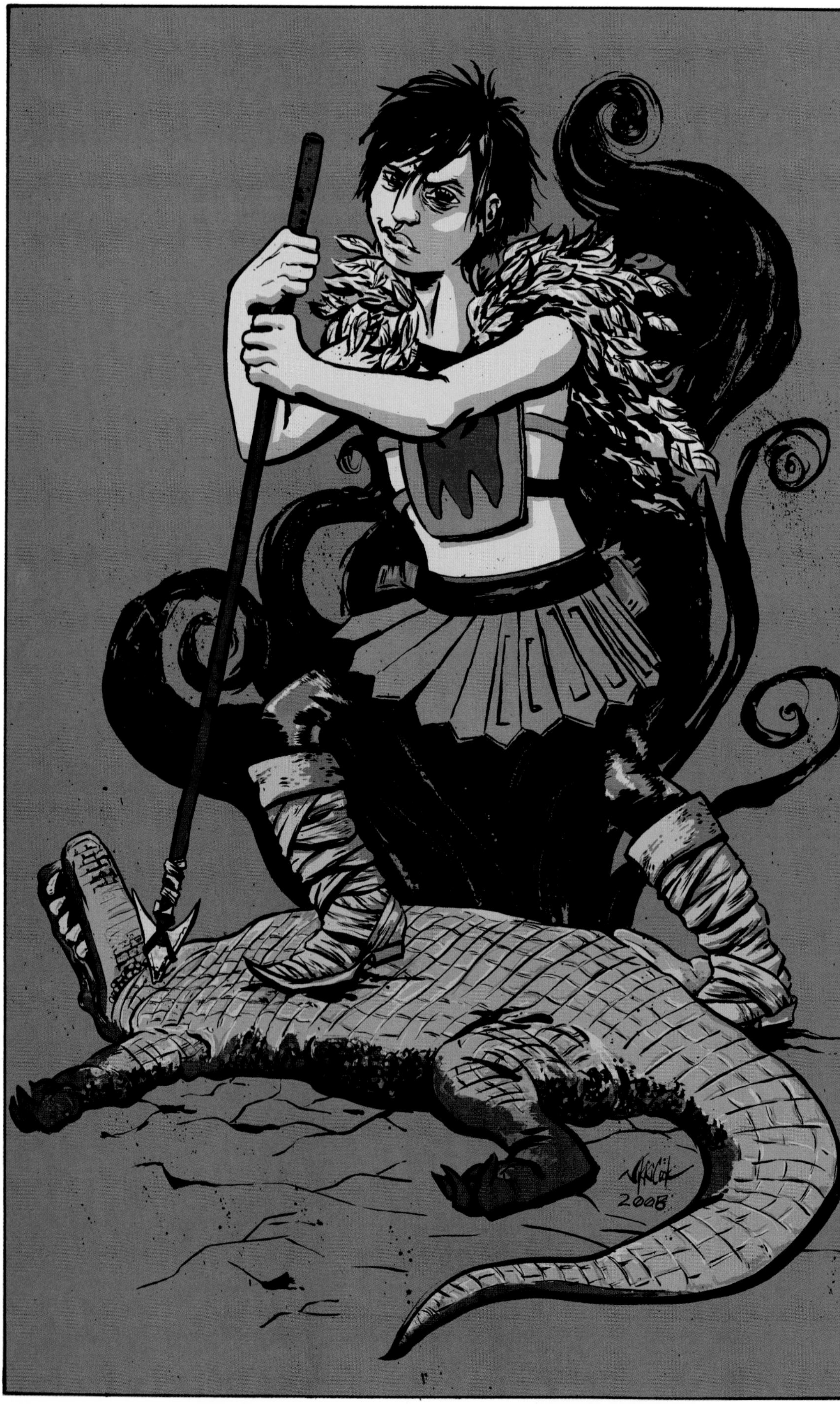
2008

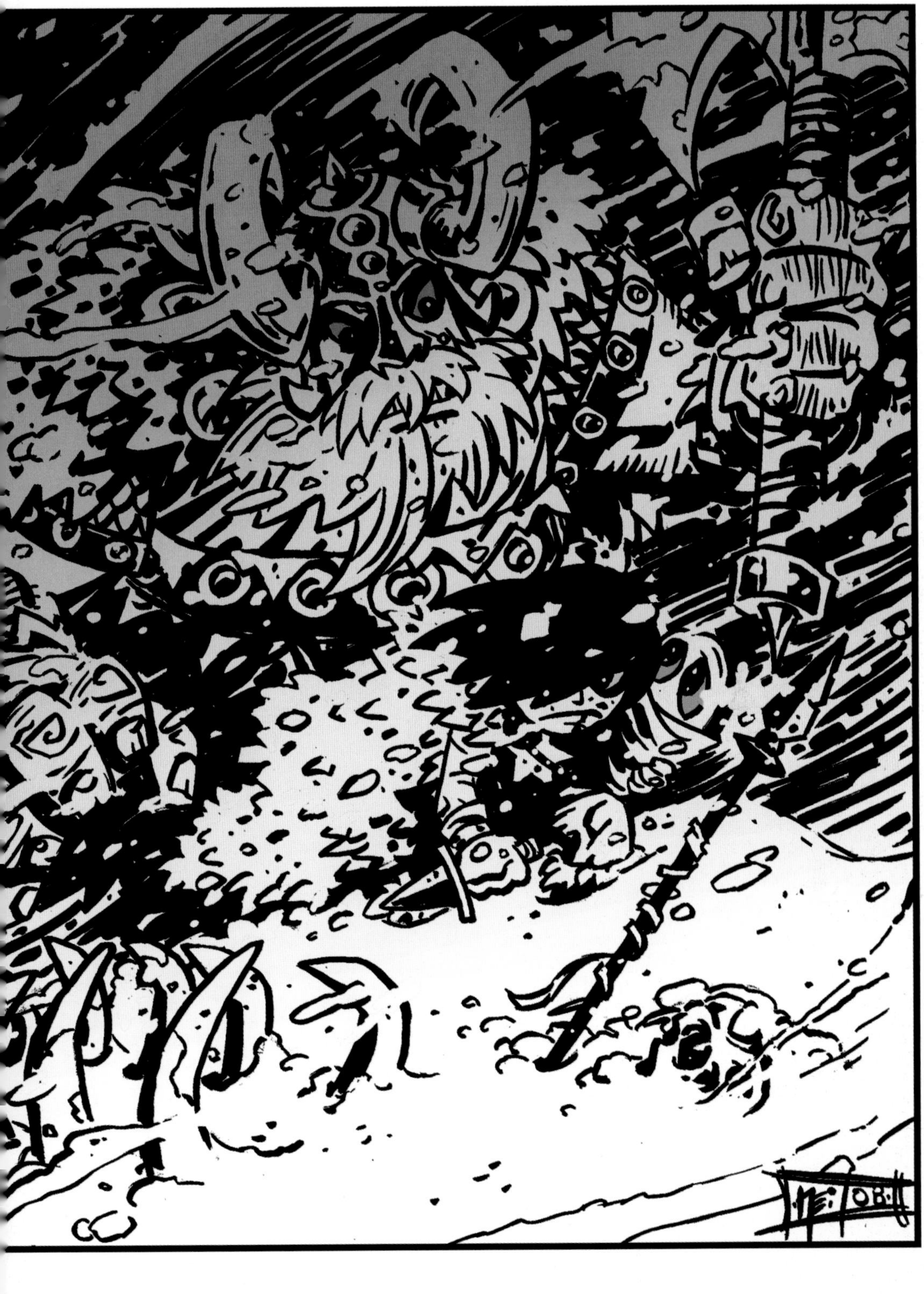

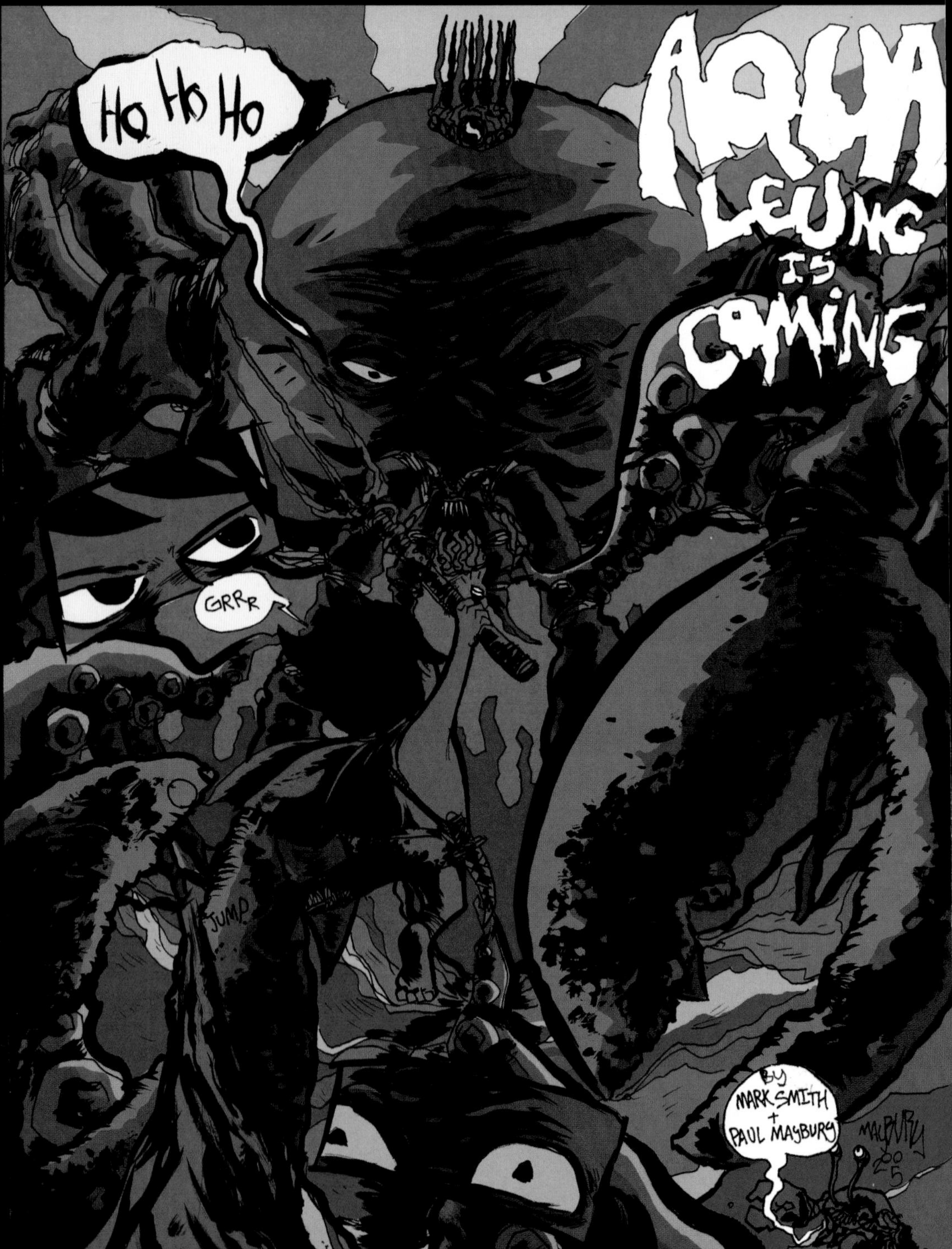
HO HO HO
AQUA LEUNG IS COMING
GRRR
JUMP
BY MARK SMITH + PAUL MAYBURY
MAYBURY 2005

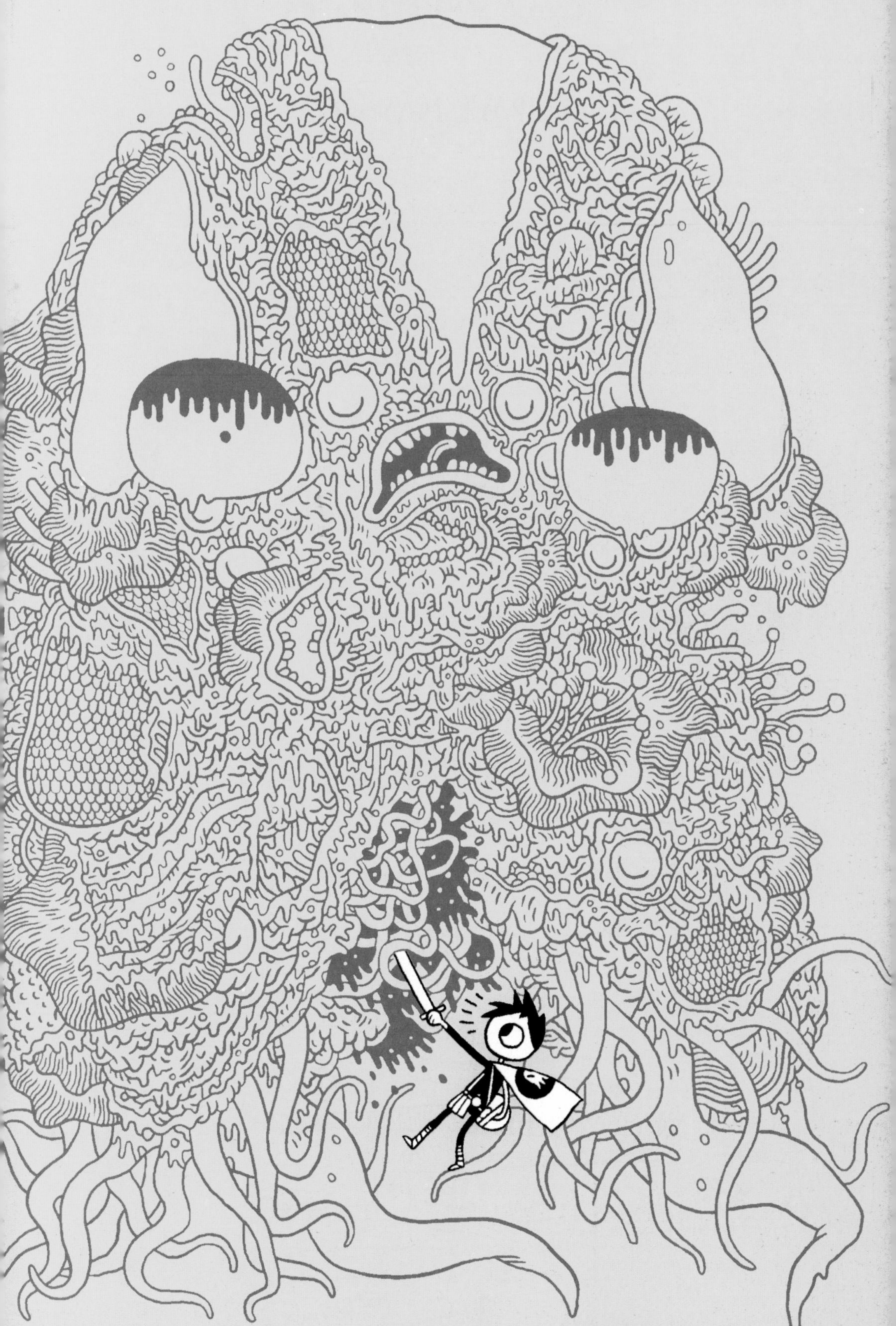

LAYOUT PAGES

BY

PAUL MAYBURY

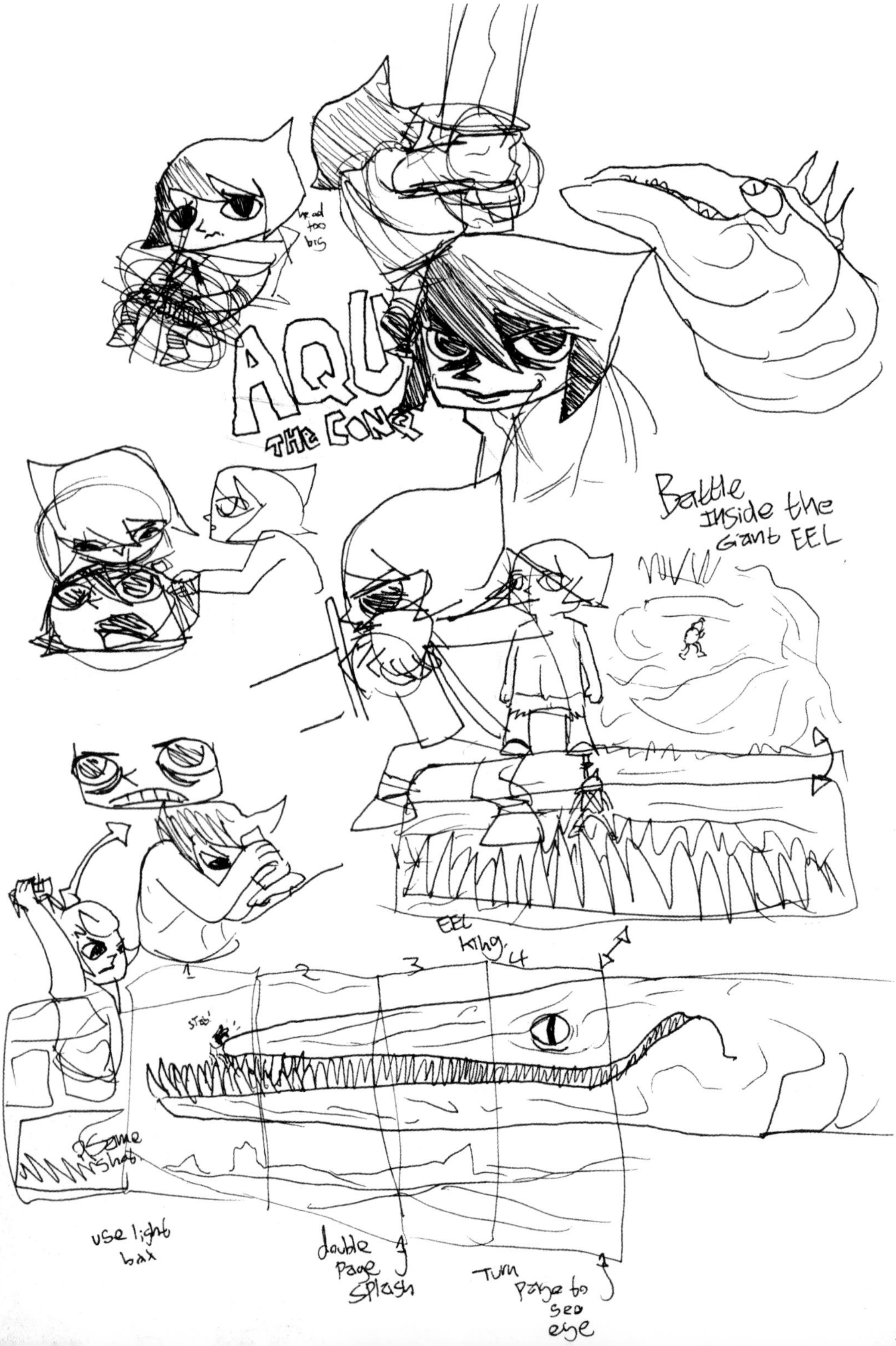

head too big
AQU
the Conq
Battle inside the Giant EEL
EEL King
1
2
3
4
Stab!
Same shot
use light box
double page splash
Turn page to see eye

AQUA COVERS

front, back n two flaps

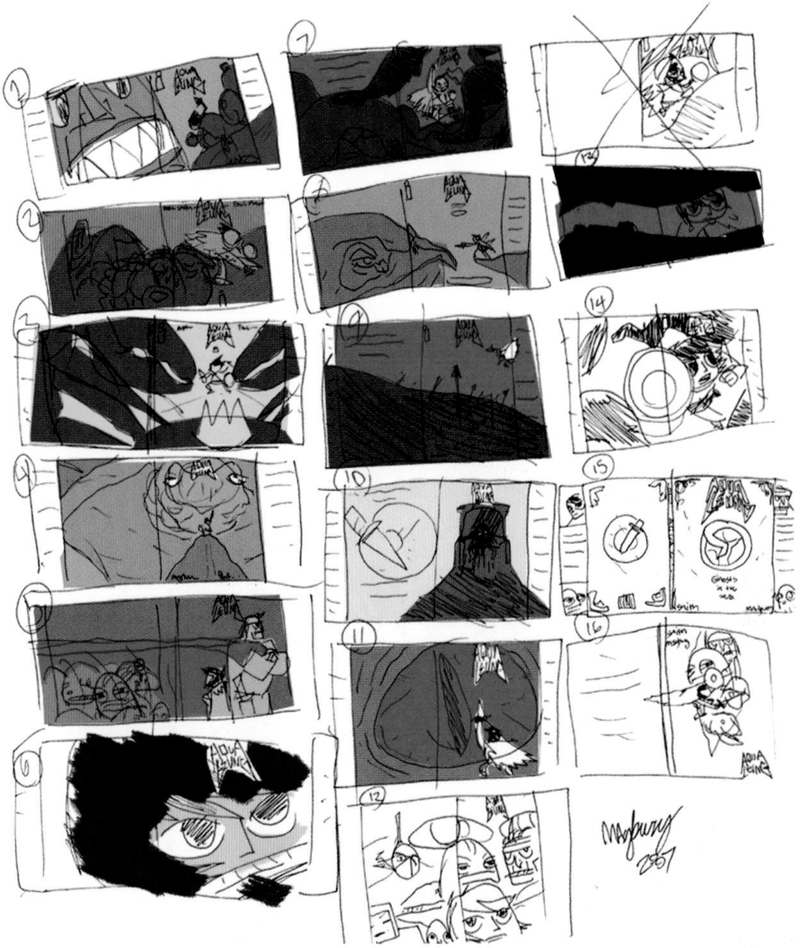

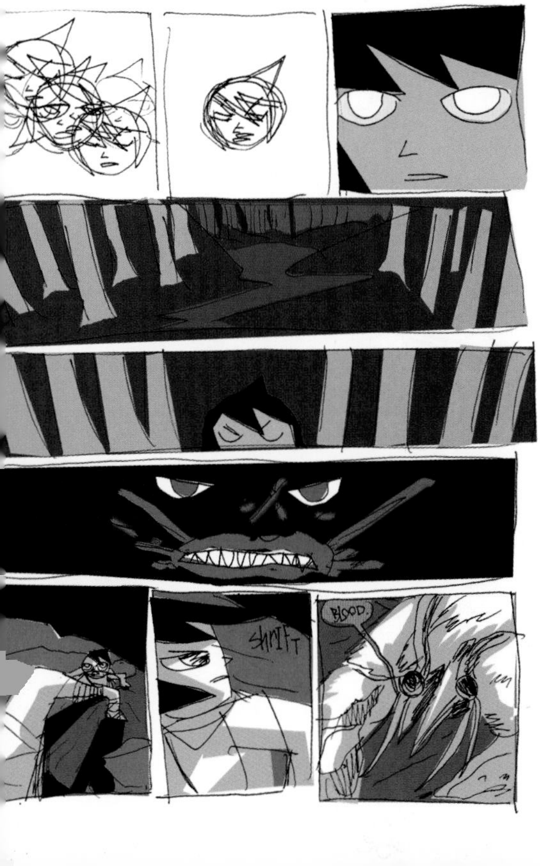
BLOOD.

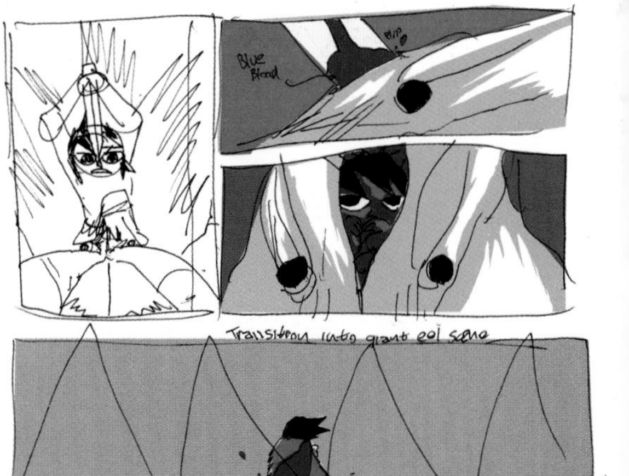
Blue Blood
Transition into giant eel scene

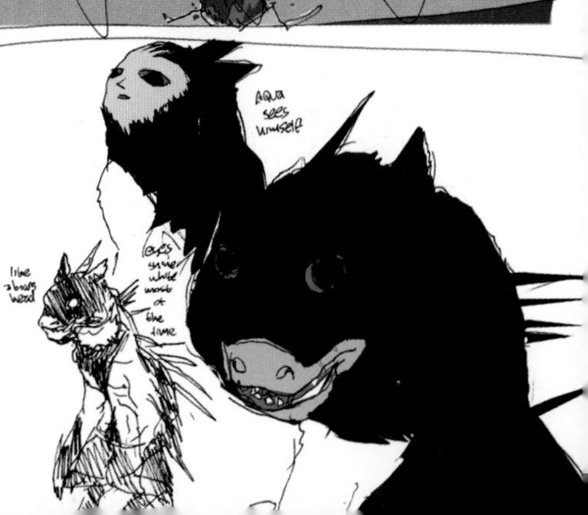
Aqua sees himself